Assessment, Testing and Evaluation in English-Medium Education from a Global Perspective

NEW PERSPECTIVES ON LANGUAGE AND EDUCATION

Founding Editor: Viv Edwards, *University of Reading, UK*

Series Editors: Phan Le Ha, *University of Hawaii at Manoa, USA,* Joel Windle, *Monash University, Australia* and Kyle R. McIntosh, *University of Tampa, USA.*

Two decades of research and development in language and literacy education have yielded a broad, multidisciplinary focus. Yet education systems face constant economic and technological change, with attendant issues of identity and power, community and culture. What are the implications for language education of new 'semiotic economies' and communications technologies? Of complex blendings of cultural and linguistic diversity in communities and institutions? Of new cultural, regional and national identities and practices? The New Perspectives on Language and Education series will feature critical and interpretive, disciplinary and multidisciplinary perspectives on teaching and learning, language and literacy in new times. New proposals, particularly for edited volumes, are expected to acknowledge and include perspectives from the Global South. Contributions from scholars from the Global South will be particularly sought out and welcomed, as well as those from marginalized communities within the Global North.

All books in this series are externally peer-reviewed.

Full details of all the books in this series and of all our other publications can be found on http://www.multilingual-matters.com, or by writing to Multilingual Matters, St Nicholas House, 31–34 High Street, Bristol, BS1 2AW, UK.

NEW PERSPECTIVES ON LANGUAGE AND EDUCATION: 131

Assessment, Testing and Evaluation in English-Medium Education from a Global Perspective

Edited by
Jack Pun, Samantha Curle and Pramod K. Sah

MULTILINGUAL MATTERS
Bristol • Jackson

For our families

DOI https://doi.org/10.21832/PUN9179
Library of Congress Cataloging in Publication Data
A catalog record for this book is available from the Library of Congress.
Library of Congress Control Number: 2025012010

British Library Cataloguing in Publication Data
A catalogue entry for this book is available from the British Library.

ISBN-13: 978-1-80041-917-9 (hbk)

Multilingual Matters
UK: St Nicholas House, 31–34 High Street, Bristol, BS1 2AW, UK.
USA: Ingram, Jackson, TN, USA.
Authorised Representative: Easy Access System Europe – Mustamäe tee 50, 10621 Tallinn, Estonia, gpsr.requests@easproject.com.

Website: https://www.multilingual-matters.com
X: Multi_Ling_Mat
Bluesky: @multi-ling-mat.bsky.social
Facebook: https://www.facebook.com/multilingualmatters
Blog: https://www.channelviewpublications.wordpress.com

Typeset by SAN Publishing Services.

Contents

Tables and Figures

Tables

Figures

Contributors

Editors

Jack Pun is Associate Professor in the Department of English at the Chinese University of Hong Kong, Hong Kong SAR, China. He completed his DPhil at the University of Oxford, which explored the teaching and learning process in EMI science classrooms, with a special focus on classroom interactions, use of code switching, and teachers' and students' views of EMI. His research interests lie in EMI and health communication. His research has been published in journals such as *ELT Journal, Language Teaching, RELC Journal, Journal of English for Academic Purposes* and *International Journal of Bilingual Education and Bilingualism*. He is associate editor of *Journal of Research in Science & Technological Education*, and published five books about EMI including: *English Medium Instruction in Secondary Education: Policy, Challenges and Practices in Science Classrooms; Teaching and Learning in English Medium Instruction: An Introduction* (with Jack C. Richards) by Routledge and *Research English Medium Instruction: Quantitative Methods for Students and Researchers* (with Samantha Curle) by Cambridge University Press.

Samantha Curle (DPhil, FHEA, FRSA) is a Reader in Education (Applied Linguistics), Director of all MRes programmes (Faculty of Humanities and Social Sciences), and Institutional Academic Lead for the South-West Doctoral Training Partnership (SWDTP) at the University of Bath. She is also Adjunct Professor at Khazar University (Azerbaijan) and an Associate Member of the English Medium Instruction (EMI) Oxford Research Group. Dr Curle's research interest lies in factors affecting academic achievement in EMI in higher education, such as English proficiency and psychological constructs. She has published seven edited books on EMI (one forthcoming) and her EMI-related research has been published in journals such as *Language Teaching, Applied Linguistics Review, Studies in Higher Education, Journal of Engineering Education, Journal for the Psychology of Language Learning, Journal of English for Academic Purposes and Language Teaching.* Her research spans across four continents (Africa, Asia, Europe, South America), and has been funded by the European Commission, the national Research Councils in Hong Kong and Turkey, the British Academy Newton Fund, as well as the British Council. Dr Curle is also a Fellow of the Higher Education Academy and the Royal Society of Arts (UK).

Pramod K. Sah is an Assistant Professor of English Language Education at The Education University of Hong Kong. He also holds an Honorary Norham Fellow position at the Department of Education, University of Oxford. Before joining EduHK, he worked as a Postdoctoral Associate at the University of Calgary. He completed his PhD study in Language and Literacy Education at the University of British Columbia, Canada, where he was also a Killam Laureate. He serves as an Editor-in-Chief of the *Journal of Education, Language, and Ideology*. His primary area of scholarly focus revolves around investigating how colonial and liberal ideologies in language policy and practices create socioemotional and educational disparities among diverse students. The central goal of his research is to conceptualize anti-oppressive and asset-based alternatives for pedagogies (e.g. linguistically and culturally sustaining pedagogies and critical translanguaging), research and policies. His research has appeared in many international journals, including *TESOL Quarterly*, *Learning and Instruction*, *Linguistics and Education, Journal of Multilingual and Multicultural Development*, *RELC Journal*, *Applied Linguistics Review* and *Current Issues in Language Planning*. He has also edited the books, *Policies, Politics, and Ideologies of English-Medium Instruction in Asian Universities: Unsettling Critical Edges* and *Pedagogies of English-Medium Instruction Programs in Asian Universities,* both with Fan Fang.

Authors

Siyan Dang is an Assistant Professor of Japanese Language Education at Chang'an University, China. She received her PhD in Sociolinguistics from Waseda University, with a specialization in the linguistic practices of international students in English-Medium Instruction (EMI) settings in Japan. Her research interests lie in multilingualism, language policy, and the role of social factors in multilingual education.

Slobodanka Dimova is a Professor at University of Copenhagen. Her research interests include language testing, English-medium instruction (EMI) and L2 speaking production. She has published several articles and volumes on EMI, most recently an edited volume *EMI Classroom Communication: A Corpus-Based Approach* (Routledge, 2024) with Branka Drljača Margić and Joyce Kling.

Shuang He is Associate Professor of English Applied Linguistics at the School of Foreign Languages, China University of Geosciences (Wuhan), China. Her main research interests cover academic English writing, mixed online and offline teaching, and teaching English as an international language. She publishes widely in Chinese journals such as *Foreign Language World*, *Chinese Journal of Language Policy and Planning*, *Journal of Language and Literature Studies*, etc.

Masakazu Iino is a professor of Sociolinguistics at the School of International Liberal Studies (SILS) and the Graduate School of International Culture and Communication Studies (GSICCS), Waseda University. His research interests include ELF (English as a Lingua Franca), EMI (English-Medium Instruction) in higher education, translanguaging in multilingual/contact situations, and technology and language use.

Wenyun Jia is a doctoral student researcher in the Department of English at the City University of Hong Kong. Her research interests lie in English medium instruction (EMI), disciplinary literacy education, learning strategies, and translanguaging. Her research on EMI has been published in journals such as *RELC Journal and International Review of Applied Linguistics in Language Teaching* and presented at conferences such as RELC, AILA and AAAL.

Joyce Kling is an Associate Professor at Lund University. Her research interests include English-medium instruction (EMI), teacher cognition, and language testing. She has published several articles and volumes on EMI, most recently an edited volume EMI Classroom Communication: A Corpus-Based Approach (Routledge, 2024) with Slobodanka Dimova and Branka Drljača Margić.

Pınar Koçer is a teaching assistant at the School of Foreign Languages at Tekirdağ Namık Kemal University. Her research interests involve language assessment, programme evaluation, learner differences and teacher beliefs. She is specifically interested in assessment literacy, English Medium Instruction (EMI) in higher education, learner autonomy and motivation. Her research has been published in journals such as *The Literacy Trek, ELT Research Journal, Journal of Foreign Language Education and Technology, Journal of Language and Linguistic Studies, International Journal of Languages' Education and Teaching.*

Mo Li is a lecturer at the School of Foreign Languages of University of Electronic Science and Technology of China. Her research focuses on English medium instruction (EMI) and teacher assessment literacy as well as language teaching and learning. She has published several journal articles in *Applied Linguistics Reviews*, *International Journal of Educational Research*, *Journal of Multilingual and Multicultural Development* and *Linguistics and Education*.

Yuen Yi Lo is an Associate Professor in the Faculty of Education at The University of Hong Kong. Her research focuses on bilingual education programmes such as English-medium instruction (EMI) and Content and Language Integrated Learning (CLIL). She is particularly interested in cross-curricular collaboration, assessment and teachers' professional development in these programmes.

Ron Martinez, PhD, has been a leader in EMI development and research in Brazil since 2016, His interests in the internationalization of higher education also extend to research publication, and was responsible for the installation of writing centres in ten different universities in Brazil to support faculty and doctoral researchers. Ron has been an English Language Specialist for the U.S. Department of State since 2018, and until 2024 was a Senior Faculty Development Specialist at the Center for Faculty Excellence at the University of Oklahoma, as the Faculty Writing Coach. Ron is currently a professor at the Universidade Federal do Paraná (UFPR) in Brazil, and is also co-Editor-in-Chief of the journal *Applied Linguistics*.

Karna Rana, PhD in e-learning from the University of Canterbury in New Zealand, MA in Education from the University of Bedfordshire in England, and MEd in English Education from Tribhuvan University in Nepal, is an Online Learning Designer at Lincoln University in New Zealand. Before this role, he, as Assistant Professor of ICT and E-learning, was a Coordinator of MPhil in English Education and BEd.in Pedagogical Sciences at Nepal Open University in Nepal. His areas of research interest include online learning design, technology in education, education policy and leadership, Indigenous knowledge, language education, medium of instruction and culture.

Barry Lee Reynolds is Associate Professor of English Language Education at the University of Macau. He has taught EGP, EAP, ESP and trained language teachers at thirteen institutions in the USA, Taiwan and Macau. His current research interests include second language vocabulary learning, written corrective feedback, CALL and English teacher education.

Larissa Giordani Schmitt is an Associate Professor of English Language Teaching in Brazil (Western Parana State University – Unioeste). Her main research interests lie in factors affecting professors' teaching performance, as well as professors' and students' confidence in English Medium Instruction (EMI) in higher education. Following postdoctoral research with this focus conducted in 2022, her efforts were applied to a graduate-level EMI course. In addition, she has been involved in early scholar development programmes at her institution, promoting the development of research among undergraduate and graduate students exploring EMI processes at the university.

Prithvi N. Shrestha is a Senior Lecturer in English Language at The Open University, UK. Shrestha has led or co-led many funded international research projects. He has published over 65 research outputs, including one research monograph (*Dynamic Assessment of Students' Academic Writing* (Springer, 2020)), covering CALL, academic literacy and disciplinary writing, academic writing assessment in distance education, language assessment, English language education in developing countries, English medium instruction. His research interests include application of social justice, critical theories, systemic functional linguistics and sociocultural theory in the above areas.

Yonghua (Yoka) Wang is a lecturer at the School of Foreign Languages, Jimei University, China. His primary research interests lie in teacher beliefs, teacher wellbeing, teacher development and language education. His publications have appeared in *System*, *British Journal of Educational Studies*, *Language and Intercultural Communication*, *British Journal of Psychology*, among others. He also serves as a research associate in research project funded by the National Social Science Fund of China.

Weihong Wang holds a PhD in Education (Applied Linguistics) from The University of Hong Kong. Currently, she works as Professor of Applied Linguistics at the School of Foreign Languages, China University of Geosciences (Wuhan), China. Her research interests include English medium instruction, teaching English for academic purposes and language policy and planning. Her publications can be seen in *Applied Linguistics Review*, *Current Issues in Language Planning*, *Journal of English for Academic Purposes*, *Language, Culture and Curriculum*, *International Journal of Bilingual Education and Bilingualism*, *System*, etc.

Winfred Xuan is an Assistant Professor in the School of Education and Languages at Hong Kong Metropolitan University. Dr XUAN obtained his PhD in Systemic Functional Linguistics from the Hong Kong Polytechnic University. His research interests include systemic functional linguistics, applied linguistics, second language writing, English for academic purposes and teaching English/Chinese as a second language. His works appear in *The Journal of Babel*, *Functional Linguistics*, *Applied Linguistics Review*, *Australian Review of Applied Linguistics* and *The Asia-Pacific Education Researcher.*

Jieting Jerry Xin is a PhD candidate in the Faculty of Education at The University of Hong Kong. His research interest includes Content and Language Integrated Learning (CLIL) and teacher professional development.

Melissa H. Yu was a part-time lecturer at Newcastle University, UK (2016–2017). She was a postdoctoral research fellow at the Faculty of Education, University of Macau (2019–2020). Her research interests include English as a lingua franca (ELF), English language teaching, learning materials, curriculum development and teacher education.

Rui (Eric) Yuan is an associate professor at the Faculty of Education of the University of Macau. His research focuses on English medium instruction in higher education and language teacher education. He has published more than 100 research works, including journal articles and book chapters, in international journals such as *TESOL Quarterly*, *Language Teaching Research* and *Teaching and Teacher Education*. He currently serves as Associate Editor of *TESOL Journal* and is an editorial board member of *TESOL Quarterly*.

Qiuyi Zhu is an Economics major and a former EMI Economic teacher in mainland China. She is currently as a researcher at the University of Hong Kong, specializing in CLIL (content-language integrated learning) and English medium instruction (EMI) education to bridge the realms of economics and language education.

Acknowledgements

This book provides access for researchers and practitioners to a growing interest in assessing, testing and evaluation in the context of English Medium Education (EME). Each chapter brings different perspectives on the role of assessment in the EME classroom. It also provides a collection of up-to-date methods and practices of assessment, testing and evaluation in the area of English as the medium of instruction.

We would like to express our sincerest gratitude to all the contributors in this edited volume. We are grateful to the many thoughtful and constructive suggestions we received from our colleagues and collaborators, which have had a significant impact on the content of the included chapters. Special thanks to Ms Wenyun Jia for her editorial support in preparing this book as well as the introduction chapter. Lastly, we would like to thank all the reviewers, whose comments and useful suggestions greatly enhanced the quality of this edited volume.

Also, we would like to express our sincere gratitude to the staff at Multilingual Matters, especially Anna Roderick, for guiding us through and assisting with the editing process from start to finish.

We hope this volume will offer valuable insights to scholars in the field of educational linguistics, particularly in English language teaching, content-based instruction, content and language integrated learning, as well as English medium instruction (EMI).

This book is dedicated to our Beloved Partners.

Introduction

Jack Pun, Samantha Curle and Pramod K. Sah

English-medium education (EME) refers to the broader framework of using English as the primary language of education in contexts where it is not the native language. Within this framework, English-medium instruction (EMI) focuses specifically on teaching non-linguistic academic subjects in English, such as mathematics or science, in higher education or other educational settings (Dearden, 2018; Macaro *et al.*, 2018; Yüksel *et al.*, 2022). EMI is a subset of EME and represents the practical implementation of this approach in classrooms, where subject content and language intersect. Recent research and practice in EMI have increasingly centered on how to meaningfully implement it in real-world classrooms. These classrooms are inherently multilingual and multicultural, presenting implicit language learning goals alongside specific teaching and learning challenges (Dafouz *et al.*, 2023; Galloway *et al.*, 2017; Rose *et al.*, 2023). There is an urgent need for a more contextual and comprehensive investigation to improve EMI education quality. This is vital for preparing students, who learn English as a foreign language, to become global citizens capable of engaging in cross-cultural knowledge exchange (Dafouz & Smit, 2016).

Effective implementation of assessment in education can significantly benefit learning mastery and teaching efforts (Guskey, 2007). However, this aspect remains surprisingly understudied in the realm of EMI (Hultgren *et al.*, 2022). The development of EMI assessments that accurately gather evidence of learning and reflect real-world tasks is a complex issue. For instance, testing data may be misleading if students, unable to read, write or listen effectively in English, cannot demonstrate their learning in content areas (Kopriva, 2000). This creates a dilemma for content teachers, especially those without training in applied linguistics, about whether to focus assessments on language abilities or content knowledge.

This edited volume aims to provide a collection of current methods and practices in assessment, testing and evaluation in EMI. It features contributions from experienced educators across various disciplines (Science, Maths, Engineering, Technology, Social Science) and researchers in educational linguistics (ESL, EFL, TESOL, EMI, CLIL). The book offers an accessible overview of the nature of assessment, testing and evaluation in EMI classrooms, spanning both basic and higher education. It serves as a comprehensive resource, combining views from educational linguistics researchers, content specialists and language educators on best practices for assessing, testing, or evaluating students' learning outcomes in EMI settings. By exploring issues, challenges and coping strategies, this book provides research-informed practices for effective assessment, testing and evaluation in EMI contexts.

Each chapter of this volume promises to contribute to the theory, policy, research and classroom practices of EMI assessment. It is highly relevant to scholars in educational linguistics, particularly in English language teaching, content-based instruction, CLIL and EMI. The book is also pertinent for education policymakers, curriculum and textbook developers, research students and students majoring in English and education. Additionally, the annotated examples of assessment, testing and evaluation, which demonstrate good practices in EMI, will be invaluable to frontline EMI teachers in content subjects and English, EMI coordinators, and instructors involved in EMI professional development courses.

Background

With the developing empirical knowledge regarding how to improve the education quality of globally expanding EMI settings, researchers have come to a consensus on the critical role of assessment in EMI teaching (Dimova & Kling, 2022; Macaro *et al.*, 2019) given that the role of assessment in improving performance of both students and teachers (Wiggins, 2010). This review serves to establish a foundation for the subsequent empirical studies by elaborating on four key topics in EMI assessment research: assessment purposes; assessment in specific language skills in EMI content learning; teachers' perspective and assessment practices; and assessment policy.

Purposes of EMI assessment

The literature identifies several purposes of EMI assessment, addressing the needs of both students and teachers (Dimova & Kling, 2022). These purposes can be broadly categorized into ***placement, formative assessment*** and ***teacher certification assessments,*** although it is important to acknowledge the complexity inherent in assessment classification. Assessments often serve multiple purposes simultaneously, and it is crucial to avoid narrowly compartmentalizing their functions within a single framework (Newton, 2007). ***Placement assessments*** aim to evaluate whether students possess sufficient English proficiency to succeed in an EMI environment. This involves determining students' qualifications for entry into EMI programs, which is widely documented in the literature (e.g. Stuers, 2019). Many universities require evidence from recognized

English proficiency tests, such as TOEFL or IELTS, whereas others rely on alternative indicators like prior education in English or graduation certificates (Galloway & Ruegg, 2020). In some cases, institutions implement entrance exams or preparatory courses designed to ensure students' readiness for EMI programs (Wächter & Maiworm, 2014). Despite these efforts, ongoing debates persist regarding the establishment of standardized benchmarks for EMI, including the appropriate level of English proficiency required for admission. For instance, Schoepp (2018) highlighted that an IELTS score of 6.0 might serve as a useful benchmark, though further research into predictive validity and context-specific thresholds is necessary. Other studies, such as Masrai *et al.* (2022) and Rahman (2020), emphasize the critical role of vocabulary knowledge, proposing that mastery of the first 5000 word families and technical or aural vocabulary may significantly impact academic achievement.

Formative assessments, on the other hand, focus on supporting students' ongoing learning and development in EMI contexts. These assessments provide feedback that helps students identify areas for improvement and adjust their learning strategies accordingly (Inbar-Lourie, 2022). Unlike placement assessments, which determine entry qualifications, formative assessments are conducted during the learning process to enhance students' academic success. ***Teacher certification assessments*** are designed to ensure that instructors in EMI programs have the requisite English proficiency and pedagogical skills to teach effectively. These assessments often serve as a quality control mechanism for institutions implementing EMI. Although this purpose is briefly mentioned in this section, detailed discussions of teacher certification assessments are provided in subsequent sections for clarity. Lastly, Soruç *et al.* (2021) argue that discussions of language thresholds to mitigate linguistic challenges should be discipline specific, as language demands and proficiency requirements vary significantly across academic fields. This highlights the need for nuanced and context-sensitive approaches when defining the purposes and applications of EMI assessments.

Despite the acknowledged importance of English proficiency to EMI academic achievement, factors other than English proficiency are also critical to successful learning experiences in EMI (Curle *et al.*, 2023), such as lecture comprehension, lecturers' language use in teaching and English language proficiency gains (Rose *et al.*, 2020). This highlights the need for formative assessment and lecturer quality evaluation. EMI assessment for formative purposes is in line with the overarching concept of 'educational assessment for learning'. This approach prioritizes enhancing students' learning over summative objectives such as accountability, ranking, certifying competence or determining learning achievement status (Baird *et al.*, 2017). A recent comprehensive review by Schellekens *et al.* (2021) underscores the inherent coherence among 'assessment for, as, and of learning' emphasizes the importance of adopting an integrated perspective to cultivate an assessment culture that maximizes learning outcomes. Therefore, to understand how EMI learning-oriented assessment can be designed and implemented, we employ a synthesized understanding of the common characteristics of assessment for, as and of learning. According to their synthesis, the common features include:

(1) emphasis on enhancing the teaching and learning process to benefit all students;
(2) measurement and judgment of assessment activities to inform decision-making about student achievement;
(3) students engage in self-assessment and take ownership of their learning;
(4) students' and teachers' collaborative roles and responsibilities;
(5) students' and teachers' continuous collection and reflection on various sources of information to monitor progress and inform actions;
(6) students and teachers possess assessment literacy and understand quality standards;
(7) teachers adapt to individual student needs and preferences;
(8) students feel secure to take risks and are encouraged to engage in assessment.

While the knowledge and effectiveness of learning-oriented assessment has been well established in applied linguistics, discussion on EMI assessment from this perspective remains scant (Hultgren *et al.*, 2022; Inbar-Lourie, 2022; Li & Ruan, 2015). These scholars argued that viewing assessment as a means for learning, with an awareness of the pivotal role of language in academic studies, can help address current EMI teaching challenges and add value in supporting and sustaining content learning. Regarding learning-oriented assessment in actual practice, Kao and Tsou (2017) found that 95% of the lecturers use assessments for summative purposes across all subjects, which could be influenced by the traditional institutional norms. They also recommended several tools for assessment for/of learning, such as online interactive discussion for monitoring students' learning processes with immediate feedback and self/peer-assessment to foster student autonomy. However, their classification of assessment tools (e.g. written exam for summative purposes) can be more flexibly interpreted, as assessment tools do not inherently determine their purposes (Newton, 2007), and traditionally viewed summative test (e.g. final course exams) can become integral to the learning process (Kao, 2023). For instance, teachers can provide transparent grading criteria, offer helpful feedback and encourage reflection on teaching quality. This indicates that further research is needed to understand how EMI lecturers and students exert their agency to navigate between available assessment tools and their own purposes.

The role of teaching in EMI assessment

Scholars have highlighted the roles of teachers and students in assessment, emphasizing the importance of teachers understanding students' learning difficulties and students engaging in metacognitive processes (Kao & Tsou, 2017; Li & Wu, 2021). However, more discussions are warranted on the conceptualization of in-depth, contextually relevant, learning-oriented EMI assessment, particularly with regard to language aspects (Li & Wu, 2021), alongside studies investigating the effectiveness of these assessment tools in enhancing EMI learning (Barés *et al.*, 2022). EMI assessment also extends to evaluating teachers' certification in delivering courses, with particular attention on their communicative patterns in the classroom (e.g. Dimova, 2017; O'Dowd, 2018). For instance, Klaassen and Bos (2010) assessed the language proficiency levels of scientific staff and the feasibility of attaining a C1 proficiency level in English to teach EMI courses. The findings corresponded to O'Dowd (2018) and showed that, although the majority of scientific staff met the C1 proficiency level, achieving the higher C2 level proved challenging. Their language proficiency was generally stronger in reading and writing compared to oral and listening skills. While this study did not delve into assessment design tailored to disciplinary instruction needs and school context, it emphasized the importance for universities to enhance lecturers' English proficiency to support students' development of global citizenship. An example of in-house development to tailor teacher assessment to contextual relevance is the Test of Oral English Proficiency for Academic Staff (TOEPAS). This is an oral performance test based on a simulated lecture to certify EMI lecturers for oral English proficiency and raise awareness about their communication strengths and weaknesses at the University of Copenhagen, Denmark (Kling & Stæhr, 2011). However, scrutiny of its native-English-norms in scoring and how teachers respond to the assessment results is necessary. Dimova's (2017, 2020) studies have contributed to these issues by revising the TOEPAS scale and feedback formatting (e.g. removing native speaker references) and advocating for multilingual-based assessment norms aligned with real classroom practices. She also emphasized to incorporate more descriptors related to pragmatic teaching rather than phonology and lexicogrammar accuracy, and advocated comprehensible and contextualized formative feedback for lecturers to enhance awareness of their oral English strengths and weaknesses. Additionally, in response to the multilingual shift in EMI, Solano-Flores (see Shohamy & Menken, 2015) proposed integrating translanguaging elements into assessing teachers' classroom language usage, such as linguistic heterogeneity and text localization.

These various EMI assessment purposes manifest researchers' strong emphasis on the inseparable connection between content and language in EMI teaching and learning, highlights the need for a broader scope in assessment to incorporate heightened language awareness and to support discipline-specific learning (Kaya *et al.*, 2023). Therefore, it becomes imperative to thoroughly comprehend and explicitly address the interconnectedness of language, content and context in both EMI assessment research and practical application.

EMI assessment in specific language skills

The call for increased attention to language in EMI assessment necessitates an exploration of how specific language skills crucial for content learning are assessed. Sánchez-Pérez (2021) measured 136 laboratory reports of EMI university students regarding their disciplinary literacy abilities (including cohesive devices, vocabulary and macro-structure) and content proficiency, and revealed a close relationship in between. This indicates that a more nuanced approach from language skills and disciplinary literacy perspectives is necessary to inform assessment criteria design and interpretation of results, thereby facilitating mutual reinforcement of language and content learning. Mancho-Barés *et al.*'s (2022) study presented a model example of using genre analysis framework to compare lecturers' expected disciplinary laboratory report writing and students' actual writing performance on the assessment task. Findings showed students' lack of awareness of how to organize a laboratory report. More importantly, the instruction, assessment rubric and feedback given were inconsistent particularly in evaluating disciplinary-specific moves and providing language-and-genre-based feedback. This suggests the potential of genre analysis as a valuable tool to scrutinize EMI assessments and enhance lecturers' assessment literacy in addressing disciplinary needs and relevant literacy skills.

In studies on EMI students' self-regulated listening strategies, Zhou and Thompson (2023) argued the efficacy of credit-bearing summative assessments, coupled with feedback and reflective tutorials, in encouraging students to evaluate their listening strategies and knowledge acquisition. Regarding reading assessment, Holzknecht *et al.* (2022) proposed that EMI tests should consider reading ability separately rather than as part of overall general language proficiency. The tests should also authentically reflect the real-world EMI learning (e.g. integrating reading with speaking and writing tasks, including texts from various complexity levels). Furthermore, text lengths and specifications (e.g. specific scientific journals and genres) should also be considered. In classroom-based assessment, Kao and Tsou (2017) advocated for employing multiple language-based measures to obtain a comprehensive view of student performance. For instance, small group presentations could assess content comprehension, English speaking proficiency and academic literacy skills, such as coherent argumentation. However, despite the importance of these language skills in disciplinary literacy development and content learning, there is still only scarce knowledge about their demands in specific EMI contexts and how they can be assessed, especially for formative purposes.

EMI lecturers' perspectives on assessment and practices

The assessment literacy of EMI lecturers – their knowledge, skills and understanding of effective assessment principles – plays a critical role in shaping their teaching and evaluation practices (Black & Wiliam, 1998). However, research has consistently highlighted gaps in assessment literacy among EMI lecturers, particularly in relation to language-sensitive assessment practices. Aguilar (2017) and Li and Wu (2018) reported that many lecturers perceive themselves as less skilled in assessing language production, which is a critical component in EMI settings. These gaps in assessment literacy often lead to resistance among lecturers to take on responsibilities typically associated with language teaching, as well as reluctance to engage in interdisciplinary collaboration for assessment design and implementation (Derakhshan *et al.*, 2021).

For example, Li and Wu (2018) found that lecturers struggled with adopting self-assessment, implementing learning-oriented assessment, and designing test items targeting higher-order cognitive abilities. These challenges underscore a lack of familiarity with assessment frameworks and methodologies tailored to EMI contexts, which can hinder the realization of assessment's potential as a tool for learning enhancement. In practice, the assessment approaches employed by EMI lecturers often reflect their limited assessment literacy. Kao and Tsou's (2017) study revealed a heavy reliance on summative assessments aimed at evaluating learning outcomes at the end of a unit, with little attention to the integration of language-focused elements. Similarly, Molino *et al.* (2022) observed that the lack of resources designed for the multilingual nature of EMI classrooms led lecturers to rely on ad-hoc strategies, such as arbitrary translanguaging during exams. This highlights the need for professional development to equip lecturers with the skills to design assessments that address both content and language objectives effectively. A significant barrier to improving assessment literacy lies in the difficulty of transitioning to formative and learning-oriented assessment approaches. Kruiper *et al.* (2022) noted challenges in engaging content lecturers in EMI-specific assessment training, while Wicking (2020) emphasized the social and institutional resistance to shifting from traditional score-oriented norms to more holistic, learning-focused assessment cultures. These findings underline the importance of fostering a comprehensive understanding of assessment principles among EMI lecturers to support their ability to design, implement, and interpret assessments that cater to the unique demands of EMI contexts.

Another challenge lies in the incongruence between lecturers' perceptions and practices, as well as between instruction and assessment (e.g.

Gronchi, 2023). The former mismatch emerges from lecturers' perceived importance of English and the absence of language elements in testing practices (Kao & Tsou, 2017). Despite some lecturers acknowledging the significance of clear and fluent English language in EMI assessment, the actual assessment tools and scoring criteria often do not reflect this perception. Conversely, Melchor and Walsh (2022) revealed a contradiction between lecturers' stated preference for content-only assessment and the implicit evaluation of students' English communicative skills (e.g. textual cohesion and coherence) in practice. The latter misalignment pertains to untaught language knowledge in the classroom compared to implicitly or explicitly assessed language knowledge and language objectives in evaluation rubrics (Dimova & Kling, 2022; Gronchi, 2023). These issues not only stem from the inherent integration of language proficiency and content acquisition in EMI learning but also from a pervasive lack of assessment rubrics or policies. However, these incongruences can lead to confusion in lecturers' assessment practices and undermine the validity (the test does not measure what it intends to measure and lacks clear directions) and reliability (the test lacks clear directions and uniform rubrics for scoring) of assessments (Brown & Abeywickrama, 2019). Therefore, these studies can perhaps inform lecturers and policymakers to consistently and reflectively consider the requirements of successful EMI learning, curriculum mandates and assessment design.

A growing body of research is also focused on the role of teacher assessment literacy to unpack the assessment skills practitioners require for conducing sound assessment in addressing these current issues and challenges (e.g. Lo & Leung, 2022). For instance, from a learning-oriented assessment perspective, Inbar-Lourie (2022) proposed four areas for EMI teacher assessment literacy, which include:

(1) contextual and policy literacies;
(2) the role of language in facilitating content learning;
(3) formative assessment for learning orientations;
(4) awareness and understanding of students' linguistic and content needs.

These four components can assist lecturers in elucidating assessment purposes, clarifying what needs to be assessed, acquiring knowledge of formative assessment principles and strategies, and critically and creatively situating these intentions, skills, and knowledge within their sociocultural and educational contexts.

EMI policy on assessment

EMI assessment practices and lecturers' perceptions are deeply influenced by policies operating at various levels, from institutional to broader educational frameworks. A multi-level analysis of policy implementation – macro, meso and micro – offers a more nuanced understanding of how policy shapes and is shaped by EMI assessment. At the **macro level**, national and regional policies establish overarching goals and priorities for EMI programs, often emphasizing the promotion of bilingualism or multilingualism. However, as Hultgren *et al.* (2022) highlighted, a lack of resource allocation and institutional buy-in at this level can hinder the adoption of research-based 'assessment for learning' approaches with greater language awareness. Policymakers often overlook the necessity of embedding language-sensitive objectives within broader educational goals, leaving implementation gaps at lower levels.

At the **meso level**, institutions translate these broad policies into specific guidelines and practices. Institutional policies play a critical role in shaping assessment strategies by allocating resources, offering professional development, and setting expectations for language use. For example, Baker and Hope (2019) demonstrated how a university's bilingual language policy – requiring bilingualism as part of promotion and tenure criteria – encouraged lecturers to incorporate bilingual listening tasks into assessments. This policy, while promoting 'passive' bilingualism (i.e. comprehension and communication in a second language), illustrates the potential of top-down initiatives to foster multilingual, research-based assessment practices. However, Gronchi (2023) noted that inadequate institutional investment in teacher training and explicit language policies can lead lecturers to rely on their personal beliefs about language learning, resulting in assessments with limited focus on language-sensitive objectives.

At the **micro level**, teacher agency plays a crucial role in interpreting and enacting these policies. While institutional guidelines provide a framework, it is ultimately up to individual lecturers to implement assessments in their classrooms. Teacher agency – their capacity to adapt, innovate and make professional decisions – can either enhance or limit the effectiveness of policy-driven assessment practices. For instance, lecturers with strong assessment literacy may actively integrate language-sensitive approaches despite limited institutional support, whereas those with less expertise may struggle to move beyond traditional score-oriented methods. This highlights the need for ongoing professional development and collaboration opportunities to empower teachers in navigating policy demands. To summarize, increasing awareness among both policymakers and lecturers of learning-oriented and language-sensitive assessments can serve as a promising starting point for promoting high-quality EMI education (Thompson *et al.*, 2022). The review underscores the importance of aligning policy objectives at all levels with the realities of classroom practices, fostering students' academic success and supporting teachers' instruction. Ensuring consistency between what is taught, what is assessed and how it is evaluated requires comprehensive and contextualized considerations of EMI purposes. Despite progress in EMI assessment research, many questions remain unanswered. This edited volume seeks to advance understanding of EMI assessment by exploring these dynamics across diverse perspectives and contexts.

Chapter Synopses

This edited volume comprises an introduction and 13 chapters that present original contributions on EMI assessment from a diverse group of emerging and established academics worldwide. These chapters are organized thematically to address critical issues, including assessment design, teacher agency, the role of policy, collaborative practices and emerging technologies. The introduction chapter delineates background information for researching students' learning outcomes in EMI classrooms. It then provides an overview of the subsequent chapters and underscores the significance of research in EMI assessment.

Chapter 1 by Samantha Curle and Pınar Koçer provides a comprehensive overview of the current state of research in EMI assessment, critically addressing three core questions: (a) what evidence exists on the efficacy of EMI assessment; (b) what challenges educators face in assessment design and (c) what gaps remain in the EMI assessment literature. By synthesizing empirical studies and theoretical insights, the chapter examines how EMI assessment practices impact learning outcomes and evaluates their alignment with educational goals. The chapter underscores the dual challenges of assessing content mastery and language proficiency in EMI settings, highlighting the complexities of balancing these interrelated components. It identifies persistent issues such as the lack of alignment between language demands and assessment tasks, variability in assessment literacy among educators and the limited integration of formative practices. Through a critical review of existing research, the authors point to the need for more longitudinal studies, cross-contextual comparisons and investigations into the role of formative assessment in fostering both content and language learning. Curle and Koçer also advocate for context-sensitive and inclusive approaches to EMI assessment that accommodate diverse student needs and linguistic backgrounds. They call for professional development initiatives to enhance educators' assessment literacy and propose integrating collaborative and technologically enhanced assessment methods. This chapter sets the stage for subsequent contributions in the volume, framing the discussion around emerging trends, methodological innovations, and practical implications for policymakers, researchers and EMI practitioners.

Chapter 2, authored by Winfred Xuan, examines the role of translanguaging practices among Hong Kong undergraduates during collaborative writing tasks, with a focus on EMI assessment. This study, situated within the Marketing BA program at a Hong Kong university, investigates how students navigate linguistic and disciplinary challenges in an EMI context. Data were collected from six working groups of third-year undergraduates, whose assignments and group discussions were analyzed to explore how translanguaging practices influenced the quality of their collaborative writing – a crucial element of EMI assessment. Follow-up interviews provided additional insights into students' language use, illuminating its impact on their written outcomes. The findings reveal that translanguaging, which involves the strategic use of multiple linguistic resources, supports students in overcoming language barriers, deepening content understanding and fostering creativity in collaborative writing. Xuan demonstrates how integrating translanguaging into assessment design can enhance language learning and improve academic writing performance, particularly in multilingual EMI contexts. The chapter offers practical recommendations for embedding translanguaging practices into EMI assessments to create more inclusive and effective evaluation methods.

Chapter 3, authored by Karna Rana and Pramod Sah, focuses on online EMI testing in Nepali universities, examining university teachers' experiences with virtual assessments. The chapter delves into the technological and pedagogical challenges faced by educators, including issues of student language proficiency, test design, and the reliability of e-proctored exams. It highlights how these challenges are exacerbated in a multilingual context like Nepal, where students often lack sufficient proficiency in English, creating barriers to fair assessment. The authors propose strategies to improve the reliability and validity of online EMI testing, such as leveraging bilingual or multilingual test frameworks and enhancing teacher training. By integrating insights from interviews and observational data, the chapter underscores the need for a contextualized approach to EMI assessments that aligns with the linguistic realities of students and educators, aiming to improve both teaching outcomes and educational equity.

In Chapter 4, Jieting Xin and Yuen Yi Lo present a multiple-case study that investigates EMI teachers' assessment practices in Hong Kong and Mainland China, addressing critical concerns about the validity and fairness of assessing students' content knowledge in a less proficient language. These concerns stem from the dual challenge of evaluating both subject content and language proficiency, alongside insufficient professional training in assessment design. Against this backdrop, Xin and Lo explored how EMI teachers assess content knowledge while navigating the interplay between language and subject matter. The study involved a qualitative multiple-case analysis of three experienced teachers from international high schools in Hong Kong and Mainland China. Data were gathered through in-depth interviews and a detailed examination of the teachers' assessment materials. The authors identified a range of effective strategies employed by EMI teachers, such as integrating formative and summative assessments, tailoring assessment formats to suit diverse learner needs, and leveraging assessment data to refine instructional practices. However, the study also revealed significant challenges, including the difficulty of disentangling content knowledge from language proficiency and the lack of adequate professional training in EMI-specific assessment methods. Additionally, the findings underscore the role of personal and contextual factors – such as teachers' professional development experiences, institutional policies and student demographics – in shaping assessment practices. The chapter advocates for enhancing assessment literacy among EMI educators, emphasizing the need for targeted training programs that address the unique demands of EMI settings. By highlighting both effective practices and persistent challenges, this chapter offers valuable insights for improving assessment strategies in EMI and other bilingual education contexts worldwide.

Chapter 5, co-authored by He *et al.* delves into the washback effects of assessment in EMI classrooms, focusing on how different types of assessment influence undergraduates' language acquisition and content learning. Employing a multi-case study design, the authors explored the impact of various assessment methods on student outcomes, uncovering key dynamics that shape the relationship between assessment practices and learning processes. The study reveals that assessment exerts significant washback effects on learners, with the nature, degree and scope of these effects varying based on the type of assessment implemented. Factors such as individual learner differences, course-specific requirements and the alignment between assessment and instructional objectives were identified as mediators of these effects. The findings suggest that well-designed assessments can foster positive washback, motivating students to engage more deeply with both language and content, while poorly aligned assessments may hinder their progress. The chapter provides actionable recommendations for promoting positive washback in EMI classrooms, such as incorporating formative assessments that emphasize feedback, designing assessments that integrate language and content goals, and tailoring assessment strategies to accommodate diverse learner needs. By offering insights into the interplay between assessment and learning, this chapter contributes to a deeper understanding of effective assessment practices in EMI and highlights strategies for enhancing both teaching and learning in bilingual education settings.

Chapter 6, authored by Prithvi Shrestha, investigates EMI assessment practices in low- and middle-income countries, with a particular focus on social justice issues in Nepal. Drawing on a mixed-methods approach, Shrestha critically examines how socioeconomic and linguistic factors shape assessment outcomes in higher education, specifically through the lens of Honneth's theory of mutual recognition. The chapter analyses data from a TOEFL academic reading test project conducted in an EMI university setting, exploring students' academic reading practices, lived experiences, and assessment challenges. The study reveals that EMI assessments, often grounded in English monolingual ideologies, marginalize students from Nepali-medium education backgrounds and exacerbate inequities. It highlights the misrecognition of students' translingual capabilities and the lack of institutional support for academic English proficiency, leading to significant social injustices. Shrestha underscores the necessity of incorporating translingual practices into assessment, making assessment policies transparent and contextualizing language tests to align with students' disciplinary and cultural realities. The chapter concludes with actionable recommendations for promoting equity in EMI assessments, such as leveraging diagnostic tools rather than high-stakes tests like TOEFL for certification purposes. By situating EMI assessments within broader conversations on equity and social justice, Shrestha provides critical insights into fostering more inclusive and fair assessment practices in multilingual, non-English-dominant settings.

In Chapter 7, Siyan Dang and Masakazu Iino delve into the role of artificial intelligence (AI) in EMI assessment through a qualitative study that addresses three critical questions: (a) how students incorporate AI into their academic tasks, (b) how evaluators perceive AI's role in EMI assessment and (c) how assessment efficiency can be maintained in the era of rapid AI adoption. Conducted at a Japanese private university, the study involved semi-structured interviews with eight students and seven professors. Using Activity Theory as an analytical framework, the authors unpack the complexities of AI integration in EMI settings, focusing on its implications for pedagogy, assessment, and academic integrity. The findings reveal a range of student perspectives on AI in assessment. While some students appreciate AI's utility in language learning, task efficiency and overcoming linguistic barriers, others highlight challenges, such as maintaining originality and navigating ethical concerns. Professors expressed a mix of optimism and apprehension, recognizing AI's potential to enhance learning while voicing concerns about its impact on the reliability and fairness of student evaluations. They stressed the importance of developing fair assessment practices and providing clear guidelines to ensure responsible AI use. Dang and Iino's study offers significant contributions to the evolving discourse on AI in education, particularly within the context of EMI. It highlights the need for stakeholders to reconsider traditional evaluation systems and adopt diverse, equitable assessment practices that balance the benefits of AI with the cultivation of critical thinking and originality. By addressing the transformative potential and challenges of AI, the chapter provides valuable insights for practitioners and policymakers navigating the future of EMI assessment in Japan and beyond.

Chapter 8, authored by Mo Li and Rui Yuan, explores EMI teachers' perceptions and implementation of assessment in content-area classrooms at a Chinese university. Through a qualitative case study involving six teachers, the chapter examines how assessment practices are shaped by course types and pedagogical beliefs, offering insights for aligning assessments with instructional goals to support both content and language learning. The study categorizes courses into skill-based and competence-based types. Skill-based courses prioritize disciplinary knowledge and technical skills, employing summative assessments such as quizzes and exams with a focus on teacher-led practices. In contrast, competence-based courses emphasize workplace-relevant competencies, using performance-based tasks like projects and simulations that allow greater flexibility in language use and encourage active student participation. Language assessment approaches differ as well, with skill-based courses focusing on terminology and subject-specific English, while competence-based courses adopt a broader perspective, integrating communication and pragmatic skills into assessments. Their findings highlight the importance of constructive alignment between instructional objectives and assessment practices, emphasizing the need for tailored approaches in EMI contexts. The chapter provides actionable recommendations, such as incorporating authentic, performance-based tasks in competence-oriented courses and enhancing EMI teachers' professional development to balance content and language goals effectively.

In Chapter 9, Barry Lee Reynolds and Melissa Yu provide a comprehensive review of EMI assessment frameworks, with a focus on their application in Taiwan. The chapter situates EMI assessment within the sociopolitical, curricular and linguistic contexts of Taiwanese higher education, highlighting the need for localized adaptations of established frameworks. By integrating both local and international perspectives, the authors propose a nuanced approach to developing contextually relevant practices that enhance the efficacy of EMI assessments in diverse educational settings. The authors examine how English functions as an assessment medium, facilitating the delivery and reception of content while addressing the interplay between language proficiency and subject learning. They underscore the dual role of EMI assessments in promoting content mastery and language development, while also addressing challenges such as examination-oriented practices and limited teacher training. Through this analysis, the chapter advocates for integrating classroom assessment as a dynamic component of EMI pedagogy, emphasizing its potential to foster meaningful learning and bridge the gap between global standards and local needs.

Chapter 10, Joyce Kling and Slobodanka Dimova examine the critical role of assessment literacy in EMI classrooms, focusing on the intersection of content and language assessment in multilingual and multicultural contexts. The authors emphasize the challenges faced by EMI educators, such as distinguishing language proficiency issues from disciplinary knowledge gaps and adapting assessment practices to diverse educational cultures. They argue that enhanced EMI assessment literacy (EMIAL) is essential, encompassing contextual and policy literacy, language and content integration, formative assessment strategies and an awareness of students' diverse needs. Drawing on a study of business management teachers in an international dual-degree graduate program, the chapter highlights the importance of professional development in equipping teachers to balance content and language goals effectively. It showcases collaborative assessment practices, such as formative feedback and performance-based tasks, as key strategies for fostering both language and disciplinary competencies. By advocating for an integrated approach to assessment, the chapter offers valuable insights for EMI educators and institutions aiming to enhance teaching and learning outcomes in globalized educational settings.

In Chapter 11, contributed by Ron Martinez and Larissa Giordani Schmitt, examines perceptions of EMI among Brazilian students and instructors across varying levels of English proficiency. Using a qualitative, multiple-case study design, the authors explore the challenges and opportunities presented by EMI in a context where both students and faculty often lack advanced proficiency in English. Data were collected from three public universities in Brazil, involving interviews, questionnaires and standardized English proficiency tests (TOEFL iBT).The findings reveal that while students and instructors initially faced challenges, such as comprehension difficulties and gaps in confidence, these eased over time with increased exposure to EMI. The study highlights the role of interactive teaching strategies, flexible use of the first language (Portuguese), and translanguaging practices in supporting both engagement and learning. Importantly, the authors emphasize the motivational aspects of EMI, with participants expressing a sense of achievement and a desire to continue their engagement with English as an academic medium. By proposing context-specific strategies to address varying proficiency levels and sustain engagement, the chapter offers practical insights for improving EMI outcomes in under-resourced settings like Brazil.

Chapter 12, authored by Wenyun Jia and Qiuyi Zhu, investigates teacher–researcher collaboration in assessing students' disciplinary-specific comprehension ability in an EMI high school economics course in China. The study explores how collaborative efforts between two researchers and two high school economics teachers inform the design and implementation of learning-oriented assessments that integrate content and language. Through a four-phase process – co-exploration of problems, co-design of assessments, co-evaluation of outcomes and co-reflection on instruction – the collaboration aimed to address challenges in assessing students' English-mediated comprehension of economics texts. The findings highlight the complementary roles of teachers and researchers in overcoming assessment challenges. Teachers contributed practical knowledge of students' needs and curriculum alignment, while researchers provided theoretical frameworks and assessment expertise. The collaboration resulted in co-designed assessments, including a multiple-choice reading comprehension test and stimulated recall interviews, which identified gaps in students' language proficiency and disciplinary knowledge. The chapter underscores the potential of teacher–researcher collaboration in enhancing EMI assessment practices and improving instructional strategies to support students' content learning and language development in secondary EMI classrooms.

The concluding chapter, authored by Slobodanka Dimova, synthesizes key findings from the volume and identifies critical emerging needs in EMI assessment. It highlights challenges such as integrating language and content in assessment practices, addressing gaps in stakeholders' EMI assessment literacy (EMIAL), and ensuring assessments are contextually relevant in non-English-dominant settings. The chapter provides a comprehensive analysis of thematic and methodological gaps, advocating for research that moves beyond descriptive studies to explore the consequences of EMI assessment on teaching and learning outcomes. Dimova underscores the importance of designing assessments that reflect the multilingual and translingual realities of EMI classrooms, emphasizing the need for collaboration among educators, policymakers and researchers. By aligning assessment practices with local and global contexts, the chapter offers actionable directions for future research, including developing integrated constructs for assessing language and disciplinary content and expanding the use of diagnostic tools to support student learning. Through these insights, Dimova calls for a reimagining of EMI assessment to better align with the diverse linguistic, cultural, and disciplinary needs of students and educators. This edited volume has come out at a crucial time, given the growing concerns about the validity and fairness of assessment in EME. The original contributions that comprise the volume arguably provide the reader with an extensive and in-depth discussion of EMI assessment. We hope that the volume will foster a deeper understanding of valid assessment design and effective pedagogy in EMI.

References

Aguilar, M. (2017) Engineering lecturers' views on CLIL and EMI. *International Journal of Bilingual Education and Bilingualism* 20 (6), 722–735.

Aizawa, I., Rose, H., Thompson, G. and Curle, S. (2020) Beyond the threshold: Exploring English language proficiency, linguistic challenges, and academic language skills of Japanese students in an English medium instruction programme. *Language Teaching Research*. http://doi.org//1362168820965510

Baird, J.A., Andrich, D., Hopfenbeck, T.N. and Stobart, G. (2017) Assessment and learning: Fields apart? *Assessment in Education: Principles, Policy and Practice* 24 (3), 317–350.

Baker, B. and Hope, A. (2019) Incorporating translanguaging in language assessment: The case of a test for university professors. *Language Assessment Quarterly* 16 (4–5), 408–425.

Barés, G.M. (2022) EMI at a medium-sized Catalan university: Implementing EMI throughout the past 10 years and ahead. In *III Simposio del grupo regional ICLHE España: diferentes perspectivas sobre la sostenibilidad de ICLHE en la educación superior española* (p. 14). Editorial Universidad de Almería (edual).

Black, P. and Wiliam, D. (1998) Assessment and classroom learning. *Assessment in Education: Principles, Policy & Practice* 5 (1), 7–74.

Brown, H.D. and Abeywickrama, P. (2019) *Language Assessment: Principles and Classroom Practices* (3rd edn). Pearson Education.

Curle, S., Lin, Y. and Aizawa, I. (2023) English medium instruction in Japan: Changes and challenges faced by faculty and students. In P. Sah and F. Fang (eds) *Policies, Politics, and Ideologies of English-Medium Instruction in Asian Universities* (pp. 33–47). Routledge.

Curle, S., Yuksel, D., Aizawa, I., Thompson, G. and Rakhshandehroo, M. (2024) Academic success in English Medium Instruction programmes in Turkey: Exploring the effect of gender, motivation, and English language proficiency. *International Journal of Educational Research* 123, 102288.

Dafouz, E. and Smit, U. (2016) Towards a dynamic conceptual framework for English-medium education in multilingual university settings. *Applied Linguistics* 37 (3), 397–415.

Dafouz, E., López-Serrano, S. and Pérez-Paredes, P. (2023) Students' views of disciplinary literacies in internationalised English-medium higher education: Step-by-step survey development. *Research Methods in Applied Linguistics* 2 (3), 100073.

Dearden, J. (2018) The changing roles of EMI academics and English language specialists. In Y. Kırkgoz and K. Dikilitas (eds) *Key Issues in English for Specific Purposes in Higher Education* (pp. 323–338). Springer.

Derakhshan, A., Rakhshanderoo, M. and Curle, S. (2021) University students and instructors' attitudes towards English medium instruction courses: Voices from Iran. In *English-Medium Instruction in Higher Education in the Middle East and North Africa: Policy, Research and Practice*. Bloomsbury Publishing.

Dimova, S. (2017) Life after oral English certification: The consequences of the Test of Oral English Proficiency for Academic Staff for EMI lecturers. *English for Specific Purposes* 46, 45–58.

Dimova, S. (2020) Language assessment of EMI content teachers: What norms. *Language Perceptions and Practices in Multilingual Universities* (pp. 351–378). Palgrave Macmillan.

Dimova, S. and Kling, J. (2022) Emerging assessment needs and solutions in EMI in higher education. *Journal of English-Medium Instruction* 1 (2), 137–152.

Galloway, N., Kriukow, J. and Numajiri, T. (2017) Internationalisation, higher education and the growing demand for English: An investigation into the English medium of instruction (EMI) movement in China and Japan. *British Council ELT Research Papers* 17 (2), 1–39.

Gronchi, M. (2023) Language assessment in EMI: Unravelling the implicit-explicit dichotomy. *Educational Linguistics* 3 (2), 238–257.

Guskey, T.R. (2007) Using assessments to improve teaching and learning. *Ahead of the Curve: The Power of Assessment to Transform Teaching and Learning* (pp. 15–29). Solution Tree.

Holzknecht, F., Guggenbichler, E., Zehentner, M., Yoder, M., Konrad, E. and Kremmel, B. (2022) Comparing EMI university reading materials with students' reading proficiency: Implications for admission testing. *Journal of English-Medium Instruction* 1 (2), 180–203.

Hultgren, A.K., Owen, N., Shrestha, P., Kuteeva, M. and Mežek, Š. (2022) Assessment and English as a medium of instruction: Challenges and opportunities. *Journal of English-Medium Instruction* 1 (1), 105–123.

Inbar-Lourie, O. (2022) EMI programs and formative assessment: Implications for the assessment literacy of content lecturers. *Journal of English-Medium Instruction* 1 (2), 204–231.

Kaya, S., Yuksel, D. and Curle, S. (2023) The effects of language learning and math mindsets on academic success in an engineering program. *Journal of Engineering Education* 112 (1), 90–107.

Kao, Y.T. (2023) Exploring assessment for learning: Assessment tools and approaches in Taiwanese CLIL classes. *The Language Learning Journal* 52 (6), 662–676.

Kao, Y.T. and Tsou, W. (2017) EMI course assessment: A survey study of the issues. In W. Tsou and S-M. Kao (eds) *English as a Medium of Instruction in Higher Education. English Language Education* (Vol. 8). Springer.

Klaassen, R.G. and Bos, M. (2010) English language screening for scientific staff at Delft University of Technology. *HERMES-Journal of Language and Communication in Business* 45, 61–75.

Kling, J.M. and Stæhr, L.S. (2011) Assessment and assistance: Developing university lecturers' language skills through certification feedback. In R. Cancino, K. Jæger and L. Dam (eds) *Policies, Principles, Practices* (pp. 213–245). Cambridge Scholars Publishing.

Kopriva, R. (2000) *Ensuring Accuracy in Testing for English Language Learners.* Council of Chief State School Officers.

Kruiper, S.M., Leenknecht, M.J. and Slof, B. (2022) Using scaffolding strategies to improve formative assessment practice in higher education. *Assessment & Evaluation in Higher Education* 47 (3), 458–476.

Li, C. and Ruan, Z. (2015) Changes in beliefs about language learning among Chinese EAP learners in an EMI context in Mainland China: A socio-cultural perspective. *System* 55, 43–52.

Li, N. and Wu, J. (2018) Exploring assessment for learning practices in the EMI classroom in the context of Taiwanese higher education. *Language Education & Assessment* 1 (1), 28–44.

Li, N. and Wu, J.R. (2021) Assessment practices in the EMI classroom in Chinese-speaking higher education contexts: Challenges and considerations. In L.I. Su, H. Cheung and J.W. Wu (eds) *Rethinking EMI* (pp. 124–140). Springer.

Lo, Y.Y. and Leung, C. (2022) Conceptualising assessment literacy of teachers in Content and Language Integrated Learning programmes. *International Journal of Bilingual Education and Bilingualism* 25 (10), 3816–3834.

Macaro, E., Curle, S., Pun, J., An, J. and Dearden, J. (2018) A systematic review of English medium instruction in higher education. *Language Teaching* 51 (1), 36–76.

Macaro, E., Hultgren, A.K., Kirkpatrick, A. and Lasagabaster, D. (2019) English medium instruction: Global views and countries in focus: Introduction to the symposium held at the Department of Education, University of Oxford on Wednesday 4 November 2015. *Language Teaching* 52 (2), 231–248.

Mancho-Barés, G., Khan, S. and Aguilar-Pérez, M. (2022) An EMI lecturer's assessment practices with engineering laboratory reports. *Journal of English-Medium Instruction* 1 (2), 232–254.

Masrai, A., El-Dakhs, D.A.S. and Yahya, N. (2022) What predicts academic achievement in EMI courses? Focus on vocabulary knowledge and self-perceptions of L2 skills. *SAGE Open* 12 (2), https://doi.org/10.1177/21582440221101044.

Melchor, M.D.R. and Walsh, A.S. (2022) "I'm really not assessing the language": EMI lecturers' perceptions of their implicit and explicit assessment of students' language production. *Ibérica: Revista de la Asociación Europea de Lenguas para Fines Específicos (AELFE)* 44, 345–368.

Molino, A., Dimova, S., Kling, J. and Larsen, S. (2022) *The Evolution of EMI Research in European Higher Education*. Routledge.

Newton, P.E. (2007) Clarifying the purposes of educational assessment. *Assessment in Education* 14 (2), 149–170.

O'Dowd, R. (2018) The training and accreditation of teachers for English medium instruction: An overview of practice in European universities. *International Journal of Bilingual Education and Bilingualism* 21 (5), 553–563.

Rahman, A. (2020) Receptive vocabulary size as a predictor of undergraduates' overall cumulative grade point average with English as Medium of Instruction in universities. *Asia-Pacific Social Science Review* 20 (3), 56–75.

Rose, H., Curle, S., Aizawa, I. and Thompson, G. (2020) What drives success in English medium taught courses? The interplay between language proficiency, academic skills, and motivation. *Studies in Higher Education* 45 (11), 2149–2161.

Rose, H., Macaro, E., Sahan, K., Aizawa, I., Zhou, S. and Wei, M. (2023) Defining English medium instruction: Striving for comparative equivalence. *Language Teaching* 56 (4), 539–550.

Sánchez-Pérez, M. (2021) Predicting content proficiency through disciplinary-literacy variables in English-medium writing. *System* 97, 1–12.

Schellekens, L.H., Bok, H.G., de Jong, L.H., van der Schaaf, M.F., Kremer, W.D. and van der Vleuten, C.P. (2021) A scoping review on the notions of Assessment as Learning (AaL), Assessment for Learning (AfL) and Assessment of Learning (AoL). *Studies in Educational Evaluation* 71, 101094.

Schoepp, K. (2018) Predictive validity of the IELTS in an English as a medium of instruction environment. *Higher Education Quarterly* 72 (4), 271–285.

Shohamy, E. and Menken, K. (2015) Language assessment: Past to present misuses and future possibilities. In W. Wright, S. Boun and O. García (eds) *The Handbook of Bilingual and Multilingual Education* (pp. 253–269). Wiley-Blackwell.

Soruç, A., Altay, M., Curle, S. and Yuksel, D. (2021) Students' academic language-related challenges in English medium instruction: The role of English proficiency and language gain. *System* 103, 102651.

Stuers, S. (2019) *Access to and Experience of English-Medium Instruction in Higher Education in Germany: A Study into English Language Entry Requirements and their Relevance*. Open University (United Kingdom).

Thompson, G., Curle, S. and Aizawa, I. (2022) It's worth the extra effort: Behind student perceptions of success in the study of content via English-Medium instruction in Japan. In J. McKinley and N. Galloway (eds) *English-Medium Instruction Practices in Higher Education: International Perspectives*, 213. Bloomsbury.

Wächter, B. and Maiworm, F. (eds) (2014) *English-Taught Programmes in European Higher Education: The State of Play In 2014*. Lemmens Medien GmbH.

Wicking, P. (2020) Formative assessment of students from a Confucian heritage culture: Insights from Japan. *Assessment & Evaluation in Higher Education* 45 (2), 180–192.

Wiggins, G. (1998) *Educative Assessment. Designing Assessments To Inform and Improve Student Performance*. Jossey-Bass Publishers.

Yüksel, D., Altay, M. and Curle, S. (2022) English Medium Instruction programmes in Turkey: Evidence of exponential growth. In S. Curle, H.I. Holi Ali, A. Alhassan and S. Saleem Scatolini (eds) *English-Medium Instruction in Higher Education in the Middle East and North Africa: Policy, Research and Practice* (pp. 1–10). Bloomsbury Publishing.

Zhou, S. and Thompson, G. (2023) A longitudinal study on students' self-regulated listening during transition to an English-medium transnational University in China. *Studies in Second Language Learning and Teaching* 13 (2), 427–450.

1 Exploring the Frontier: Efficacy, Challenges and Future Directions in English Medium Instruction Assessment Practices

Samantha Curle and Pınar Koçer

1.1 Introduction

In the evolving landscape of global education, the phenomenon of English medium instruction (EMI) has emerged as a transformative force, redefining educational practices across continents. EMI, defined as the use of English to teach academic subjects in countries where English is not the majority's first language (Macaro, 2018: 18), has proliferated in recent years, significantly impacting the dynamics of teaching and learning in diverse geographical regions.

1.1.1 The global surge of EMI: A phenomenon of the 21st century

The last decade has witnessed an unprecedented rise in the adoption of EMI, particularly in higher education. This global surge is intricately tied to the phenomena of globalisation and academic mobility (Curle *et al.*, 2020a). The role of English as a lingua franca in professional and academic settings further catalyses its adoption (Curle, 2018; Rose *et al.*, 2021). Macaro *et al.* (2018) highlight EMI's growing prevalence in universities and schools across Europe, Asia, Africa and Latin America. The world-wide spread use of EMI reflects not only the internationalisation of education but also the strategic positioning of institutions and nations in the global knowledge economy.

1.1.2 The critical role of assessment in EMI

In the EMI context, assessment assumes a pivotal role, transcending traditional academic evaluations to encompass a dual focus on content mastery and language proficiency. The distinct nature of EMI necessitates a nuanced approach to assessment, one that acknowledges the complexities of learning subject content through a non-native language. As Hamid *et al.* (2015) point out, effective assessment in EMI settings is paramount in ensuring that educational outcomes are equitable and representative of (at a minimum) academic subject understanding and, possibly as well, linguistic understanding. This duality poses unique challenges, highlighting the need for assessments that are not only linguistically accessible but also academically rigorous.

1.1.3 Objectives and scope of this chapter

This chapter aims to synthesise the latest empirical research to provide a comprehensive overview of current practices and emerging trends in EMI assessment. To ensure clarity and transparency, the chapter incorporates a detailed review of current studies related to three fundamental aspects.

(1) **The efficacy of EMI assessment:** This section evaluates the effectiveness of current assessment practices within EMI settings and their alignment with educational goals. It draws on empirical studies encompassing both quantitative and qualitative research, identifying key patterns and variations in efficacy.
(2) **Challenges in EMI assessment design:** This section identifies and analyses the challenges faced in designing and implementing effective assessments in EMI contexts. The analysis highlights common themes across studies, including resource constraints, language proficiency considerations and cultural factors influencing assessment design.
(3) **Exploration of research gaps:** This section highlights areas lacking in-depth study and suggests directions for future research that could contribute to the enhancement of EMI assessment practices. It maps the coverage of existing research, noting overlaps and underexplored areas across the aforementioned aspects.

Throughout the chapter, the methodology for identifying, categorising and analysing studies is clearly outlined, providing readers with an understanding of how the literature was selected and grouped by relevance to these aspects. The review also summarises the extent of coverage observed, indicating whether studies addressed one, two or all three aspects, and where significant overlaps or gaps were found. This approach ensures a robust and transparent synthesis, offering valuable insights for educators, policymakers and academic researchers, while paving the way for future studies to address identified gaps.

1.2 Methodology of the Literature Review

1.2.1 Approach to literature selection

The literature review for this chapter was conducted with a systematic and rigorous approach to ensure comprehensive coverage of the relevant research on EMI assessment (Chong & Plonsky, 2024). The selection criteria were designed to include peer-reviewed articles, seminal books and authoritative reports published primarily within the last decade, to reflect the most current trends and findings in the field. Special attention was given to studies that offer empirical data, critical analyses and case studies from diverse educational contexts.

1.2.2 Data sources and search strategy

The search for relevant literature was conducted across several academic databases, including JSTOR, ERIC, Google Scholar, Scopus and Web of Science. Keywords used in the search included 'English Medium Instruction', 'EMI Assessment', 'EMI in Higher Education', 'Globalisation and EMI', 'EMI Challenges' and 'EMI Efficacy'. These terms were combined with Boolean operators to refine the search results. The search was also extended to bibliographies of key articles and books to identify additional relevant sources (Velez-Estevez *et al.*, 2023).

1.2.3 Method of analysis and synthesis

Once the literature was collected, it was subjected to a thematic analysis to identify and categorise key themes and patterns. This process involved an initial reading to gain an understanding of the general content, followed by a more detailed review to extract specific information related to EMI assessment practices, challenges, efficacy and research gaps. The analysis aimed to synthesise findings from various studies to present a coherent and comprehensive overview of the state of EMI assessment. Emerging trends, common challenges and innovative practices were highlighted (Curle & Pun, 2023). The synthesis also involved a critical examination of the methodologies used in the studies to ensure the reliability and validity of the findings presented.

1.2.4 Inclusion and exclusion criteria

Studies were included in the review if they provided direct insights into assessment practices within EMI settings, addressed challenges or efficacy of EMI assessment, or discussed policy and implementation aspects relevant to EMI assessment. Exclusion criteria involved studies that were not in English, those that focused solely on English language instruction without a direct connection to EMI content assessment, and older publications that did not reflect the current context of EMI. This methodology ensured a thorough and balanced review of the literature, providing a solid foundation for the subsequent sections of the chapter. The resulting synthesis offers a nuanced understanding of the current state of EMI assessment, grounded in empirical evidence, and contemporary scholarly discourse.

1.3 The Efficacy of EMI Assessment

1.3.1 Overview of key findings

The efficacy of assessment in EMI settings has been a focal point of recent academic discourse (Arslan & Curle, 2021; Hultgren *et al.*, 2022). EMI assessment is particularly complex as the main focus is to assess academic content knowledge; however, the influence of English language proficiency on this assessment poses a significant challenge (Graham *et al.*, 2018). This challenge is not trivial; it requires a nuanced approach to ensure that the assessment accurately reflects students' understanding of the subject matter without their language proficiency unduly influencing the outcome.

1.3.2 Comparative analysis with non-EMI settings

In comparing EMI with non-EMI settings, a study in Italy by Costa and Mariotti (2017) examined EMI Economics students' ($n = 214$) learning outcomes. The students' performance, based on marks obtained in two comparable written exams, showed no significant difference in learning outcomes between the L1 and L2 instruction groups. This suggests that the medium of instruction (Italian or English) did not notably impact the students' academic performance. Del Campo *et al.* (2015) found that students studying Business Administration through EMI in Spain outperformed their peers in relation to academic content, compared with those studying Business through Spanish. However, the authors did note the small sample size, and therefore lack of ability to generalise. There is a debate on whether this improvement comes at the expense of content understanding. Aguilar and Muñoz (2014) suggest that while EMI can lead to higher language proficiency, it may initially pose challenges in content comprehension, a gap that tends to narrow over time with adequate support and adaptation.

1.3.3 Balancing content and language in EMI assessment

Successful EMI assessment practices often involve innovative approaches that integrate content and language learning. Dafouz and Smit (2020) illustrate this in a European university where EMI assessments were designed to evaluate content understanding while simultaneously supporting language development. This approach aligns with findings from Dearden's (2014) research, which advocates for assessments that are sensitive to students' language proficiency levels without compromising on the rigor of content evaluation. The balance between content and language proficiency in EMI assessment is critical. Research by Kao and Tsou (2017) in the Taiwanese context shows that effective EMI assessments are those that acknowledge students' language challenges while maintaining academic standards. Findings from interviews with 29 tertiary EMI teachers revealed a careful design of assessment tasks that are linguistically accessible yet intellectually demanding.

1.3.4 The role of formative assessment

Formative assessment is increasingly recognised as a crucial component in the effectiveness of EMI, primarily owing to its role in providing ongoing feedback and facilitating the continuous progression of learning. Otto and Estrada Chichón (2021) have highlighted the significance of formative assessments in supporting students' academic development within EMI contexts. This type of assessment, characterised by its iterative and responsive nature, enables educators to tailor their teaching to meet the evolving needs of their students.

Inbar-Lourie (2022) brings to light the paucity of research specifically dedicated to formative assessment practices within EMI programmes. There is a clear gap in the scholarship regarding how formative assessment is being implemented, its efficacy and the impact it has on both language and content learning within EMI environments. Through the lens of sociocultural theory, which posits that learning is a socially mediated process, the study identifies four pivotal areas that are essential to developing a robust framework of assessment literacy for EMI programmes. These areas include:

(1) **Contextual and policy literacies:** This involves an understanding of the educational context, including institutional policies and the sociopolitical climate that influences and shapes the practice of assessment in EMI. Recognising these factors is crucial for developing assessments that are not only educationally sound but also culturally and politically responsive.
(2) **The role of language in facilitating content learning:** Language is not merely a medium of instruction in EMI; it plays an active role in shaping students' comprehension and engagement with the content. Thus, assessments must be designed to discern and support the intertwined development of language and content knowledge.
(3) **Formative assessment for learning orientations:** Formative assessments should be oriented towards learning, which means they should

be used not just to measure students' performance but to actively promote and enhance learning. This implies a shift from summative assessment practices towards a more formative approach, emphasising ongoing feedback and adjustment.

(4) **Awareness and understanding of students' linguistic and content needs:** Educators must be acutely aware of their students' specific linguistic and content needs. This awareness should be reflected in the design and implementation of assessments to ensure they are equitable and supportive of all students' learning.

Inbar-Lourie (2022) underscores the imperative for targeted training in assessment for lecturers who teach EMI content courses. Such training should focus on integrating continuous, feedback-led assessment strategies to effectively address the unique challenges of the EMI content-language integrated framework. By fostering a thorough understanding of formative assessment practices within the theoretical framework of sociocultural theory, EMI programmes can enhance their pedagogical approaches, leading to improved educational outcomes.

1.3.5 Considerations for fair and valid assessments

At the heart of this EMI assessment training should be fairness and validity, as these are paramount in EMI assessments. Hamid *et al.* (2019) emphasise the need for assessments that are equitable and representative of students' capabilities in both language and content. This necessitates a mindful approach to assessment design – one that rigorously accounts for the varied linguistic backgrounds of students and actively seeks to mitigate any biases that might unfairly impact non-native English speakers. Moreover, the theoretical framework for such assessments should be anchored in the notion of inclusive assessment practices (Nieminen, 2022; Yuksel *et al.*, 2021). These practices should be geared towards providing all students, irrespective of their first language, with an equal opportunity to demonstrate their understanding and mastery of the subject matter. Teachers need to be equipped with the strategies and tools to construct and implement assessments that are not only content-valid but also linguistically accessible. This dual-objective approach ensures that the assessment process is a fair measure of student learning outcomes, truly reflective of the diverse EMI classroom environment.

In conclusion, effective assessment in EMI is critical for accurately reflecting students' content understanding while accommodating their English proficiency. Comparative studies, such as those by Costa and Mariotti (2017) and Del Campo *et al.* (2015), indicate that the instructional language does not significantly affect academic outcomes, although initial challenges in content comprehension can be mitigated over time with appropriate support, as suggested by Aguilar and Muñoz (2014). Research by Otto and Estrada Chichón (2021) and Inbar-Lourie (2022) highlights the importance of formative assessment in EMI, advocating for ongoing feedback and adjustment to meet students' learning needs. The imperative for fairness and validity in EMI assessments, emphasised by Hamid *et al.* (2019), calls for inclusive practices that are sensitive to linguistic diversity and that promote equitable learning opportunities for all students. Continued research and innovative practices are essential for optimising the efficacy of EMI assessment.

1.4 Challenges in EMI Assessment Design

1.4.1 Linguistic proficiency and assessment outcomes

One of the foremost challenges in EMI assessment design is accommodating the varying levels of students' English language proficiency. Studies by Curle *et al.* (2020b) illustrate how differences in linguistic competence can significantly affect students' performance, particularly in assessments that do not account for these disparities. This mixed-methods study at a public university in Turkey investigated academic success in an Economics programme, comparing EMI and Turkish Medium Instruction (TMI) among fourth-year students (n = 159). It found that while general English proficiency wasn't a significant predictor of EMI success, academic achievement in TMI courses did predict success in EMI courses, demonstrating how the first language enhance learning outcomes. The challenge of English language proficiency therefore necessitates a careful consideration of language support mechanisms within EMI assessment design to ensure fairness and inclusivity.

1.4.2 Balancing content knowledge and language ability

Another critical issue is the balance between assessing subject knowledge and English language skills. A study by Airey (2016) highlights the risk of content knowledge being overshadowed by language proficiency demands. Effective EMI assessments should therefore strive to evaluate content understanding without letting language proficiency unduly influence the outcomes. This balance is crucial to the validity of the assessment process in EMI settings. Differentiating between language assessment and content assessment in EMI poses a unique challenge. A systematic review by Thippayacharoen *et al.* (2023) indicates the need for clarity in what is being assessed – language proficiency or content knowledge. This differentiation is essential for the development of fair and effective assessment criteria in EMI programmes.

1.4.3 Institutional and logistical challenges

Institutional and logistical challenges are significant barriers to the successful implementation of EMI assessments. At the core of these challenges is the resource allocation for developing appropriate assessment materials that align with the dual demands of language and content proficiency (Earl, 2013). Institutions often grapple with the scarcity of qualified personnel who possess the requisite expertise in both the subject matter and English language, which is essential for the creation and execution of EMI assessments (Dearden, 2015). Another pressing concern is the standardisation of assessment practices, which is especially complex in diverse educational contexts with varying standards and student needs (Doiz *et al.*, 2013). These challenges necessitate not only significant strategic planning but also the fostering of a collaborative environment where stakeholders can work together to develop robust, adaptable and fair assessment strategies that are sensitive to the EMI context (Altay *et al.*, 2022). Without addressing these institutional and logistical hurdles, the potential benefits of EMI assessments may not be fully realised, underscoring the need for concerted efforts to overcome these obstacles to support the advancement of EMI programmes.

1.4.4 Diversity and inclusivity in assessment practices

In EMI programmes, the diversity of student backgrounds presents a unique set of challenges, particularly in the realm of assessment. The design and implementation of assessments in such settings require a nuanced approach that acknowledges and accommodates the varied cultural and educational backgrounds of students (Ismailov *et al.*, 2021). Dearden (2015) emphasises, assessments in EMI contexts should not only test content knowledge but also be sensitive to the diverse linguistic and cultural backgrounds of the students. This involves an understanding of different learning styles, as well as the cultural nuances that may influence how students interpret and respond to assessment tasks. Furthermore, Dunn and Griggs (2000) highlight the importance of adapting teaching and assessment methods to cater to diverse learning styles, suggesting that this adaptation can significantly enhance student performance and engagement. In EMI settings, where students come from various linguistic and cultural backgrounds, such adaptability becomes even more crucial. EMI students also need acclimatisation to the norms and expectations of their EMI academic environment. Ryan and Carroll (2005) discuss the concept of 'academic socialisation', which refers to this process. In EMI contexts, where students may be unfamiliar with the educational norms of the medium language, assessments need to be designed in a way that supports this socialisation process, helping students to understand and meet the academic expectations. For example, a significant number of students in an EMI programme at a foreign university may come from educational backgrounds that did not emphasise critical thinking and independent analysis, which are often key components of Western educational norms (Sellars *et al.*, 2018). In such a scenario, directly introducing these students to standard Western-style assessments (like essays requiring critical analysis or open-ended research projects) might lead to confusion and poor performance, not necessarily because of a lack of understanding of the content, but owing to unfamiliarity with these types of assessment formats. To support these students, EMI instructors could implement a scaffolded approach to assessments. Initially, assessments might start with more structured tasks that are familiar to the students, such as short-answer questions or exercises that require recalling and summarising information. Gradually, as the course progresses, the assessments could incorporate elements that require higher-order thinking skills, like critical analysis or application of concepts to new scenarios. This approach not only assesses students' understanding of the course material but also supports their adaptation to the educational norms of the EMI context, enhancing their overall academic success (Yuksel *et al.*, 2022). The development of culturally sensitive and inclusive assessment practices in EMI programmes is essential. Such practices should not only accommodate the diverse linguistic abilities of students but also their cultural and educational backgrounds, learning styles and the need for academic socialisation. By doing so, educators can ensure that assessments are fair, equitable and truly reflective of student learning.

1.4.5 Concluding comments

Designing EMI assessments requires careful consideration of students' varied linguistic proficiencies, alongside the need for institutional support in developing and implementing these evaluations (Dearden, 2015). As academic performance is intertwined with language competence, educators must craft fair assessments that accurately reflect both content knowledge and linguistic ability (Curle *et al.*, 2020b). Moreover, embracing the concept of 'academic socialisation' (Ryan & Carroll, 2005) can guide the development of assessments that not only test knowledge but also help students acclimate to the academic norms of an EMI environment. Successfully addressing these challenges is crucial for the advancement of EMI programmes, ensuring that assessments are valid, inclusive and supportive of the diverse student body that characterises these educational settings.

1.5 Research Gaps in EMI Assessment

1.5.1 Under-explored research areas in EMI assessment

In the landscape of EMI research, several domains warrant further scholarly investigation to enhance our understanding of EMI's efficacy and impact. In the realm of assessment, the following might be suggested avenues of research to investigate:

- The long-term academic and linguistic trajectories of students enrolled in EMI programmes, demanding diligent, longitudinal monitoring to evaluate the sustained influence of EMI on learner achievement and language proficiency.
- The impact of EMI on different academic disciplines, scrutinising how EMI intersects with discipline-specific literacies and shapes subject understanding.
- The socioemotional dimensions within EMI environments, including student perspectives, attitudes, experiences, motivational factors and the potential for anxiety and stress among learners when taking their EMI assessment.
- The perspectives of EMI educators on EMI assessment, including the challenges and practices in designing and implementing culturally and linguistically appropriate assessment methods, and the impact of professional development tailored to EMI environments on assessment practices.
- The interplay between EMI, identity development and formation, and acculturation processes, and how these shape learning outcomes.
- The validity and effectiveness of assessment tools in EMI settings, especially in relation to their ability to accommodate learner diversity and demonstrate cultural responsiveness and adaptability across diverse EMI educational contexts.
- The adequacy of assessment in gauging teacher readiness and professional growth within EMI contexts, which is critical for addressing the distinct challenges presented to educators.
- The ramifications of EMI adoption on assessment policies, which require careful scrutiny of the educational and sociopolitical impacts at both institutional and national strata.
- The integration of digital technologies (including artificial intelligence (AI)) in EMI assessment, investigating the impact of technological tools and resources on EMI learning outcomes.

To fully harness the potential of EMI, it is imperative to address these gaps in EMI assessment research. By delving deeper into these under-explored areas, we can enhance student learning outcomes, ensuring that EMI practices are tailored to effectively meet the diverse educational needs of both learners and educators. Some of these aspects will now be further elaborated.

1.5.1.1 The need for longitudinal, comparative and cross-cultural studies

In relation to the long-term academic and linguistic trajectories of students enrolled in EMI programmes, there is a pressing need for diligent, longitudinal monitoring to evaluate the sustained influence of EMI on learner achievement and language proficiency. Longitudinal research (see Yuksel *et al.*, 2023) tracking the academic and linguistic development of students over extended periods, is imperative. This approach would provide a more nuanced understanding of how EMI influences learners' academic performance and language proficiency over time. It is particularly important to examine how students' language skills evolve in tandem with their academic knowledge in EMI settings, and how these trajectories differ across diverse cultural and educational landscapes.

A critical gap identified in the literature is the dearth of comparative studies across different educational contexts. Highlighted by Macaro *et al.*, back in 2018, despite the vast number of EMI empirical studies, there remains a notable shortfall in studies that compare EMI outcomes in varied cultural and linguistic environments. Such studies are imperative to examine how EMI is implemented and experienced in various cultural and academic settings to fully grasp its pedagogical implications and effectiveness. These studies would offer valuable insights into how contextual factors influence the efficacy of EMI and are essential to understand the global applicability and adaptability of EMI practices.

By conducting longitudinal, comparative and cross-cultural studies, researchers can gain a comprehensive understanding of the multifaceted impact of EMI, thereby informing more effective and context-sensitive EMI strategies and policies.

1.5.1.2 Practitioner-oriented research

Another significant gap is the limited focus on practitioner experiences and perspectives in EMI assessment research. A primary area of interest is the adaptation of assessment methods by educators in EMI settings, a challenge highlighted by Earls (2016), who stresses the need for assessments that are linguistically and culturally appropriate for diverse student populations. This includes balancing content knowledge and language proficiency in assessments, a complex task that necessitates professional development tailored to the unique demands of EMI environments. Such professional development should focus on equipping educators with skills in differentiated instruction and formative assessment techniques, crucial for multilingual classrooms (Deroey, 2023). Furthermore, the beliefs and perceptions of teachers regarding EMI assessments, as Hultgren *et al.* (2022) note, significantly influence their assessment practices. Investigating teacher-student interactions during the assessment process can shed light on the communication of assessment criteria and feedback, essential for ensuring fairness and inclusivity.

Another vital aspect, particularly relevant to practitioner-oriented research in EMI, is the exploration of collaborative assessment practices, such as peer and self-assessment. Andrade *et al.* (2019) highlight the potential of these methods to significantly enhance student engagement and learning outcomes. For educators, understanding the nuances and effectiveness of these approaches in EMI contexts is crucial. It involves examining how peer and self-assessment can be effectively integrated into diverse subject areas, the ways in which they influence student' language proficiency and content understanding, and the extent to which they foster a more interactive and reflective learning environment. Therefore, investigating the training and support educators need to implement these methods effectively is essential. This research could reveal how collaborative assessments can be tailored to meet the specific linguistic and academic needs of students in EMI programmes, potentially leading to more dynamic and student-centred learning experiences.

Additionally, the influence of various assessment formats on learning outcomes within EMI contexts represents a significant, yet under-researched, area. As Jenkins and Leung (2017) have pointed out, there is a crucial need to investigate how different types of assessments – such as project-based, oral presentations, written exams and digital assessments – affect students' understanding and engagement with both the subject matter and the English language. This exploration is essential not only to gauge the effectiveness of these varying formats in accurately measuring student learning but also to understand how they cater to or challenge the linguistic and cognitive abilities of students in EMI settings. Such research could provide valuable insights into developing more effective and inclusive assessment strategies that align with the diverse needs of learners in in the dynamically diverse landscape of EMI.

1.5.1.3 Integrating technology (including AI) in EMI assessment

With the rise of digital technology in education, there is a growing need to explore how technology can be effectively integrated into EMI assessment. Recent works by Tekir (2023) discuss the potential of digital tools in enhancing EMI assessment but note that empirical research in this area is still budding. Studies focusing on the use of technology in EMI assessment can shed light on innovative practices and their impact on learning outcomes.

The infusion of AI into EMI assessment is pioneering a transformative shift towards more individualised and accurate student evaluations. The insights from Cropley (2023) illuminate how machine learning algorithms underpinning AI can tailor assessments to the unique learning journeys of each student, providing a nuanced and adaptive assessment landscape. Such assessments can adapt to each student's comprehension level, learning speed and language proficiency, offering a more equitable evaluation method in the diverse classrooms of EMI settings. This approach not only accommodates different learning styles but also yields detailed data on student learning, aiding educators in customising their teaching methods. AI assessments can also help overcome language barriers in EMI, supporting both content understanding and language development. This work thus signals a shift towards a more personalised, responsive and comprehensive assessment framework in EMI programmes through the use of AI and machine learning technologies.

1.5.2 AI and language proficiency

The research conducted by Rusmiyanto *et al.* (2023) highlights a groundbreaking approach in the realm of language proficiency assessment within EMI contexts, leveraging the power of AI. These AI-driven language assessment tools offer a profound depth in evaluating students' linguistic capabilities. They extend beyond traditional methods, providing detailed insights into various aspects of language skills such as grammar, vocabulary, pronunciation and fluency. This enables a more nuanced understanding of each student's linguistic strengths and weaknesses, facilitating a tailored approach to language learning and development. In EMI settings, where English language proficiency is often a key determinant of academic success, the implementation of AI in language assessment can be particularly impactful. These tools not only enhance the precision of language evaluations but also contribute significantly to a more supportive and individualised educational experience for learners. Educators can gain valuable insights from these assessments, allowing them to adapt their instructional methods to better suit the linguistic needs of their students. Rusmiyanto *et al.*'s study (2023) thus points towards a future where AI not only improves the accuracy and efficacy of language assessments but also fosters a more encompassing and successful language learning environment within EMI programmes. This advancement aligns with the primary goals of EMI, to deliver quality education while supporting language development, showcasing the potential of technology as a vital tool in EMI educational settings.

1.5.3 Challenges of integrating AI in EMI

The integration of AI into EMI assessment is not without its institutional and ethical challenges. The considerations of reliability and fairness, as raised by Bannister *et al.* (2023) are paramount in ensuring AI tools serve all students equitably, particularly in the linguistically diverse settings of EMI. A primary concern raised by the authors revolves around the issues of reliability and fairness of AI tools in assessments. In EMI contexts, where students come from a variety of linguistic backgrounds, the need to ensure that AI-driven assessments are equitable and unbiased is critical. The study emphasises the importance of developing AI systems that can accurately and fairly evaluate students' academic and linguistic abilities, irrespective of their native language or cultural background. This challenge is compounded by the inherent complexities in programming AI to understand and assess human language in a nuanced and context-sensitive manner. Furthermore, the potential exists for AI to inadvertently perpetuate existing inequalities. If AI tools are not carefully designed and implemented, they could disadvantage students who may not have the same level of familiarity or comfort with such technology, or those whose linguistic nuances (e.g. pronunciation) might not be as easily recognised by AI algorithms. This raises substantial concerns regarding social justice in education, particularly in ensuring that AI in EMI assessments do not become a tool that widens the gap between different student groups. There should therefore be a concerted effort for a collaborative effort between technologists, linguists, educators and policymakers to address these challenges. There will be a need to for rigorous testing and continuous refinement of AI tools, coupled with a robust ethical framework to guide their development and implementation in EMI assessment. By doing so, AI can be harnessed to support an educational setting that is fairer and more welcoming to all learners, aligning with the core objectives of EMI to provide quality education accessible to all learners.

These avenues promise to unlock innovative practices that recognise the multilingual capabilities of students and the practical implications for educators in EMI environments. The forward trajectory of EMI assessment therefore lies in the confluence of AI advancements with a deeper understanding of the educator and student experiences. This synergy is set to redefine educational evaluation in EMI programmes, fostering a future where technology and pedagogy coalesce to create a more inclusive, accurate and effective assessment paradigm.

1.5.4 Concluding comments

Addressing these research gaps is essential for advancing our understanding of EMI assessment and enhancing the effectiveness of EMI. Future research should focus on longitudinal and comparative studies, deepen our understanding of the practitioners' role in assessment, and explore the intersection of digital technology such as AI and EMI assessment. Such efforts can contribute significantly to the development of more robust, inclusive and efficient EMI assessment strategies.

1.6 Conclusion

In this chapter on assessment in EMI, it is evident that the field is at a crucial juncture, brimming with potential yet facing significant challenges. The incorporation of innovative technologies like AI presents exciting opportunities to create assessments that are more adaptive, personalised and reflective of individual student needs. This technology has the potential to not only enhance the fairness and effectiveness of assessments but also to support the unique linguistic and educational backgrounds of a diverse EMI student body. However, the integration of such advancements must be approached with caution. The ethical implications, the need for equitable access and the potential for AI to inadvertently perpetuate educational inequalities are critical concerns that must be addressed. This will require a collaborative effort among all EMI stakeholders.

Moreover, the broader issues surrounding EMI assessment, such as the differentiation between language proficiency and content knowledge, institutional and logistical challenges, and the need for diversity and inclusivity in assessment practices, remain paramount. These challenges highlight the necessity for a multifaceted approach to assessment in EMI that is sensitive to the needs of a global and diverse student population. As we look to the future, it is clear that the evolution of EMI assessment will be shaped by the dynamic interplay between technological advancements and a deepening understanding of the educational experiences of both educators and students. This synergy is poised to redefine educational evaluation in EMI programmes, paving the way for a more inclusive, accurate and effective assessment paradigm. Continued research and exploration in this field are therefore imperative, focusing on longitudinal and comparative studies, and further probing into the intersections of digital technology and EMI assessment. Such efforts will be instrumental in developing robust, inclusive and efficient EMI assessment strategies, ultimately aligning with the core objectives of EMI to provide quality education accessible to all learners.

References

Aguilar, M. and Muñoz, C. (2014) The effect of proficiency on CLIL benefits in Engineering students in Spain. *International Journal of Applied Linguistics* 24 (1), 1–18.

Airey, J. (2016) EMI, CLIL, and CBI: Differing approaches and goals. *Content and Language Integrated Learning* 2 (1), 30–43.

Altay, M., Curle, S., Yuksel, D. and Soruç, A. (2022) Investigating academic achievement of English medium instruction courses in Turkey. *Studies in Second Language Learning and Teaching* 12 (1), 117–141. https://pressto.amu.edu.pl/index.php/ssllt/article/view/26179

Andrade, H.L., Bennett, R.E. and Cizek, G.J. (eds) (2019) *Handbook of Formative Assessment in the Disciplines*. Routledge.

Arslan, S. and Curle, S. (2021) The Sustainable Development Goals in the English language high school curriculum in Turkey. *European Journal of Education*. https://onlinelibrary.wiley.com/doi/10.1111/ejed.12473

Bannister, P., Santamaría-Urbieta, A. and Alcalde-Peñalver, E. (2023) A Delphi study on generative artificial intelligence and English medium instruction assessment: Implications for social justice. *Iranian Journal of Language Teaching Research* 11 (3), 53–80.

Chong, S.W. and Plonsky, L. (2024) A typology of secondary research in Applied Linguistics. *Applied Linguistics Review* 15 (4), 1569–1594. https://doi.org/10.1515/applirev-2022-0189.

Costa, F.G. and Mariotti, C. (2017) Differences in content presentation and learning outcomes in English-medium instruction (EMI) vs. Italian-medium instruction (IMI) contexts. In J.A.W.R. Valcke (ed.) *Integrating Content and Language in Higher Education* (pp. 187–204). https://doi.org/10.3726/978-3-653-07263-1

Cropley, D.H. (2023) Making an impact: Fit-for-purpose creativity assessment. In F.K. Reisman (ed.) *Unpacking Creativity: Culture, Innovation, and Motivation in Global Contexts* (pp. 154–174). KIE Publications.

Curle, S. (2018) Developing and validating a Japanese English Medium of Instruction Attitude Scale (JEMIAS). *The Journal of Asia TEFL* 15 (4), 900–1238. http://dx.doi.org/10.18823/asiatefl.2018.15.4.24.1195

Curle, S.M. and Pun, J.K. (eds) (2023) *Qualitative Research Methods in English Medium Instruction for Emerging Researchers: Theory and Case Studies of Contemporary Research*. Routledge.

Curle, S., Jablonkai, R., Mittelmeier, J., Sahan, K. and Veitch, A. (2020a) English Medium Part 1: Literature review. In N. Galloway (ed.) *English in Higher Education (Report No. 978-0-86355-977–8)*. British Council. https://www.teachingenglish.org.uk/article/english-higher-education-%E2%80%93-english-medium-part-1-literature-review

Curle, S., Yuksel, D., Soruç, A. and Altay, M. (2020b) Predictors of English medium instruction academic success: English proficiency versus first language medium. *System* 95, 102378.

Dafouz, E. and Smit, U. (2020) *ROAD-MAPPING English Medium Education in the Internationalised University*. Springer International Publishing.

Dearden, J. (2014) *English as a Medium of Instruction – A Growing Global Phenomenon*. British Council.

Dearden, J. and Macaro, E. (2016) Higher education teachers' attitudes towards English medium instruction: A three-country comparison. *Studies in Second Language Learning and Teaching* 6 (3), 455–486.

Del Campo, C., Cancer, A., Pascual-Ezama, D. and Urquía-Grande, E. (2015) EMI vs. Non-EMI: Preliminary analysis of the academic output within the INTE-R-LICA Project. *Procedia-Social and Behavioral Sciences* 212, 74–79.

Deroey, K.L. (2023) English medium instruction lecturer training programmes: Content, delivery, ways forward. *Journal of English for Academic Purposes* 101223.

Doiz, A., Lasagabaster, D. and Sierra, J.M. (eds) (2013) *English-Medium Instruction at Universities: Global Challenges*. Multilingual Matters.

Dunn, R. and Griggs, S.A. (2000) *Practical Approaches to Using Learning Styles in Higher Education*. Bloomsbury Publishing.

Earl, L.M. (2013) *Assessment as Learning: Using Classroom Assessment to Maximize Student Learning* (2nd edn). Corwin Press.

Earls, C.W. (2016) *Evolving Agendas in European English-Medium Higher Education: Interculturality, Multilingualism and Language Policy*. Springer.

Graham, K.M., Choi, Y., Davoodi, A., Razmeh, S. and Dixon, L.Q. (2018) Language and content outcomes of CLIL and EMI: A systematic review. *Latin American Journal of Content and Language Integrated Learning* 11 (1), 19–37.

Hamid, M.O., Nguyen, H.T.M. and Baldauf, R.B. (2015) Medium of instruction in Asia: Context, processes and outcomes. In M.O. Hamid, H.T.M. Nguyen and R.B. Baldauf (eds) *Language Planning for Medium of Instruction in Asia* (pp. 1–15). Routledge.

Hultgren, A.K., Owen, N., Shrestha, P., Kuteeva, M. and Mežek, Š. (2022) Assessment and English as a medium of instruction: Challenges and opportunities. *Journal of English-Medium Instruction* 1 (1), 105–123.

Inbar-Lourie, O. (2022) EMI programs and formative assessment: Implications for the assessment literacy of content lecturers. *Journal of English-Medium Instruction* 1 (2), 204–231.

Ismailov, M., Chiu, T.K., Dearden, J., Yamamoto, Y. and Djalilova, N. (2021) Challenges to internationalisation of university programmes: A systematic thematic synthesis of qualitative research on learner-centred English Medium Instruction (EMI) pedagogy. *Sustainability* 13 (22), 12642.

Jenkins, J. and Leung, C. (2017) Assessing English as a lingua franca. *Language Testing and Assessment* 7, 103–117.

Kao, Y.T. and Tsou, W. (2017) EMI course assessment: A survey study of the issues. In W. Tsou and S.M. Kao (eds) *English as a Medium of Instruction in Higher Education: Implementations and Classroom Practices in Taiwan* (pp. 183–205). Springer.

Macaro, E., Curle, S., Pun, J., An, J. and Dearden, J. (2018) A systematic review of English medium instruction in higher education. *Language Teaching* 51 (1), 36–76.

Nieminen, J.H. (2022) Assessment for inclusion: Rethinking inclusive assessment in higher education. *Teaching in Higher Education* 29 (4), 841–859. https://doi.org/10.1080/13562517.2021.2021395

Otto, A. and Estrada Chichón, J.L. (2021) Analysing EMI assessment in higher education. *Revista Tempos E Espaços Em Educação* 14 (33), 1–11.

Rose, H., McKinley, J. and Galloway, N. (2021) Global Englishes and language teaching: A review of pedagogical research. *Language Teaching* 54 (2), 157–189.

Rusmiyanto, R., Huriati, N., Fitriani, N., Tyas, N.K., Rofi'i, A. and Sari, M.N. (2023) The role of artificial intelligence (AI) in developing English language learner's communication skills. *Journal on Education* 6 (1), 750–757.

Ryan, J. and Carroll, J. (2007) 'Canaries in the coalmine': International students in Western universities. In J. Carroll and J. Ryan (eds) *Teaching International Students* (pp. 15–22). Routledge.

Sellars, M., Fakirmohammad, R., Bui, L., Fishetti, J., Niyozov, S., Reynolds, R. ... and Ali, N. (2018) Conversations on critical thinking: Can critical thinking find its way forward as the skill set and mindset of the century? *Education Sciences* 8 (4), 205.

Tekir, S. (2023) Technology enhanced active learning: A promising model for low language readiness to study at an EMI university. *International Journal of Educational Reform*, 10567879231155872.

Thippayacharoen, T., Hoofd, C., Pala, N., Sameephet, B. and Satthamnuwong, B. (2023) Assessing language or content? A systematic review of assessment in english medium instruction classrooms in different contexts. *LEARN Journal: Language Education and Acquisition Research Network* 16 (2), 548–571.

Velez-Estevez, A., Perez, I.J., García-Sánchez, P., Moral-Munoz, J.A. and Cobo, M.J. (2023) New trends in bibliometric APIs: A comparative analysis. *Information Processing & Management* 60 (4), 103385.

Yuksel, D., Altay, M. and Curle, S. (2022) English Medium Instruction programmes in Turkey: Evidence of exponential growth. In S. Curle, H. Ali, A. Alhassan and S. Scatolini (eds) *English-Medium Instruction in Higher Education in the Middle East and North Africa: Policy, Research and Practice*. Bloomsbury.

Yuksel, D., Curle, S. and Kaya, S. (2021) What role do language learning mindsets play in english medium instruction? A comparison of engineering and business administration in turkey. *Journal for the Psychology of Language Learning* 3 (1), 50–62. https://www.jpll.org/index.php/journal/article/view/yukseletal

Yuksel, D., Soruç, A., Altay, M. and Curle, S. (2023) A longitudinal study at an English medium instruction university in Turkey: The interplay between English language improvement and academic success. *Applied Linguistics Review* 14 (3), 533–552.

2 Understanding College Students' Translanguaging Practice in Collaborative Writing from an ESP Course: Voices from Hong Kong

Winfred Xuan

2.1 Introduction

Translanguaging, a pedagogical approach that encourages the use of multiple languages in the learning process, has been widely recognized and implemented in language education, particularly within classroom settings (Li, 2018). However, there is a dearth of research exploring its application and impact in other contexts, such as group projects involving collaborative writing. This chapter seeks to fill this research gap by examining the practice of translanguaging among college students in Hong Kong, specifically during group projects. The central premise of this study is that translanguaging can significantly enhance the quality of students' group assignments. To validate this argument, a mixed-methods approach is employed, involving a class of 30 third-year Bachelor of Arts in Marketing students from a college in Hong Kong. The study analyzes group discussions, conducts follow-up interviews and evaluates students' written work, focusing on their translanguaging practices. The findings of this research aim to provide valuable insights into the potential benefits of translanguaging in collaborative writing tasks, contributing to the growing body of research on this pedagogical approach and offering practical implications for educators.

2.2 Literature Review

2.2.1 Defining translanguaging

The increasing globalization and integration of our world has led to a significant diversification in terms of race, language, culture and education. One notable outcome of this globalization is the use of multiple languages within the same community. This is particularly evident in metropolises such as New York, Hong Kong and London, where hundreds of different languages are used daily. Consequently, the official language of these regions is no longer the sole medium of communication and work. This mixed use of different languages in daily life has given rise to a new concept in applied linguistics known as translanguaging (Li, 2022).

Translanguaging is not an entirely new concept, but rather a term that evolved from the observations made by Williams (1994) in his teaching practice. Williams and his team from Wales, UK, discovered that students whose first language was Welsh often used a significant amount of Welsh to understand English language and grammar when learning it as a second language. Initially, Williams referred to this linguistic behavior as codeswitching, viewing it as a valuable pedagogical tool that aided his Welsh students in better understanding his English instruction. This led to the publication of his dissertation, 'an evaluation of teaching and learning methods in the context of bilingual secondary education' (Williams, 1994).

Since then, codeswitching has been widely used and developed in the field of language education, becoming a renowned pedagogical tool in first, second or foreign language education. Initially, this tool was perceived as a means for students to use two languages simultaneously for communication (Li, 2018).

However, García further developed and expanded this concept, asserting that it is not merely a tool for multilingual settings, such as New York. García and her team proposed that codeswitching should be reframed and reconceptualized as translanguaging. They argued that it involves more than just using two languages in communication (García, 2014). They posited that the use of multiple languages in daily life and educational settings is a common linguistic phenomenon. Users of multiple languages, they found, have integrated these languages into their cognitive processes, creating a mixed linguistic repertoire rather than maintaining separate languages in their minds. Consequently, García *et al.* broadened the concept of codeswitching to translanguaging, defining it as

> the complex discursive practices of all bilinguals and the pedagogies which build on these discursive practices to releases ways of speaking, being and knowing of bilingual subaltern communities. (2012: 51)

Since its inception, this perspective on languaging has gained widespread acceptance in the field of applied linguistics and has been extensively utilized in classroom teaching and learning. Originating in England, this concept has been expanded and reframed with more liberal perspectives. For instance, García and her team discovered that promoting this pedagogical tool in multilingual educational settings has empowered students from diverse ethnic and linguistic backgrounds, providing them with a voice to express themselves and fostering a sense of respect (García *et al.*, 2012). Beyond giving students a voice, Yilmaz (2021) contends that this approach also aids schools and educators in promoting educational equity in multilingual and multicultural settings. Consequently, numerous research studies have been conducted in various academic, linguistic and social settings.

2.2.2 Translanguaging as a pedagogical tool

Translanguaging has been widely accepted and utilized in various multilingual and multicultural educational settings, serving as a tool for teaching and learning, and has garnered positive feedback globally. A significant area of study using this approach is the promotion of educational equity in multilingual and multicultural settings. Spain, for instance, has been a focal point of such investigations. Cenoz and Gorter (2022) found that translanguaging (Basque language and Spanish) can serve as a comprehensive pedagogical tool in the Basque region of Spain to promote educational equity. For example, by implementing this approach, students can better develop their identities through multilingual practices, fostering social harmony within the school setting.

Additionally, this approach has been employed to enhance literacy development among new immigrants in a new country. Arteagoitia and Howard (2015) discovered that allowing students, particularly new immigrants in the US school setting, to use their mother tongues in English enhancement classes can expedite their English language learning process, thereby facilitating their adaptation to the US educational system. Similar findings have been reported in an English as a Foreign Language (EFL) context in Japan, where students learning English as a foreign language found it easier to master English grammar when they used Japanese to understand the language (Aoyama, 2020).

Translanguaging has also been applied in the context of language across the curriculum. For instance, in Hong Kong's secondary education system, where English is the medium of instruction in half of the schools and 90% of students' mother tongue is Cantonese, Lin and He (2017) found that translanguaging is widely used in secondary classrooms. Students often use their mother tongue to understand concepts and theories from their content classroom learning, such as chemistry and biology. Her findings indicate that both teachers and students engage in translanguaging in their classrooms, and this pedagogical tool greatly facilitates the teaching and learning process, receiving very positive feedback from their projects. Similar positive findings have been reported in the English for Academic Purpose (EAP) context (Mbirimi-Hungwe, 2016).

2.2.3 Translanguaging in the writing classroom

In recent years, an increasing number of studies in second language (L2) writing have adopted the theoretical framework of translanguaging. Examples include research on translanguaging and bilingual writing, academic writing and dialogic teaching (Motlhaka & Makalela, 2016), feedback in L2 writing (Sun & Zhang, 2022) and English for Specific Purposes (ESP) writing quality (Chen *et al.*, 2019). Velasco and García (2014) posited that translanguaging is not merely a pedagogical tool in a bilingual education setting that aids language teaching. They found that translanguaging as a linguistic practice helps primary school students better organize and write their bilingual compositions. Specifically, their findings indicate that allowing students to employ translanguaging strategies in their learning enhances their biliteracy development in a multilingual and multicultural educational setting.

Conversely, the use of translanguaging as a pedagogical tool in EAP writing has yielded positive results in a South African study (Motlhaka & Makalela, 2016). The study found that using translanguaging in EAP writing classes helps students better understand the metalinguistic knowledge used in EAP writing and facilitates their mastery of the concept of voice in EAP writing classes. Ultimately, students' learning outcomes were significantly improved. In a similar context, translanguaging has been applied to ESP writing instruction in Taiwan, where it was found to help students generate more in-depth ideas, express more information and engage more in the writing process using their diverse linguistic resources.

Regarding feedback provision in online teaching contexts, translanguaging has also been employed, as in the process of providing feedback (Sun & Zhang, 2022). Their study found that using translanguaging to give feedback to students in the first round of writing and revision was more beneficial than feedback provided solely in English. However, the significance of this advantage was less apparent in the second and third drafts. The study concluded that incorporating translanguaging in this context benefits multilingual learners, provided that student agency and motivation are taken into account.

Previous studies have demonstrated that translanguaging is a practical and useful pedagogical tool in language education, particularly in L2 writing. However, most studies have focused on the use of this tool within classroom L2 writing instruction and learning. Few studies have explored how this tool is used beyond the classroom in an L2 writing context, particularly in collaborative writing. To address this gap, the present study aims to investigate how translanguaging can assist L2 writers in completing their collaborative writing tasks. The hypothesis is that translanguaging will facilitate students in producing higher quality essays in their ESP learning beyond classes.

2.2.4 Defining collaborative writing

Collaborative writing is a pedagogical approach in writing education that involves multiple writers in the writing process (Li, 2013). This approach originated in the 1990s when writing scholars investigated student writing in a second language (L2) context and discovered that this form of writing task significantly enhanced L2 writers' fluency and abilities. It has since been widely adopted in educational and business settings, as it encourages diverse writers to contribute different ideas to the writing process, thereby enhancing the professionalism and success of their writing (Li, 2013; Li & Zhang, 2023).

Numerous studies in the field of L2 writing have explored this context. For instance, research has examined how this collaborative dynamic can help learners better organize their writing products (Li, 2020), how it can improve writing output (Storch, 2011) and how it facilitates students in complementing each other's expertise and skills (Shehadeh, 2011). Over the past decades, a wealth of studies has focused on this writing method and yielded positive findings (Zhang *et al.*, 2021).

While previous studies have concentrated on how this approach can enhance writing quality, foster better team dynamics and examine student interactions, the use of language and languaging practices during the planning process remains unexplored. Therefore, this study aims to unravel the linguistic behaviors of these multilingual writers during their discussion process, specifically their use of the translanguaging strategy. The following objectives guide this project:

(1) To explore the practice and impact of translanguaging in collaborative writing tasks among Hong Kong college students.
(2) To understand students' perceptions and attitudes towards the use of multiple languages in their project discussions.
(3) To investigate the differences in the use of translanguaging between high and low achievers.
(4) To assess the potential of translanguaging as a pedagogical tool in Hong Kong undergraduate classroom teaching.

2.3 Methodology

2.3.1 Research context

The current study was conducted in a four-year, self-financed private college in Hong Kong. The term 'self-financed' refers to institutions that are not publicly funded and rely on student tuition for operation. In Hong Kong, higher education is divided into two categories: government-funded and self-financed. Government-funded institutions typically have more resources and attract higher-performing students due to their financial capabilities. In contrast, self-financed institutions must manage their finances independently, resulting in fewer resources and a lower preference among students. This context explains why the participants in this study generally have lower academic performance compared to students from public universities. For instance, students from public universities typically achieve IELTS scores of 6 or 6.5, while the students in this study group generally score around 5 or 5.5.

The participants were a class of 25 students majoring in BA Marketing, Finance and Accounting. Given their relatively lower academic performance, these students were enrolled in an ESP course titled 'Effective Professional Communication in English' to enhance their English proficiency in business writing. This course aims to prepare students to be proficient users of professional English in a business context. The syllabus encompasses both spoken (job interviews, problem-solving discussions) and written (report, proposal and email writing) learning tasks. All learning materials are developed based on real business scenarios in the Hong Kong business context and are tailor-made for students to learn before they transition into professional roles. One of the three assessments for this course is a collaborative writing task: team report writing. The current study focuses on how students utilize various multilingual resources in the writing of this business project.

The participants of this study come from diverse linguistic and cultural backgrounds. The majority are local Hong Kong students, with one-fifth from mainland China and one-tenth from other parts of the world, including India, the Philippines, the US and Pakistan. Their mother tongues vary, including English, Cantonese, Mandarin, Pakistani and Tagalog. This diversity provides a rich linguistic context for students to practice translanguaging, especially during project discussions.

2.3.2 Data collection and analysis

The current study focuses on the group work assessment task of report writing, which requires collaborative writing among team members. This task, which constitutes 25% of the final course grade, is to be submitted at the end of the semester. Students are provided with a hypothetical context that includes a problem to be solved. They are expected to discuss this context with their classmates before commencing their group writing.

All students participating in this research project signed a consent form prior to the start of the project. They were instructed to record the entire process of their project discussions. A total of five hours of recordings were collected. In addition to these recordings, students' written work was also collected as samples for linguistic analysis to support the identification of high and low achievers. This was done to investigate students' translanguaging practices affect their writing quality.

The high and low achievers are identified based on their grades from the course lecturer. The rubrics consist of several sections, including completion of the genre, lexicogrammatical resources and APA usage.

All data collected for this study were stored in accordance with the requirements of the college's research office. The recorded discussions were transcribed into scripts, and themes related to linguistic behavior were identified. Additionally, the quality of the written products was compared in terms of their performance. This comprehensive approach to data collection and analysis provides a robust foundation for understanding the role of translanguaging in collaborative writing tasks.

2.3.3 The writing prompt

2.3.3.1 Context

You are the head of the marketing department of a local supermarket. Your company has planned to expand its business on facial mask section. Your shop manager has asked you to conduct market research on five brands.

Please use the result of your investigation to write a short report to recommend three brands.

Write a short report

review findings of your investigation
propose practical recommendations to your company
include a title, headings, and sub-headings

Word limit
Each student should write about 150 words. (Total: 600–750)
Task Arrangement:
Form a group of 4 to 5 students.
You and your group members should make even contribution to the report writing

Here are the data of your market research:

Table 2.1 Information for five top-rated masks

Brand	Type of mask	Colours/Style	Package	Price (HK$) Per mask
Smart Mask	three-ply surgical face masks BFE: 95% PFE: 95% Level 1	3 colours pink, black, and white (Each box has one colour)	bulk pack Pack of 50	0.6

Table 2.1 (Continued)

Brand	Type of mask	Colours/Style	Package	Price (HK$) Per mask
Hello Kids	four-ply surgical face masks BFE: 98% PFE: 98% Level 2	The size is for kids ages eight and over. Three colors	bulk packs Pack of 24	1.5
Fancy Fam	three-ply surgical face masks BFE: 95% PFE: 95% Level 1	Stylish on-trend patterns with 5 colours in a box	Individually Wrapped Pack of 45	2
PW Perfect	Cloth mask (reusable) Brand-name mask	Stylish on-trend patterns with 7 colours	Individually Wrapped Pack of 1	65
Super PRO	five-ply medical-grade surgical face masks BFE > 99% PFE > 99% VFE > 99% Level 3	One colour White	Individually Wrapped Pack of 20	5

Note
BFE: Bacterial Filtration Efficiency; PFE: Particle Filtration Efficiency; VFE: Viral Filtration Efficiency (Not all brands list this item in their package)

Chart 1. Factors for mark choice (in percentage)

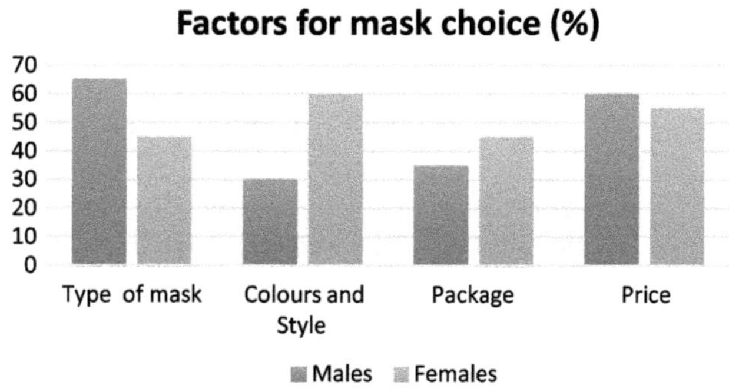

Customers review

Smart Mask

'The mask is thin and breathable, and best yet it has the metal nose piece! Fits my entire family, just twist the straps (which aren't ear tugging) to make it fit a child. I looked high and low and many different sites to find some that were reasonably priced as many have price gouged. Smart Mask is one of the more affordable options. I'll say I'm okay paying roughly 60 cents per mask especially with kids going back to school.'

'Is this the best mask I've worn? No, N95 masks will always take that title, but for a non-N95 mask this is pretty fantastic. I hope they come out with more colors! These are my go-to masks now. They are breathable.'

Hello Kids

'It's been tough to find masks that fit my 12-year-old. These ones fit him great. He wears them to school daily, so we've been through several boxes. The quality is consistent, and the patterns are fun. They're pricier than other disposable masks, but I think they're worth it.'

'I hope these masks have cute cartoons and more colours to attract children. Because I have three children, I am looking for a more affordable option'

Fancy Fam

'My wish to own a stylish medical-grade mask can now be a reality thanks to Fancy Fam. It has many beautiful colours that match with my clothes. Great product for bad times. I've worn a lot of Fancy Fam'.

'Personally, I don't mind the style of a mask. I would prefer a cheaper brand with the same quality. I think this brand is a little too expensive although it has more stylish cutting and colours.'

PW Perfect

'I love the feel of these on my skin, and the design is great too'.

'This mask is less breathable, and the elastic straps are a little too tight and put some strain on my ears.'

'I love the idea that this mask can be reusable. It is environmentally friendly and affordable. I can wear another disposable mask inside of it when I need more protection.'

Super Pro

'These are the best masks I've tried. They are thick to where I feel safe, but they are also very breathable, and I can work out in them easily. My dad also loves them now because they don't fog his glasses!'

'Nice masks and good quality. They were well packaged when received. The fabric used is of good quality. I feel very safe to wear this brand.'

'The mask is quite expensive to my family. I hope we can have more colours.'

2.4 Findings and Discussions

The results of our analysis reveal that the majority of students acknowledge the use of multiple languages in completing their assignments. In general, the practice of translanguaging is prevalent among this group of students.

The subsequent section will present findings from both high and low achievers regarding their views on translanguaging in the context of their group project. Our findings suggest that high and low achievers have distinct perspectives and strategies when it comes to utilizing their linguistic repertoire.

2.4.1 Performance of high achievers

Group 1, which achieved the highest grade in this assignment, consists of three students: Amy, Bob and Calvin. They received an 'A' for their final result. These students have different mother tongues. While Amy and Bob share Cantonese as their mother tongue, Calvin, a student from mainland China, communicates exclusively in Mandarin and English during his group project.

Insights gleaned from the interviews with these high achievers are summarized as follows: How do you perceive translanguaging in doing your group project?

Student Amy

- *I won't just use English. This is because sometimes using **multiple languages** helps us **organize our thoughts faster**, especially using our native language Cantonese.*
- *I use Cantonese when **sharing my thoughts and arguing with my teammates**.*

Student Bob

- *In the exam, I will only use English; but the usual discussions are mainly in Chinese because I can **convey my thoughts faster**.*
- *If I use English only, I'm worried about **misunderstanding** what other people are saying. Or I can't understand the words that others use but are unfamiliar to me.*
- *When directly discussions with others, it may take more time to **think, express and clarify the ideas**. In addition, it is also necessary to **double-confirm** what other people mean to avoid misunderstanding problems.*

Student Calvin:

- *I think it is ok to use mother tongue cause sometimes our groupmates may **be shy or embarrassed** to speak in English, but it shouldn't be an always event.*
- *Mostly **Cantonese**, sometimes use **English**, often **Mandarin**.*
- *Because when we speak English in discussion groupmates **can't catch up** the group progress, so I have to repeat in other language.*

From the interview excerpts, it becomes clear that the high-achieving students, who secured an 'A' grade, are not just open to, but actively embrace the practice of translanguaging in their working language. Amy, one of the students, highlighted that this practice significantly aids her in organizing her thoughts more efficiently. This perspective is in line with previous research findings, which suggest that translanguaging can expedite the writing process and enrich the expressiveness of L2 writers. These findings are corroborated by studies conducted in Taiwan, where English is taught as a foreign language, further validating the benefits of translanguaging.

Bob, another local student, shared that the use of multiple languages in his group project serves as a valuable tool for double-checking and clarifying intricate points. This becomes particularly beneficial when the discussion revolves around complex topics that require clear and precise communication among team members. This practice of using multiple languages contributes to the well-structured, logical and coherent nature of their written work, thereby enhancing the overall quality of their assignments.

Calvin, a mainland student in the group, offered a unique perspective on his use of translanguaging. He confessed to feeling apprehensive about using English in the group project due to his perceived lack of proficiency in the language. As a mainland student studying in Hong Kong, he often compares his English skills to those of local students and feels at a disadvantage. This leads him to resort to Mandarin during group projects, as he believes it enables him to engage more effectively in discussions, given that all group members understand Mandarin. He also mentioned that he sometimes finds English challenging to follow, leading him to prefer Mandarin for discussions.

In conclusion, high-achieving students demonstrate an open-minded approach towards using multiple languages in their projects. They effectively employ translanguaging as a strategic tool to facilitate group discussions during their assignment writing. This results in their written work being more logical, professional, and well-organized. For these students, translanguaging is not just a practice but a valuable tool that aids in accomplishing their tasks. They do not fixate on the language used during discussions; instead, they focus on whether it serves the purpose of the discussion and contributes to the successful completion of their project.

2.4.2 Low achievers' view points

This group, consisting of Kay, Raymond and Yolanda, received a 'C' grade in the final assessment. Kay and Raymond are local students from Hong Kong, while Yolanda hails from mainland China.

When it comes to the use of multiple languages in their project discussions, their perspectives significantly diverge from those of the previously discussed high-achieving group.

Student Raymond:

- *It is OK to use mother tongue for the group project. However, I still think that* ***English is more recommendable*** *for the channel to finish the discussion.*
- *At most of time, I will try to English to discuss. Because* ***I think it is useful for*** *my both spoken and written English.*

Raymond holds the view that students should primarily use English for group project discussions, given that this is an English course. He encourages students to speak and practice English more through these discussions. When asked about the rationale behind his viewpoint, Raymond revealed that his perspective was shaped by his secondary school education in a public school in Hong Kong.

In Hong Kong, about a decade ago, most schools and teachers did not accept the practice of translanguaging. It has only recently become more acceptable. However, the majority of schools still advocate for the use of English in English classes. This educational approach has deeply influenced Raymond's ideology and his perspective on language use in academic settings.

Student Kay:

- *Actually I think using English in the group project is* ***quite important*** *because in our daily life we seldom have time to practice on the English*

Similarly, Kay mentioned in her interview that she seldom has time to practice her English in her life. So she limits herself to speak English in the project discussion.

Student Yolanda:

- *First of all, I think English is a very important course, I think most of the time we should use English to discuss, only* ***a small part of popular and rare words*** *we need to use a simple way to understand, such as Mandarin*

Yolanda, a mainland student, also advocates for the use of English in project discussions. However, she provides a slightly more nuanced perspective on the use of multiple languages. In her opinion, resorting to Mandarin is advisable when encountering technical terms or unfamiliar words during discussions. Apart from these instances, she does not generally recommend the use of languages other than English. Despite this, Yolanda acknowledges that the use of multiple languages during group discussions has proven beneficial.

The findings and discussions above indicate that translanguaging serves as a useful tool in assisting students with their collaborative writing tasks. The majority of students hold a liberal view towards this linguistic behavior and endorse this approach. According to the findings of this small-scale study, translanguaging is not considered taboo among Hong Kong college students.

However, the study also reveals that the practice of translanguaging is employed differently by high and low achievers. High achievers generally have a more democratic perspective on this linguistic phenomenon. These findings are consistent with literature from other contexts. For instance, high achievers utilize multiple languages to practice translanguaging during discussions. They also view translanguaging as a beneficial linguistic strategy for sharing ideas, arguing points, clarifying misunderstandings, organizing thoughts more quickly, and overcoming shyness.

In contrast, 'C' grade learners mostly agree that the use of translanguaging is acceptable during project discussions. However, they believe it should only be used when explaining new words. Most of these students maintain that English remains the most suitable language for their English project discussions.

2.5 Implications

The findings of this study have several implications for both pedagogical practice and future research.

Firstly, while the practice of translanguaging shows promise for collaborative writing tasks, its specific impact on the quality of group discussions and written work requires further empirical validation. The study highlighted students' perceptions of translanguaging as a beneficial tool for organizing ideas and clarifying points during discussions. However, future research should include a detailed analysis of translanguaging instances and their direct relationship to aspects such as coherence and structure in written outputs, as well as a comparison of rubric scores to substantiate these claims. Educators could cautiously incorporate translanguaging into collaborative writing activities, ensuring its use aligns with specific learning goals.

Secondly, translanguaging holds potential as a pedagogical tool for making language learning more explicit and accessible. By encouraging the use of multiple languages, teachers can help students bridge linguistic gaps and better articulate complex ideas, thereby enhancing their language proficiency. However, these implications should be explored further by examining the pedagogical strategies that most effectively integrate translanguaging into classroom settings and assessing their long-term impact on learning outcomes.

Lastly, the study indicates that translanguaging is viewed as generally acceptable among students, challenging traditional monolingual approaches in English language learning. This finding underscores the importance of fostering more inclusive and flexible attitudes toward language use in educational settings. Educators and institutions could benefit from targeted training to effectively implement translanguaging strategies, while future research should investigate how this approach can be adapted to different contexts and learner needs.

In conclusion, while the findings highlight the potential of translanguaging as a valuable tool in collaborative writing and language learning, further research is needed to better understand its specific effects on student outcomes and how it can be systematically incorporated into pedagogical practice.

2.6 Future Research

The findings of this study open up several avenues for future research.

Firstly, future studies could benefit from a longer time frame. This would allow researchers to observe the impact of translanguaging over a more extended period and provide a more comprehensive understanding of its effects on students' language learning and collaborative writing tasks.

Secondly, future research could involve a more diverse range of participants. This study primarily focused on students from Hong Kong and mainland China. Including participants from different cultural and linguistic backgrounds could offer a broader perspective on the use and benefits of translanguaging. It would be interesting to explore how students from different linguistic backgrounds utilize translanguaging and how it impacts their learning experiences.

Lastly, future research could focus on the practical application of translanguaging as a pedagogical tool in classroom teaching. This could involve designing and implementing teaching strategies that incorporate translanguaging and evaluating their effectiveness in enhancing students' language learning and collaborative writing skills. Such research could provide valuable insights for educators seeking to incorporate translanguaging into their teaching practices.

In conclusion, while this study provides valuable insights into the use and benefits of translanguaging, there is still much to explore in this area. Future research should continue to investigate the potential of translanguaging as a pedagogical tool and its impact on students from diverse cultural and linguistic backgrounds.

References

Arteagoitia, I. and Howard, E.R. (2015) The role of the native language in the literacy development of Latino students in the United States. *Multilingual Education* 61–83.

Aoyama, R. (2020) Exploring Japanese high school students' L1 use in translanguaging in the communicative EFL classroom. *Tesl-Ej* 23 (4), n4.

Cenoz, J. and Gorter, D. (2022) Pedagogical translanguaging and its application to language classes. *RELC Journal* 53 (2), 342–354.

Chen, F., Tsai, S.C. and Tsou, W. (2019) The application of translingual practice in a college ESP writing. *English Teaching & Learning* 43 (1), 65.

García, O. (2014) Countering the dual: Transglossia, dynamic bilingualism and translanguaging in education. *The Global-Local Interface, Language Choice and Hybridity*, 100–118.

García, O., Zakharia, Z. and Otcu, B. (eds) (2012) *Bilingual Community Education and Multilingualism: Beyond Heritage Languages in a Global City*. Multilingual Matters.

Li, M. (2013) Individual novices and collective experts: Collective scaffolding in wiki-based small group writing. *System* 41 (3), 752–769.

Li, M. (2020) Languaging in wiki-based collaborative writing. *Languaging In Language Learning and Teaching: A Collection of Empirical Studies* 55, 149.

Li, M. and Zhang, M. (2023) Collaborative writing in L2 classrooms: A research agenda. *Language Teaching* 56 (1), 94–112.

Li, W. (2018) Translanguaging as a practical theory of language. *Applied Linguistics* 39 (1), 9–30.

Li, W. (2022) Translanguaging as method. *Research Methods in Applied Linguistics* 1 (3), 100026.

Lin, A.M. and He, P. (2017) Translanguaging as dynamic activity flows in CLIL classrooms. *Journal of Language, Identity & Education* 16 (4), 228–244.

Sun, P.P. and Zhang, L.J. (2022) Effects of translanguaging in online peer feedback on Chinese university English-as-a-foreign-language students' second language writing performance. *RELC Journal* 00336882221089051.

Storch, N. (2011) Collaborative writing in L2 contexts: Processes, outcomes, and future directions. *Annual Review of Applied Linguistics* 31, 275–288.

Shehadeh, A. (2011) Effects and student perceptions of collaborative writing in L2. *Journal of Second Language Writing* 20 (4), 286–305.

Mbirimi-Hungwe, V. (2016) Translanguaging as a strategy for group work: Summary writing as a measure for reading comprehension among university students. *Southern African Linguistics and Applied Language Studies* 34 (3), 241–249.

Motlhaka, H.A. and Makalela, L. (2016) Translanguaging in an academic writing class: Implications for a dialogic pedagogy. *Southern African Linguistics and Applied Language Studies* 34 (3), 251–260.

Velasco, P. and García, O. (2014) Translanguaging and the writing of bilingual learners. *Bilingual Research Journal* 37 (1), 6–23.

Williams, C. (1994) Arfarniad o Ddulliau Dysgu ac Addysgu yng Nghyd-destun Addysg Uwchradd Ddwyieithog, [An evaluation of teaching and learning methods in the context of bilingual secondary education]. Unpublished doctoral thesis, University of Wales, Bangor.

Yilmaz, T. (2021) Translanguaging as a pedagogy for equity of language minoritized students. *International Journal of Multilingualism* 18 (3), 435–454.

Zhang, M., Gibbons, J. and Li, M. (2021) Computer-mediated collaborative writing in L2 classrooms: A systematic review. *Journal of Second Language Writing* 54, 100854.

3 University Teachers' Experiences of Online Testing in English-Medium Instruction Programmes in Nepal

Karna Rana and Pramod K. Sah

3.1 Introduction

In recent years, the use of English as a medium of instruction (EMI) has become commonplace in Nepali higher education settings. The growing prevalence of EMI in Nepali colleges indicates its widespread acceptance in higher education. Despite having 124 languages, including Nepali, the only language of administration (Central Bureau of Statistics, 2022), EMI has become a de facto medium of instruction in higher education institutions (Sah, 2022). Nepali universities, including Nepal Open University, where this study was conducted, have adopted EMI in their instructional and assessment practices. Discussions at crossroads have raised doubts about the viability of online testing after the institutional decision to implement EMI. In online instruction, concerns arise around how university instructors administer exams to students completing coursework and tests in English. As the administration of proctored online exams requires a thoughtful and appropriate approach to the reliability of digital technologies, universities need to utilise proper software and execute simulations to assess and mitigate technological interferences (Kharbat & Abu Daabes, 2021). Both teachers and technicians can pilot EMI tests, analyse results and develop proctored online exam systems collaboratively (Martins *et al.*, 2019). It is essential to have a standard framework for the implementation of EMI testing in an online environment (Otto & Estrada Chichón, 2021). In addition, teachers and students must have a comprehensive understanding of the EMI testing framework.

Many studies (e.g. Khati, 2016; Phyak, 2013; Poudel & Choi, 2021; Sah & Li, 2018) have shown problems with EMI implementation in schools, including teachers and students' poor English proficiency. However, EMI continues to be misunderstood as a way to enhance education quality. These problems are also evident at universities (Rana & Sah, 2023). EMI is expected to internationalise higher education institutions, increasing the chances of jobs for graduates globally. However, concerns about the implementation of EMI, especially about how teachers administer EMI tests and how students take the tests, are reported in some studies (Ghanbari & Nowroozi, 2021; Macaro *et al.*, 2017). Nevertheless, the cultural sensitivity in EMI testing may be overlooked, and the EMI standard may be misunderstood as a global framework (Yuksel *et al.*, 2023). Particularly in non-English language contexts, these concerns are highlighted, emphasising the need for adequate support for teachers (McKinley *et al.*, 2023). The current literature on EMI covers various aspects such as language policies, learning difficulties and English language pedagogies; however, research on university teachers' experiences giving EMI tests in an online setting is either lacking or has been overlooked, particularly in the Nepali context. This research fills this gap by analysing Nepali university teachers' experiences designing and administering EMI tests online. This research answers the following question: how is the experience of university teachers regarding the design and administration of online testing in EMI programmes? This question enabled us to explore relevant literature and organise it in the following section.

3.2 EMI Testing in Higher Education

Many studies have highlighted the challenges and opportunities in assessing EMI in higher education. Hichour (2022) reveals that teachers have doubts about the quality of online tests, fearing a high chance of student cheating. Ismailov *et al.* (2021) identify challenges, such as insufficient English proficiency and weak management for administering tests online. Moreover, implementing online exams is criticised for having issues, including a lack of technological facilities, insufficient technological and pedagogical knowledge among teachers (Gan & Lam, 2020), and a lack of online assessment training for teachers (Zainal & Yunus, 2022). Teachers, particularly those of the older generation, choose face-to-face paper-and-pen tests mainly because they lack the understanding and skills to manage online assessments (Li & Wu, 2018). The essence of standardised EMI tests for the online environment (Dimova, 2020), the need for EMI teachers' professional development (Macaro *et al.*, 2020) and the impact of EMI tests on teachers' capability and students' performance (Marcjanik, 2023) are overlooked. Even though EMI has been identified as a substantial barrier to learning and achievement in terms of students' inadequate proficiency in English, its implementation in higher education is rapidly increasing worldwide (Macaro *et al.*, 2017). McKinley *et al.* (2023) argue that, although the universities decide to implement online tests in EMI, they are likely to fail to achieve educational outcomes in non-English language contexts through the EMI approach.

Despite the technological challenges of implementing EMI tests in the online environment, it can be an opportunity to transform the closed-book test system into an open-book assessment system (Pun & Curle, 2022). University teachers can take the opportunity to design an alternative assessment system that is highly practicable in terms of time and space flexibility (Ghanbari & Nowroozi, 2021). For example, Selwyn *et al.* (2023) found that students appreciated online tests because they offered them flexibility, reduced their anxiety and provided them with immediate feedback. Particularly, online tests became practicable while the COVID-19 pandemic accelerated the use of web technologies in education (Borisov *et al.*, 2020). Kharbat and Abu Daabes (2021) contend that, despite concern about student cheating in online tests, which can be minimised by asking creative questions, they lessen human errors and anxiety. Parker *et al.* (2021) argue that because traditional closed-book assessments are criticised for being a source of stress and a separated entity from continuous teaching and learning activities, the open-book assessments that are administered in the online environment allow teachers to assess learning in real time and demonstrate their efforts of teaching and managing courses. However, Macaro *et al.* (2020) argue that implementing EMI testing online, especially when English is taught for academic purposes, requires a high level of English proficiency in teachers, ensuring they have sufficient e-learning knowledge and experience.

Implementing online assessment requires adequate development of teachers' professionalism and ICT infrastructure (García-Peñalvo *et al.*, 2021). Otto and Estrada Chichón (2021) and Li and Wu (2018), for example, highlight the necessity of providing EMI teachers with enhanced training and assistance, specifically in designing and executing learning-oriented assessment procedures. Simbolon (2023) emphasises this even more, pointing out that cooperation and well-defined plans are essential for EMI teachers. It is essential to equip teachers with technological, pedagogical and EMI content knowledge to implement online assessments (Dang *et al.*, 2023). Hou *et al.* (2013) focus on the EMI programme, which should cover the training of EMI teachers, EMI test design and online assessments. Kukić (2021) emphasises the necessity of implementing virtual assessments, taking into account the perspectives and experiences of the teachers. From a technology standpoint, Martins *et al.* (2019) highlight the significance of having excellent education management information systems (EMIS) to create online platforms and manage online assessments. The proper development of web-based assessment systems, especially real-time observation, monitoring and evaluation technologies in language testing is essential to make them more effective than traditional ones (Resdiana & Yulientinah, 2023). However, it is crucial to take into account the quality of EMI (Yiwei, 2021), as well as learner readiness and challenges (Shifat *et al.*, 2021) when administering online exams. Dang *et al.* (2023) contend that developing a viable online examination system is essential. Im and Kim (2015) suggest incorporating a blended learning concept in the EMI programme to implement EMI testing in the online environment effectively.

Students who are not accustomed to the online environment, have inadequate technological skills, or need to be proficient in English are more likely to struggle with EMI testing (Paudyal & Rana, 2021). Furthermore, the success of online testing appears to be influenced by the design of online tests, IT infrastructure and support services (Acharya *et al.*, 2022). Students who must study in EMI in non-English language environments struggle not only to comprehend the material but also greatly fear making mistakes and performing poorly on tests (Hibatullah, 2019; Trinh & Pham, 2021). Studies (Han *et al.*, 2019; Rohliah *et al.*, 2023; Sah, 2023) have revealed that anxiety related to foreign languages is a common occurrence for these students. This anxiety manifests itself in several forms, such as test anxiety, communication anxiety and fear of receiving a poor evaluation. Their study programmes' intricate and difficult linguistic requirements may worsen this worry (Russell *et al.*, 2022). Dafouz and Camacho-Miñano (2016) suggest that individualised instruction that adjusts materials, activities and assessments based on students' language skill levels can reduce fear and enhance learning outcomes. In her discussion of the necessity of translating tests for students who do not understand English, Goldsmith (2003) highlights the significance of offering evaluations in languages other than English. Furthermore, Stansfield (2003) highlights the qualities that a test needs to have, implying that when creating a test, one should consider the diversity of students' native tongues and their usage of the English language.

There is a paucity of information regarding EMI testing in higher education, particularly in Nepal, even though there is ample international literature regarding the use of EMI in higher education. We created a research strategy to fill this gap and carried out this investigation.

3.3 Research Procedure

In this qualitative study, we employed semi-structured interviews with university teachers to understand their experiences of designing and administering online tests in an EMI programme. We also discussed the observational phenomena, the evidence found in the natural setting (synchronous activities in this case) and the interview data obtained from the participants. In particular, the first author who worked at the study site corroborated and discussed observational data. Existing collegial relationships (Cohen *et al.*, 2018; Rana *et al.*, 2019) enabled us to approach the study participants, plan data collection strategies and conduct interviews.

Initially, we invited 12 teachers from the Business Studies and Social Science departments to participate in this study. However, only seven of them accepted to participate in the interview. We obtained informed consent from them before interviewing. We emailed them a Google form with open-ended questions and asked them to answer them. After analysing their responses on the Google form, we invited them for an online interview via MS Teams to further discuss the issues they raised in their written responses. We conducted the online interviews primarily in Nepali, although all the participants answered our written questions in English. In addition, the first author gathered information by invigilating e-proctored exams to triangulate the information gathered through the Google form questionnaire and follow-up online interviews. For this, he invigilated ten online exams managed on MS Teams in a semester and developed a diary of the observations.

A thematic approach to data analysis (Braun & Clarke, 2006) was adopted. First, we transcribed the interview records and organised all data to proceed with the analysis. Second, following an inductive coding approach, we developed preliminary codes by reading the data gathered through the online questionnaire, follow-up interviews and observations of e-proctored exams. Third, we identified commonalities between the codes and grouped them into themes. Fourth, we revised the themes in line with the research questions. Fifth, we read the data under each theme and renamed the themes. This process allowed us to critically reflect on the themes we finalised for presenting the data analysis. We then interpreted the data in the story form and developed this research report. The first author collected, organised and analysed the data to prepare the initial draft, while the second author revised and finalised it.

Throughout several rounds of data analysis, both authors collaborated on the draft, engaging in multiple revisions to ensure that the knowledge presented in this report is highly trustworthy. All original names are replaced with pseudonyms to maintain anonymity in this paper.

3.4 Results

The data analysis presented in the following sections has offered ideas about how university teachers construct tests in English, administer online proctored exams of different courses and interpret the impact of EMI testing on students' achievement. The analysis revealed the following three themes: 'Students' lack of understanding of questions in English'; 'Teachers' capability in using understandable English in test'; and 'Impact on students' achievement'.

3.4.1 Students' lack of understanding of questions in English

In their interviews, the teachers expressed their worries about the university's use of EMI for non-English language courses and about providing exams in English. They underscored that non-major English-learning students would undoubtedly struggle to comprehend academic English. Additionally, they stated how difficult it was for them to present lessons in EMI and how they frequently had to switch to Nepali to clarify the material. Students had to utilise both Nepali and English simultaneously since they had trouble understanding English, especially regarding subject-specific terms. Their accounts of imparting knowledge in EMI prompted inquiries about what their students comprehended from exam questions in English and what they wrote in their English answers. For example:

> They have difficulties to understand the instruction given to them and the intent of the question. In the online environment, they have very little opportunity to ask someone to explain questions. They write whatever they understand. Language is the main barrier to them to express their understanding of the content. (Anmol)

These comments indicate that students seem to fail to learn different courses and attempt exams in EMI because English is not their major subject. Participants in our follow-up interviews expressed concern about EMI in Nepali higher education for various reasons, including that English was neither the students' mother tongue nor their specialisation subject. Their comments reminded our observational experiences of online proctored examinations in that students frequently asked invigilators to clarify questions in Nepali so that they could answer those questions. We observed that invigilators often tried to assist them by translating English terminologies and giving hints in Nepali. These exam behaviours raised concerns about how these students wrote their ideas in English and achieved learning outcomes. In our interviews, participants further shared their stories, for example:

> In online exams, some of the students' answers are totally irrelevant to questions and sometimes even misguided. It is pretty much clear they have English language problems to understand questions. (Gagan)

> Students were not habituated, and they felt it unusual and less practicable at the beginning. Tests in English is not so effective in terms of student's ability to understand questions and write in English. But they must answer questions in English. (Hom)

Gagan's comments indicate that due to a lack of understanding of English, students in online exams struggle to understand and answer questions appropriately. Moreover, Hom's stance underscores the impractical EMI tests, raising the issue of evaluating students' abilities. Bijay highlighted an issue of e-proctored exams: because students had difficulty understanding questions in English, they sought help from their friends, breaching the exam rules. He said:

> It is necessary to create an environment where students cannot communicate with other unwanted people. If they are not strictly observed online and if they are provided a longer duration to answer questions, it is likely to increase the chance of students' unethical conversations with others. (Bijay)

Bijay's remarks, for instance, provide an indirect venue for conjecturing how students find it challenging to study for and take tests in English because of the requirement of EMI testing.

3.4.2 Teachers' capability in using understandable English in tests

Participants emphasised using academic terminologies in the questions to help students comprehend and respond to questions. Specifically, they concentrated on making instructions for questions explicit so that students could be sure to answer them accurately. For instance, Ekendra stated, 'Offer alternative arrangements for students with limited access to devices or the internet. Provide precise assessment criteria and guidelines.' However, none of the participants in this study explicitly articulated the essence of the examiners' strong command of English. Instead, they frequently floated to the types of test items (questions) they included in the exams when we asked them how they ensured understandable language in tests.

> Online examination can be effective if questions are properly designed, and a proper testing environment is created. Time-bound objective and short-answer questions can be appropriate if students are familiar with technology use. E-proctored examinations can be equally effective. Students' diverse backgrounds and learning styles are addressed by designing subjective and issue-based questions where they can write in the way they choose. Optional questions will address such diversity issues. (Bijay)

It was unclear from their expressions what level of understanding they had of academic English. During our conversations, we kept asking them about the exact methods they used to create practicable EMI exams. All of them, however, failed to provide a clear explanation of how to ensure that the English on tests is understood by students who do not major in the language. Rather, they tended to show off their extensive theoretical understanding of the test-building process, as Anmol said:

> I focus on the objectives of the course and the contents I taught to them. I shall provide alternative items in case of internal test. I provide clear instructions and rubrics before they sit in the examination.

Anmol's comments indicate that teachers are accustomed to clarifying questions for students in the exam hall, although they are not permitted even to read tests. In particular, they expected the proctored online exam environment to be flexible so that students could get explanations or translations of EMI tests in understandable English or Nepali. We had doubts about these teachers' awareness of exam conditions. Their actions during the proctored online exam, including translating questions and explaining English terminology to students, raised suspicions about their capacity to choose understandable English for assessments. Moreover, participants' comments triggered the issue of how students would answer questions in English and what impact they had on their minds and performance.

3.4.3 Impact on students' achievement

The analyses of results in the above sections illustrate how non-major English approach their coursework and EMI tests. In addition to making it difficult for students to study and attempt tests, using EMI also resulted in poor performance. These educators expressed concern about the efficacy of EMI pedagogies, which they believed impeded students' ability to demonstrate their knowledge and grasp of the material. They acknowledged that EMI implementation in higher education is not a wise decision. For example:

> Students' level of English proficiency contributes to differences in student performance or engagement during EMI testing in the online environment compared to face-to-face settings. (Dev)

> Despite students' appreciation for the online testing system, many students perform poorly due to the language barrier. If we make some supporting mechanisms to implement EMI testing, the students could perform better. I've seen some students copy answers from somewhere in an online exam. (Chun)

We could sense how challenging EMI proved to be for students to learn and take tests and for professors to impart courses. Sadly, academics in universities, including the one in this study, would not oppose the legacy of EMI teaching and testing. Most likely, because of these reasons, teachers emphasised the need to support students with English language difficulties in online proctored exams. Priya, among others, emphasised the necessity of examining the efficacy of EMI in tertiary education.

> My students always ask the meaning of questions in exam halls. I feel it is a serious case to investigate and rethink EMI. Most of the students other than English major fail exams and leave university. All maths may not be proficient in using EMI. (Priya)

However, none of the participants in this study researched students' experiences in taking tests in English. In response to our question about what feedback they got from students about EMI pedagogies and testing, they responded that they had never gathered student feedback. We, thus, doubted their ability to understand EMI pedagogies and test student learning in English. During our follow-up interviews, Bijay and Kumar voiced their strong belief that using EMI could significantly contribute to university dropout rates in Nepal. They said:

> EMI testing can be a more effective way to assess student learning outcomes in some cases, particularly when it comes to assessing students' ability to use English in a communicative context. EMI tests can also be more motivating for students, as they can see the real-world relevance of the skills they are being assessed on. (Bijay)

> Even teachers are weak in English. How can they teach in English? I think we are missing the fact that we have our own language. EMI is a barrier to many for education. It is okay for a job and international communication, but practically using a foreign language as a teaching method is impractical. EMI stops many from going to higher education. Why don't we think in a way that every student has own choice of learning? EMI breaks their way. I can't express a lot of things in English. My mind goes translating thoughts into English. Just confused with terms and writing. I think most teachers don't want to follow EMI. (Kumar)

Bijay believed that EMI testing might be relevant in assessing students' English communication skills. However, Kumar critiqued that while teachers like him might face challenges in understanding subject-specific English terminologies and have to use their mother tongue to explain content, students would struggle to learn and take tests in EMI. He expressed concerns about the impact of EMI testing on both students and teachers who struggled with their low level of English proficiency. This implies that universities, including the one in this study, need to be practical in choosing EMI pedagogies and testing in the Nepali context.

3.5 Discussion

The analysis of teachers' EMI testing experience reveals the practical challenges of implementing EMI tests in an online environment for some reasons, such as low level of English proficiency in teachers and students and teachers' limited knowledge about EMI test construction and administration. Findings indicate that implementing EMI in higher education seems to impact teachers' and students' psychology and performance, discouraging using their mother tongue. However, the universities, including the one in this study, have ignored the issue of EMI, promoting the use of English only in higher education. In particular, the university tends to establish EMI as the only medium of instruction by administering EMI tests and ignoring teachers' and students' low levels of English proficiency. Using English only in online tests in a holistic approach without considering teachers and students from non-English specialisation backgrounds seems to encourage the ideological practice of EMI in higher education (Rana & Sah, 2023). More than just the language barrier, the root cause of these consequences seems to be an ideological practice of EMI and discriminatory language policies in education (Phyak, 2013; Poudel & Choi, 2021; Sah, 2022; Sah & Li, 2018). In addition, the expectation of raising education quality (van den Hoven & Carroll, 2020) and internationalising the university (Walkinshaw *et al.*, 2017), evident in similar contexts, appear to have some connections with the implementation of EMI in higher education in Nepal.

From the observations of online exam environments where we watched students straining to comprehend and respond to questions in English, we could speculate on the potential difficulty of taking EMI testing. Students asking for explanations of questions, particularly English terminologies, and teachers helping them with translations or explanations in proctored online exams illustrate the challenges of EMI testing. Based on teachers' statements and our observations of proctored online exams, it is difficult to predict these tests' validity, dependability and fairness (Shraim, 2019). It is questionable why higher education institutions in non-English-speaking countries adopt the assessment criteria of native-English-speaker norms (Dimova, 2020). As a monolingual standard might not be accepted for the EMI environment, the assessment tool would be developed to achieve learning outcomes in such a way that would ease students' understanding of questions and respond to them correctly (Lasagabaster & Doiz, 2020). However, professional learning support for teachers is required, including creating exams for EMI programmes and applying EMI pedagogies (Dang *et al.*, 2023; Fang & Sah, 2024).

The lack of adequate experience in EMI test construction for online environments (Rambousky *et al.*, 2015), limited knowledge of bilingual approach to test design for EMI contexts (Stansfield, 2003) and lack of understanding of the complexity of EMI contexts (Jinghui, 2023) seem to be significant problems with the teachers involved in this study. The adjunct instruction in EMI tests might increase students' achievement (Roquet *et al.*, 2022). Using students' language along with English (Goldsmith, 2003) and individualised instruction in tests (Dafouz & Camacho-Miñano, 2016) would ease the administration of EMI tests in an online environment and increase students' performance. However, when creating EMI tests, examiners should possess a strong command of the English language (Yuksel *et al.*, 2023). In our previous study (Rana & Sah, 2023), we found that Nepali higher education institutions adopted EMI without analysing its practicality in the multilingual context. We argue that, despite the lack of clear higher education policy in EMI, colleges and universities have used EMI as an instrument to attract students and increase their business (Sah, 2022). Although international studies (Dang *et al.*, 2023; Sanahuja Vélez *et al.*, 2020) have reported a lack of evidence to prove the improvement of education quality and international student exchanges, the university involved in this study seems to be motivated by this motive. The authority of this university seems to be either unaware of or has ignored recent research evidence of Russell *et al.* (2022), who have found that the requirement of EMI in non-English language contexts increases students' learning and test anxiety.

The suggestion of international studies (Kirkpatrick, 2017; Lasagabaster & Doiz, 2020; McKinley *et al.*, 2023) to use mother-tongue-based bilingual or multilingual pedagogies seems to be either ignored by the authorities or unknown to them. Although EMI has been highly criticised owing to its impact on students' learning and performance (Aizawa & McKinley, 2020; Simbolon, 2023), the university in this study did not seem to realise it. Also, the recommendation of using bilingual teaching methods and testing systems in our recent study (Rana & Sah, 2023) at the same university did not seem to be implemented. The findings of this study, also resonate with the findings of Sah and Fang (2024), indicate that institutions in multilingual Nepal should consider the diversity of languages spoken by their students, as well as their degree of English proficiency, before introducing EMI in higher education, especially in exams.

3.6 Conclusion

Examining the context of online test administration in an EMI programme drawing on university teachers' viewpoint has provided four key ideas: (a) the complexity of teaching and testing in EMI, (b) the difficulty of understanding exam questions supplied in English, (c) the challenges of achieving learning outcomes and (d) the practical issues with EMI implementation. Firstly, not all students enrolled in courses like educational leadership, business management, psychology, sociology, mathematics and business have a degree in English. As a result, they likely find it challenging to understand learning materials in English and teachers' lectures in EMI. Science teachers frequently used Nepali in their explanations of the material and exam questions, it was clear that instructors did not select EMI as their preferred teaching method, nor was it a practical choice for students.

Another issue in this study was students' poor comprehension of exam questions. In online proctored tests, students often asked the invigilators to clarify confusing English terms and questions so that they could be certain to answer them. In this situation, teachers comfortably assisted them with translating and explaining Nepali. This suggests that universities, including the one involved in this study, have face-masked the practical issues of implementing EMI in higher education. The facade of EMI in non-English multilingual countries like Nepal offers nothing but fake beauty, covering the real face of higher education institutions.

Findings suggest that there may be a problem with the achievement of learning outcomes. Teachers indicated a decline in their students' performance because of EMI. Teachers' low level of practical knowledge of EMI test construction and administration raises questions about the validity and trustworthiness of EMI testing in the online environment. Universities would not be able to change their educational system in general, or EMI testing in particular, by having online versions of traditional physical hall exams.

This study highlights the practical challenges of EMI implementation in higher education in addition to our previous research findings (Rana & Sah, 2023). Findings indicate that teachers' understanding of EMI pedagogies in multilingual contexts like Nepal was especially inadequate. Their interpretation of EMI was the use of English only, which many scholars have problematised for various reasons, including that it is an illogical instructional medium and an impractical teaching approach in non-English speaking contexts. Findings show that low- and middle-income nations like Nepal have created a space for foreign-led ideologies by implementing EMI in higher education (Sah, 2022).

The findings will impact the usefulness of EMI tests administered via online mode in higher education. They imply that higher education institutions may amend their policies regarding the medium of instruction and select a suitable medium based on the context. The findings also suggest that these institutions might consider using a bilingual test construction strategy if it fits their institutional environments.

References

Acharya, B.N., Khadka, T.B., Lamichhane, R.P. and Sharma, R.K. (2022) Experiences of online university examinations: A case of Nepal. In E.J. Valeau, R. Raby and U. Gaulee (eds) *Shaping a Humane World Through Global Higher Education: Pre-Challenges and Post-Opportunities During a Pandemic* (pp. 105–118). STAR Scholars.

Aizawa, I. and McKinley, J. (2020) EMI challenges in Japan's internationalization of higher education. In H. Bowles and A.C. Murphy (eds) *English-Medium Instruction And The Internationalization of Universities* (pp. 27–48). Springer. https://doi.org/10.1007/978-3-030-47860-5_2

Borisov, E.A., Petrenko, E.G.e., Zatsarinnaya, E.I., Romanov, A., Cherkina, V.M. and Sotnikova, L.V. (2020) Organization of taking exams of university students in online format: Problems and opportunities. *E3S Web of Conferences* 217, 08005. https://doi.org/10.1051/e3sconf/202021708005

Braun, V. and Clarke, V. (2006) Using thematic analysis in psychology. *Qualitative Research in Psychology* 3 (2), 77–101. https://doi.org/10.1191/1478088706qp063oa

Central Bureau of Statistics (2022) *National Population and Housing Census 2022 (National Report)*. National Planning Commission Secretariat, Central Bureau of Statistics, Government of Nepal.

Cohen, L., Manion, L. and Morris, R. (2018) *Research Methods in Education* (8th edn). Routledge.

Dafouz, E. and Camacho-Miñano, M.M. (2016) Exploring the impact of English-medium instruction on university student academic achievement: The case of accounting. *English for Specific Purposes* 44, 57–67. https://doi.org/10.1016/j.esp.2016.06.001

Dang, T.K.A., Bonar, G. and Yao, J. (2023) Professional learning for educators teaching in English-medium-instruction in higher education: A systematic review. *Teaching in Higher Education* 28 (4), 840–858. https://doi.org/10.1080/13562517.2020.1863350

Dimova, S. (2020) Language assessment of EMI content teachers: What norms. In M. Kuteeva, K. Kaufhold and N. Hynninen (eds) *Language Perceptions and Practices in Multilingual Universities* (pp. 351–378). Palgrave Macmillan

Fang, F. and Sah, P.K. (eds) (2024) *Pedagogies of English-Medium Instruction Programs in Asian Universities*. Routledge.

Gan, L. and Lam, R. (2020) Understanding university English instructors' assessment training needs in the Chinese context. *Language Testing in Asia* 10 (1), 11. https://doi.org/10.1186/s40468-020-00109-y

García-Peñalvo, F.J., Corell, A., Abella-García, V. and Grande-de-Prado, M. (2021) Recommendations for mandatory online assessment in higher education during the COVID-19 pandemic. In D. Burgos, A. Tlili and A. Tabacco (eds) *Radical Solutions for Education in a Crisis Context: COVID-19 as an Opportunity for Global Learning* (pp. 85–98). Springer. https://doi.org/10.1007/978-981-15-7869-4_6

Ghanbari, N. and Nowroozi, S. (2021) The practice of online assessment in an EFL context amidst COVID-19 pandemic: Views from teachers. *Language Testing in Asia* 11 (1), 27. https://doi.org/10.1186/s40468-021-00143-4

Goldsmith, S.M. (2003) Lost in translation: Issues in translating tests for non-English speaking, limited English proficient, and bilingual students. In J.E. Wall and G.R. Walz (eds) *Measuring Up: Assessment Issues for Teachers, Counselors, and Administrators* (pp. 127–146). ERIC.

Han, Y., Gao, X. and Xia, J. (2019) Problematising recent developments in non-English foreign language education in Chinese universities. *Journal of Multilingual and Multicultural Development* 40 (7), 562–575. https://doi.org/10.1080/01434632.2019.1571072

Hibatullah, O.F. (2019) The challenges of international EFL students to learn English in a non-English speaking country. *Journal of Foreign Language Teaching & Learning* 4 (2), 88–105. https://doi.org/10.18196/ftl.4240

Hichour, H. (2022) Teachers' experience in e-assessment: Case study of EFL teachers in Algerian universities. *Arab World English Journal (AWEJ)* 13 (1), 450–461. https://doi.org/10.2139/ssrn.4085864

Hou, A.Y.C., Morse, R., Chiang, C.-L. and Chen, H.-J. (2013) Challenges to quality of English medium instruction degree programs in Taiwanese universities and the role of local accreditors: A perspective of non-English-speaking Asian country. *Asia Pacific Education Review* 14 (3), 359–370. https://doi.org/10.1007/s12564-013-9267-8

Im, J.H. and Kim, J.-y. (2015) Use of blended learning for effective implementation of English-medium instruction in a non-English higher education context. *International Education Studies* 8 (11), 1–15. http://doi.org/10.5539/ies.v8n11p1

Ismailov, M., Chiu, T.K.F., Dearden, J., Yamamoto, Y. and Djalilova, N. (2021) Challenges to internationalisation of university programmes: A systematic thematic synthesis of qualitative research on learner-centred English medium instruction (EMI) pedagogy. *Sustainability* 13 (22), 12642. https://doi.org/10.3390/su132212642

Jinghui, S. (2023) Lost in the EMI trend: Language-related issues emerging from EMI practice. *SAGE Open* 13 (3), 21582440231181494. https://doi.org/10.1177/21582440231181494

Kharbat, F.F. and Abu Daabes, A.S. (2021) E-proctored exams during the COVID-19 pandemic: A close understanding. *Education and Information Technologies* 26 (6), 6589–6605. https://doi.org/10.1007/s10639-021-10458-7

Khati, A.R. (2016) English as a medium of instruction: My experience from a Nepali hinterland. *Journal of NELTA* 21 (1–2), 23–30. https://doi.org/10.3126/nelta.v21i1-2.20198

Kirkpatrick, A. (2017) The languages of higher education in east and southeast Asia: Will EMI lead to Englishisation? In B. Fenton-Smith, P. Humphreys and I. Walkinshaw (eds) *English Medium Instruction in Higher Education in Asia-Pacific: From Policy to Pedagogy* (pp. 21–36). Springer International Publishing. https://doi.org/10.1007/978-3-319-51976-0_2

Kukić, M. (2021) Testing the English language in the online environment during the imposed Covid-19 era. *Zbornik Radova Univerziteta Sinergija* 22 (7), 47–52. https://doi.org/10.7251/zrsng2101010k

Lasagabaster, D. and Doiz, A. (2020) Epilogue: Multilingualism in northern European universities—reflections from the south. In M. Kuteeva, K. Kaufhold and N. Hynninen (eds) *Language Perceptions and Practices in Multilingual Universities* (pp. 379–394). Palgrave Macmillan. https://doi.org/10.1007/978-3-030-38755-6_15

Li, N. and Wu, J. (2018) Exploring assessment for learning practices in the EMI classroom in the context of Taiwanese higher education. *Language Education & Assessment* 1 (1), 28–44. https://doi.org/10.29140/lea.v1n1.46

Macaro, E., Akincioglu, M. and Han, S. (2020) English medium instruction in higher education: Teacher perspectives on professional development and certification. *International Journal of Applied Linguistics* 30 (1), 144–157. https://doi.org/10.1111/ijal.12272

Macaro, E., Curle, S., Pun, J., An, J. and Dearden, J. (2017) A systematic review of English medium instruction in higher education. *Language Teaching* 51 (1), 36–76. https://doi.org/10.1017/S0261444817000350

Marcjanik, M. (2023) EMI in higher education: Current challenges. *ANGLICA-An International Journal of English Studies* 32 (2), 137–155. https://doi.org/10.7311/0860-5734.32.2.07

Martins, J., Branco, F., Gonçalves, R., Au-Yong-Oliveira, M., Oliveira, T., Naranjo-Zolotov, M. and Cruz-Jesus, F. (2019) Assessing the success behind the use of education management information systems in higher education. *Telematics and Informatics* 38, 182–193. https://doi.org/10.1016/j.tele.2018.10.001

McKinley, J., Rose, H. and Curdt-Christiansen, X.L. (2023) EMI in Chinese higher education: The muddy water of 'Englishisation'. *Applied Linguistics Review* 14 (6), 1475–1481. https://doi.org/doi:10.1515/applirev-2022-0015

Otto, A. and Estrada Chichón, J.L. (2021) Analysing EMI assessment in higher education. *Revista Tempos e Espaços em Educação* 14 (33), e15475. https://doi.org/10.20952/revtee.v14i33.15475

Parker, A.M., Watson, E., Dyck, N. and Carey, J.P. (2021) Traditional versus open-book exams in remote course delivery: A narrative review of the literature. *Proceedings of the Canadian Engineering Education Association (CEEA)*. https://doi.org/10.24908/pceea.vi0.14845

Paudyal, G.R. and Rana, K. (2021) How university lecturers and students interpret opportunities and challenges of online mode of learning. *International Journal of Research in Education and Science (IJRES)* 7 (4), 1006–1022. https://doi.org/10.46328/ijres.2383

Phyak, P. (2013) Language ideologies and local languages as the medium-of-instruction policy: A critical ethnography of a multilingual school in Nepal. *Current Issues in Language Planning* 14 (1), 127–143. https://doi.org/10.1080/14664208.2013.775557

Poudel, P.P. and Choi, T.-H. (2021) Policymakers' agency and the structure: The case of medium of instruction policy in multilingual Nepal. *Current Issues in Language Planning* 22 (1–2), 79–98. https://doi.org/10.1080/14664208.2020.1741235

Pun, J.K.H. and Curle, S. (2022) The use of technology in English medium education. In J.K.H. Pun, S. Curle and D. Yuksel (eds) *The Use of Technology in English Medium Education* (pp. 1–9). Springer International Publishing. https://doi.org/10.1007/978-3-030-99622-2_1

Rambousky, R., Bausen, A., Lange, S. and Sabath, F. (2015) IEMI-testing of electronic systems in critical infrastructure surrounding. *2015 IEEE International Symposium on Electromagnetic Compatibility (EMC)*, Dresden, Germany, 2015, 1057–1062. https://doi.org/10.1109/ISEMC.2015.7256314

Rana, K. and Sah, P.K. (2023) Policy development for English medium instruction at a Nepali university: Unpacking hidden motivations and agendas. In P.K. Sah and F. Fang (eds) *Policies, Politics, and Ideologies of English-medium Instruction in Asian Universities* (1st edn, pp. 48–62). Routledge. https://doi.org/10.4324/9781003173120-5

Rana, K., Greenwood, J., Fox-Turnbull, W. and Wise, S. (2019) Challenges in accessing fieldwork in rural Himalayas: An emerging researcher's experiences. *Waikato Journal of Education* 24 (1), 67–77. https://doi.org/10.15663/wje.v24i1.605

Resdiana, W. and Yulientinah, D.S. (2023) Designing English language testing using a web-based monitoring platform. *Journal of English Education, Linguistics and Literature (JEELL)* 9 (2), 41–48. https://doi.org/10.32682/jeell.v9i2.2838

Rohliah, L., Lestari, P., Ningsih, W. and Hutagalung, G.U. (2023) Non-English major students' foreign language anxiety: A study case. *Global Expert: Journal Bahasa dan Sastra* 11 (1), 7–16. https://doi.org/10.36982/jge.v11i1.3201

Roquet, H., Vraciu, A., Nicolás-Conesa, F. and Pérez-Vidal, C. (2022) Adjunct instruction in higher education: Examining the effects on English foreign language proficiency. *International Journal of Bilingual Education and Bilingualism* 25 (4), 1377–1398. https://doi.org/10.1080/13670050.2020.1765967

Russell, B., Barron, C., Kim, H. and Jang, E.E. (2022) A mixed-method investigation into international university students' experience with academic language demands. *Frontiers in Education* 7, 1–18. https://doi.org/10.3389/feduc.2022.934692

Sah, P.K. (2022) English medium instruction as neoliberalism endowment in Nepal's higher education: Policy-shaping practices. In J. McKinley and N. Galloway (eds) *English Medium Instruction Practices in Higher Education: International Perspectives* (pp. 71–83). Bloomsbury. https://doi.org/10.5040/9781350167889.ch-006

Sah, P.K. (2023) Emotion and imagination in English-medium instruction programs: Illuminating its dark side through Nepali students' narratives. *Linguistics and Education* 75, 101150. https://doi.org/10.1016/j.linged.2023.101150

Sah, P.K. and Fang, F. (2024) Decolonizing English-medium instruction in the Global South. *TESOL Quarterly*. https://doi.org/10.1002/tesq.3307

Sah, P.K. and Li, G. (2018) English medium instruction (EMI) as linguistic capital in Nepal: Promises and realities. *International Multilingual Research Journal* 12 (2), 109–123. https://doi.org/10.1080/19313152.2017.1401448

Sanahuja Vélez, G., Ribes Giner, G. and Moya Clemente, I. (2020) A systematic review of English as a medium of instruction in higher education institutions: The case of a business school. In M.L. Carrió-Pastor (ed.) *Internationalising Learning in Higher Education: The Challenges of English as a Medium of Instruction* (pp. 35–61). Springer International Publishing. https://doi.org/10.1007/978-3-030-21587-3_3

Selwyn, N., O'Neill, C., Smith, G., Andrejevic, M. and Gu, X. (2023) A necessary evil? The rise of online exam proctoring in Australian universities. *Media International Australia* 186 (1), 149–164. https://doi.org/10.1177/1329878x211005862

Shifat, N.F., Khan, M.E.I. and Chowdhury, M.S.A. (2021) Learner acumens of online EFL classes at the private universities in Bangladesh. *European Journal of Open Education and E-learning Studies* 6 (2), 39–54. https://doi.org/10.46827/ejoe.v6i2.3838

Shraim, K. (2019) Online examination practices in higher education institutions: Learners' perspectives. *Turkish Online Journal of Distance Education* 20 (4), 185–196. https://doi.org/10.17718/tojde.640588

Simbolon, N.E. (2023) English medium instruction (EMI) in higher education: Insights from Indonesian vocational lecturers. *Utamax: Journal of Ultimate Research and Trends in Education* 5 (1), 11–20. https://doi.org/10.31849/utamax.v5i1.9973

Stansfield, C.W. (2003) Test translation and adaptation in public education in the USA. *Language Testing* 20 (2), 189–207. https://doi.org/10.1191/0265532203lt252oa

Trinh, N.B. and Pham, D.T.T. (2021) Challenges in speaking classrooms among non-English majors. *Vietnam Journal of Education* 5 (2), 37–42. https://doi.org/10.52296/vje.2021.52

van den Hoven, M. and Carroll, K.S. (2020) English-medium policy and English conversational patterns in the UAE. *World Englishes* 40 (2), 205–218. https://doi.org/10.1111/weng.12508

Walkinshaw, I., Fenton-Smith, B. and Humphreys, P. (2017) EMI issues and challenges in Asia-Pacific higher education: An introduction. In B. Fenton-Smith, P. Humphreys and I. Walkinshaw (eds) *English Medium Instruction in Higher Education in Asia-Pacific: From Policy to Pedagogy* (Vol. 21, pp. 1–18). Springer. https://doi.org/10.1007/978-3-319-51976-0_1

Yiwei, Y. (2021) Research on online teaching quality during the epidemic period in Chinese universities-based on student feedback of English course in Glasgow College, UESTC. *2021 International Conference on Education, Information Management and Service Science (EIMSS)*, Xi'an, China, 16–18 July 2021, 141–144. https://doi.org/10.1109/EIMSS53851.2021.00038

Yuksel, D., Soruç, A., Altay, M. and Curle, S. (2023) A longitudinal study at an English medium instruction university in Turkey: The interplay between English language improvement and academic success. *Applied Linguistics Review* 14 (3), 533–552. https://doi.org/10.1515/applirev-2020-0097

Zainal, N. and Yunus, M.M. (2022) Asian university students' perspectives on online English courses during COVID-19: A systematic review. *International Journal of Evaluation and Research in Education* 11 (2), 888–896. https://doi.org/10.11591/ijere.v11i2.22420

4 A Multiple-Case Study of Teachers' Assessment Practices in EMI

Jieting Jerry Xin and Yuen Yi Lo

4.1 Introduction

English medium instruction (EMI) has been defined as 'the use of the English language to teach academic subjects (other than English itself) in countries or jurisdictions where the first language (L1) of the majority of the population is not English' (Macaro, 2018: 19). Recent decades have witnessed a rapid spread of EMI in European countries, probably driven by the desires to facilitate language learning, promote global student mobility and internationalisation of education (Rose *et al.*, 2022). EMI has often been juxtaposed with other bilingual education programmes, particularly Content and Language Integrated Learning (CLIL), a term coined in the 1990s and can be defined as 'any type of pedagogical approach that integrates the teaching and learning of content and second/foreign languages' (Morton & Llinares, 2017: 1). Although both programmes share the key characteristic of teaching content subjects through an L2, one can also infer some differences from their definitions – the L2 is specified as English in EMI while it can be others in CLIL, although English is the target L2 in many CLIL programmes (Dalton-Puffer *et al.*, 2022); language learning is highlighted in CLIL, but not in EMI. That probably explains why, on continuums of different variants of bilingual programmes, EMI is usually regarded as more 'content-oriented' while CLIL seems to balance content and language learning, that is somewhere in the middle (Macaro, 2018). However, it should be noted that whether the 'ideal' form of CLIL, that is integrating/balancing content and language teaching can be achieved in programmes labelled as CLIL is still controversial (Morton & Llinares, 2017), while EMI teachers are being urged to incorporate more language teaching to their content subject lessons (Lyster & Ruiz de Zarobe, 2018). Hence, the differences or boundaries between EMI and CLIL are somewhat blurry, and it has been proposed that CLIL can be used as an umbrella term that comprises a variety of teaching methodologies combining both content and language to various extents (Dalton-Puffer *et al.*, 2014).

This blurry boundary and balance between content and language teaching in EMI and CLIL also raises questions about assessments. Although EMI emphasises content learning outcomes and hence the content subject curriculum tends to determine assessment designs (Hönig, 2010), the role of using an L2 in mediating students' ability to express their content knowledge in assessments cannot be overlooked (Attar *et al.*, 2022; Lo *et al.*, 2023). At the same time, if learning English is an implicit goal of EMI (Macaro, 2018), teachers may also need to evaluate students' English development, at least academic English associated with EMI subjects, so that teachers can diagnose students' learning progress and provide support if necessary. This is indeed an important function of assessment, i.e. to collect data to evaluate the effectiveness of teaching and learning so as to inform teaching (Leung, 2014). Despite the considerable research efforts in EMI and CLIL (e.g. An *et al.*, 2019; Hennebry & Gao, 2021; Ouazizi, 2016), assessment remains an under-explored area. This chapter sets out to investigate how EMI teachers assess their students' content knowledge in L2 and what potential factors affect their assessment practices. By doing so, this chapter can enhance understanding of issues related to EMI assessment practices and teacher assessment literacy, thereby providing salient implications for future EMI teacher professional development. It should be noted that our research focus is on EMI in school settings, though we acknowledge that EMI is more often used in some contexts to refer to the practice in higher education. As defined above, EMI is characterised by students' learning content subjects through English in non-Anglophone countries. It is predominantly content-oriented and EMI teachers are typically content specialists. In some parts of the chapter, we would use the term CLIL, especially when referring to specific studies. However, those studies on CLIL reviewed also tend to be more content-oriented and so are similar to EMI in real practice.

4.2 Literature Review

4.2.1 Assessment issues in EMI

When deciding effective assessment, one key principle is to align assessment with learning goals and instructional practices, so that the assessment data collected can monitor teaching and learning effectiveness, and inform teaching (Shepard, 2019). This can also ensure the accountability, validity and reliability of assessment. However, it is not easy to achieve this alignment in EMI and other content-oriented CLIL programmes. One reason can be the dual focus on developing both content knowledge and L2, which leaves most EMI/CLIL teachers in dilemma concerning how to balance the assessment domains. Kao (2023) investigated the assessment practices employed by EMI teachers in Taiwanese elementary schools. The results indicate that questioning, worksheets, peer and self-assessment, and formative use of summative tests were frequently used in EMI classrooms. However, the teacher participants in this study reported several challenges such as whether they should place emphasis on content knowledge or academic language, how to manage time and efforts from both teachers and students, and how to ensure the effectiveness of assessment for learning techniques on each student. Barrios and Milla Lara (2020) conducted a SWOT analysis of CLIL programmes in Spain, including the aspect of assessment. It was observed by all parties involved that a discrepancy existed between the actual implementation of assessment in schools and official guidelines which stated that content learning should be prioritised over language competence in assessment.

The second reason explaining the complexity of EMI assessment is the mediating role of L2 in content learning, which could bring about validity issue. Otto and Estrada (2019) examined the role L2 played in CLIL assessment. The findings showed that students' level of language proficiency could impact teachers' grading of students' assessment performance. Lo and Fung (2020) explored the interplay of linguistic and cognitive demands students may face through analysing the questions in EMI assessment tasks in Hong Kong. The findings indicated that junior secondary assessment tasks required lower cognitive (i.e. recall of knowledge) and lower linguistic demands (i.e. no production or word-level production), while senior secondary assessment tasks imposed higher cognitive (i.e. application and analysis of knowledge) and linguistic demands (sentence-level or text-level production) on students. Based on the same analytical framework, Lo *et al.* (2023) further analysed the potential impact of different cognitive and linguistic demands on students' performance in content subjects in a high-stakes public examination in Hong Kong. Their results showed that linguistic demands, particularly productive demands at the text level, impeded EMI students' performance. These studies, therefore, underscored the validity issue in EMI assessment, which concerns whether students' academic achievement could be underestimated because of their L2 proficiency.

Apart from the alignment of assessment with learning goals (content and/or language), another EMI assessment issue concerns fairness. Considering the mediating role of L2 in students' performance in content subjects, it may not be fair to compare the assessment results between EMI students and their counterparts who take assessment through their familiar/dominant language (L1), especially when it comes to summative, high-stakes assessments used for selection purpose. Otto and Estrada's (2019) study revealed the dilemma faced by some CLIL teachers – out of concerns over fairness, those CLIL teachers adopted the same assessment tools for both CLIL and non-CLIL students, which were usually written tests consisting of essay questions, even though the teachers were aware that other assessment tools (e.g. oral presentations) may better capture CLIL student learning.

Facing these assessment issues, EMI teachers need sufficient knowledge and skills to make informed decision on the design and implementation of assessment (Lo & Leung, 2022). In other words, they have to be assessment literate, which leads to the notion of 'teacher assessment literacy'.

4.2.2 Teacher assessment literacy

Assessment can provide valuable information for instructional decision-making and support student learning (Baird, 2013). Seeing its essential role in education, teacher assessment literacy, which is defined as a collection of knowledge about educational assessment and the skills required to employ that knowledge to measure student learning (Stiggins, 1991), has been viewed as an important component of teacher professionalism (O'Neill & Adams, 2014). The conceptualisation of teacher assessment literacy has been evolving thanks to continuous research efforts. Some researchers (e.g. Brookhart, 2011; Stiggins, 1991) explicated what knowledge and skills teachers should have to become assessment literate, such as understanding the purposes and uses of the range of available assessment options and be skilled in using them; analysing classroom questions, test items and performance assessment tasks to ascertain the specific knowledge and thinking skills required for students to do them; providing effective, useful feedback on student work. Some researchers (e.g. Cowie *et al.*, 2014; Forsberg & Wermke, 2012) explored mediating factors that can influence teachers' assessment practices, such as teaching experience, collaboration with colleagues and teacher training. Through a sociocultural lens, Xu and Brown (2016) reconceptualised teacher assessment literacy with a hierarchical model named Teacher Assessment Literacy in Practice. This model includes six aspects, namely, knowledge base, teacher conceptions of assessment, micro- and macro-contexts, teacher assessment literacy in practice, teacher learning and teacher identity (re)construction as assessor. In a nutshell, teacher assessment literacy has been shifted from a one-dimensional understanding towards a social–cultural, multi-dimensional conceptualisation that views teachers as growing professionals and active agents in making assessment decisions (DeLuca *et al.*, 2019).

4.2.3 EMI/CLIL teacher assessment literacy

Despite the evolvement of teacher assessment literacy, existing frameworks on the notion are too general to reveal the specific competencies required in specific disciplines. As Xu and Brown (2016) argue, teacher assessment literacy should be situated. In terms of teacher assessment literacy in EMI or other content-oriented CLIL programmes, it is important to recognise that it involves more than just the combination of assessment literacy in content subjects and language education. Rather, it needs to entail the organic integration of these two aspects in alignment with the specific classroom and educational context. Hence, it is imperative to develop a framework for teacher assessment literacy that reflects the complexities caused by the co-existence of content and language learning goals (despite not always being balanced) and students' use of their less proficient language in content subject assessment. In this regard, Lo and Leung (2022) and Liu *et al.* (2023) proposed a conceptual framework for assessment literacy of teachers in bilingual education programmes. Although they specified 'CLIL' in their framework, it is intended to encompass different variants of bilingual education programmes, by capturing the interaction between teachers' conceptions and knowledge of assessment, contextual factors (e.g. educational contexts, programme learning goals) and teachers' decision-making and assessment practices. The framework consists of the following components (Figure 4.1), and they are illustrated with the context of EMI below:

(1) **Teacher conceptions**: This is related to teachers' views of teaching and learning, as well as the values and principles of assessment they perceive. In EMI programmes, what teachers should be particularly cautious about is how they understand the integration of content knowledge and language learning and how they actualise it in teaching, learning and assessment. Teachers should also pay attention to the issues of validity and fairness in EMI assessment due to the inseparability of content and language in EMI programmes.
(2) **Teachers' assessment knowledge**: This includes knowledge of *assessment purposes* (e.g. to diagnose students' learning progress and difficulties in content and language, to inform instruction and support students' learning in content and language, to motivate students' self-assessment and learning, to evaluate and grade students' achievements at a certain point of time), knowledge of *assessment dimensions* (e.g. content knowledge, language skills, cognitive skills, integration of content, cognition and language), knowledge of *assessment strategies* (e.g. assessment techniques, design of assessment tasks, assessment criteria and marking), knowledge of *assessment interpretation and action-taking* (e.g. understanding assessment results, helping students to make sense of the results, informing instruction).
(3) **Potential mediation of contextual factors**: There are some contextual factors mediating the relationship between teachers' conceptions and knowledge of assessment and their actual assessment practices. These factors can be geographical, institutional or related to the educational contexts.

(4) **Teacher decision-making and practices**: Based on their assessment knowledge and conceptions, and through making compromise to some potential contextual factors, teachers make decisions on the design and implementation of assessment in EMI classrooms.

It can be argued that the essence of this conceptual framework is capturing the interaction between teachers' 'cognitive domain' (including conceptions and knowledge), contextual factors and real assessment practices. Lo and Leung (2022) briefly illustrated such interaction by showing

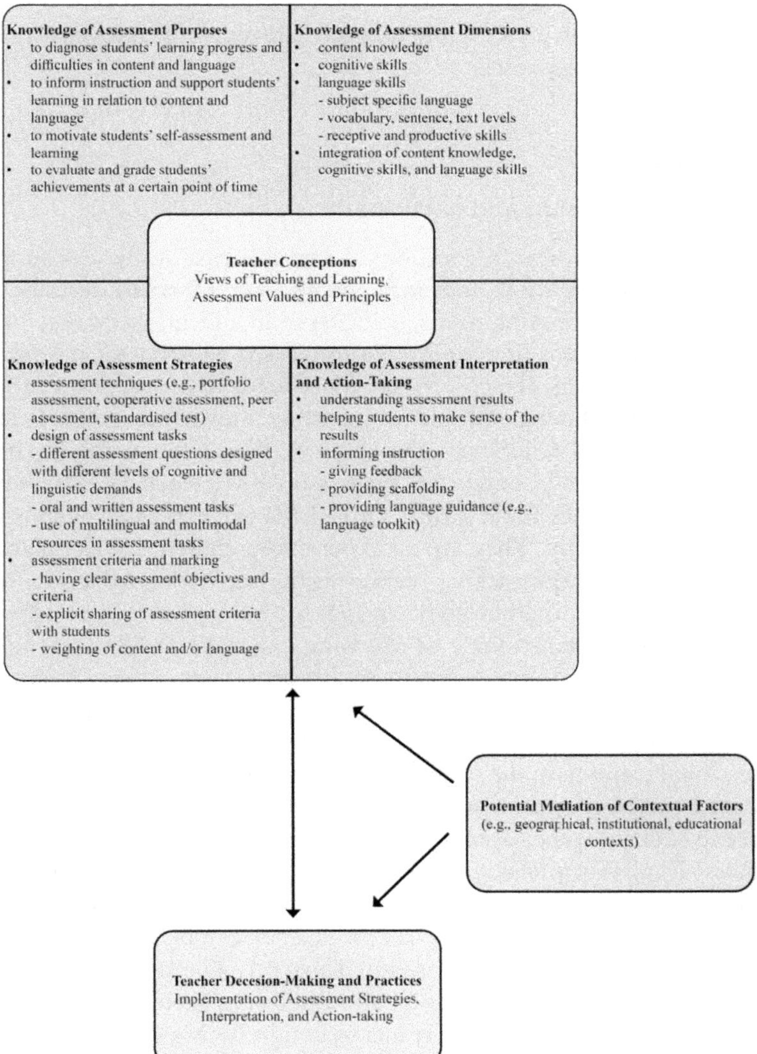

Figure 4.1 Framework of CLIL Teacher Assessment Literacy

how a Geography teacher in an EMI school in Hong Kong applied her language awareness and knowledge of assessment to designing appropriate assessment tasks for her students, with the aim of supporting students in both content and language development, which was aligned with the school's strategic planning. To further explore the intriguing relationship between the various components of EMI teacher assessment literacy, this study seeks to examine the implementation of assessment by EMI teachers and the potential impact of different factors. The research questions of this study are as follows:

(1) How do teachers assess students' content knowledge in L2?
(2) What are the potential factors that mediate teachers' assessment practices in EMI classrooms?

4.3 Methodology

4.3.1 Research design and participants

To answer the research questions, a multiple case study was adopted in this study. A case study approach enables researchers to describe and expand the understanding of a specific issue in education (Stake, 1995). As teacher assessment literacy is conceptualised as situated, interacting with different factors, the case study approach is appropriate to capture such interaction. Having multiple cases further allows researchers to identify similarities and differences among cases, thereby inferring the influence of personal and contextual factors on EMI teachers' assessment practices (Creswell & Poth, 2016). Three EMI teachers were purposively selected for this study. They are all experienced content subject teachers (with over seven years of teaching), delivering the International Baccalaureate (IB) curriculum in different international secondary schools in different cities in China. The rationale of choosing experienced EMI teachers is that they should have more exposure to different types of assessments and assessment strategies, which can provide richer insights for the research questions, compared to novice teachers. The three EMI teachers received professional training in the subjects they teach. In other words, they were all content subject specialists. Among them, Ms A also got a master's degree in education specialising in CLIL. We did not explicitly ask for the teachers' English proficiency level. However, considering the fact that international schools in China mainly hire native or near-native English speakers, the three teachers' English proficiency can be regarded as high. The teachers' profile is summarised in Table 4.1. The students taught by the teachers use Chinese as their L1 and English as their L2. Yet, according to the teachers' comments, students taught by Ms A's have a higher level of L2 proficiency, while those taught by Mr B and Ms C have diverse L2 proficiency levels.

Table 4.1 Profile of three EMI teacher participants

	Ms A	Mr B	Ms C
Nationality	China	India	China
City	Hong Kong	Shanghai	Foshan
Subject	Economics	Chemistry	Economics
Grade	G11–12	G10–12	G9–10
Years of Teaching	8 years	10 years	7 years

4.3.2 Data collection and analysis

Semi-structured interview and assessment materials (e.g. assessment tasks, marking rubrics, teachers' feedback) were collected for each case. Interviews provide an opportunity to gather in-depth information related to teachers' assessment literacy in a nuanced manner, while assessment materials provide tangible evidence of teachers' assessment practices. Having both interview and artefacts data can enhance the trustworthiness of the findings through triangulation and provide a more comprehensive understanding of EMI teachers' assessment practices and the potential mediation of various factors. Each semi-structured interview, which lasted for nearly one hour, was conducted in either English or Chinese, depending on the participants' preference. The major interview questions included (1) What assessment domains do EMI teachers pay attention to? (2) How do EMI teachers design assessment tasks and implement assessment? (3) What actions do EMI teachers take after assessment? The interview data were transcribed verbatim and checked before analysis.

Data analysis of this study included two phases: within-case analysis and cross-case analysis (Stake, 2005). During the within-case analysis, each teacher's interview and assessment materials were put into NVivo software and coded thematically (Braun & Clarke, 2022). The thematic analysis was done in both deductive and inductive way so that a comprehensive understanding of each EMI teacher's assessment practices could be developed. Specifically, the deductive coding was based on different components of the framework of CLIL Teacher Assessment Literacy (Figure 4.1). At the same time, new themes and sub-themes emerging from the data were allowed and named (e.g. resources for assessment design, use of multilingual/multimodal resources as assessment scaffolding, interdisciplinary collaboration on EMI assessment). The coding scheme was first piloted by two research team members with a small amount of data. Each of them then analysed half of the data, and discussed any uncertainties after coding. One researcher re-analysed the data and achieved an intra-coder reliability of 75%. The second researcher then joined the discussion, and the research team reached consensus on the coding results. Following the within-case analysis, cross-case analysis was used to explore the similarities and differences among the three EMI teachers so as to identify any good EMI assessment practices and determine the potential factors that influenced their assessment practices.

4.4 Results

This section starts by providing an overview of the three EMI teachers' assessment practices with the key components of the CLIL Teacher Assessment Literacy framework, i.e. what domains they assess, what strategies they use, how they mark students' work, how they interpret assessment data, and what actions they take. This is then followed by cross-case analysis.

4.4.1 Overview of three EMI teachers' assessment practices

Ms A

When **deciding on assessment domains**, Ms A adhered to IB assessment criteria. In doing so, she considered the integration of Economics knowledge, cognitive skills (e.g. application, analysis, evaluation, etc.), and academic language. In terms of **assessment strategies**, apart from summative assessment (which is co-created by all Economics teachers within the department), Ms A also employed various assessment techniques such as classroom-based assessment, interactive assessment, peer assessment and self-assessment. Among the assessment questions, essay writing is the most difficult task, so Ms A prepared scaffolding like generic essay structure for her students before assessment. Regarding marking, since IB exams are high-stakes and students answer the questions in L2, Ms A would have a thorough discussion with colleagues on how to mark students' answers with rubrics in a consistent manner. She prioritised content over language when marking students' work. **In terms of assessment interpretation and action-taking,** Ms A gave students written feedback on both content knowledge mastery and language use after summative assessment, reminded students of their common L2 grammatical mistakes in subsequent lessons, and had one-to-one consultation with lower achievers to learn about their learning difficulties. Figure 4.2 shows Ms A's written feedback on a student's essay script. It can be seen that her feedback prioritised content (e.g. the relationship between increasing pollination and farm harvest). As for action-taking, she modified her teaching in subsequent lessons or teaching units based on the assessment results.

Mr B

When **deciding on assessment domains**, Mr B also followed IB assessment criteria, taking Chemistry knowledge, cognitive skills and communication into consideration. **Concerning assessment strategies**, in addition to summative assessment (which is co-created by all Chemistry teachers

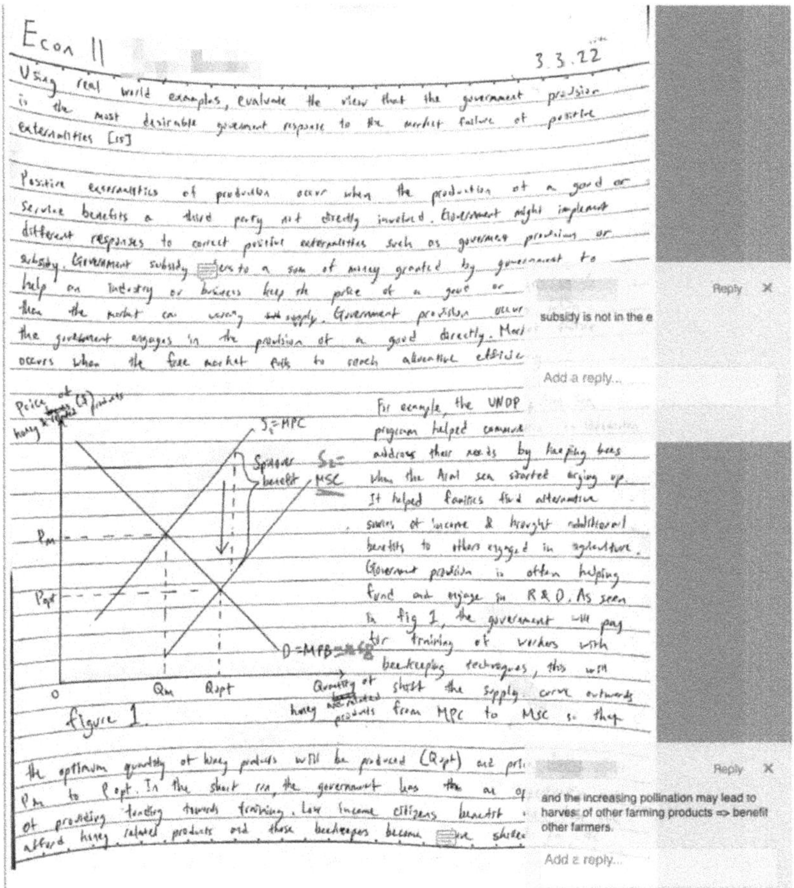

Figure 4.2 Ms A's written feedback on students' EMI assessment

within the department), he used various formative assessment tasks like regular quizzes, oral presentations and group work. Although he motivated his students to communicate in L2, he understood some students were too shy to speak in L2. He did not share the same L1 with his students, either. Hence he allowed drawing diagrams as a means of communication in formative assessment. Doing Chemistry experiments and writing lab reports are challenging, so Mr B often broke down the assessment tasks and provided students with sample answers, consultation and language support. English teachers would come to support their students' academic writing. Like Ms A, Mr B discussed with his colleagues on the marking rules and ensured consistency in their marking practice. They attempted to seek for a balance between assessing content knowledge and academic language. One interesting practice which may reflect his language awareness is that Mr B fine-tuned the marking rules which were

第一个期末考试 First End-term	
List which paper(s), topics, and/or sections were examined **列出试卷号、主题及考试部分**	
Topic 11.1 and 11.2: Measurement and Graphing Topic 1: Stoichiometry Topic 2: Atomic Structure Topic 3: Periodicity Topic 10.1: Organic Nomenclature Topic 5: Energetics	
List which paper(s) were examined **列出试卷号**	
Paper 1: Multiple Choice Questions Paper 2: Free Response Questions Paper 3: Section A: Experimental and Data Analysis Questions	
Student Performance **学生考试表现**	**Action Steps** **跟进举措**
T3,5,10 Low familiarity with terminology (electronegativity, isomer, homologues series, standard enthalpy change of combustion or formation, temperature rise)	Provide activity which requires students to generate questions with correct command terms, given definitions and terms. Introduce terminology once a week in a 5 min formative assessment.
T2 and T5 Knowledge covered in G10 was not reviewed by students. T10 Students improved in draw structural formula of organic compound, compared with SA. However, students were confusing with the group of atoms in bracket of condensed structural formula	the determination of the sign of enthalpy change. Create merged T5 questions in T4's formative quiz. For condensed structural formula, more examples and illustration in class and give more practiced questions.
Students were not able to apply graphical drawing skills from theory to practical. Students were not able answer Paper 3 questions which assess the conditions that is not usually focused or discussed well.	Standards for drawing scientific diagram. For future labs and IA, analyze the reason and evaluate the procedures, observations, results carefully in classroom practical and IA.

Figure 4.3 Assessment report provided for students in Mr B's school

related to the language performance at students' different learning stages, from lenient at the beginning to increasingly rigorous when students got used to the bilingual education and were closer to college application. **With respect to assessment interpretation and action-taking,** he worked with his colleagues in the same department to analyse students' performance and generate a report which listed students' major weaknesses and solutions to help them make improvements. Figure 4.3 is an extract from the report on an examination. For example, in this exam, the teachers found that students were not familiar with some subject-specific terms (e.g. *electronegativity, isomer*) and the teachers suggested designing activities for students to '*generate questions with correct command terms, give definitions and terms*'. After interpreting the assessment data, Mr B adjusted his teaching and provides additional learning materials according to students' needs.

Ms C

Ms C considered the **assessment domains** in accordance with the IB assessment criteria, which covered Economics knowledge, cognitive skills and communication. **As for assessment strategies,** in addition to employing summative assessment, Ms C used formative assessment through different techniques, including questioning, guessing games, group presentations and knowledge competitions. Given that quite a few of her students had difficulties with their L2, she offered language scaffolding during assessments to support their learning process. For instance, she permitted her students who had lower L2 proficiency to use their L1 during formative assessments. Likewise, she discussed with her colleagues regarding the use of rubrics to ensure consistency in their marking. When evaluating students' works, she prioritised the accuracy of content knowledge over their language performance. **Regarding assessment interpretation and action-taking,** after each summative assessment, she had a talk with her students in order to ascertain whether their learning difficulties pertained to the subject matter or language barriers. Drawing upon her diagnosis, she provided students with recommendations to tackle their learning challenges.

4.4.2 Cross-case analysis of three EMI teachers' assessment practices

Similarities

Although these three EMI teachers worked in different teaching contexts, they shared some similar assessment practices. When deciding on **assessment domains,** they all integrated content knowledge, cognitive skills and communication, thereby ensuring the tasks were aligned with the expectations of the IB exams. When implementing **assessment strategies,** they used a mixture of summative and formative assessment tasks. The formative assessment tasks were in diversified forms, so that they not only assessed students' content knowledge in L2, but also facilitated the development of multiple generic skills (e.g. collaboration, communication, self-evaluation). Seeing that IB exams are high-stakes and teachers need to rely on the official rubrics to mark students' work, these teachers had close intra-disciplinary collaboration with their colleagues on designing exam papers and discussing how to use the rubrics for reliable marking. EMI students encounter challenges from both content and language, so the three teachers provided scaffolding (e.g. essay structure) before assessment to support students in demonstrating their content knowledge through L2. **As for assessment interpretation and action-taking after assessment**, the three teachers diagnosed students' learning issues to identify whether students needed support in content and/or language and offered them solutions accordingly.

Differences

When implementing formative assessment, apart from teacher being the assessor, Ms A adopted peer assessment and self-assessment. By teaching students how to use the rubrics to review peers' work and use the checklists to self-evaluate their learning outcomes, students got more familiarised with the assessment criteria and took more responsibility for their learning. Ms A believed this pedagogical guidance can engage students in learning, which brings positive effects on their learning outcomes (Smith *et al.*, 2013). She explained her practice in this way:

> Ms A: I will use marking codes, for example, 'too vague', or 'lack of explanation' ... and let them know how to do the marking... and then they will imitate the way of our marking. Later **they will start to remind each other's work with the marking codes** and then I think this is a very **funny** and **interesting** practice because the **students are able to understand the exam requirements.**

The L2 proficiency levels of students in Mr B's and Ms C's classes were diverse, so both teachers allowed the use of multimodality or L1 in formative assessment:

> **Mr B:** The other thing we do is on a regular basis, ... do the small whiteboard (activity). Let's say, I am teaching them a topic, which involves some calculation. ... Then I will be like: 'Guys, get a new group, now whiteboarding activity' ... So, you need to solve this question on your whiteboard, and you need to **draw a graph** and you need to **present it**. ... **Because sometimes students are shy to talk**, I mean, but they're very good at writing. So, **I tried to** like, you know, **change it up**, so that **not only one strategy is being assessed for language all the time**.
> **Ms C:** For some students whose English language proficiency is not high, they will answer the questions in Chinese in some formative assessments. But I just need to interpret their performance in L1... **Allowing the use of L1** on some occasions is a kind of **motivation for learning**...

Mr B highlighted the fact that CLIL teachers should not only assess students' learning with the language mode. Depending on different disciplines, teachers can check students' content knowledge and skills with other meaning-making resources (e.g. doing calculation, drawing graphs). In a similar vein, Ms C acknowledged the potential language barriers some students may face when expressing their answers in L2. Hence, she allowed students to use their familiar language. This not only helped them overcome the language barriers, but also enhance their *learning motivation*. These assessment practices echo the recent advocacy for multimodal and multilingual assessments in EMI/CLIL, so that students' content knowledge can be assessed in a more valid way (e.g. Gorter & Cenoz, 2017; Leontjev & deBoer, 2022).

To support students' academic writing, cross-curricular collaboration was practised in Mr B's school. As most EMI teachers are not professionally prepared for teaching *both* content and language, cross-curricular collaboration between content teachers and L2 teachers is advocated to help teachers effectively integrate content and language instruction in bilingual education programmes (Lin, 2016). Mr B claimed that this was also beneficial for students' assessment performance:

> **Mr B**: There is a lot of **collaboration** for sure, like our English department. … For example, they spend a lot of time on **supporting students' academic research report writing**. They teach students how to cite an article correctly and how to go about not plagiarising. … When they come to Chemistry report writing … it's **extremely beneficial**…

When marking students' work, both Ms A and Ms C prioritised content over language by following the rubrics strictly, while Mr B showed attentiveness to students' language use and tweaked his marking rules considering students' L2 proficiency at different learning stages. He justified his decision in this way:

> **Mr B**: … they don't have too much experience with English…, **so initially** when we mark them for the first middle exam or the first mid-term exam, **we are a little lenient with them, not very strict with the spellings, with the language**. … And then, **as we progress further and further, especially when it comes close to the college application**, we make sure that we have trained them, given them enough practice, and then **we start becoming more strict, we start paying attention to terminology, how the answer is constructed**…

The way Mr B balanced content and language in marking demonstrates his language awareness (Andrews & Lin, 2017), particularly his understanding of students' learning difficulty, and how he applied such awareness to EMI assessment practices.

Regarding assessment interpretation and action-taking, while Mr B diagnosed students' learning issues with his colleagues, Ms A and Ms C did that through one-to-one talk with their students. The subject disciplines (Humanities or Science) could help explain the different ways Economics teachers and Chemistry teachers identified students' learning problems. Generally speaking, Humanities subjects are more language-oriented than Science subjects (Lo, 2014). They in turn impose higher language demands on students when they express ideas in Humanities subjects (e.g. Economics) in L2. This may make it more difficult for teachers to detect whether students' learning issues stem from content, language or both. As Ms C explained:

> **Ms C**: I will talk with my students after assessment to know about how they thought at that time when they were answering the questions. Some students would let me know that they understood the content knowledge in fact. **Looking at their answer sheets while listening to their explanation, I can finally understand what the students really wanted to express in the exam**. Later, **I will tell them how to use more subject-related language** to answer the questions in the exams.

After analysing students' assessment data, Mr B and his colleagues provided their students with a report telling their weaknesses and providing suggestions. Additionally, they provided tutoring workshops for students in need. Such collaboration and follow-up action were some usual practice in the school Mr B worked in.

Last but not the least, Ms A and Mr B adjusted their instruction after assessment, which revealed their awareness of using assessment data to inform teaching and improve students' learning (Shepard, 2019).

To summarise the assessment practices of the three teachers, a Venn diagram is provided (see Figure 4.4). Factors such as students' L2 ability, school policies, high stakes examinations, teachers' belief in specific assessment techniques, teachers' language awareness were found to influence teachers' assessment practices.

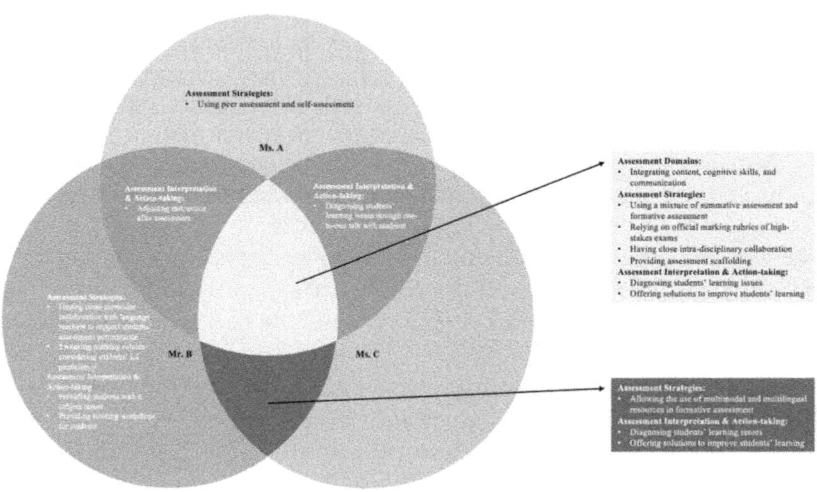

Figure 4.4 Comparative analysis of three EMI teachers' assessment practices

4.5 Discussion

Through comparing and contrasting three cases in this study, similarities and differences of three EMI teachers' assessment practices are identified, which reveal some good assessment practices and the potential mediation of some factors on how EMI teachers implement assessment.

The shared assessment practices among the three EMI teachers echo some key principles of assessment in EMI/CLIL programmes, where students learn content subjects through an L2:

- integrating both content and language in assessment (Mehisto & Ting, 2017);
- setting objectives and criteria and sharing them with students (Xavier, 2020);
- using a mixture of formal and informal assessment (Coyle *et al.*, 2010);
- providing students with language scaffolding (Lo & Fung, 2020);
- providing feedback and supporting students' progress (Xavier, 2020).

Some assessment practices from individual EMI teachers also correspond to some proposals of EMI/CLIL researchers:

- taking students' developmental stage into consideration (Massler, 2011);
- seeking cross-curricular collaboration between content teachers and language teachers on assessment (Lin, 2016);
- involving students in peer assessment and self-assessment (Xavier, 2020);
- allowing the use of multimodal and multilingual resources for meaning-making in assessment (Leontjev & deBoer, 2022; Saito, 2020);
- adjusting teaching strategies based on interpretation of students' assessment data (Liu *et al.*, 2023).

These good practices match with the key components of Liu *et al.*'s (2023) conceptual framework of CLIL Teacher Assessment Literacy, including knowledge of assessment dimensions, assessment purposes, assessment strategies and assessment interpretation and action taking. The empirical evidence and examples reported by the three EMI teachers in this study help explicate these key components, particularly when it comes to the fundamental question of what to assess (content vs language) and how to assess in the EMI context. While it can still be observed that the three EMI teachers placed more emphasis on the content aspect (especially when it comes to marking), they were still aware of the language aspect, but this is mainly manifested by their awareness of the language barriers that students may face and their provision of scaffolding before and after the assessment. This may not be surprising, considering the content-oriented nature of EMI and the teachers' professional training.

The cross-case analysis in this study also reveals the potential influence of contextual factors at different levels on teachers' assessment practices. First, it is noted that Mr B and Ms C allowed their students to use drawing or L1 in assessment owing to students' diverse L2 proficiency. The nature of the subjects could also explain why Ms A and Ms C tended to diagnose students' learning issues through one-to-one interaction. These two factors can be regarded as micro-level factors, as they concern individual's subject discipline and classroom context. Second, Mr B's school implemented policies related to action-taking after assessment (e.g. generating exam reports for students) and fostered cross-curricular collaboration. Hence, Mr B's students received academic language support from English teachers and more personalised tutoring. These conditions related to the school culture and policies can be regarded as meso-level factors. Third, given that IB exams are high stakes, all the teachers in this study adhered to the assessment criteria when deciding on assessment domains and grading students' work. Close collaboration within their department was observed in designing test papers and ensuring marking consistency. This factor functions at the macro level, as it concerns the external expectations from an international exam system. Apart from contextual factors, some personal factors can also be identified from this study. For example, Ms A's beliefs in peer assessment and self-assessment motivated her to use those strategies to facilitate her students' learning. Without a shared L1 with his students, Mr B was limited to utilising multimodal resources in some assessments as a strategy to accommodate his students' language needs. His language awareness and student-centred mindset influenced his 'differentiated' marking practices on students' language performance according to students' stages of learning. Thus, by tapping into teachers' conceptions of assessment, knowledge of assessment in different dimensions, examining their assessment practices, and understanding their personal beliefs, experience and working contexts, this study has illuminated the interaction between teachers' cognition, personal and contextual factors, as well as real assessment practices. This further validates the CLIL Teacher Assessment Literacy Framework.

4.6 Conclusion

Adopting a qualitative multiple case study design, this study reported how three EMI teachers assess students' content knowledge in L2 and explored the role of potential factors on their assessment practices. The findings highlight some good EMI assessment practices, including designing assessment tasks based on assessment criteria (learning objectives), seeking intra- and inter-disciplinary collaboration, providing students with scaffolding, employing diversified assessment strategies, balancing content knowledge and academic language, diagnosing EMI students' learning issues, providing feedback and suggestions, and adjusting pedagogical instructions to support students' learning. The findings also indicate how personal factors (e.g. (un)shared linguistic repertoire between teachers and students, teachers' language awareness, teachers' pedagogical knowledge) and contextual factors (e.g. the level of students' L2 proficiency, natures of different subjects, school policies, high stakes exams) influence EMI teachers' decision-making and implementation of assessment. All these reflect the interrelationship among EMI teachers' assessment conceptions, assessment knowledge, assessment practices and factors at various levels and from various sources.

This study is not without limitations. One of them lies in the lack of classroom observations owing to the pandemic. Classroom data could have provided additional insights into the actual assessment implementation. Another limitation is the reliance on self-reported interview data, which may be influenced by recall bias. Despite the limitations, this study has shed light on EMI teacher education. There have been calls for more professional development programmes for EMI teachers, so as to help them understand why and how to integrate content and language in instruction. Such understanding should be extended to the assessment dimension, so that EMI teachers can broaden their assessment knowledge and sharpen their skills in utilising various assessment strategies according to the instructional goals and student needs. Future professional development programmes should also empower EMI teachers to identify, understand and address the contextual factors that hinder or facilitate their assessment practices, so that they can better apply their conceptions and knowledge to their practices and to support their students' learning.

References

An, J., Macaro, E. and Childs, A. (2019) Language focused episodes by monolingual teachers in English Medium Instruction science lessons. *Journal of Immersion and Content-Based Language Education* 7 (2), 166–191.

Attar, Z., Blom, E. and Le Pichon, E. (2022) Towards more multilingual practices in the mathematics assessment of young refugee students: Effects of testing language and validity of parental assessment. *International Journal of Bilingual Education and Bilingualism* 25(4), 1546–1561.

Andrews, S. and Lin, A.M. (2017) Language awareness and teacher development. In *The Routledge Handbook of Language Awareness*. Routledge.

Baird, J.A. (2013) The currency of assessments. *Assessment in Education: Principles, Policy & Practice* 20 (2), 147–149.

Barrios, E. and Milla Lara, M.D. (2020) CLIL methodology, materials and resources, and assessment in a monolingual context: An analysis of stakeholders' perceptions in Andalusia. *The Language Learning Journal* 48 (1), 60–80.

Braun, V. and Clarke, V. (2022) *Thematic Analysis: A Practical Guide*. Sage.

Brookhart, S.M. (2011) Educational assessment knowledge and skills for teachers. *Educational Measurement: Issues and Practice* 30 (1), 3–12.

Cowie, B., Cooper, B. and Ussher, B. (2014) Developing an identity as a teacher-assessor: Three student teacher case studies. *Assessment Matters* 7 (6), 64–89.

Coyle, D., Hood, P. and Marsh, D. (2010) *CLIL: Content and Language Integrated Learning*. Cambridge University Press.

Creswell, J.W. and Poth, C.N. (2016) *Qualitative Inquiry and Research Design: Choosing among Five Approaches* (4th edn). Sage.

Dalton-Puffer, C., Hüttner, J. and Llinares, A. (2022) CLIL in the 21st century: Retrospective and prospective challenges and opportunities. *Journal of Immersion and Content-Based Language Education* 10 (2), 182–206.

Dalton-Puffer, C., Llinares, A., Lorenzo, F. and Nikula, T. (2014) "You can stand under my umbrella": Immersion, CLIL and bilingual education. A response to Cenoz, Genesee & Gorter (2013). *Applied Linguistics* 35 (2), 213–218.

DeLuca, C., Coombs, A., MacGregor, S. and Rasooli, A. (2019) Toward a differential and situated view of assessment literacy: Studying teachers' responses to classroom assessment scenarios. *Frontiers in Education* 4. https://doi.org/10.3389/feduc.2019.00094

Forsberg, E. and Wermke, W. (2012) Knowledge sources and autonomy: German and Swedish teachers' continuing professional development of assessment knowledge. *Professional Development in Education* 38 (5), 741–758.

Gorter, D. and Cenoz, J. (2017) Language education policy and multilingual assessment. *Language and Education* 31 (3), 231–248.

Hennebry, M. and Gao, X. (2021) Interactions between medium of instruction and language learning motivation. *International Journal of Bilingual Education and Bilingualism* 24 (7), 976–989.

Hönig, I. (2010) *Assessment in CLIL: Theoretical and Empirical Research*. VDM Verlag Dr. Müller.

Kao, Y.T. (2023) Exploring assessment for learning: Assessment tools and approaches in Taiwanese CLIL classes. *The Language Learning Journal* 1–15. https://doi.org/10.1080/09571736.2023.2217435

Leontjev, D. and deBoer, M.A. (2022) Multimodal mediational means in assessment of processes: an argument for a hard-CLIL approach. *International Journal of Bilingual Education and Bilingualism* 25 (4), 1275–1291.

Leung, C. (2014) Classroom–based assessment: Issues for language teacher education. In A. Kunnan (ed.) *Companion to Language Assessment* (Vol. 3, pp. 1510–1519). Wiley-Blackwell.

Lin, A.M. (2016) *Language Across the Curriculum & CLIL in English as an Additional Language (EAL) Context: Theory and Practice*. Springer.

Liu, J.E., Lo, Y.Y. and Xin, J.J. (2023) CLIL teacher assessment literacy: A scoping review. *Teaching and Teacher Education* 129, 104150. https://doi.org/10.1016/j.tate.2023.104150

Lo, Y.Y. (2014) L2 learning opportunities in different academic subjects in content-based instruction – evidence in favour of "conventional wisdom." *Language and Education* 28 (2), 141–160.

Lo, Y.Y. and Fung, D. (2020) Assessments in CLIL: The interplay between cognitive and linguistic demands and their progression in secondary education. *International Journal of Bilingual Education and Bilingualism 23* (10), 1192–1210.

Lo, Y.Y., Fung, D. and Qiu, X. (2023) Assessing content knowledge through L2: Mediating role of language of testing on students' performance. *Journal of Multilingual and Multicultural Development* 44 (10), 1013–1028.

Lo, Y.Y. and Leung, C. (2022) Conceptualising assessment literacy of teachers in Content and Language Integrated Learning programmes. *International Journal of Bilingual Education and Bilingualism* 25 (10), 3816–3834.

Lyster, R. and de Zarobe, Y.R. (2018) Introduction: Instructional practices and teacher development in CLIL and immersion school settings. *International Journal of Bilingual Education and Bilingualism* 21 (3), 273–274.

Macaro, E. (2018) *English Medium Instruction: Language and Content in Policy and Practice*. Oxford University Press.

Massler, U. (2011) Assessment in CLIL learning. In S. Ioannou-Georgiou and P. Pavlou (eds) *Guidelines for CLIL Implementation in Primary and Pre-Primary Education* (pp. 114–136). Cyprus Pedagogical Institute.

Mehisto, P. and Ting, Y.L.T. (2017) *CLIL Essentials for Secondary School Teachers.* Cambridge University Press.

Morton, T. and Llinares, A. (2017) Content and language integrated learning (CLIL): Type of programme or pedagogical model? Paper presented at the Applied linguistics perspectives on CLIL.

O'Neill, J. and Adams, P. (2014) The future of teacher professionalism and professionality in teaching. *New Zealand Journal of Teachers' Work* 11 (1), 1–2.

Otto, A. and Estrada, J.L. (2019) Towards an understanding of CLIL assessment practices in a European context: Main assessment tools and the role of language in content subjects. *CLIL. Journal of Innovation and Research in Plurilingual and Pluricultural Education* 2 (1), 31–42.

Ouazizi, K. (2016) The effects of CLIL education on the subject matter (Mathematics) and the target language (English). *Latin American Journal of Content and Language Integrated Learning* 9 (1), 110–137.

Rose, H., Macaro, E., Sahan, K., Aizawa, I., Zhou, S. and Wei, M. (2022) Defining English Medium Instruction: Striving for comparative equivalence. *Language Teaching* 56 (4), 539–550.

Saito, H. (2020) Gearing teaching and assessment towards CLIL: Theorizing assessment for learning in the Junior High School Soft CLIL Classrooms in Japan. In M. DeBoer and D. Leontjev (eds) *Assessment and Learning in Content and Language Integrated Learning (CLIL) Classrooms* (pp. 167–188). Springer.

Shepard, L.A. (2019) Classroom assessment to support teaching and learning. *The ANNALS of the American Academy of Political and Social Science* 683 (1), 183–200.

Smith, C.D., Worsfold, K., Davies, L., Fisher, R. and McPhail, R. (2013) Assessment literacy and student learning: The case for explicitly developing students 'assessment literacy'. *Assessment & Evaluation in Higher Education* 38 (1), 44–60.

Stake, R.E. (1995) *The Art of Case Study Research.* Sage.

Stake, R.E. (2005) *Multiple Case Study Analysis.* The Guilford Press.

Stiggins, R.J. (1991) Assessment literacy. *Phi Delta Kappan* 72 (7), 534–539.

Xavier, A. (2020) Assessment for learning in bilingual education/CLIL: A learning-oriented approach to assessing english language skills and curriculum content in Portuguese primary schools. In M. DeBoer and D. Leontjev (eds) *Assessment and Learning in Content and Language Integrated Learning (CLIL) Classrooms* (pp. 109–136). Springer.

Xu, Y. and Brown, G.T. (2016) Teacher assessment literacy in practice: A reconceptualization. *Teaching and Teacher Education* 58, 149–162.

5 The Washback Effects of Assessment in a Chinese University EMI Programme

Shuang He, Weihong Wang and
Yonghua (Yoka) Wang

Washback, or the consequence of test use on teaching and learning, is an indispensable element of assessment that has to be faced in educational systems and has, thus, been widely studied in the field of education. However, scant research has been seen discussing the washback effects of assessment on students' learning in university English-medium instruction (EMI) courses. The study takes up the issue by focusing on a Business Management programme at a Chinese university. To internationalise higher education and enhance students' competitiveness, the programme enacts EMI for all its disciplinary core courses with the vision of promoting students' learning of both subjects and English at the same time. The study adopts a multi-case study design to investigate the impacts of assessment in such courses on students' language and subject content learning. Findings reveal that assessment exerts significant washback effects on learners' content as well as language learning, and the washback effects vary in direction and intensity. Further analyses find that the effects are mediated by a series of individual and contextual factors, including learners' motivation, self-perceived language proficiency, projected identity, peer influence and the nature of courses. Based on the findings, implications for university EMI pedagogy, in particular the assessment of EMI courses, are discussed.

5.1 Introduction

The new millennium has witnessed an exponential expansion of English medium instruction (EMI) around the globe, especially in European and Asia-Pacific countries (Lei & Hu, 2023; Macaro *et al.*, 2018). Meanwhile, research on EMI has also increased dramatically in recent decades. A plethora of topics pertinent to EMI have been investigated, ranging from EMI policies (Sah & Fang, 2023), perceptions (Song,

2019) and impacts (Thompson *et al.*, 2022) to EMI classroom practices (Fang & Sah, 2023), challenges and strategies (Doiz *et al.*, 2013) and instructor professional development (Chen & Peng, 2019). However, as a critical component of EMI practice, the testing or assessment adopted by EMI courses and its correspondent washback effects are comparatively under-researched in the literature. Distinct from the traditionally separated language and subject courses whose goal is to learn either the language or the subject content, EMI envisions achieving both. How the dual goal of EMI is evaluated in course assessments and what impacts it has on teaching and learning are critical questions awaiting to be addressed in EMI research. To fill in the gap, the study takes an undergraduate Business Management programme in a Chinese university as a case to examine the assessment practices of EMI courses in the programme and their washback effects on learners. In the following section, we will first review what has been done on assessment washback in the literature and then elaborate on this study's research design and findings.

5.2 Assessment and Washback

The strong influence of assessment on education, be it high-stakes test, summative or formative assessment, has long been recognised in the field of education (Madaus, 1988; Resnick & Resnick, 1992). It influences not only the teaching and learning practices of individual teachers and learners at the micro level but also the educational system or even society at the macro level, such as school, curriculum, textbook, parents and policymakers, to name but a few (Bachman & Palmer, 1996; Wei, 2017). However, it is *impact* or *consequence* that are often used in discussing the influence of assessment on education; we choose to use the term *washback* in this paper because it has a narrower focus on the impacts of assessment on micro-level practices in the literature, which is more in line with our focus on assessment and students' learning.

It is the shift of focus in language assessment that spurs researchers' interest in assessment washback. In the late 20th century, language assessment shifted its emphasis from testing primarily learners' linguistic competence to communicative competence, that is, their ability to apply language-related knowledge, skills and abilities for real-world communication. At the same time, views towards test validity have also shifted to have systematic validity, that is, whether integrating a test in education can improve teaching and learning, as a major concern of a test. The two aspects of movements in test design have led researchers to attend to the influence of tests on teaching and learning, or in other words, washback, a term first put forward by Hughes (1989) in his book *Testing for Language Teachers*. Hughes (1989) highlighted washback, or backwash as he called it, as a key concern for teachers. His seminal work boosted researchers' interest in developing washback research into a legitimate research area.

Ever since, a number of models have been put forward as theoretical frameworks for washback studies. Alderson and Wall (1993) proposed 15 hypotheses for washback research, which covered a variety of issues around assessment washback, such as the test effects on teachers and teaching, learners and learning, the intensity of washback, and so on. Hughes (1993: 2) grouped the 15 hypotheses into a washback mechanism, which distinguished between 'participants, process and product in teaching and learning'. Bailey (1996) also proposed to examine the interactions between tests, participants, processes and products, but she particularly highlighted two concepts: washback to the learners and washback to the programme. The former referred to the impacts of 'test-derived information provided to the test-takers and having a direct impact on them'; and the latter appertained to 'results of test-derived information provided to teachers, administrators, curriculum developers, counsellors, etc. (Bailey, 1996: 263–264). Green (2007) further expanded Bailey's (1996) model by adding two dimensions to his washback model: direction and intensity. In terms of direction, washback can be either positive or negative, depending on whether assessments are well designed and properly applied; as for intensity, washback can be either strong or weak, which has a close relationship with the stakes of assessments (cited in Xu & Liu, 2018).

However, given the term was first used by language teachers in language education, empirical studies on washback have accumulated in this area as well. For instance, Cheng (1997) examined the washback effects of the Hong Kong Certificate of Education Examination in English in Hong Kong secondary schools and found that teachers tended to select in-class teaching content and activities aligned with those required in the examination syllabus. Cheng (2002, 2005) further noticed that changes in the assessment for the Hong Kong Certificate of Education Examination led to publishers' development of new textbooks and resources (Cheng, 2002), which, in turn, influenced secondary school English teachers' teaching content and practices in classroom (Cheng, 2005). The studies have shed light on assessment washback on language teachers, teaching practices and the use of teaching materials in the classroom but failed to uncover the influences of tests on learners and learning. As Green (2006: 113) argued, 'The washback effects of tests on teaching have attracted considerable attention over recent years, but the critical question of how this translates into washback on learning remains under-explored'.

To address Greens' (2006) concern, an increasing number of studies have shifted their attention to the washback effects of assessment on learners and their learning experiences since the 2010s. However, a majority of these studies have placed their emphases on international or national high-stakes tests, such as TOEFL iBT (Sadeghi *et al.*, 2021), the Chinese proficiency test of *Hanyu Shuiping Kaoshi* (HSK) for international Chinese learners (Kong & Zhang, 2024), the Test for English Majors

(TEM) in China (Xu & Liu, 2018) and the Chinese National Matriculation English Test (Zhang & Bournot-Trites, 2021). For example, Zhang and Bournot-Trites's (2021) study on the Chinese National Matriculation English Test found that the test did help students learn college English based on data from questionnaire surveys and semi-structured interviews. Kong and Zhang (2024) explored the washback effects of HSK on 1,616 Chinese as a second language learners. Both positive and negative impacts of the test were identified, but the positive effects (offering clear learning goals, fostering a positive attitude towards Chinese learning, developing learning strategies, and improving Chinese language proficiency) outweighed the negative ones (leading to worse classroom performance, causing exam pressure, and selecting surface learning methods). Also, the results revealed stronger assessment impacts on students at a lower level of Chinese proficiency and weaker impacts on students at a higher level. The study of Andrews *et al.* (2002) on the Hong Kong Advanced Supplementary 'Use of English' oral examination found that the test indeed helped improve students' performance in the spoken English test but did not fundamentally improve learners' language learning.

Besides examining the effects of washback, recent studies have begun to explore the mediating factors centred around assessment washback. Among them, learners' language proficiency is identified as a predominant factor affecting learners' test preparation such as their test preparation strategies, intensity and time investment (Fox & Cheng, 2007; Shih, 2007). However, the direction of their influence on washback effects is still unclear. Some studies reveal a positive relationship between learner's language proficiency and washback intensity (Pan, 2014), while others report the opposite (Fox & Cheng, 2007). In addition, learners' examination knowledge, test-taking experiences and attitudes towards test design are also found as possible intrinsic factors affecting washback effects (Tsang & Isaacs, 2022; Xie & Andrews, 2013). For instance, in Sato (2019), the washback effects of Japanese high-stakes university entrance examinations on students' English learning were mediated by learners' views on examinations, personal strengths and weaknesses and learning methods.

Extrinsic factors mediating washback effects on learners are identified as well. For instance, Gosa (2004) highlighted teachers as the most significant mediating factor influencing assessment washback on learners at the school level. Green's (2006) study further pointed out that the washback effects on learners were subjected to their teachers' beliefs about teaching content and test preparation courses. Likewise, in Zhan and Wan's (2016) study, student participants reported that teachers' rigid control over their test preparation affected their English learning. Outside the school context, Cheng *et al.* (2011) found that parents' perceptions of assessments play a considerably direct role in shaping their children's beliefs about assessments and their learning behaviours in and outside class. Tsang and Isaacs (2022) even identified societal factors such as posts on social media and the examination-oriented culture as mediating factors affecting the washback effects of assessment on learners.

Taken together, although much has been done to unveil the washback effects of assessment on learners and the various intrinsic and extrinsic factors affecting such effects, most studies focus on large-scale high-stakes tests. Scant research explores the washback effects of regional or local tests. A few extant studies disclose that even local or low-stakes tests also have washback effects on students. For example, in Fan *et al.*'s (2014) study, students reported that the Fudan English Test, a university-based test, gave them motivation and pressure to learn the English language, but the test provoked limited washback on their actual learning behaviours. As to research on the washback effects of course-based tests, scant studies have been seen in the literature. Besides, current research on mediating factors tends to examine them in a separate manner. How these factors work together on individual learners in specific contexts, in other words, the socially situated nature of the washback phenomenon is still under-researched. Furthermore, current research has been accumulated in language assessment. As washback is inherent in assessment, it is necessary to move washback research beyond the language-only type of assessment. In light of these considerations, the study took university EMI courses as our focus to examine the washback effects of course assessment on learners' learning of both subject content and English as a foreign language in a Chinese university context.

5.3 The Study

As an extension of washback research from large-scale high-stakes language tests to assessment in local courses, the study selected Chinese university EMI courses as our subjects because these courses are not limited to language learning and only target at students who take the courses, the two features of which are distinct from those oft-examined large-scale high-stakes language tests. Studies on these courses have the potential to add new value to current washback research. Moreover, unlike large-scale high-stakes tests, which are often designed by entities outside classrooms, assessment in these local courses is often designed by course teachers. Hence, its washback effects might be more visible on learners rather than on teachers. Therefore, this study centres on learners and is guided by the following research questions:

(1) How are the EMI courses assessed?
(2) What impacts the assessment of the EMI courses have on learners and their learning?
(3) What factors (internal or external) mediate the impacts of assessment on learners and their learning of the EMI courses?

Given that the washback phenomenon is socially situated, as revealed in previous research (Tsang & Isaacs, 2022), we situate our study in a specific university EMI programme. To gain a holistic and context-specific understanding of assessment washback in EMI courses, we adopt a multi-case study design (Yin, 2009) by focusing on individual learners who undertake EMI courses in the selected university.

5.3.1 The site

In response to the heightened role of English in globalisation and the worldwide practice of implementing EMI for the internationalisation of higher education, Chinese universities have also expanded their provision of EMI courses (Wang & Curdt-Christiansen, 2019). By referring to EMI, we follow Macaro's (2018: 19) understanding as 'the use of the English language to teach academic subjects (other than English itself) in countries or jurisdictions where the first language (L1) of the majority of the population is not English'. However, as McKinley *et al.* (2023: 1476) point out:

> In China, ... the growth of EMI provision at some universities amounts to teaching partial courses, whole courses, and entire programs in English, muddling the understanding of EMI in the region (e.g. Sahan *et al.*, 2022). Expectations surrounding language learning in EMI are not well-defined, but research in China often states a dual aim: to learn discipline content and to improve students' academic English proficiency (Zhou *et al.*, 2021). This dual purpose, ... might more accurately capture the actual practice of implementing EMI in Chinese higher education, in which bilingual education practices are common. (Hu, 2008)

What McKinley *et al.* (2023) have described about the practices of EMI in China is basically true for the site of this study. There are around 1,270 higher education institutions in China. Among them, around 145 are key universities directly under the administration of central agencies. The focal university is one of the 145 key national universities, and it is located in central China. In response to the national call for EMI for non-language courses, it provides EMI for around 5–10% of all its courses. There is even one undergraduate degree programme – Business Management in the Faculty of Economics and Management – that enacts EMI for most of its core disciplinary courses. Our study was situated in this programme.

5.3.2 Participants and data collection

Since most of the disciplinary core courses in this programme are delivered in Years 2 and 3, our study selected participants from these two cohorts. The study was conducted during the autumn semester of 2023.

We first contacted a student from the undergraduate Business Management programme and asked her to invite volunteers to participate in the study. In total, six participants (three Year 2: Alice, Jim and Lily; three Year 3: Cindy, Daisy and Mandy) agreed to participate in our study (all were pseudonyms). The six participants were then interviewed by the first author at the beginning, in the middle and at the end of the semester, respectively. The interviews were semi-structured under the guidance of three aspects of questions: (1) how the course was assessed; (2) how and why they were influenced by the assessment in the content learning; (3) how and why they were influenced by the assessment in the learning of English. Each interview lasted about 40 minutes and was conducted in both the interviewer and interviewee's mother tongue, Chinese. During the interview, if students mentioned certain materials that were helpful in understanding the impacts of assessments, those materials were collected afterwards. Besides, some complementary data were collected via the instant online chatting and sharing app, QQ, when we ran upon certain unclear points during the process of data analysis and needed to seek clarification from the participants.

We also shadowed the participants in three of their EMI courses. For second-year students, we sat with them in one session of their *Principles of Economics* and *Marketing* courses, respectively. For the third-year students, we observed one session of their *Project Management* course. Prior to these observations, we contacted their course teachers and got their permission first. After observing the courses, we talked with the teachers of the three courses to gain more information on their assessment practices for the courses.

In the end, interviews with the six students, which lasted 12 hours 40 minutes, were collected as our primary data, and 10 pages of fieldwork notes, three textbooks, three sets of courseware, two sets of assignments, one set of groupwork materials presented by participants and six sets of QQ chatting records were also collected to facilitate our understanding of the interview data.

5.3.3 Data analysis

Based on the data, we first categorised the types of assessment adopted in the three EMI courses. Then, we developed a coding scheme (Table 5.1) to conduct thematic analysis of our data first case by case, and then across cases.

To be specific, we first identified the impacts of assessment on each participant's content and English learning and the factors contributing to the impacts, respectively. Then, we referred to Hughes' (1993) trichotomy of the backwash model to divide the impacts into categories of attitudes, actions and outcomes. The mediating factors were also coded and classified. After analysing each case, we compared and contrasted six cases to synthesise similarities and identify differences. Then, we tried to build links across categories to achieve an integrative understanding of the phenomenon.

Table 5.1 Coding scheme for data analysis

I Assessment practices	I-1 Formative assessment	I-1a Attendance I-1b Assignments I-1c In-class performance I-1d Projects
	I-2 Summative assessment	I-2a Exam items in English and answer in English I-2b Exam items in English and answer in Chinese I-2c Exam items in Chinese and answer in English I-2d Exam items in Chinese and answer in Chinese
II Washback effects of assessment	II-1 Effects on content learning	II-1a Attitudes II-1b Actions II-1c Outcomes
	II-2 Effects on English learning	II-2a Attitudes II-2b Actions II-2c Outcomes
III Factors mediating the washback effects	III-1 Internal factors	III-1a Learners' motivation III-1b Self-perceived language proficiency III-1c Projected identity III-1d Others
	III-2 External factors	III-2a Peer influence III-2b Nature of courses III-2c Others

For each step of the analysis, the first two authors did the initial analysis, respectively, and the comparison of their analysis revealed a 93% agreement across all cases. Then, the disagreements were examined and discussed with the third author until final agreements were achieved among all three authors.

5.4 Findings and Discussions

5.4.1 The three observed courses and their assessment practices

The three EMI courses we followed were delivered by Chinese subject teachers with 5 to 14 years of teaching experience and 1 to 4 years of overseas study experience. The textbooks that the courses adopted were English ones published by international publishing houses. As to lecturers' courseware and instructional language, the three courses differed.

The *Principles of Economics* course for Year 2 students consisted of two parts: the *Microeconomics* part was delivered by a male lecturer in English initially and switched to Chinese later on, whereas the *Macroeconomics* part was delivered by a female lecturer primarily in Chinese. The courseware for both parts was in English throughout. The two lecturers explained that they began using Chinese for about two-thirds of the course time after noticing students' difficulties in learning in English (*Fieldnote taken after talking with the Macroeconomics teacher*).

In the Year 2 *Marketing* course, the courseware was presented bilingually in both English and Chinese, in particular for those key terms and concepts in marketing, whereas the lecturer's teaching was mainly delivered the course in Chinese. The course teacher explained that it was her first time teaching bilingually and that her previous experience of learning the course was in Chinese. Therefore, she chose to deliver the course in Chinese so as to better explain subject knowledge to students (*Fieldnote taken after talking with the course teacher*). The *Project Management* course for Year 3 students was delivered by a female returnee from Australia in a co-existence of both English and Chinese and the courseware was also presented bilingually. The lecturer explained that she believed both academic English and Chinese were equally important for students' subject learning and future work in the profession (*Fieldnote taken after talking with the Project Management teacher*).

As to assessment practices, all three courses followed the university requirement of incorporating both formative and summative assessment, with each accounting for 50% of students' final scores for a course. The formative assessment for a course usually includes attendance, assignments, in-class performance and projects. The summative assessment was conducted in the format of final exams, which usually focused on evaluating students' mastery of subject knowledge. The assessment methods were often announced by course teachers at the very beginning of the courses. Although the three courses followed similar assessment patterns, the detailed assessment practices in each course varied.

In *Principles of Economics*, assignments and in-class performance were measured mainly through students' responses to questions about the main content of individual lessons. Questions in assignments were in English. Students were required to answer in English as well. The in-class questions were in English, but students were to decide to answer in either Chinese or English. The project of this course was to complete an online quiz in the formats of multiple choices and true-or-false questions. The quiz was written in English, and the objective of the quiz was to examine students' mastery of economic knowledge and the application of economic theories or principles in analysing economic phenomena. The final exam for the course included multiple-choice questions, calculation questions and essay questions. All questions were given in English and required to be answered in English, except one essay question, which was given in Chinese, and students could answer in Chinese or English.

In *Marketing*, the assignments were two marketing research projects. The students were required to make a marketing case analysis by using academic knowledge acquired in the course. The projects were to be done in Chinese. The first project was to be published on a WeChat public account, and the teacher evaluated students' performance by checking the likes and followers of each post. The second project was to be completed in groups and then presented in Chinese in class. The in-class performance was evaluated by a question–answer session at the beginning of each class to examine students' mmastery of content from previous lectures. Both questions and answers were delivered in Chinese. The question types of the final exam were term explanations, true or false questions, multiple choices and marketing case analysis. All questions were delivered in English and required to be answered in English, except the last marketing case analysis, which was delivered in Chinese, and students were free to answer in Chinese or English.

In *Project Management*, the assignments in the formative assessment were short-answer questions, which were assigned to students twice in one semester in the format of a spot check to assess students' mastery of lecture content in class. Students had to review the last lecture and get ready to be checked at the beginning of the next lecture if they expected to get a decent score in the assignments. In-class performance was measured by answering teachers' questions during each lecture. And the small-group project was to ask students to analyse a real-life project management case with knowledge learned in class. For all these exercises, teachers would provide questions and requirements in English with Chinese explanations, whereas students were free to answer in English or Chinese. The final exam for the course was an open-book test. Students could refer to their textbooks, handouts, courseware, and other learning materials during the test. The question types in the test included multiple choice, true or false questions, short-answer questions, calculation questions and essay questions. All questions were written in English and required to be answered in English.

5.4.2 The washback effects of assessment in the three courses

Given that the envisioned goal of EMI was to learn both content and English, the washback effects of assessment in these courses were also examined in the two aspects. And for each aspect of research, we followed Hughes's (1993: 2) trichotomic model to approach the effects of assessment on participants in three dimensions: their 'perceptions and attitudes towards their work', 'actions undertaken' by them to complete learning tasks, and 'learning outcomes and the quality of learning'. From the themes we identified in each individual participant, we noticed that the six participants had more sharedness than divergence. Therefore, we reported their similarities instead of differences.

As to the washback effects of assessment on students' content learning, we found that all six participants held positive attitudes towards content learning in EMI courses. As seen in the assessment practices of all three courses, no matter whether it was the formative or summative assessment, the students' mastery of content knowledge was assessed. Take the *Principles of Economics* course as an example. In the very first class, the course teacher made it clear in class and on PPT slides the constituents of formative assessment for this course, and the final exam focused on 'the essentials of economic theories and principles and their application in analysing economic phenomena' *(Conversation with the Microeconomics teacher)*. Though English was required in some of the assessments, the teacher highlighted that their assessment depended mainly on students' performance in content learning instead of language proficiency (*Fieldnote taken after talking to the Macroeconomics teacher*). Therefore, in student interviews, all six participants agreed that the main objective of the courses was to learn subject knowledge.

Because of participants' firm belief in subject content learning in EMI courses, when asked what and how they learnt the courses in the semester, their interview answers revealed that the methods they mentioned were all relevant to content learning. All six reported that they previewed textbook chapters before class and reviewed teachers' courseware after class. Three even reinforced that they would at least read teachers' courseware more than three times. Five students admitted that they had resorted to Chinese textbooks or other Chinese resources online to facilitate their understanding of subject content in EMI courses. Four participants mentioned discussing with teachers and classmates as an effective way to clarify some difficult knowledge points in textbooks. For example, in the interview, Lily told us, 'Though it is difficult for me to understand those economic principles, I can find different ways to master them. I read my English textbook repeatedly, refer to PPT provided by the teacher, watch Chinese online classes, discuss with my roommates, and so on' *(Third interview with Lily)*. Findings revealed that all participants exerted agency in taking positive actions to learn content knowledge.

As to the outcomes engendered by such assessment practice, participants agreed that they mastered most of the basic and core content knowledge of the three courses. For instance, Alice shared with us her experiences in preparing the *Marketing* research project:

> We are required to analyse a case comprehensively by using all we have learned in the course. The more employment of knowledge we have learned in class, the better. Once we get the group task, all group members discuss with each other and compete in providing cases to be analysed. We are all devoted to the task during the whole week. Throughout the process, we basically go over all the course content, in particular those key marketing theories and principles several times, together with our group members. What's more, by applying class learning to case analysis, I strongly feel that my understanding of certain knowledge has been deepened and expanded. *(Third interview with Alice)*

The excerpt points to the role of assessment in driving students to consolidate their learning through addressing real-world issues.

To sum up, the assessments made participants attach great importance to content learning, encouraged them to take positive actions to learn content and eventually led them to master basic and key content knowledge of the course. This echoes the findings of Brown and Bradford (2017) that EMI is mainly concerned with content learning, and the assessment practices in the courses further reinforce the point. However, we also noticed that students tended to ignore content that was not core to a subject or might not be covered in exams. As Jim justified that 'I would only memorise the definitions of some key terms in *Marketing*, because there were only five terms to be tested in the final exam. There is no opportunity for the teacher to include some unimportant terms in the exam, I predict' (*Second interview with Jim*). It seems the disclosure of test formats breeds a test-oriented learning culture for some students.

There are also three shared themes identified regarding the effects of assessment on students' English learning. First, the engagement of English in assessment enhanced participants' awareness of the importance of English, in particular specialised English expressions, in subject learning. The questions in assignments and the question–answer sessions were primarily in English. Test papers were also mainly written in English. Students realised that they had to maintain a state of English learning through, for example, reading English textbooks so as to understand exam questions in English. Daisy even recognised 'knowing subject-related terms and expressions as the most rewarding part of English learning in EMI courses' (*Third interview with Daisy*).

With the upholding of such belief, students' efforts in English learning were mainly put on specialised English expressions. We noticed in class observations that students' most frequent actions in English learning were adding Chinese counterparts to specialised terms or expressions in their English textbooks. In the interviews, students also expressed their puzzles about understanding long and complex sentences in textbooks. However, given no specific lecture on language learning in EMI courses, they themselves did not know how to deal with the difficulty.

As to the outcome of English learning in EMI courses, all students reported that their English reading ability was improved under the influence of assessment requirements. We observed that teachers seldom provided language support in lectures or corrected students in their English assignments or presentations. Students had to solve English-related problems by themselves. The course teachers explained that they were not language teachers and were incompetent in English teaching. They also mentioned that language was not the primary concern of the course, so they chose to ignore it (*Fieldnote after talking with teachers*). The study further noticed that assessment practices in the three courses exerted limited impacts on students' English speaking and listening because 'these two aspects of English ability are not required in assessment' (*First interview with Mandy*). Although the participants expressed the importance of English listening and speaking, they still ignored improving them because they were not required to do so in the final exam. In other words, the current way of engaging English in assessment did not stimulate students' effort to improve their English listening and speaking.

5.4.3 Factors mediating the effects of assessment washback in EMI courses

Besides identifying shared washback effects of assessment in the EMI courses, variations also occurred. Our reiterated analyses of variations across cases and factors leading to the variations reveal that the following five internal and external factors may account for the variations – learners' motivation, self-perceived language proficiency, projected identity, peer influence and the nature of courses.

It was found that students displayed two basic orientations toward their studies: grade orientation and learning orientation (Svinicki, 2005). Students showing grade orientation would concentrate on achieving scores in learning, while those displaying learning orientation would focus on mastering knowledge or skills. In the interview, we found that participants' motivations for EMI learning differed. Mandy explicitly expressed that her immediate learning goal was to get good scores, so she prioritized learning content that might be included in the assessment. For English learning, she thought it was enough to learn only subject-related English expressions so as to help her comprehend questions in assessment and answer questions in simple English. The other five, however, stated that although getting satisfactory scores was important for them, their fundamental goal was to learn content and language. They not only mastered what might be included in the assessment but also attempted to extend content learning to integrate English. As Lily expressed, she wanted to enhance her English by taking EMI courses. Hence, in daily learning, she chose to 'memorise and review English vocabulary' and 'consult additional resources to know how to effectively understand long English sentences' in doing assignments and preparing for the final exam in the *Principles of Economics* course; her English reading ability was also 'greatly improved because of my effort' (*Third interview with Lily*). Likewise, Daisy planned to further her studies in future and wanted to write and publish in English. Therefore, even though English was optional in formative and summative assessments, she forced herself to use English whenever she was given choices between English and Chinese. The examples indicate that variations in motivation may lead to students' different assessment preparation efforts in EMI courses.

Students' self-perceived language proficiency was found to be a second oft-mentioned mediating factor. In the interviews, four participants *(Alice, Cindy, Daisy and Mandy)* believed that their present English proficiency was sufficient for them to deal with language-related problems in assessment if they learned some additional subject-related English expressions. In practice, they reported that their way to prepare for exams was to browse the English textbook and courseware to review course content and at the same time note down specialised English vocabulary. With content knowledge and specialised English vocabulary, they said they would understand and answer questions properly in exams. While two participants *(Jim and Lily)* were unsure that their English was enough for course assessment, they made particular efforts to learn English in the EMI courses. They mentioned they would read the English textbooks carefully, not only to know subject-related English vocabulary but also to understand English phrases and even sentences. The difference seems to indicate that English proficiency plays a role in students' preparation for assessment in EMI courses.

The third mediating factor we identified was students' projected identities. Three participants *(Cindy, Daisy and Lily)* mentioned that since they were taking the EMI-based Business Management programme, they should be distinct from those who took the normal Business Management programme. One distinguished feature of their programme was that they learned disciplinary courses in English, so they should excel at English in comparison with others. They said that they 'should show their advantage in English' (*Second interview with Cindy*). That's why Cindy told us that she chose to answer questions voluntarily in English in the *Project Management* course, though either English or Chinese was acceptable. In contrast, the other three participants did not think they should be labelled better English learners. If the teacher did not ask them to answer the questions in English, they 'naturally answered the questions in Chinese' (*Second interview with Alice*). The different projections of the two groups of participants led them to different efforts in test preparations.

Besides individual factors, external factors such as peer influence also play a role in mediating participants' learning for assessment in EMI courses. In interviews, five out of six participants referred to roommates or schoolmates in certain ways when they were probed into responses to assessment requirements in EMI courses. For instance, Daisy mentioned that at the beginning of the *Project Management* course, she consulted one previous schoolmate who once took the course and was told that, although English was not compulsory in completing course assignments and the final exam, many students who took the course previously talked of getting higher scores in the end; the teacher would not be particular at students' language mistakes but provided generous bonus scores for their extra effort in answering questions in English. The consultant's words impressed Daisy deeply; thus, she mentioned that she had tried her best to use English on most occasions in the course. The case seems to reveal that peers play a critical role in university students' learning behaviours.

Another prominent external factor was the nature of the courses. In the study, we noticed two courses with distinct features: *Marketing* was practice-oriented, whereas *Principles of Economics* was more theory-oriented. In *Marketing*, there were many case analyses on topics closely related to students' real-life experiences in the economic world of China. Therefore, they could understand English easily. Therefore, although the course teacher relied heavily on Chinese in lectures, two participants reported reading English textbooks and consulting English resources in preparing their marketing analysis projects. By contrast, the *Principles of Economics* course involved heavy economic theories and principles which were originally conceptualised in English. The *Microeconomics* teacher also preferred to teach in English. However, students found it difficult to understand abstract and professional expressions in English, and all three participants agreed that they relied more on Chinese in learning the course, in particular in the later *Macroeconomics* part. Some EMI courses were theoretical, while others were practical. The different reactions of the same three participants to the two courses indicate that course nature exerts impacts on learners' learning to a certain degree.

While learners' motivation, self-perceived language proficiency, projected identity, peer influence and the nature of courses were five prominent factors mediating the washback effects of EMI assessment, they did not always function simultaneously and equally for every participant. Instead, these factors interacted with each other and yielded different impacts on individual participants. For example, Year 2 Lily projected herself as an EMI-programme taker and believed firmly in developing English skills and excelling in English. Thus, she first read the English textbook only in the *Principles of Economics* course and refused to refer to any Chinese materials when she did the assignments. However, later on, she found that some theories in English were beyond her understanding, and it was hard for her to complete the assignments in total English. She switched to Chinese gradually.

5.5 Pedagogical Implications

Though the study is based on only six cases and is rather limited at present, the findings of the study may have three aspects of implications for EMI pedagogy.

Firstly, explicit instructional objectives and assessment arrangements for students' English learning need to be included in EMI courses. The study finds that students indeed have a desire to learn English in EMI, but the practices of English learning in EMI courses seem to be rather casual. There are only loose requirements of using or not using English in practice. As to what, when and how English should be incorporated in EMI courses, no specific planning is identified in the study.

Secondly, the training of content instructors should be given due attention. The study reveals varied practices among teachers and courses in the EMI programme. It seems that instructors of EMI courses do not receive specific training on how to teach EMI courses. Admittedly, EMI courses are neither similar to conventional subject courses nor language courses.

Necessary training is needed for the successful implementation of EMI courses. Apart from training content instructors on how to teach EMI courses, they also need to receive systematic training on assessments to improve their assessment literacy and agency in designing EMI-specific assessment practices. How to engage students in academic English learning in EMI courses could also be a possible consideration in teacher training programmes.

Last but not least, learners' factors should never be neglected when implementing EMI education. The study shows that learners' motivation, self-perceived language proficiency and projected identities are important factors mediating their attitudes, actions and outcomes in EMI learning. While improving contextual factors such as teachers and teaching, it is also necessary to know our learners and the internal factors that give rise to positive learning in EMI courses. Without their commitment, whatever efforts teachers have made would not take effect.

References

Alderson, J.C. and Wall, D. (1993) Does washback exist? *Applied Linguistics* 14 (2), 115–129.

Andrews, S., Fullilove, J. and Wong, Y. (2002) Targeting washback: A case-study. *System* 30 (2), 207–223.

Bachman, L. and Palmer, A. (1996) *Language Testing in Practice*. Oxford University Press.

Bailey, K.M. (1996) Working for washback: A review of the washback concept in language testing. *Language Testing* 13 (3), 257–279.

Brown, H. and Bradford, A. (2017) EMI, CLIL, & CBI: Differing approaches and goals. In P. Clements, A. Krause and H. Brown (eds) *Transformation in Language Education* (pp. 328–334). JALT.

Chen, Y. and Peng, J. (2019) Continuing professional development of EMI teachers: A Chinese case study. *Journal of Education for Teaching* 45 (2), 219–222.

Cheng, L. (1997) How does washback influence teaching? Implications for Hong Kong. *Language and Education* 11 (1), 38–54.

Cheng, L. (2002) The washback effect on classroom teaching of changes in public examinations. In S.J. Savignon (ed.) *Interpreting Communicative Language Teaching: Contexts and Concerns in Teacher Education* (pp. 91–111). Yale University Press.

Cheng, L. (2005) *Changing Language Teaching Through Language Testing: A Washback Study*. Cambridge University Press.

Cheng, L., Andrews, S. and Yu, Y. (2011) Impact and consequences of school-based assessment in Hong Kong: Views from students and their parents. *Language Testing* 28 (2), 221–250.

Doiz, A., Lasagabaster, D. and Sierra, J.M. (eds) (2013) *English-Medium Instruction at Universities: Global Challenges*. Multilingual Matters.

Fan, J., Ji, P. and Song, X. (2014) Washback of university-based English language tests on students' learning: A case study. *The Asian Journal of Applied Linguistics* 1 (2), 178–191.

Fang, F. and Sah, P.K. (2023) (eds) *English-Medium Instruction Pedagogies in Multilingual Universities in Asia*. Routledge.

Fox, J. and Cheng, L. (2007) Did we take the same test? Differing accounts of the Ontario Secondary School Literacy Test by first and second language test-takers. *Assessment in Education* 14 (1), 9–26.

Gosa, C.M.C. (2004) Investigating washback: A case study using student diaries [Unpublished doctoral thesis]. Lancaster University.

Green, A. (2006) Washback to the learner: Learner and teacher perspectives on IELTS preparation course expectations and outcomes. *Assessing Writing* 11 (2), 113–134.

Green, A. (2007) *IELTS Washback in Context: Preparation for Academic Writing in Higher Education*. Cambridge University Press.

Hughes, A. (1989) *Testing for Language Teachers*. Cambridge University Press.

Hughes, A. (1993) Washback and TOEFL 2000 [Unpublished manuscript]. University of Reading.

Kong, F. and Zhang, Y. (2024) Investigating the washback of the Chinese Language Proficiency Test (HSK): From the perspective of CSL students. *SAGE Open* 14 (1), 1–15.

Lei, J. and Hu, G. (2023) Research on English-medium instruction in the Asia-Pacific: Trends, foci, challenges, and strategies. In W.O. Lee *et al.* (eds) *International Handbook on Education Development in the Asia-Pacific* (pp. 637–659). Springer.

Macaro, E. (2018) *English Medium Instruction*. Oxford University Press.

Macaro, E., Curle, S., Pun, J., An., J. and Dearden, J. (2018) A systematic review of English medium instruction in higher education. *Language Teaching* 51 (1), 36–76.

Madaus, G.F. (1988) The influence of testing on the curriculum. In L.N. Tanner (ed.) *Critical Issues in Curriculum: Eighty-Seventh Yearbook of the National Society for the Study of Education* (pp. 83–121). University of Chicago Press.

McKinley, J., Rose, H. and Curdt-Christiansen, X.L. (2023) EMI in Chinese higher education: The muddy water of 'Englishisation'. *Applied Linguistics Review* 14 (6), 1475–1481.

Pan, Y.C. (2014) Learner washback variability in standardized exit tests. *TESL-EJ* 18 (2). Retrieved March 27, 2024.

Resnick, L.B. and Resnick, D.P. (1992) Assessing the thinking curriculum: New tools for educational reform. In B.R. Gifford and M.C. O'Connor (eds) *Changing Assessments: Alternative Views of Aptitude, Achievement and Instruction* (pp. 37–73). Kluwer Academic Publishers.

Sadeghi, K., Ballıdağ, A. and Mede, E. (2021) The washback effect of TOEFL iBT and a local English Proficiency Exam on students' motivation, autonomy and language learning strategies. *Heliyon* 7 (10), 1–9.

Sah, P.K. and Fang, F. (2023) *Policies, Politics, and Ideologies of English-Medium Instruction in Asian Universities: Unsettling Critical Edges*. Routledge.

Sato, T. (2019) An investigation of factors involved in Japanese students' English learning behavior during test preparation. *Papers in Language Testing and Assessment* 8 (1), 69–95.

Shih, C.M. (2007) A new washback model of students' learning. *Canadian Modern Language Review* 64 (1), 135–161.

Song, Y. (2019) English language ideologies and students' perception of international English-medium instruction (EMI) master's programmes: A Chinese case study. *English Today* 35 (3), 22–28.

Svinicki, M.D. (2005) Student goal orientation, motivation and learning. *The IDEA Centre*. Paper#41.

Thompson, G., Aizawa, I., Curle, S. and Rose, H. (2022) Exploring the role of self-efficacy beliefs and learner success in English medium instruction. *International Journal of Bilingual Education and Bilingualism* 41 (2), 368–384.

Tsang, C.L. and Isaacs, T. (2022) Hong Kong secondary students' perspectives on selecting test difficulty level and learner washback: Effects of a graded approach to assessment. *Language Testing* 39 (2), 212–238.

Wang, W. and Curdt-Christiansen, X.L. (2019) Translanguaging in a Chinese-English bilingual education programme: A university-classroom ethnography. *International Journal of Bilingual Education and Bilingualism* 22 (3), 322–337.

Wei, W. (2017) A critical review of washback studies: Hypothesis and evidence. In R. Al-Mahrooqi, C. Coombe, F. Al-Maamari and V. Thakur (eds) *Revisiting EFL assessment: Critical Perspectives* (pp. 49–67). Springer.

Xie, Q. and Andrews, S. (2013) Do test design and uses influence test preparation? Testing a model of washback with Structural Equation Modeling. *Language Testing* 30 (1), 49–70.

Xu, Q. and Liu, J. (2018) *A Study on the Washback Effects of the Test for English Majors (TEM): Implications for Testing and Teaching Reforms*. Springer.

Yin, R.K. (2009) *Case Study Research: Design and Methods* (4th edn). Sage.

Zhan, Y. and Wan, Z.H. (2016) Test takers' beliefs and experiences of a high-stakes computer-based English listening and speaking test. *RELC Journal* 47 (3), 363–376.

Zhang, H. and Bournot-Trites, M. (2021) The long-term washback effects of the National Matriculation English Test on college English learning in China: Tertiary student perspectives. *Studies in Educational Evaluation* 68 (3), 100977.

6 Students' Academic Reading in EMI and Assessment *for* Social Justice: The Case of a University in Nepal Through the Lens of Honneth's Mutual Recognition

Prithvi N. Shrestha

6.1 Introduction

Assessment probably plays the most influential role in student learning in higher education (Ajjawi, 2023). Therefore, it is essential to understand assessment policies and practices which have life-changing impacts on students. Language plays a crucial role in assessment because the language of teaching and assessment (e.g. English) may not be students' first language and thus can be challenging to them. The global hegemony of English language means education at all levels is affected by this hegemony, particularly in non-English speaking regions. Specifically, in the Asian context, there is a noticeable growth of English as a medium of instruction (EMI) across all levels of education but more increasingly in higher education (HE) due to the drive towards internationalisation, the legacy of British imperialism, perceived economic benefits of English, lack of textbooks in local/ national languages and government education policy changes (Galloway *et al.*, 2020; Walkinshaw *et al.*, 2017).

Although EMI in many non-Anglophone countries is a recent development, EMI in HE in South Asia including Nepal, the context of this chapter, is not a new phenomenon. It resulted from politicohistorical processes due to the region being a British colony for 200 years (e.g. see Mahboob, 2017) and the insertion of an English medium education. Beyond 1949, in a number of subjects in HE, the language of teaching, learning and assessment has been English (Linn *et al.*, 2021; McCulloch *et al.*, 2020) in the region although the language in education policies may still be obscure and English language remains to be a foreign language to HE students in Nepal. In recent years, pure EMI in HE in contexts such as Nepal has been questioned due to its negative impact on equity and social justice (Linn *et al.*, 2021; Phyak & Sah, 2022; Shrestha *et al.*, 2024). However, the issue of social justice in assessment in EMI is under-researched generally and particularly in Nepal. The most recent volume on EMI and social justice in South Asia (Giri *et al.*, 2024), for example, includes only one chapter that discusses university admissions language test in Bangladesh (Roshid *et al.*, 2024). Therefore, there is an urgent need for more scholarly work in the area of assessment and social justice in EMI contexts as highlighted in recent EMI scholarship (Hultgren *et al.*, 2022; Sah, 2022).

HE has long served both public and private purposes, including advancing knowledgebase, fostering democratic equality and meeting industry needs (public), and social mobility (private) (Cuellar *et al.*, 2021). It is the social mobility and democratic equality purposes that this chapter is broadly concerned with as they are linked with *social justice* in HE. I define social justice as a fair (re)distribution of resources and opportunities available, *mutually recognising* the diverse needs of individuals' lived realities (Gale & Molla, 2015; Honneth, 2004; Sen, 2010; Singh, 2011).

Through the lens of *assessment for social justice* (McArthur, 2016), which focuses on students' lived experiences, this chapter will examine assessment in EMI in HE in Nepal. Drawing on the data from a recent larger TOEFL academic reading test in EMI contexts project (Owen *et al.*, 2021), this chapter specifically aims to examine academic reading and high-stakes English language reading testing in an EMI university setting in Nepal and the unique challenges facing those who are studying in a language other than their L1 by focusing on their lived experiences. Although social justice angles have been applied to EMI in HE (e.g. see many chapters in Giri *et al.*, 2024; Zheng & Qiu, 2023) and studies on (English language) assessment in EMI contexts have been conducted (e.g. Dimova, 2020; Dimova & Kling, 2018; Iliovits *et al.*, 2022), to my knowledge, the research in this chapter is the first attempt to examine assessment in the EMI context through a *social justice* perspective. It thus makes a significant contribution to EMI research. Social justice in assessment is too important to be ignored if we want to promote equity and fairness in EMI in HE.

This chapter will begin by providing a brief account of *assessment for social justice* and the theories behind it. Next, it will historically situate assessment in HE in Nepal by surveying the existing scant literature (e.g. Owen *et al.*, 2021; Phyak & Ojha, 2019). Then it will present the current

EMI situation examining existing language in education policy documents to contextualise the study and EMI students' academic reading practices, experiences and their TOEFL reading test performance in an EMI university setting in Nepal drawing on relevant empirical data. The data are based on a recent Educational Testing Service (USA) funded research project (Owen *et al.*, 2021) assessing the use of TOEFL academic reading tests in EMI contexts (Nepal and Sweden) of which the author was a co-investigator. The EMI situation will be scrutinised in relation to social justice by applying the notion of social justice for assessment drawing on Honneth's theory of mutual (mis)recognition (Honneth, 2004; McArthur, 2018) as explained next. The chapter will conclude with implications for assessment in EMI and social justice in HE.

6.2 A Notion of Assessment for Social Justice

The term social justice has widely been used by scholars embracing critical perspectives/pedagogies in education including HE to discuss the purpose of education (McArthur, 2010). Social justice has also appeared as a key theme in a recent volume on assessment in HE (Ajjawi *et al.*, 2023) but chapters in the volume are not specifically related to EMI although their contexts may have been EMI. Many scholars have drawn on capability theories to evaluate social justice in education (e.g. Shrestha *et al.*, 2024; Singh, 2011; Walker & Unterhalter, 2007) while many others employ social critical theories (e.g. Naidoo, 2004; Phyak & Sah, 2022; Rana & Sah, 2023). The ultimate goal of each of these theories is furthering social justice. Social justice theories, however, have rarely been applied to examine assessment in HE despite the notion of fairness and equality being advocated in the sector for many years (McArthur, 2016). It is worth noting that within language assessment scholarship, there are concepts such as *test fairness* (Kunnan, 2000) and *critical language testing* (Shohamy, 2001), which share some concerns with the social justice paradigm. They are, nevertheless, limited to language assessment, technicalities and policies. Thus, EMI requires a radically different notion to promote social justice related to lived realities of students and teachers and their (mis)recognition to uncover individuals' lived experiences and struggles of those at the receiving end (i.e. students) in HE EMI settings.

To address this lacuna, I employ McArthur's aspiring notion of *assessment for social justice* in HE (McArthur, 2016, 2018). She states that the notion was inspired by recent developments in learning-oriented assessment (Boud & Falchikov, 2006; Carless, 2015) and developed by adapting concepts from a plural social justice theory advocated by the German critical theorist, Axel Honneth. Of significance is Honneth's social justice notion of *mutual recognition,* namely, 'the conditions of a just society through the aim of recognizing the individual dignity of all individuals' (Honneth, 2004: 352). Mutuality is central to his conception of social justice as he argues that 'The justice or wellbeing of a society is measured according to the degree of its ability to secure conditions of mutual recognition in which personal identity formation, and hence individual self-realization, can proceed sufficiently well' (Honneth, 2004: 254). Honneth contends that human relations and interactions are complex and intersubjective, forming an individual's social/mutual recognitions (identity and self-relations) with certain patterns. Social injustice occurs when these recognitions believed to be legitimate are withheld.

Honneth (2004) proposes a plural theory of social justice to reflect the complexity of human interactions. It includes three differentiated spheres of recognition: *love* (affective) recognition, *respect* (legal) recognition and *esteem* (traits, abilities, contributions to society) recognition. McArthur (2018) applies this theory by using five concepts to assessment practices and policies examples: trust, honesty (love, affect), responsibility (legal, regulations, procedures), forgiveness and responsiveness (respect, esteem). Although Honneth's three spheres of recognition may apply to all five, each of them embraces one more clearly than others as shown in parenthesis. In this chapter, Honneth's *mutual recognition* will be applied to assessment in EMI when I discuss the findings and draw on McArthur's interpretation where relevant. This novel look at assessment in EMI enables hitherto under-researched social (in)justice issues to be revealed and makes a significant contribution to EMI research.

6.3 Literature Review

6.3.1 Social justice and assessment in EMI settings in Nepalese higher education

Nepal is a highly multilingual country where at least 123 languages are spoken[1] (Phyak, 2016; Sah & Li, 2018; Shrestha, 2008). English has always enjoyed a higher symbolic status and value than the local languages including the national language Nepali. The English language is the most widely used foreign language in the country and has gained currency in the last few decades in all spheres of life, including education often at the expense of indigenous languages (Phyak & Sah, 2022; Shrestha & Gautam, 2022).

In the current education system, English is taught as a compulsory subject from Grade 1 through the undergraduate level. Students must pass the subject to progress to the next level. In addition to being a compulsory subject, it is also a language of instruction in many schools and HE. EMI is adopted by default in almost all private schools (29% of total schools (Shrestha & Gautam, 2022)) and increasingly, several community or state schools have shifted to EMI from Nepali-medium instruction in recent years (Ojha, 2018). In HE, predominantly EMI is used in science, technology, engineering, maths (STEM) and disciplines such as medicine and forestry where assessment is conducted through English. EMI is not experienced by students equitably due to their school backgrounds (i.e. Nepali or English medium) and access to resources, and thus the use of EMI has become a social justice issue.

While EMI was originally confined to private schools, it has gained prominence recently (Phyak, 2016; Shrestha, 2008). This is because of parental demand and the Education Act, which since 2010 has permitted EMI alongside Nepali medium education (NME) in state schools as well (Sah & Li, 2018). In contrast to the case in pre-tertiary education, the Nepalese government has never had a clear policy on the medium of instruction in HE. The most recent education policy from 2019 remains surprisingly silent about this. Tribhuvan University (TU), the current research context, seems to have adopted EMI from 1918 till 1990 and then shifted to Nepali and English (Watkins & Regmi, 1990), although the university-level policy and practices appear to be haphazard and invisible, often driven by neoliberal ideologies and commodification of English (Rana & Sah, 2023; Sharma & Phyak, 2017). Only Kathmandu University (autonomous and self-funded) seems to have a clear EMI policy, which is considered an expensive university. Nationally, EMI is more widespread in STEM, medicine and forestry, whereas NME is prevalent in the social sciences and humanities, in line with the disciplinary variation observed in other countries (Linn *et al.*, 2021; Phyak & Ojha, 2019). The renewed interest in EMI appears to be driven by internationalisation and globalisation ambitions. In practice, however, not all teachers are well prepared to teach and assess their subjects through EMI and are thus unlikely to be able to provide English language support to those students who need it. The situation worsens when students from both NME and EMI schools come together to study in HE. Students attending from NME schools have typically received no English language support due to their socioeconomic status which may significantly disadvantage them in terms of academic achievement demonstrated through assessment compared to those from EMI school backgrounds (Onta, 2023).

Research on assessment in EMI settings is extremely sparse globally; assessment for social justice yet more so. This paucity of scholarship is not surprising given that most foci have been on EMI policies and EMI efficacies (Hultgren *et al.*, 2022). Only in the last 5–6 years has assessment in EMI received attention although commercial English language tests used in EMI contexts have been scrutinised in some studies from critical perspectives by examining their sociopolitical and economic implications in society (e.g. see contributions in Mirhosseini & De Costa, 2021). However, most language testing literature concentrates on linguistic and cognitive constructs, and psychometric measurements. There are a limited number of studies related to assessment in EMI contexts. These include studies which examine teacher English language proficiency (Dimova & Kling, 2018), student English language requirements for admissions (Dimova,

2020; Roshid *et al.*, 2024) and the relationship between students' English language test scores and academic language related challenges (Soruç *et al.*, 2021).

In Nepalese HE, references to assessment in some EMI programme subjects (e.g. sciences) are made in a handful of studies (Linn *et al.*, 2021; Phyak & Ojha, 2019). Noteworthy is the lack of any published research on assessment in the Nepalese HE EMI settings. To date, none of the studies on assessment in EMI contexts exclusively investigate social justice issues. For instance, the latest edited volume, which is entirely dedicated to HE policies and perspectives in Nepal, does not examine assessment (see chapters in Bista *et al.*, 2019). Therefore, there is an urgency to disseminate research into assessment in Nepalese HE to build our knowledgebase and reveal any social justice issues.

6.4 A Case Study of EMI Settings in a Large Nepali State University

6.4.1 Methodology

This study which draws on the data in the larger TOEFL academic reading test in EMI contexts (see Owen *et al.*, 2021) investigated assessment of reading for academic purposes in two broad EMI disciplines (sciences and business) through sequential mixed-methods research incorporating qualitative and quantitative methods. Following the research ethics approval, this study was conducted at Tribhuvan University (TU), Nepal. The data consisted of the reading practices of EMI students through their reading logs (types and lengths of texts and languages in their reading for three weeks), responses to a reading survey, TOEFL iBT reading test performances (all quantitative) and semi-structured interviews (qualitative) (For details about the instruments, see Owen *et al.*, 2021.)

In total, there were 69 EMI students who volunteered to participate in the survey: 35 males and 34 females; 44 sciences and 25 business students, and a mean age 23.5. The survey was paper-based and administered in the participants' campuses. All 69 students sat a paper version of the TOEFL iBT reading test before the survey. TOEFL iBT is found to be suitable for assessing students' English language proficiency in EMI universities (O'Dwyer *et al.*, 2018) and therefore, this test was used in the current study. Nineteen of the survey respondents had also submitted their reading logs of three weeks prior to the survey. Interview participants included 15 EMI students. Eight of them studied in science disciplines and seven in business administration (eight females and seven males). The interviews ranged from 14 to 25 minutes, were audio recorded in Nepali or English based on student choices and were subsequently transcribed and translated. While the survey data were statistically analysed, all interview data were thematically coded using NVivo.

6.5 EMI Reading Assessment, (Mis)Recognition and Social (In)Justices

In this section, I report findings and discuss them by applying Honneth's (2004) notions of *mutual recognition* to scrutinize social justice issues. Particularly, I will be drawing on *respect recognition* and *esteem recognition*. The data did not indicate remarkably about *love recognition* (love or care), although there may have been caring and loving EMI lecturers who could boost the EMI students' self-confidence/self-worth or there may be EMI lecturers who neglect EMI students' identity and damage their self-confidence through assessment as assessment can often be emotional (Shrestha, 2020) and can leave lasting damaging psychological effects on students. As McArthur (2018) argues, trust (love recognition) between teachers and students regarding assessment could also be examined. However, this sphere of recognition seemed invisible in the data. Therefore, the other two spheres of recognition are used to scrutinise the findings and any social (in)justice.

6.5.1 EMI assessment policies and practices, academic reading practices and (dis)respect of students

As noted earlier, EMI policies at TU are unclear and invisible for any discipline. None of the curriculum documents by central departments (e.g. Chemistry) or university-level policy documents indicate the medium language of instruction or assessment. This means they are hidden from students and appear to be passed on as tacit knowledge to lecturers and students. The only policy document that mentions the medium language of instruction and assessment is *Tribhuvan University Vision 2030* (Tribhuvan University, 2019). For instance, as its strategic priority, it aims to strengthen the semester system by adopting 'flexible policy in the medium of instruction and providing options for the students to use either English or Nepali in their exams' (2019: 50). It also mentions them when it refers to its vision for 'world ranking and internationalisation': 'Strictly enforce English as the medium of instruction in the programs where there are international students … Make English language test scores mandatory for programs targeting to international students' (2019: 53). However, the same does not appear in any curriculum documents and English continues to be the language used in assessment which is a colonial legacy of the British education system influence in South Asia (Shrestha *et al.*, 2024). Although the 'flexible policy' *recognises* many Nepalese students' education background as Nepali medium and their socioeconomic background, the actual practice *disrespects* and *invisibilises* them by requiring them to use English in assessment in the EMI settings. This situation privileges those students who come from EMI school and affluent backgrounds. The second quote above exclusively relates to internationalisation/marketisation of the university to attract international students and English language and English language test scores are used as instruments to achieve this. Nevertheless, the policy document or individual departments do not provide English language support to students in need, which is supported by student interview data. Thus, the students who come from Nepali medium backgrounds are *misrecognised* and *disrespected* again as illustrated below:

> *In BBS only I have to study in English medium else I haven't studied in English other than compulsory subjects because from village only I cleared my +2. S.L.C and +2 are from village, it was taught completely in Nepali medium, compulsory English was only taught in English, that's why I don't know much about English. I feel very difficult to understand when they teach here in English.* (translated, female BBS student)

> *I finished my high school education in Nepali, then right now a Master's in English medium. That's why I'm facing lots of problems, more problems, I can't understand. Maybe one article while I'm reading, two or more times I need to read to understand what is there.* (translated, male MSc student)

This experience consequently could mean losing self-respect as they are not treated equitably.

From among 69 reading survey respondents, 19 students submitted reading logs of three weeks, prior to the reading survey as summarised in Table 6.1.

The participants reported that approximately half of their reading over the course of a three-week period consisted of academic materials, of which the vast majority was in English. The majority of the reading requirements were in English, with a minority of Nepali and some materials in more than one language, supported by both the reading practices survey data and the student interviews. From a reading point of view, the overwhelming majority of texts encountered represented a standard variety of English (British

Table 6.1 Reading log overview: Material read in each language (in pages and percent)

Student reading logs (*n* = 19)

Source	Language	Pages	Percent
Academic	English	2008	45.75
	Nepali	129	2.94
	English/Nepali (mixed)	155	3.53
Non-academic	English	999	22.77
	Nepali	1382	31.48
Total	All	4390	100

Table 6.2 Questionnaire section 1 results. [Figures in (...) are percentages]

Proportion of English		**Options**				
Please put a tick (✓) in the column to reflect how much English is used.		**0%**	**25%**	**50%**	**75%**	**100%**
1.1	What proportion of the courses on your study programme is delivered in English?	0 (0.00)	2 (2.90)	9 (13.04)	38 (55.07)	20 (28.99)
1.2	What proportion of the reading material is in English?	0 (0.00)	1 (1.45)	6 (8.70)	17 (24.64)	45 (65.22)
1.3	What proportion of the assessment material (exams, assignments, etc.) is in English?	0 (0.00)	2 (2.90)	7 (10.14)	11 (15.94)	49 (71.01)

or American) which misrecognises the English language variety (known as *Nenglish*) used by Nepalese students (Giri, 2020). The reading log data indicated students' translingual reading practices (Canagarajah, 2013) showing the fluidity of languages instead of being monolingual practices. The monolingual ideology demonstrated by 'English only' EMI assessment practices in the disciplines examined again misrecognise students' translingual academic reading practices, benefitting only those students who come from English medium and affluent backgrounds.

Reading log findings are supported by reading practices survey results. A total of 69 students participated in the survey. Table 6.2 shows the findings for section 1, which asked participants to estimate what proportions of their learning occurred through the medium of English.

As shown in Table 6.2, students reported that their courses were not always delivered in English, with most respondents reporting about 75% of delivery through the medium of English (item 1.1). However, there was greater agreement regarding reading materials, with 65% of the students reporting that all of their materials were in English (item 1.2). Greater consensus was reached regarding assessment materials, with most students (>85%) reporting their assessments were undertaken in English (item 1.3). The interview data corroborate translingual EMI classroom reading practices by using both Nepali and English for discussions:

> *English, umm, 50 to 75% is English and 25% percent, since we are Nepali, of course Nepali will be used.* (male, BBS student)

> *Sometimes we also use Nepali, umm, since English is not our mother tongue, some words passages are difficult to understand, in that case we prefer Nepali as well.* (female MSC student)

However, all the student interviewees unanimously reported that assessment was entirely in English, not allowing any use of other languages such as Nepali. This again reinforces English monolingual ideology ingrained in assessment as reported in a recent media piece about assessment in the

Table 6.3 Questionnaire section 3 results. [Figures in (...) are percentages]

Reading course material in English		**Level of agreement**				
Please put a tick (✓) in the column that best describes your reading of course material in English.		**Never**	**Rarely**	**Sometimes**	**Frequently**	**Always**
3.1	I read the required English course material	1 (1.45)	1 (1.45)	3 (4.35)	17 (24.64)	47 (68.12)
3.2	I understand the English course material that I read	0 (0.00)	3 (4.41)	2 (2.94)	38 (55.88)	25 (36.76)
3.3	I wish the course material was in my first language	4 (5.88)	8 (11.76)	21 (30.88)	14 (20.59)	21 (30.88)
3.4	Lecturers provide guidance on appropriate reading strategies for each text	1 (1.47)	13 (19.12)	19 (27.94)	20 (29.41)	15 (22.06)

journalism subject (Onta, 2023) and *disrespects* the students' translingual academic reading identity recognised by the lecturers in the classroom. This EMI assessment practice privileges only the few students with an EMI school background.

Students were asked about their experiences of reading in English, their reading habits and level of support from course lecturers (Table 6.3).

Despite professing confidence in their English reading ability, a majority of the students (51.47%) agreed or strongly agreed with the statement 'I wish the course material was in my first language'. Approximately half of the participants also reported feeling that they did not receive sufficient guidance although they were more likely to report that they did receive such guidance overall. The interview data indicate that the only form of English language support provided by the lecturers was translation from English to Nepali. Often the interviewees reported relying on their classmates for understanding a reading text as below:

> *Or we can also ask friends if we are not that much good with the teachers, we can ask friends. And so, they make us understand in Nepali also.* (male MSc student)
>
> *Mostly, umm, normally I prefer to discuss with my friends at first.* (female MSC student)

English language proficiency is essential for the success of students' studies in EMI contexts which emphasise a monolingual assessment policy. Despite many interviewees reporting a good confidence level regarding English academic reading, many of them who came from Nepali medium education backgrounds shared their struggles when reading and writing for assessment. Although Nepali is the most widely used national language, for many of the interviewees, it is their second language (e.g. first language being Tamang, Doteli) and thus, English is a third language which poses additional difficulties. For example, a Doteli first language speaker student said:

> *... sometimes seniors from there come to us and it becomes very difficult for us to do the communication [in English], like within ourselves also with my friends, I feel that my communication part is weak. Though my academic performance is good, but my performance in English is not that satisfactory. I feel like I couldn't get such opportunities.* (male, MSc student)

Similarly, another male MSc student expressed his frustration and struggles:

> *Personally, sometimes I feel very difficult. I even don't get anything by consulting dictionaries, by consulting internet, by guessing from the text, sometime that gets very difficult.*

The sheer emphasis on English monolingual assessment policies and practices, as revealed by the data, continue to *misrecognise* the identities of the translingual students in this study and their struggles. Equally, the institution *disrespects* these EMI students by not taking the *responsibility* (McArthur, 2018) to provide academic English language support to them and not allowing them to use their rich translingual repertoire in EMI assessment. These EMI students are systematically *invisibilised.* Consequently, these students often feel vulnerable in assessment and continue to lose self-respect and struggle in their studies unlike their counterparts with EMI education backgrounds.

6.5.2 EMI academic reading assessment (TOEFL iBT) and esteem (mis)recognition of students

In this section, findings regarding English academic reading assessment are discussed as reflected by TOEFL iBT reading test scores which are widely used in EMI universities (O'Dwyer *et al.*, 2018), and related survey and interview data. I do this by applying Honneth's (2004) *esteem recognition* (abilities, traits, contributions to society) to the findings.

The reading section of the TOEFL iBT test was completed by 69 students. The test is divided into three sections each containing one text and uses standard US variety of English. The first text has 14 questions, the second has 13 and the third has 14. Basic comprehension and inferencing items are dichotomous (correct/incorrect). There are three reading to learn items, two of which are worth two points and the third worth three points. Therefore, the maximum score that could be obtained in the test is 45 points (29 for basic comprehension, 9 for inferencing and 7 for reading-to-learn). Descriptive statistics are outlined in Table 6.4.

As Table 6.4 shows, the total mean score (20.41) for the group is relatively low. This means the students' English language proficiency is quite

Table 6.4 Test score statistics

Items		N	Max score	Mean	SD
Total		69	45	20.41	8.17
Reading purpose	Basic comprehension	69	29	14.62	5.49
	Inferencing	69	9	3.20	1.89
	Reading to learn	69	7	2.58	1.84

low and thus may not be sufficient for EMI programmes. Additionally, the high standard deviation (8.17) suggests that the test is sensitive to significant individual variations within contexts, a potential indication of the students' EMI and NME backgrounds. While the test scores may have boosted the self-esteem of the students with high scores, the students with low scores would have lost self-esteem. The TOEFL test contained three passages, of which one related to Psychology, one to Biology and one to Palaeontology. These topic areas favour certain students, especially science students and those who are from private EMI school backgrounds as they would be familiar with these topics and related specialist vocabulary in English as reflected by the interview data. Thus, the low test scores would *exclude* and *ignore* NME students, making them feel a loss of their *dignity* and become an outsider within their community of practice (i.e. their disciplinary community).

The TOEFL suitability questionnaire was composed of Likert-type items as in Table 6.5. It shows the extent to which students agree with a number of statements about the TOEFL iBT reading test.

The participants broadly expressed positivity regarding the relationship between the types of questions in the reading section of the TOEFL iBT test and the academic English reading skills required for their academic programmes. However, most students expressed uncertainty or disagreement regarding the suitability of the reading test for them including their reading proficiency, text topics, its predictive and face validity despite previous studies indicating high predictive validity of the test (e.g. O'Dwyer *et al.*, 2018). Therefore, the test is likely to *misrecognise* and *invisibilise* their esteem although they believe they have the capability to study in their respective discipline. Given that these students are not in an English-dominant context, the test (ab)use may perpetuate social injustices in HE in Nepal which is already fraught with EMI and NME divisions (Shrestha *et al.*, 2024) if it is used for high stakes decision-making rather than diagnostic purposes.

Interviews with participants further examined their attitudes towards the reading section of the TOEFL test. Interviews were conducted immediately or within 24 hours after they had taken the test so that their perspectives of the text and tasks remained fresh. Students offered nuanced comments regarding their impressions of the reading section of the TOEFL

Table 6.5 TOEFL suitability questionnaire results. [Figures in (...) are percentages]

TOEFL iBT Reading test		**Level of agreement**				
Please put a tick (✓) in the column that best describes your reading of course material in English.		**Strongly disagree**	**Disagree**	**Uncertain**	**Agree**	**Strongly agree**
5.1	The different types of questions in the TOEFL reflect the English reading skills needed for my course	0 (0.00)	0 (0.00)	3 (4.55)	38 (57.58)	25 (37.88)
5.2	A university can learn a lot about a person's English reading ability from their TOEFL performance	0 (0.00)	4 (5.97)	9 (13.43)	34 (50.75)	20 (29.85)
5.3	The TOEFL test is an accurate reflection of my English reading ability	0 (0.00)	6 (8.82)	15 (22.06)	35 (51.47)	12 (17.65)
5.4	The TOEFL reading texts were difficult to understand	8 (13.56)	12 (20.34)	23 (38.98)	13 (22.03)	3 (5.08)
5.5	People who perform well in the TOEFL reading test will do well in university	2 (3.33)	19 (31.67)	22 (36.67)	14 (23.33)	3 (5.00)
5.6	A bad performance in the test shows that your reading ability is limited	14 (23.33)	36 (60.00)	6 (10.00)	3 (5.00)	1 (1.67)
5.7	The TOEFL examines English reading skills I will never use	0 (0.00)	5 (8.33)	7 (11.67)	29 (48.33)	19 (31.67)
5.8	Performance in the test depends on text topic	2 (3.33)	5 (8.33)	33 (55.00)	19 (31.67)	1 (1.67)
5.9	I feel that my English reading ability is better than my performance will indicate	0 (0.00)	2 (3.33)	25 (41.67)	28 (46.67)	5 (8.33)

iBT test and its suitability for making claims about reading proficiency within their EMI context. Students made a large number of comments relating to the context validity of the reading section of the TOEFL iBT test. The overwhelming majority of these comments related to the suitability of the passage topic and the perceived impact of content knowledge on test performance. Nearly all comments coded 'negative' related to the appropriacy of text topics. Students' perceptions were influenced by their academic pathway. As mentioned earlier, the reading test contained three passages, of which one related to Psychology, one to Biology and one to Palaeontology. Students undertaking science courses were satisfied with the appropriacy of the latter two texts but perceived their performance may have been hindered by a lack of familiarity with the terminology related to Psychology.

> *The second and third passages were related to fish and biology, fossils, I understood it very well, my performance was good on those but first one was difficult to understand.* (male MSc student)

But if it is not of the field of your study, then I think it's not good to evaluate someone by putting some questions which is not of interest of them. I found comfortable to answer the question which were in Science, but I found it extremely difficult to write the answers or tick the sentences for the another one. (female MSc student)

The business students reported the reading test passages being difficult to comprehend due to the topics. As a result, they lost *self-confidence* and *self-esteem* as illustrated by the quotes below:

The reading passages which I studied yesterday, most of the words were difficult for me as well. We might have studied the direct meaning of the words, but the sentence might give a different meaning. (male, BBS student)

I think it [TOEFL test] is completely different. Because there were many advanced words used, the meanings are deeply rooted. … I also found that we were not able to understand many grammatical words as well. ***I felt like I knew them, but when I sat for that test, after that I felt like I knew nothing.*** *That was the level of the test.* (emphasis added, female BBS student)

The last quote reveals how the female participant felt the loss of their *honour* and *dignity* (*esteem recognition*) as a result of her reading test experience.

Despite a previous study not supporting that text topic influences test performance (Liu, 2011), participants' perceptions of the suitability of text topic is an important issue of face validity. Students perceived the relevance of passage content as an issue of test fairness as the content of the test should reflect the kinds of texts they engage with in their academic programme. It is an important social justice issue (i.e. *misrecognition of student esteem*) as well in the context of English non-dominant translingual EMI contexts if the test use is for decision making.

Interview data were coded as 'cognitive validity' when they referred to the mental activities undertaken in the action of reading. Cognitive validity includes the processing of text and the higher-order strategic decisions readers make about how to engage with specific texts. Students' comments covered both the kinds of processes undertaken to complete specific tasks, the kinds of strategies they employed and the relevance of these to their contexts. Students perceived that the reading load imposed by the test tasks was heavy and this was affected by the timed conditions. A lack of understanding of the difficult text meant that students re-read texts several times to ensure comprehension:

This is also quite difficult for me. I need to read more than two or three times, but time is too much limited in that section, I think. I need to need, if I read an article like my course related articles, to understand that article, what is inside there, what is the main objectives, more than two/ three times I need to read. After that I was to consult with seniors, Google search, also talk seniors that I will solve the problem. That's why I need to finish in limited time, that's why I'm quite confused. (male Nepali MSc student)

The MSc student perceived the timed test conditions to be dissimilar to the nature of reading in their context. This means the test does not reflect the reality of the EMI context the students study in although some students reported that the test could encourage them to develop their English academic reading skills. If the test taker cannot see the relevance of the test to their real world including their profession, the test may *misrecognise* their *esteem* and disadvantage them.

6.6 Conclusion

This chapter makes an important contribution to the EMI scholarship on assessment in translingual contexts where communication and meaning-making transcend individual languages, promoting fluidity and 'code-meshing' (Canagarajah, 2013). It innovatively examined social justice for assessment in assessment in university EMI settings in the largest university in Nepal through the lens of Honneth's notions of *mutual recognition* (2004). Particularly, the spheres of *respect (mis)recognition* and *esteem (mis)recognition* were applied to the findings and discussed regarding university EMI assessment policies, pedagogical practices and the students' lived experiences of the TOEFL iBT reading test. I reported that the EMI assessment policies and practices *misrecognise* NME students' *(self)respect* and *(self)esteem* by privileging the students with the EMI backgrounds although the EMI pedagogical practices *recognise* the students' translingual repertoire. Owing to the English monolingual ideology in assessment, NME students experienced the loss of their *dignity* and *honour* and an inability to contribute to their community (*esteem misrecognition*), which was exacerbated by the lack of institutional academic English language support (*respect recognition*). The findings also showed that the TOEFL iBT reading test *misrecognises* students' academic reading abilities (*esteem misrecognition*) due to its decontextualised nature of reading texts and that it is not appropriate for their context if its use is for high-stakes decision-making rather than diagnostic purposes.

There are a number of implications of the study for similar non-English dominant and translingual EMI settings to make assessment equitable and socially just. First, it is essential to recognise students' translingual repertoire not only in classroom pedagogical practices but also in assessment, allowing and celebrating translingual assessment practices (*esteem recognition*). Second, the university EMI policy about assessment and pedagogy should be visible to both lecturers and students. Third, the university should provide academic English language support to all EMI students (*respect recognition*). Fourth, any academic English language test should be contextualised to suit the discipline and students before its use. If an external English test such as TOEFL is used, it should be used only for diagnostic/ developmental purposes rather than for certification. Finally, urgent additional research is needed which investigates assessment in EMI from social justice perspectives as such research is extremely sparse currently but essential to reveal and minimise the perpetuation of social injustices occurring in assessment in EMI settings and to promote more progressive and equitable assessment.

Acknowledgements

I would like to acknowledge that the data used in this chapter relate to the project entitled *Researching Academic Reading in two contrasting EMI (English as a Medium of Instruction) university contexts*, funded by Educational Testing Service USA (see Owen *et al.*, 2021). I am grateful to Ben Evans for his insightful comments on a previous version of the chapter. The funder of the original project, ETS, recommends using this standard text for publications related to its funded projects:

> 'This research was funded by ETS under a TOEFL Committee of Examiners research grant. ETS does not discount or endorse the methodology, results, implications, or opinions presented by the researcher(s).'

Note

(1) Please note that the Language Commission reported eight additional languages in 2020, thus making 131 languages in total. However, at the time of writing this paper, there was no published report available. Please see this news report: https://english.onlinekhabar.com/language-commission-identifies-eight-more-languages-in-nepal-taking-total-to-131.html

References

Ajjawi, R. (2023) Introduction. In R. Ajjawi, J. Tai, D. Boud and T.J. de St Jorre (eds) *Assessment for Inclusion in Higher Education: Promoting Equity and Social Justice in Assessment* (pp. 1–5). Routledge. https://doi.org/10.4324/9781003293101-1

Ajjawi, R., Tai, J., Boud, D. and De St. Jorre, T.J. (2023) *Assessment for Inclusion in Higher Education: Promoting Equity and Social Justice in Assessment*. Routledge.

Bista, K., Sharma, S. and Raby, R.L. (eds) (2019) *Higher Education in Nepal: Policies and Perspectives*. Routledge. https://doi.org/10.4324/9781351139205.

Boud, D. and Falchikov, N. (2006) Aligning assessment with long-term learning. *Assessment & Evaluation in Higher Education* 31 (4), 399–413.

Canagarajah, S. (2013) *Translingual Practice: Global Englishes and Cosmopolitan Relations* (1st edn). Routledge. https://doi.org/10.4324/9780203073889

Carless, D. (2015) Exploring learning-oriented assessment processes. *Higher Education* 69 (6), 963–976. https://doi.org/10.1007/s10734-014-9816-z

Cuellar, M.G., Bencomo Garcia, A. and Saichaie, K. (2021) Reaffirming the public purposes of higher education: First-generation and continuing generation students' perspectives. *The Journal of Higher Education* 1–24. https://doi.org/10.1080/00221546.2021.1979849

Dimova, S. (2020) English language requirements for enrolment in EMI programs in higher education: A European case. *Journal of English for Academic Purposes* 47, 100896. https://doi.org/10.1016/j.jeap.2020.100896

Dimova, S. and Kling, J. (2018) Assessing English-medium instruction lecturer language proficiency across disciplines. *TESOL Quarterly* 52 (3), 634–656. https://doi.org/10.1002/tesq.454

Gale, T. and Molla, T. (2015) Social justice intents in policy: An analysis of capability for and through education. *Journal of Education Policy* 30 (6), 810–830. https://doi.org/10.1080/02680939.2014.987828

Galloway, N., Numajiri, T. and Rees, N. (2020) The 'internationalisation', or 'Englishisation', of higher education in East Asia. *Higher Education* 80 (3), 395–414. https://doi.org/10.1007/s10734-019-00486-1

Giri, R.A. (2020) Nepali English. *The Handbook of Asian Englishes*, 317–336. https://doi.org/10.1002/9781118791882.ch13 (Wiley Online Books)

Giri, R.A., Padwad, A. and Kabir, M.M.N. (2024) *English as a Medium of Instruction in South Asia: Issues in Equity and Social Justice*. Routledge. https://doi.org/10.4324/9781003342373

Honneth, A. (2004) Recognition and justice: Outline of a plural theory of justice. *Acta Sociologica* 47 (4), 351–364. https://doi.org/10.1177/0001699304048668

Hultgren, A.K., Owen, N., Shrestha, P.N., Kuteeva, M. and Mežek, Š. (2022) Assessment and English as a medium of instruction: Challenges and opportunities. *Journal of English-Medium Instruction* 1 (1), 105–123. https://doi.org/10.1075/jemi.21019.hul

Iliovits, M., Harding, L. and Pill, J. (2022) Language use in an English-medium instruction university in Lebanon: Implications for the validity of international and local English tests for admissions. *Journal of English-Medium Instruction* 1 (2), 153–179. https://doi.org/10.1075/jemi.21009.ili

Kunnan, A.J.E. (2000) *Fairness and Validation in Language Assessment*. Cambridge University Press.

Linn, A., Shrestha, P.N., Bezborodova, A. and Hultgren, A.K. (2021) *Current Practice in English-Medium Education in Higher Education: Case Studies From Kazakhstan, Turkmenistan, Bangladesh and Nepal*. British Council.

Liu, O.L. (2011) Do major field of study and cultural familiarity affect TOEFL® iBT reading performance? A confirmatory approach to differential item functioning. *Applied Measurement in Education* 24 (3), 235–255. https://doi.org/10.1080/08957347.2011.580645

Mahboob, A. (2017) English medium instruction in higher education in Pakistan: Policies, perceptions, problems, and possibilities. In B. Fenton-Smith, P. Humphreys and I. Walkinshaw (eds) *English Medium Instruction in Higher Education in Asia-Pacific: From Policy to Pedagogy* (pp. 71–91). Springer International Publishing. https://doi.org/10.1007/978-3-319-51976-0_5

McArthur, J. (2010) Achieving social justice within and through higher education: The challenge for critical pedagogy. *Teaching in Higher Education* 15 (5), 493–504. https://doi.org/10.1080/13562517.2010.491906

McArthur, J. (2016) Assessment for social justice: The role of assessment in achieving social justice. *Assessment & Evaluation in Higher Education* 41 (7), 967–981. https://doi.org/10.1080/02602938.2015.1053429

McArthur, J. (2018) *Assessment for Social Justice: Perspectives and Practices Within Higher Education* (1st edn). Bloomsbury Publishing Plc. https://doi.org/10.5040/9781474236089

McCulloch, S., Indrarathne, B., Jahan, A., Gnawali, L., Hussain, N., Nauman, S. ... Abeyawickrama, W. (2020) *Investigating English for Academic Purposes Provision in South Asian Higher Education: Current Trends and Future Needs*. British Council.
Mirhosseini, S.-A. and De Costa, P. (eds) (2021) *The Sociopolitics of English Language Testing*. Bloomsbury Publishing.
Naidoo, R. (2004) Fields and institutional strategy: Bourdieu on the relationship between higher education, inequality and society. *British Journal of Sociology of Education* 25 (4), 457–471. https://doi.org/10.1080/0142569042000236952
O'Dwyer, J., Kantarcıoğlu, E. and Thomas, C. (2018) An investigation of the predictive validity of the TOEFL iBT® Test at an English-medium university in Turkey. *ETS Research Report Series* 2018 (1), 1–13. https://doi.org/10.1002/ets2.12230
Ojha, L.P. (2018) Shifting the Medium of Instruction to English in Community Schools: Policies, Practices and Challenges in Nepal. In D. Hayes (ed.) *English Language Teaching in Nepal: Research, Reflection and Practice* (pp. 189–198). British Council.
Onta, P. (2023, 29 September 2023) The medium language of teaching. *The Kathmandu Post*. https://kathmandupost.com/columns/2023/09/29/the-medium-language-of-teaching
Owen, N., Shrestha, P.N. and Hultgren, A.K. (2021) Researching academic reading in two contrasting English as a medium of instruction contexts at a university level. *ETS Research Report Series*. https://doi.org/10.1002/ets2.12317
Phyak, P. (2016) Local-global tension in the ideological construction of English language education policy in Nepal. In R. Kirkpatrick (ed.) *English Language Education Policy in Asia* (pp. 199–217). Springer International Publishing. https://doi.org/10.1007/978-3-319-22464-0_9
Phyak, P. and Ojha, L.P. (2019) Language education policy and inequalities of multilingualism in Nepal. In A. Kirkpatrick and A.J. Liddicoat (eds) *The Routledge International Handbook of Language Education Policy in Asia*. Routledge. https://doi.org/10.4324/9781315666235-24
Phyak, P. and Sah, P.K. (2022) Epistemic injustice and neoliberal imaginations in English as a medium of instruction (EMI) policy. *Applied Linguistics Review*. https://doi.org/10.1515/applirev-2022-0070
Rana, K. and Sah, P.K. (2023) Policy development for English medium instruction at a Nepali University: Unpacking hidden motivations and agendas. In P.K. Sah and F. Fang (eds) *Policies, Politics, and Ideologies of English-Medium Instruction in Asian Universities: Unsettling Critical Edges* (1st edn, pp. 48–62). Routledge. https://doi.org/10.4324/9781003173120-5
Roshid, M.M., Zilany, G.K. and Afroz, N. (2024) Medium of education and inequality in university admission tests: Exploring the case of a flagship university in Bangladesh. In R.A. Giri, A. Padwad and M.M.N. Kabir (eds) *English as a Medium of Instruction in South Asia: Issues in Equity and Social Justice* (pp. 57–75). Routledge. https://doi.org/10.4324/9781003342373-5
Sah, P.K. (2022) A research agenda for English-medium instruction: Conversations with scholars at the research fronts. *Journal of English-Medium Instruction* 1 (1), 124–136. https://doi.org/10.1075/jemi.21022.sah
Sah, P.K. and Li, G. (2018) English Medium Instruction (EMI) as linguistic capital in Nepal: Promises and realities. *International Multilingual Research Journal* 12 (2), 109–123. https://doi.org/10.1080/19313152.2017.1401448
Sen, A. (2010) *The Idea of Justice*. Penguin Books.
Sharma, B.K. and Phyak, P. (2017) Neoliberalism, linguistic commodification, and ethnolinguistic identity in multilingual Nepal. *Language in Society* 46 (2), 231–256. https://doi.org/10.1017/S0047404517000045
Shohamy, E. (2001) *The Power of Tests: A Critical Perspective on the Uses of Language Tests*. Longman.

Shrestha, P.N. (2008) ELT, ESP & EAP in Nepal: Whose interests are served? In M. Krzanowski (ed.) *EAP and ESP in Developing Countries: State of Play vs Actual Needs and Wants* (pp. 191–210). IATEFL ESP SIG.

Shrestha, P.N. (2020) *Dynamic Assessment of Students' Academic Writing: Vygotskian and Systemic Functional Linguistic Perspectives*. Springer. https://doi.org/10.1007/978-3-030-55845-1

Shrestha, P.N. and Gautam, G.R. (2022) *English Language Teaching, Learning and Assessment in Nepal: Current Policies and Practices in the School Education System*. British Council.

Shrestha, P.N., Rahman, S. and Shrestha, B.B. (2024) English as a medium of instruction and social justice in higher education in Bangladesh and Nepal: A capability perspective. In R.A. Giri, A. Padwad and M.M.N. Kabir (eds) *English as a Medium of Instruction in South Asia: Issues in Equity, Inclusion and Social Justice* (pp. 171–189). Routledge. https://doi.org/10.4324/9781003342373-14

Singh, M. (2011) The place of social justice in higher education and social change discourses. *Compare: A Journal of Comparative and International Education* 41 (4), 481–494. https://doi.org/10.1080/03057925.2011.581515

Soruç, A., Altay, M., Curle, S. and Yuksel, D. (2021) Students' academic language-related challenges in English Medium Instruction: The role of English proficiency and language gain. *System* 103, 102651. https://doi.org/10.1016/j.system.2021.102651

Tribhuvan University (2019) *Tribhuvan University Vision 2030*. Tribhuvan University.

Walker, M. and Unterhalter, E. (2007) *Amartya Sen's Capability Approach and Social Justice in Education*. Palgrave Macmillan US.

Walkinshaw, I., Fenton-Smith, B. and Humphreys, P. (2017) EMI issues and challenges in Asia-Pacific higher education: An introduction. In B. Fenton-Smith, P. Humphreys and I. Walkinshaw (eds) *English Medium Instruction in Higher Education in Asia-Pacific: From Policy to Pedagogy* (pp. 1–18). Springer International Publishing. https://doi.org/10.1007/978-3-319-51976-0_1

Watkins, D. and Regmi, M. (1990) Language of instruction and approach to learning: A Nepalese investigation. *Perceptual and Motor Skills* 71 (3_suppl), 1075–1078. https://doi.org/10.2466/pms.1990.71.3f.1075

Zheng, Y. and Qiu, Y. (2023) Epistemic (in)justice in English medium instruction: Transnational teachers' and students' negotiation of knowledge participation through translanguaging. *Language and Education* 1–21. https://doi.org/10.1080/09500782.2023.2248968

7 The Use of Artificial Intelligence in Japanese EMI Assessments: Under the Framework of Activity Theory

Siyan Dang and Masakazu Iino

7.1 Introduction

Recently the field of artificial intelligence (AI) has witnessed remarkable growth, marked by enhanced computational capabilities and advancements in algorithm design. These developments have significantly influenced various domains, including education and research (Niemi *et al.*, 2023; Rahman & Watanobe, 2023). An example of this impact is Open AI's release of the innovative generative AI platform, 'ChatGPT', in November 2022. Rapidly gaining popularity, ChatGPT attracted over 100 million monthly users worldwide only two months after it was launched (Wu *et al.*, 2023), showcasing the transformative potential of AI in all fields. Its ability to process large volumes of information quickly, comprehend intricate queries and offer coherent, human-like responses highlights a significant shift in the educational landscape (Zhu *et al.*, 2023). As AI applications increasingly transform the education sector, they generate a lot of challenges and concerns. A major issue facing educators and institutions is maintaining academic integrity. Given AI's capacity to answer complex queries, including those found in traditional examinations, determining the authenticity of a student's work is becoming a contentious issue (Chaudhry *et al.*, 2023).

Research on AI usage in higher education institutions has been conducted, but not much specific clarification in the English medium instruction (EMI) setting has come out yet. Compared with other situations in higher education, one typical characteristic of EMI is that English is not the dominant language of the jurisdiction, and in most cases students and teachers are not native speakers of English, implying that the lack of English proficiency among EMI students becomes one of the most recurrent obstacles to EMI implementation (Chapple, 2015; Pun *et al.*, 2023). Also, such EMI students with low English proficiency might graduate without sufficient content knowledge (Hellekjær, 2010). While students' low English proficiency is one factor hindering EMI, instructors' English proficiency must also be taken into account (Aizawa & McKinley, 2020). Students also perceived their teachers' insufficient English abilities as an obstruction to effective teaching in the EMI classroom (Galloway *et al.*, 2017).

Given the situation of insufficient language ability, the emergence of AI tools is regarded as a solution that EMI students adopt on various occasions. According to Sabzalieva and Valentini (2023), students possibly use AI to do research design, search datasets, translate sources into other languages, analyze data and write up or improve essays (Figure 7.1).

However, this contributes to the increased risk of plagiarism and cheating if students use AI tools to prepare or write essays and exams. Apart from academic integrity, Sabzalieva and Valentini (2023) also point out additional concerns related to privacy, cognitive biases, accessibility and the commercialization of education. These issues reflect the broader implications and challenges of integrating advanced AI technologies like ChatGPT in educational settings and evaluation.

This study will adopt the second generation of Activity Theory (AT) to analyze the use of AI tools in Japanese EMI assessment. On the one hand, it is essential to consider the practices of students in the proficient use of AI technologies. On the other hand, it is important to develop students' critical thinking and problem-solving skills via using these tools. This is particularly relevant in EMI contexts, where language proficiency and subject learning intersect. In the next section, the authors will provide a detailed justification for the application of AT in this context.

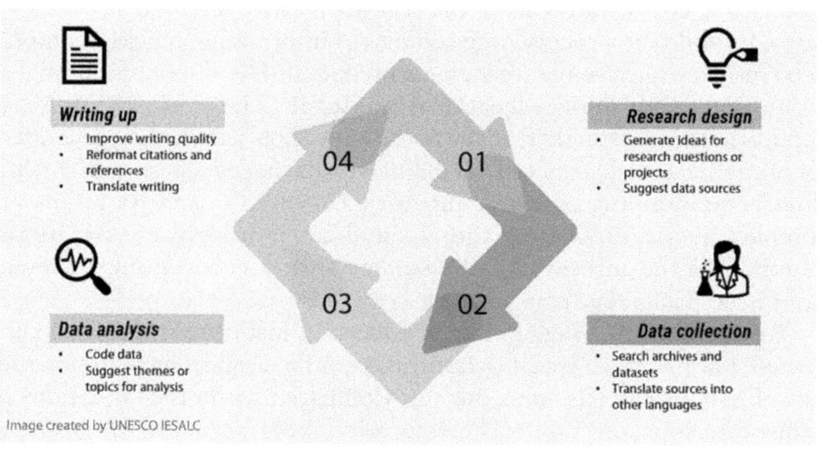

Figure 7.1 The possible ways of using AI tools in higher education (Sabzalieva & Valentini, 2023)

7.2 Literature Review

7.2.1 AT and educational research

The theoretical framework of cultural–historical activity theory, originally conceived by Lev Vygotsky in the late 1920s and early 1930s, represents a significant milestone in the field of psychology. This theory underwent further refinement and expansion through the contributions of Vygotsky's colleague and follower, Alexei Leont'ev, in the later years, particularly in 1978 and 1981. According to scholarly analysis, the development of AT can be categorized into three distinct generations of research, each building upon the foundational concepts established by its predecessors (Engeström, 2001).

Building upon the foundations of second-generation AT, Engeström's (2015) expansion of the Activity System has broadened the AT framework, enhancing its applicability in organizational studies. This evolution of AT has contributed to its widespread recognition as a robust framework for analyzing human activities, particularly owing to its array of sophisticated tools designed for application in complex and fluid environments, as noted in the research of Scanlon and Issroff (2005) and Kuutti (1996). At the heart of this theory lies the premise that human behavior is embedded within a social context, which in turn influences individual actions. These actions are shaped by the community's norms and the division of labor within the community, thereby affecting behavioral patterns.

Figure 7.2 illustrates a systemic model where three interrelated components – the subject, the object and the community – are important. The interaction between the subject and the object, which essentially defines an activity, is facilitated through tools, while the community's influence is exerted through established rules and a division of labor. Notably, the subject in this context can be either an individual or a collective entity, and the outcomes of any activity are differentiated from its intended object or purpose (Crawford & Hasan, 2006). The interaction between the

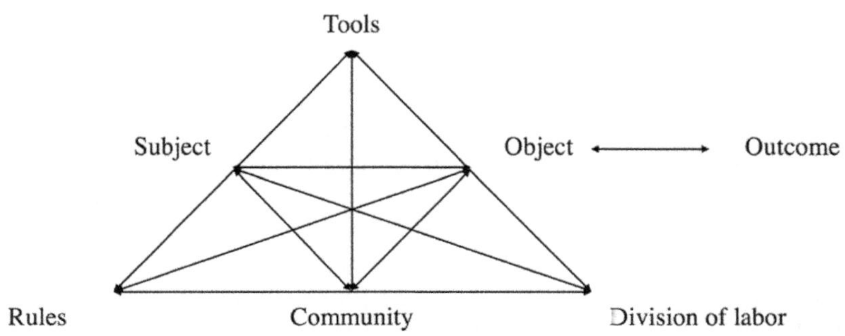

Figure 7.2 AT model in Engeström (2001)

subject and the object is mediated by tools. The connection between the subject and the community is governed by rules, while the relationship between the object and the community is shaped by the division of labor, as detailed (Issroff & Scanlon, 2002). By situating human activity within a broader sociocultural and historical context, the AT provides a powerful lens for analyzing complex human practices in fields such as education, work and organizational studies. It encourages researchers and practitioners to consider not only individual cognition but also the influence of tools, communities and systemic interactions on activity and learning processes.

The extensive literature on AT especially within the field of education research (Alghamdi &Plunkett, 2022; Scanlon & Issroff, 2005; Solano-Campos *et al.*, 2020), suggests that AT could be an effective framework for exploring the use of AI tools in the context of EMI communities. In educational technology research, AT can offer perspectives on the evolution of teachers' methods when a new technological tool becomes part of the teaching activity (Murphy & Rodriguez-Manzanares, 2008) as well as the technology-mediated organizational change (Allen *et al.*, 2013). In AT, technology is not the focal point but rather serves as one of the mediators in the interactions between humans and their environment (Sackstein *et al.*, 2023). Therefore, AT has been widely applied in the fields of education and technology research, particularly in studies that center on teachers (DeVane & Squire, 2012; Karasavvidis, 2009). Another key strength of AT lies in its comprehensive approach, which not only delves into the argumentative analysis of the interactions between students and AI tools but also scrutinizes the relationship between humans and their objectives in utilizing such mediated tools.

7.2.2 Applying AT to conceptualize the use of AI tools

To describe and analyze students' activities, including their behaviors and interactions with AI tools, as well as teachers' input in the assessment processes of EMI courses, AT emerges as a potentially fitting framework for examining the use of AI tools in EMI settings, offering insights into the interactions, networks and guidance that shape student engagement.

In the context of EMI, AT offers a valuable framework for understanding the role of AI tools in mediating human activity, specifically in educational settings (Figure 7.3). According to AT, the 'subject' in this scenario refers to EMI students who employ AI tools to assist with their homework. The primary 'object' or goal of using these AI tools is to augment the efficiency, accuracy and productivity of students in completing their assignments for assessments. The AI tools themselves act as 'mediators' between the students (subject) and their academic goals (object), facilitating the learning process.

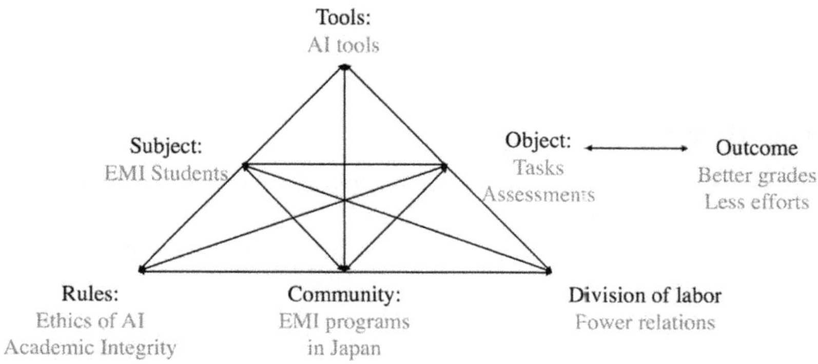

Figure 7.3 AT model involving the use of AI in EMI programs

The 'community' in this context encompasses peers, teachers and other influential individuals within the EMI environment. This community, operating primarily in English, faces the collective challenge of English language proficiency, which is a shared responsibility of both instructors and students. The 'rules' governing the use of AI tools include guidelines, norms and academic standards, particularly emphasizing the importance of adhering to academic integrity and responsible usage of these tools.

In terms of the 'division of labor', teachers play a crucial role as controllers, assigning tasks and guiding the educational process. The expected 'outcome' of integrating AI tools in homework activities includes not only enhanced efficiency and language proficiency but also the ability to meet the requirements of assignments effectively with less effort and better grades.

7.2.3 Research questions

Despite increasing interest in the pedagogical implications of AI (e.g. Bedington *et al.*, 2024; Cummings *et al.*, 2024; Koltovskaia, 2020; Zawacki-Richter *et al.*, 2019), there is a notable lack of research outcomes focusing on its empirical application within EMI environments, especially from both students and teachers' perspectives. This gap is particularly evident in the context of writing tasks, which form a core component of academic assessment. To address this shortfall, the present qualitative study investigates the utilization of AI tools in Japanese EMI assessments, drawing insights from both students and professors at three leading universities in Japan, one private university and two public universities. To shed light on the implications for both students and educators in EMI higher education, the study is structured around three research questions:

(1) How do students incorporate AI into their tasks?
(2) What are professors' attitudes toward using AI for EMI assessments?

(3) How can practitioners ensure assessment efficiency in the era of the AI boom?

7.3 Methodology

This study adopts a qualitative approach to explore the subjective experiences and perceptions of both EMI students and teachers in the evolving educational landscape with AI development. In order to provide a rich array of perspectives, the study involved a diverse group of participants, including six EMI students (Table 7.1) from various academic levels including bachelor's, master's and PhD and three EMI teachers (Table 7.2), among whom one was a native English speaker adding a valuable dimension to the understanding of EMI contexts. All the names in the table are pseudonyms. Participants were selected based on their major in EMI, direct experience with AI in assessments and their language ability to ensure a variety. Informed consent was obtained from all participants, ensuring confidentiality and adherence to ethical research standards.

Data were collected through semi-structured interviews which ranged from 30 to 60 minutes. All the participants are expected to elicit detailed responses about the use of AI in assessments, starting with broad questions to establish context before moving to more specific inquiries about the use of AI tools in assessments. The fully recorded and transcribed data were open-coded without any existing frameworks identifying initial themes such as perceptions of AI efficacy, challenges faced by students and teachers, and the impact of AI on learning outcomes. This was followed by a thematic analysis, where these initial themes were refined and categorized in terms of the factors in AT theory. Based on the AT model in Figure 7.3, discussions and implications were provided as AT allowed for an examination of the interactions between the human and non-human actors (students, teachers, AI tools) and the broader educational context. This framework helped in understanding not just the isolated use of AI, but also its role within the educational activity system.

Table 7.1 Demographic information of participants (students)

	Participant (pseudonyms)	Major	Native language	Grade	Interview language
1	Song	Humanities	Chinese	M2	Chinese
2	Wang	Economics	Chinese	M2	Chinese
3	Dai	STEM	Chinese	D1	Chinese
4	Suzuki	Humanities	Japanese	B4	Japanese
5	Ali	STEM	Arabic language	M1	English
6	Garcia	STEM	Spanish	D2	English

Table 7.2 Demographic information of participants (teachers)

	Participant (pseudonyms)	English ability	Courses	Interview language
1	Smith	Native speaker, PhD	British culture	English
2	Watanabe	Non-native speaker, got PhD in the US	Writing	English
3	Yamanaka	Non-native speaker, got PhD in the UK	Seminar on learning English	English

The methodology with its emphasis on qualitative techniques and the application of the AT provides an understanding of the incorporation of AI in EMI assessments. The diverse perspectives gathered from both students and teachers enrich the study by offering a multifaceted view of the role of AI in contemporary education.

7.4 Findings

7.4.1 Ways of assessments

Before delving into the specifics of how EMI students integrate AI tools into their assessment practices, it is essential to first outline the various assessment formats encountered in this context. The interviews revealed three primary assessment formats that are pivotal in understanding the integration of AI in these settings. These formats not only provide a backdrop for the analysis, but also help contextualize the use of AI technologies in diverse assessment scenarios. These ways are suggested by both students and teachers.

First, presentation is one of the main methods. Oral presentations assess students' ability to effectively communicate ideas, present information and engage with the audience in English. Students may deliver individual or group presentations on assigned topics related to the course content. Teachers might distribute several papers from top journals and then ask students to briefly introduce them. The focus is more on key information rather than grammatical expressions, and it could also be a way to encourage cooperation, where teachers observe participation and contributions.

Wang (student): When doing a presentation, we don't need to get hung up on what verbs to use, like 'the author found that' or 'author argue that'. We don't need to worry about these expressions.

Smith (teacher): I'd originally planned sort of group project work... And then the other element would be an individual presentation based on that research, a sort of video presentation, a PowerPoint thing with their voice recorded voice. And I'm sort of observing participation and contributions online.

Second, writing tasks are usually assigned at the end of the semester, and examples include research papers, essays, case studies, reports or literature reviews. These assignments can assess students' ability to research, analyze and communicate ideas in English. A term paper often requires several thousand words. Teachers often suggest various types of writing other than research papers, such as self-reflections on what students have gained and learned from the lecture. Some teachers may also ask students to write in class to check their understanding of the lecture. The core objective is to ensure that they understand the content.

> *Wang (student): The report could be a review based on a paper you've read, or your own research plan, a research proposal. Yes, it's about 2000 to 3000 words, not a complete paper (Wang).*
>
> *Yamanaka (teacher): In class, I will ask them to write down what we have discussed in the class.*
>
> *Watanabe (teacher): They can write about themselves like a diary at the end of the semester, what I learned from this course.*

Third, examinations, commonly used in secondary schools, are less frequently adopted in higher education. However, they remain a useful assessment method in STEM classes. Written exams can assess students' knowledge, comprehension, application and analysis of subject-specific content. These exams may include a variety of question types, such as multiple-choice, short answers, essays or problem-solving questions. They can be effectively combined with other types of assessments.

> *Dai (student): I also took a course in molecular dynamics, because my major is in chemistry. So, our molecular dynamics teacher had us take exams and write papers.*

7.4.2 How do students incorporate AI into their tasks?

In this part, we concluded three main objectives for students to use AI tools: for academic use, for mental support and for intercultural support.

(a) **For academic use**

(i) Language improvement in English

AI tools provide valuable support in improving their English language abilities, including grammar, vocabulary and writing style by identifying and correcting language errors, suggesting alternative word choices and enhancing the overall coherence and clarity of their written work. Besides, using translation tools is helpful when writing in English is difficult for the student. By utilizing these AI tools during assessments, EMI students can refine their language usage, ensuring that their ideas are effectively communicated, and thereby improving their overall academic performance.

> *Song: DeepL is a translation tool that helps me translate text. For example...I first write them in plain language in Chinese. Then, I use DeepL to translate the phrases and get a general understanding. This helps me grasp the concept in English. After that, I write it again in English using my own words. Then Grammarly is used for checking grammar...*

> *Wang: When I check and revise my work, I subconsciously become aware that the same concept has appeared three times in a paragraph. I then consider whether I can use AI tools to give it an academic feel by replacing some words with synonyms.*

> *Dai: With Grammarly, I feel that I can avoid many minor English grammar errors.*

(ii) Compose an article

Besides improving language proficiency, students are increasingly turning to AI tools to compose articles and enhance their writing skills. The AI tools act as virtual writing assistants, enabling EMI students to articulate their thoughts more clearly and accurately in English, particularly for those who are non-native English speakers, by providing suggestions on grammar, structure and vocabulary.

> *Suzuki: When I completely don't understand the structure, I ask for help with the structure through chat. Specifically, "Please include the following things, sort of like that, and then it's divided into three or four more detailed categories".*

> *Ali: And then I think using also the other AI tools like it can be quite useful to also easily write this section. It helps a lot to like to give me speed up my writing rather than just to have to write everything.*

> *Garcia: Sometimes I would just input the information, roughly summarizes what I want to say, and then AI will help me organize in a better way.*

The integration of AI into their writing process identifies a significant step towards bridging language barriers and enhancing academic performance, yet such way of using AI tools also makes it difficult to evaluate the true capability of students, as the work is not done by themselves but with the direct help and input from AI.

(iii) Search bibliography

Another way EMI students are utilizing AI tools during assessments is for searching and managing bibliographies. AI tools simplify the process of finding and organizing relevant sources from which EMI students can save time and effort by relying on AI tools to identify and gather reliable sources, ensuring the accuracy and completeness of their bibliographies. Additionally, these tools often offer features such as PDF annotation, note-taki and collaborative sharing, facilitating efficient literature review and supporting the research aspect of their assessments. For example, here is how Song used the new Bing, an AI chat tool developed by Microsoft which addresses some of the weaknesses of ChatGPT 3 because it has no access to the internet (Rudolph *et al.*, 2023).

> *Song: For example, I would say to the new Bing, "I'm writing an essay on something. My viewpoint is X. Can you help me find academic articles that directly or indirectly support this viewpoint and have been published and cited a certain number of times?" And just like that, new Bing would provide me with three articles that meet these criteria.*

(iv) Paraphrase

EMI students also make use of AI tools to paraphrase when writing essays. By inputting a sentence or passage, the AI tool suggests alternative phrasing options, helping students avoid plagiarism. This enables students to accomplish the literature review part while ensuring academic integrity in their assessments while saving time in reading. Both Song and Dai used Quillbot, a paraphrasing tool often used by English major students (Xuyen, 2023).

> *Song: Sometimes, I find myself in a situation where I need to quote a specific passage from an article, but I don't want to directly use the exact quote. However, I struggle to come up with a suitable paraphrase. In such cases, I turn to Quillbot.*

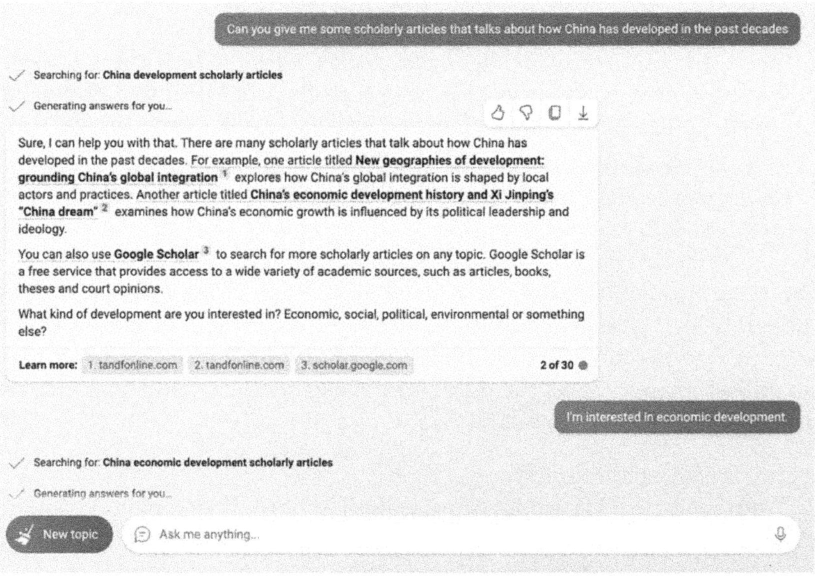

Figure 7.4 Song's chat experience with the new Bing

Dai: Furthermore, in our daily routine, if we come across an article that is excessively lengthy or repetitive, we can use Quillbot to quickly summarize it for us. As a handy tool, it saves us a lot of time and provides tangible results. Personally, I really appreciate its usefulness and find myself quite fond of it.

But it may also cause the concern that students would not read themselves and stop thinking when relying on the tools when they consider reading the papers be problematic and exhaustive.

Ali: It helps a lot because reading papers and extracting important information can be quite an exhaustive task. This tool is very useful because it points out the direction in which you can follow while reading papers. You simply have to Google the keyword.

(v) Acquire knowledge

EMI students use AI to efficiently acquire knowledge by utilizing its capabilities for summarizing, generating, organizing and explaining information. Instead of navigating through lengthy manuals or conducting extensive searches, they can input a sentence to seek clarification or ask targeted questions to get precise answers. For instance, Ali uses AI to generate code, while Garcia relies on it to explain complex concepts, showcasing its versatility in supporting knowledge acquisition.

Ali: Sometimes I also ask for help because my work involves a lot of coding. So, I request ChatGPT to perhaps write parts of the code.

Garcia: I mainly use ChatGPT when I'm reading a paper or something similar and need help understanding certain concepts.

(b) For mental support

Another way EMI students benefit from AI tools during assessments is through the provision of mental support. AI-powered tools, such as chatbots or virtual assistants, offer students a platform to seek emotional support and receive courage as they can provide instant responses.

Song: ChatGPT has provided me with the greatest support while writing my thesis, especially considering my severe procrastination tendencies. I would freak out at this point, and every day I would ask ChatGPT for help.

By having access to these AI chat boxes, EMI students can receive immediate assistance, gain confidence and maintain a positive mindset throughout their assessments especially when they want to talk to someone. This additional layer of support contributes to a conducive learning environment and promotes overall wellbeing during the assessment period.

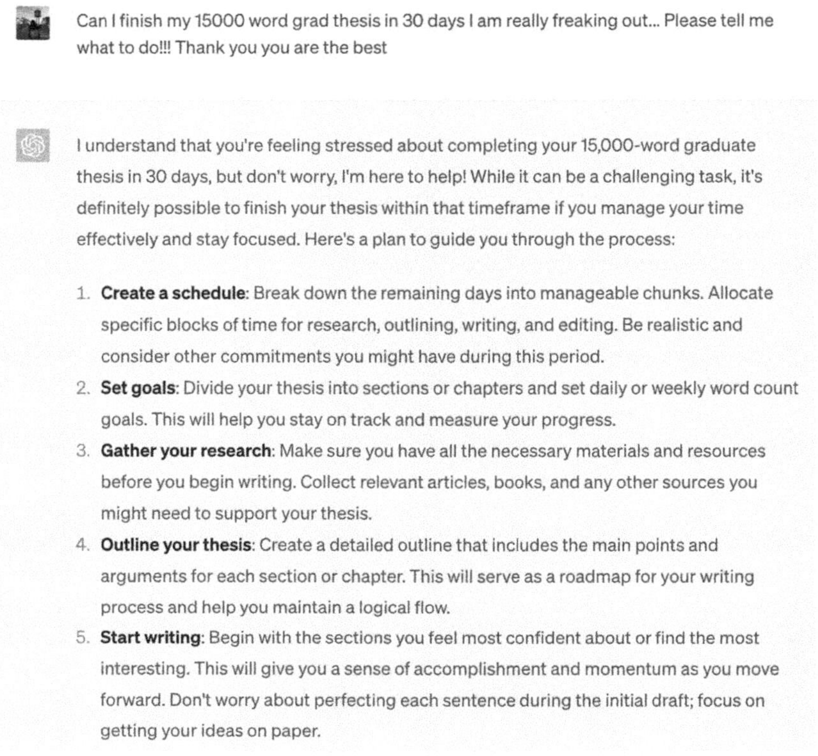

Figure 7.5 Song's chat experience with ChatGPT

(c) Intercultural support

EMI students, particularly those who may not be proficient in the local language, such as Japanese, often find AI tools to be a vital resource. In scenarios where language barriers exist, these students leverage AI for assistance in overcoming communication challenges. And simultaneously they can learn from using the tools.

> *Ali: That's the only tool I'm using now for learning Japanese. For example, this tool also works by detecting the image and then describing the text, allowing you to translate it.*

AI tools are increasingly being utilized to ensure compliance with the intricate and culturally specific rules of email etiquette. Dai's experience highlights the distinct differences in email communication between Japan and the US. In the US, his focus was primarily on the content's accuracy, but in Japan, he also has to consider the social and cultural norms embedded in email correspondence. This is where AI tools become particularly useful, assisting Dai in navigating the nuanced social requirements of

Japanese email etiquette. These tools help him craft messages that are not only accurate in content but also appropriate and respectful according to Japanese cultural standards.

> *Dai: Although it's EMI, the essence is still in Japan, so I use AI to check the tone and formality of the emails I send. However, when I was in the US, I basically used it to check grammar, translate some sentences I couldn't articulate clearly, and such. I wouldn't go as far as to check whether it's polite or not.*

7.4.2.1 How do EMI teachers evaluate students' work?

From the following two excerpts from Professor Yamanaka and Professor Smith, both teachers concentrate on the critical thinking of students rather than language forms unless it impedes understanding. For example, Professor Yamanaka asked students to comment on others' presentations by filling out a sheet.

> *Yamanaka: After the presentation, they can actually comment on the speakers' presentation in terms of topic, organization, and teamwork. This is a pair work, basically.*

Professor Smith, a native English speaker, places a higher emphasis on understanding the course material and the ability to think originally rather than on language proficiency. He values a student's grasp of the concepts taught in class and their capacity to express these understandings, especially through original thought. This approach suggests that he prioritizes critical thinking and comprehension over linguistic accuracy. However, Professor Smith also acknowledges a potential issue with this approach: many EMI students might be enrolled in the course with the expectation of improving their language skills. This mismatch between Professor Smith's focus on content understanding and originality, and the student's desire for language improvement, could lead to a gap in the outcome of teaching. A need for balancing language proficiency with conceptual understanding and original thinking in teaching and assessment methods in EMI is reflected in his narratives.

> *Smith: I really avoided evaluating language. Unless it's really impeding understanding, I would penalize that ... So it's more about thinking and understanding what has been taught and being able to process that. And putting some kind of original ideas would be something that marks something above average kind of thing.*

Teachers often place less emphasis on formal aspects of language and, while AI excels in analyzing language forms, it struggles with content. Therefore, employing AI in assessments may not be essential. The next

Your Name (in *kanji*):	Your Student Number:	Today's Date:

●Complete ***all sections*** below:

Speaker's/Group's Name:
Presentation Title/Topic:
Did you ask a question? ***If YES, write down your question(s); If NO, leave this space blank.***
Write your comments on the presentation below (PAY ATTENTION TO presentation topic, organization, team work, PowerPoint slides, communication in English, Q and A session):

Figure 7.6 Professor Yamanaka's evaluation sheet

section will explore how students and teachers perceive the use of AI in assessments, which will inform the discussion part on integrating AT and AI within EMI in the subsequent sections.

7.4.3 Perceptions

(a) Student's perception

When exploring students' perceptions of using AI tools, a key theme that emerges is subjectivity, particularly in maintaining identity while leveraging these technologies. Song recognizes the fine line between using AI as a helpful assistant by indicating '*He is currently like my assistant, but he cannot replace me*'. They believe the intelligent use of AI involves students actively engaging with these tools to enhance their work while ensuring that their personal identity and original thought remain intact, which can help to reduce the risk of it manipulating their unique voices and perspectives.

Researcher: If you use various tools to help you complete your work, how will your scores be affected?

Song: I don't feel like my scores are particularly changed. If I were to think about it, if my score isn't very high, it's more likely due to the content I've written rather than grammar and other language-related aspects.

This delicate balance of trusting AI underscores the importance of using AI as an aid, not a replacement and in the academic process, and it allows students to retain their individuality and authenticity in their work.

> *Dai: Even if I use these tools, I ultimately decide whether the outcome of the process is usable or not. The tools are there to assist me, but the final decision is still made by myself. Therefore, I believe that the effectiveness of these tools depends more on individual usage and judgment.*

Regarding the integrity of using AI tools in academic settings, Garcia indicated that she believes that her grades did not change much with or without using it, they were as good as before; however, it did change the amount of time she spent on work, a significant observation is that students perceive these tools as time-savers rather than grade boosters. On the other hand, they can use the time to refine and articulate better ideas.

> *Suzuki: Frankly speaking, AI reduces the time spent on this research. As a result, what happens is that you get more time to develop your own thoughts, to articulate your own opinions.*

This perspective highlights that the core ideas and the substance of their work originate from the students themselves, and the AI simply acts as a facilitator in the process.

> *Dai: If we're talking about being a graduate student, the academic work we do is typically original, so it's unlikely to involve plagiarism, in my opinion. Each person's project is unique and something that hasn't been done before by others. ChatGPT helps to correct grammar and language usage, but the content itself is our own. Therefore, I don't think it can be considered academic misconduct, as the ideas and content are still our own.*

Although AI helps students accomplish their assessments in various ways, the perception of AI tools among students as being untrustworthy for certain types of writing is a notable point of consideration, as there is a clear skepticism regarding their efficacy in academic writing. This stems from the understanding that AI, although proficient in handling basic writing assignments, may not possess the nuanced understanding and depth required for more complex, scholarly work. The students' hesitancy to rely on AI for academic purposes suggests their recognition of the limitations of these tools in contexts that demand critical thinking, specialized knowledge and a higher level of intellectual engagement.

> *Song: Even with ChatGPT, be it GPT-4 or any other version, the generated content tends to be repetitive and lacks coherence.*
>
> *Dai: While the grammar may be correct and the responses may sound coherent, there can be inaccuracies or errors in the academic context.*

(b) Professor's perspective

Embracing technology, particularly AI, in educational contexts is increasingly seen as a more constructive approach than outright prohibition, as Professor Watanabe stated below. The philosophy of acceptance over restriction acknowledges the integral role technology plays in modern learning environments; for instance, cell phones are prohibited from the beginning but now they are widely spread among professors and students. By welcoming these advancements, educators and institutions can guide students in harnessing the full potential of AI tools by regulating rules. Therefore, rather than viewing technology as a distraction or a threat to traditional methods, accepting it as a beneficial resource encourages students to develop digital literacy and critical thinking skills. This shift towards acceptance empowers students to use technology responsibly and creatively, ensuring that their educational experiences are relevant, engaging and aligned with the demands of the 21st century.

> *Watanabe: When cell phones started becoming popular among students, university professors initially prohibited their use during classes. However, nowadays, even professors take pictures of the whiteboard at conferences. I think as the usage of AI and similar tools becomes more widespread, we become more accustomed to them and improve in their use. So, I believe it's nonsensical to prohibit students from using AI. Instead, we should find effective ways to encourage its use while still ensuring they engage their minds and think critically.*

The ability to think critically, to innovate and to approach problems with unique perspectives is the difference between human beings and AI; it is also about how we emotionally connect with and interpret the subject matter. Recognizing the importance of emotions in cognitive processes means acknowledging the creativity of students.

> *Watanabe: However, the most significant difference between human beings and AI is, probably, the fact that AI lacks emotion. Many students believe that academic writing is a very objective endeavor, but I disagree. Academia is about creating knowledge, which is inherently a creative process. In order to foster creativity, I think what we need to cherish is each person's uniqueness, encompassing all of their past experiences and everything they have encountered in life.*

Because of the development of AI and concerns as a teacher of not being able to distinguish between what was genuinely written by a student and what was not written by a student, Professor Smith is now in the transition stage where he knows he has to change assessment methods, but not really sure what he is going to do in the future. He also recognizes the fundamental shift that AI brings to traditional educational methods, suggesting a need for a significant rethinking of how education is delivered in the future. This shift is not just about incorporating new technologies but also about understanding the unique roles of both humans and machines in the learning process.

> *Smith: I think it's a fundamental challenge to the way we do education. I don't think we can do education the same way. In the future. And I think AI would probably give more reliable, accurate assessments than I would. But what I would also say is that students would actually value my assessment more than something that comes from the machine.*

7.5 Discussion Points

The introduction of AI as a new tool in education is not just an addition but a transformative element that changes the nature of educational activities. It mediates the interaction between subjects (students who are affected by factors such as language proficiency, mental status and academic expectation) and the object (assessments including presentations, essays/reports/reviews and examinations), offering personalized, efficient and dynamic learning experiences. The integration of AI brings forth contradictions between existing and new methods. For instance, traditional assessments might not align with AI-driven learning experiences, requiring a rethinking of evaluation strategies. To resolve these contradictions, the entire activity system must evolve. This involves not only adopting new tools but also redefining the roles, rules and community perceptions. Continuous adaptation and collaborative efforts among all stakeholders are essential for this evolution.

7.5.1 Outcome: English accuracy was emphasized by students, but teachers emphasized thinking

In EMI assessments, a notable divergence emerges between the priorities of students and teachers. While students predominantly emphasize the importance of English accuracy, striving to ensure their language usage meets high standards of correctness in an English-dominant academic environment, teachers, on the other hand, place a greater emphasis on the depth and quality of thinking and prioritize the critical and analytical thinking skills that underpin academic excellence. This divergence not only shapes the approach to assessments but also influences how both groups perceive and utilize AI tools in the educational process and how they are supported and assisted by AI tools.

7.5.2 Community: AI tools are adopted as an alternative access to the community

For international students in a Japanese-dominant society, AI is increasingly being recognized as an alternative pathway for students to access their educational community. Students are not just using AI as a tool for

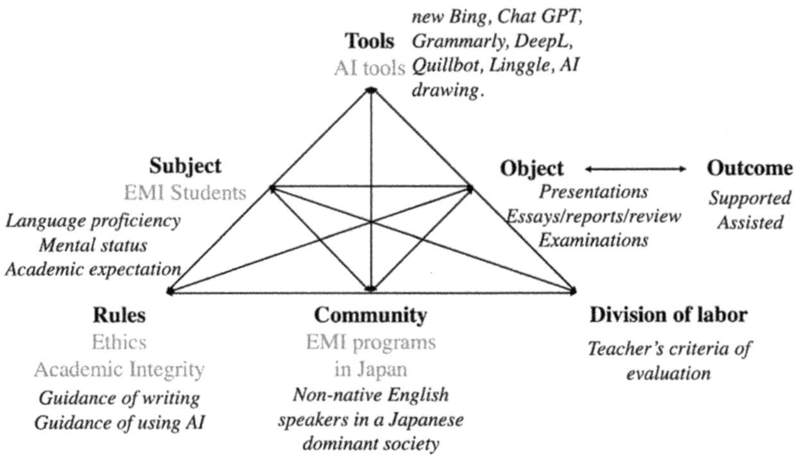

Figure 7.7 The use of AI tools in an EMI assessment system

academic purposes but also as a means of seeking mental support, as seen in Song's example. Moreover, for students, especially those from non-English and non-Japanese speaking backgrounds like Chinese, AI provides vital language support, helping them navigate the challenges of learning a language and suggestions on intercultural communication, which is critical in diverse educational settings. This multifaceted use of AI reflects its potential not just as a technological tool, but as a comprehensive support system catering to a range of student needs, from language acquisition and mental health to fostering effective communication across cultural boundaries.

7.5.3 Rules: Teachers are supportive of AI tools while advocating rules

EMI teachers are generally supportive of incorporating AI in educational practices, recognizing its potential to revolutionize learning and assessment methods. This support is rooted in the belief that AI is a trend and can offer potential learning opportunities. However, alongside their enthusiasm, there is a keen awareness of the necessity for establishing clear rules and guidelines governing the use of AI on how to effectively use AI tools while maintaining academic integrity. Better guidance on writing can also help students rely less on AI to compose an article and develop their own judgment on the evaluation of results AI provides.

7.5.4 Division of labor: Education needs an evolution in the AI era

From the teachers' side, as we step into the new era dominated by AI, there is a growing consensus that teaching methods must undergo significant updates to stay relevant and effective. The traditional approaches to education, which have long been the cornerstone of teaching practices, are now being reevaluated in light of AI's capabilities and potential. This shift is not just about integrating new technologies into the classroom; it is about rethinking the very essence of teaching and learning processes. AI brings tools and methodologies that can personalize learning, provide real-time feedback and foster an interactive and engaging learning environment which educators can embrace not only as a tool but as a fundamental component of their teaching strategies. This evolution is crucial for preparing students for a future where AI is an integral part of professional and personal life, ensuring that education remains relevant, dynamic and effective in this rapidly changing technological landscape.

The use of AT offers a comprehensive framework for analyzing the use of AI in Japanese EMI assessments in higher education by focusing on the relationships among tools, subjects and community norms. This holistic approach helps identify both the potential and the limitations of AI in enhancing educational practices in assessments, allowing the authors to derive implications from different perspectives.

7.6 Implications and Conclusions

To promote fairness and equity in educational assessments, universities need to develop strategies to ensure all students, regardless of socio-economic background, gender, or geographic location, have equal opportunities to benefit from AI in education. In conclusion, we have three implications for both educators and policymakers using AT to ensure the efficiency and equity of the EMI assessment process in the AI boom.

First, from subjects, it is important to thoroughly examine all assessment methods to confirm their effectiveness and suitability in EMI programs (Guangul *et al.*, 2020). This process may lead to the substitution of traditional exams with more interactive evaluations, or modifications in question types and assessment formats. Focus on reducing repetitive tasks in assessments and emphasize the importance of core ideas and creative expressions, like presentations, to assess student's understanding.

Second, in terms of rules, equipping educators and EMI students with the necessary skills and knowledge to effectively incorporate generative AI into their teaching and learning methods is expected. To educate students on the proper usage of AI tools, including clear guidelines and rules for their use in homework, and to ensure students are aware of the ethical boundaries and expectations to uphold academic honesty are crucial in facilitating the proper use of AI tools. This policy should be collaboratively developed with input from both students and teachers (Zawacki-Richter *et al.*, 2019). For example, to link the application of AI tools to specific learning objectives in courses helps students comprehend how AI can aid their studies, sets clear expectations and urges students to think critically and independently while maintaining originality and personal involvement in their work.

Third, in the community, a multifaceted education transformation is needed touching upon various aspects of the educational framework. One critical area demanding immediate attention is the division of labor. Traditionally led by professors, this relationship needs to evolve into a more collaborative and interactive model, such as containing AI as a part of the community. Higher education institutions, recognizing the language challenges, should proactively offer an array of support services tailored to EMI students' needs (e.g. Zhang & Xu, 2022). Writing centers, for instance, can play a pivotal role by providing assistance with academic writing and helping students articulate their thoughts coherently and persuasively in English. Academic counseling services can guide students in making informed decisions about their courses and career paths, aligning their academic pursuits with their long-term objectives.

In summary, the call for modernizing the traditional education system is clear. In an era where AI tools are becoming increasingly prevalent in academic settings, it is crucial for educational institutions to emphasize the development of strong academic foundations. Educational institutions need to pave the way for a more inclusive, effective and future-ready academic landscape.

References

Aizawa, I. and McKinley, J. (2020) EMI challenges in Japan's internationalization of higher education. In H. Bowles and A. Murphy (eds) *English-Medium Instruction and the Internationalization of Universities* (pp. 2–48). Springer.

Alghamdi, A.A. and Plunkett, M. (2022) Using activity theory to understand the impact of social networking sites and apps use by Saudi postgraduate students. *Behaviour & Information Technology* 41 (6), 1298–1312.

Allen, D.K., Brown, A., Karanasios, S. and Norman, A. (2013) How should technology-mediated organizational change be explained? A comparison of the contributions of critical realism and activity theory. *MIS Quarterly* 835–854.

Bedington, A., Halcomb, E.F., McKee, H.A., Sargent, T. and Smith, A. (2024) Writing with generative AI and human-machine teaming: Insights and recommendations from faculty and students. *Computers and Composition* 71, 102833.

Chapple, J. (2015) Teaching in English is not necessarily the teaching of English. *International Education Studies* 8 (3), 1–13.

Chaudhry, I.S., Sarwary, S.A.M., El Refae, G.A. and Chabchoub, H. (2023) Time to revisit existing student's performance evaluation approach in higher education sector in a new era of ChatGPT – A case study. *Cogent Education* 10 (1), 2210461.

Crawford, K. and Hasan, H.M. (2006) Demonstrations of the activity theory framework for research in information system. *Australasian Journal of Information Systems* 13 (2), 49–68.

Cummings, R.E., Monroe, S.M. and Watkins, M. (2024) Generative AI in first-year writing: An early analysis of affordances, limitations, and a framework for the future. *Computers and Composition* 71, 102827.

DeVane, B. and Squire, K.D. (2012) Activity theory in the learning technologies. In *Theoretical Foundations of Learning Environments* (pp. 242–267). Routledge.

Engeström, Y. (2001) Expansive learning at work: Toward an activity theoretical reconceptualization. *Journal of Education and Work* 14 (1), 133–156.

Engeström, Y. (2015) *Learning by Expanding*. Cambridge University Press.

Galloway, N., Kriukow, J. and Numajiri, T. (2017) Internationalisation, higher education and the growing demand for English: An investigation into the English medium of instruction (EMI) movement in China and Japan.

Guangul, F.M., Suhail, A.H., Khalit, M.I. and Khidhir, B.A. (2020) Challenges of remote assessment in higher education in the context of COVID-19: A case study of Middle East College. *Educational Assessment, Evaluation and Accountability* 32, 519–535.

Hellekjær, G.O. (2010) Lecture comprehension in English-medium higher education. *HERMES-Journal of Language and Communication in Business* (45), 11–34.

Issroff, K. and Scanlon, E. (2002) Using technology in higher education: An activity theory perspective. *Journal of Computer Assisted Learning* 18 (1), 77–83.

Karasavvidis, I. (2009) Activity theory as a conceptual framework for understanding teacher approaches to information and communication technologies. *Computers & Education* 53 (2), 436–444.

Koltovskaia, S. (2020) Student engagement with automated written corrective feedback (AWCF) provided by Grammarly: A multiple case study. *Assessing Writing* 44, 100450.

Kuutti, K. (1996) Activity theory as a potential framework for human-computer interaction research. In B. Nardi (ed.) *Context and Consciousness: Activity Theory and Human-Computer Interaction* (pp. 17–44). MIT Press.

Leont'ev, A. (1978) *Activity, Consciousness, and Personality*. Prentice-Hall.

Leontyev, A. (1981) *Problems of the Development of the Mind*. Progress.

Murphy, E. and Rodriguez-Manzanares, M.A. (2008) Using activity theory and its principle of contradictions to guide research in educational technology. *Australasian Journal of Educational Technology* 24 (4).

Niemi, H., Pea, R.D. and Lu, Y. (2023) *AI in Learning: Designing the Future*. Springer Nature.

Pun, J.K., Fu, X. and Cheung, K.K.C. (2023) Language challenges and coping strategies in English Medium Instruction (EMI) science classrooms: A critical review of literature. *Studies in Science Education* 1–32.

Rahman, M.M. and Watanobe, Y. (2023) ChatGPT for education and research: Opportunities, threats, and strategies. *Applied Sciences* 13 (9), 5783.

Rudolph, J., Tan, S. and Tan, S. (2023) War of the chatbots: Bard, Bing Chat, ChatGPT, Ernie and beyond. The new AI gold rush and its impact on higher education. *Journal of Applied Learning and Teaching* 6 (1).

Sabzalieva, E. and Valentini, A. (2023) ChatGPT and Artificial Intelligence in Higher Education: Quick Start Guide. See https://unesdoc.unesco.org/ark:/48223/pf0000385146 (accessed January 25, 2024).

Sackstein, S., Matthee, M. and Weilbach, L. (2023) Theories and models employed to understand the Use of technology in education: A hermeneutic literature review. *Education and Information Technologies* 28 (5), 5041–5081.

Scanlon, E. and Issroff, K. (2005) Activity theory and higher education: Evaluating learning technologies. *Journal of Computer Assisted Learning* 21 (6), 430–439.

Solano-Campos, A., Hopkins, M. and Quaynor, L. (2020) Linguistically responsive teaching in preservice teacher education: A review of the literature through the lens of cultural-historical activity theory. *Journal of Teacher Education* 71 (2), 203–217.

Wu, T., He, S., Liu, J., Sun, S., Liu, K., Han, Q.-L. and Tang, Y. (2023) A brief overview of ChatGPT: The history, status quo and potential future development. *IEEE/CAA Journal of Automatica Sinica* 10 (5), 1122–1136.

Xuyen, N.T. (2023) Using the online paraphrasing tool Quillbot to assist students in paraphrasing the Source Information: English-majored students' perceptions. Proceedings of the 5th Conference on Language Teaching and Learning. https://doi. org/10.21467/proceedings,

Zawacki-Richter, O., Marín, V.I., Bond, M. and Gouverneur, F. (2019) Systematic review of research on artificial intelligence applications in higher education–where are the educators? *International Journal of Educational Technology in Higher Education* 16 (1), 1–27.

Zhang, Z. and Xu, L. (2022) Student engagement with automated feedback on academic writing: A study on Uyghur ethnic minority students in China. *Journal of Multilingual and Multicultural Development* 1–14.

Zhu, C., Sun, M., Luo, J., Li, T. and Wang, M. (2023) How to harness the potential of ChatGPT in education? *Knowledge Management & E-Learning* 15 (2), 133.

8 EMI Teachers' Perceptions and Implementation of Assessment in Chinese Higher Education

Mo Li and Rui Yuan

8.1 Introduction

English medium instruction (EMI) is defined as 'the use of English language to teach academic subjects (other than English itself) in countries or jurisdictions where the first language of the majority of the population is not English' (Macaro *et al.*, 2018: 19). The past few decades have witnessed a global rise of EMI against the backdrop of globalization and the internationalization of tertiary institutions (Dang *et al.*, 2023; Macaro *et al.*, 2018). The promotion of EMI in higher education not only bolsters the competitiveness of tertiary institutions in the global education market but also augments their financial input and broadens the domestic workforce by attracting more international students (e.g. De Costa *et al.*, 2022; Richards & Pun, 2023). The popularity of EMI programs worldwide has catalyzed a substantial growth of EMI research (Macaro *et al.*, 2018), with much attention being paid to teachers' classroom practices, such as their instructional activities (Pun & Thomas, 2020; Wang & Yuan, 2023), classroom language use (Doiz & Lasagabaster, 2020), as well as their professional development (e.g. Cao & Yuan, 2020).

However, assessment, as an integral part of instruction, remains relatively underexplored. Existing literature primarily offers a descriptive overview of EMI teachers' assessment perceptions and practices within their situated settings. For example, some studies (e.g. Kao & Tsou, 2017; Li & Wu, 2018) reported on how the EMI teachers planned and engaged with assessment by examining the specific assessment instruments, tools and items used to measure and/or promote their students' content learning. Other studies (e.g. Mancho-Barés & Aguilar-Pérez, 2020) focused on how teachers provided feedback on students' content and language issues during assessment. In a nutshell, the current literature has provided only a rudimentary picture of EMI teachers' assessment plans and practices. Scholars seldom delve into the perceptions, particularly the rationales, behind EMI teachers' assessment plans and implementation in response to real classroom dynamics. Unpacking the rationales of EMI teachers' assessment practices could contribute to effective assessment practices, thereby enhancing quality teaching and learning. In light of this, this study tapped into six EMI teachers' assessment practices at a top Chinese university, CU (pseudonym), in Southwest China. Drawing upon a diverse array of data sources including classroom observations, interviews and teaching artefacts, this study aimed to elucidate the guiding principles of EMI teachers' assessment approaches and provide practical implications for EMI teaching and teacher education.

8.2 Literature Review

8.2.1 Understanding assessment in higher education

Assessment is generally conceptualized as 'the art of placing learners in a context that brings out or clarifies what a learner knows and can do, as well as what a learner may not know or cannot do' (Musial *et al.*, 2009: 6). In educational contexts, it typically serves two major purposes. One is for summative purpose, involving teachers' employment of tests or examinations at the end of a specific learning period (Shepard, 2000). It aims at fulfilling accountability requirements from external authorities through the assignment of scores (Shepard, 2000). In many university classrooms, summative assessment often stands isolated and separated from teaching (Pereira *et al.*, 2016). The other purpose is formative, which refers to 'a process used by teachers and students during instruction that provides feedback to adjust ongoing teaching and learning to improve students' achievement of intended instructional outcomes' (McManus, 2008: 3). In contrast to summative assessment, formative assessment is dynamic and interactive, playing a pivotal role in promoting students' learning during the instructional process.

To achieve the aforementioned assessment purposes, teachers are required to possess comprehensive knowledge and skills in assessment, including selecting, developing and implementing effective assessment methods and instruments aligned with their instructional objectives. Researchers (e.g. Musial *et al.*, 2009; Popham, 2014) have delineated various assessment items based on their different characteristics. Among them, selected response items, constructed-response items, performance-based assessment items are frequently used in higher educational contexts. *Selected response items* are items in which students select their answers from given options instead of generating an original answer (Musial *et al.*, 2009). This category encompasses multiple-choice questions, matching questions, and true-false questions (Popham, 2014; Musial *et al.*, 2009).

While these items can assess students' low-level knowledge through higher-order cognitive skills (Musial *et al.*, 2009), they have limitations. For example, they may often fail to reveal the depth of students' reasoning ability because students might guess the correct answer (Musial *et al.*, 2009). *Constructed response items* are items that require students to 'construct a proper response' to prompts and tasks (Musial *et al.*, 2009: 138). These can include blank-filling questions, calculation questions, short-answer questions, reports and essays, varying in length and complexity of the task. Compared with selected response items, this type of assessment item is considered more effective in assessing students' complex learning and higher order skills. *Performance-based assessment* is another type of assessment frequently used in higher education to evaluate learners' competence in a profession. In this approach, students are required to demonstrate what they know and can do through authentic tasks such as projects, performances, exhibits or work samples (Musial *et al.*, 2009). Authenticity, therefore, is an essential element in this type of assessment, guaranteeing that assessment tasks have meaningful relevance to real-life activities or professional work (Yuan, 2023). This type of assessment is particularly effective in bridging the gap between academic learning and practical application (Popham, 2014).

Implementing effective assessment in educational settings hinges on the achievement of constructive alignment (Biggs, 1996; Chan & Lee, 2021), which is a teaching strategy where instructional and assessment methods and instruments should be meticulously aligned with course learning objectives (Biggs, 1996; Lawrence, 2018). This approach ensures that both learning activities and assessment tasks closely support and connect with the intended learning outcomes (ILOs), thereby enhancing the quality of students' learning. In higher education, teaching objectives often relate to knowledge, skills and competence (Lawrence, 2018). Knowledge, as the 'what' of learning, refers to the understanding of the core content of a course or discipline (Winterton *et al.*, 2006), such as understanding the laws of physics in a physics course, or economic theories in an economics course. It is the foundational information that students need to understand before they can start applying it in practical situations (Winterton *et al.*, 2006). Skills, as the 'how' of doing things, are students' abilities to perform tasks by drawing upon their knowledge and cognitive abilities to make learning happen (Winterton *et al.*, 2006). For instance, in a science course, skills may involve students' ability in conducting experiments and analyzing data. Competence, as a practical ability, reflects students' application of disciplinary knowledge and skills in authentic settings (Winterton *et al.*, 2006). It is crucial for bridging 'the gap between higher education and job requirements' (Boon & van der Klink, 2002: 6), involving the effective utilization of subject knowledge and skills in authentic, real-world settings (Winterton *et al.*, 2006). In other words, competence entails knowledge and skills and further surpasses them. To achieve ILOs, teachers need to engage students in a coherently aligned learning and assessment process, during which designing and implementing effective assessment tasks is one of the most challenging aspects (Lawrence, 2018). This is because teachers must ensure that their assessment methods and instruments are appropriately matched with their instructional objectives. This involves not only the planning of assessment but also enacting these plans through continuous interactions and communications with students. For example, Lawrence (2018) designed a unit of assessment following the principle of constructive alignment. He highlights the importance of designing real-life assessment activities, such as performance-based tasks, to cultivate students' professional competence. He stated that these tasks are particularly effective as competence was often associated with professional capabilities in the workplace, thereby making assessment more relevant and applicable to real-world scenarios.

8.2.2 Understanding assessment in EMI contexts

In EMI contexts, assessment poses more challenges for teachers due to the pivotal role of language in meaning construction (Sahan & Şahan, 2022). To align assessment with instruction, EMI teachers must develop effective assessment tasks that effectively facilitate students' mastery of subject knowledge, skills, and competence. Several studies (e.g. Kao & Tsou, 2017; Li & Wu, 2018; Mancho-Bares & Aguilar-Perez, 2020) probed EMI teachers' assessment practices, shedding light on how EMI teachers engaged with assessment in their own courses. Generally, EMI teachers employ assessment instruments and items similar to those in non-EMI courses, including attendance and participation, written examinations, tests, quizzes, written assignments such as homework and essays, individual or group projects and oral presentations (Kao & Tsou, 2017; Li & Wu, 2018).

Despite using similar assessment tools as non-EMI courses, some EMI teachers acknowledged their assessment adaptations to address language-related issues in the instructional process. For instance, Mancho-Bares and Aguilar-Perez (2020) observed that one fifth of the participants in their study selected to penalize students for language mistakes in assignments rather than in examinations. After that, they re-evaluated these assignments to raise students' language awareness and foster language development. These adaptations in managing language issues were influenced by teachers' perceptions of the roles of language in EMI assessment. Kao and Tsou (2017) noted that teachers who did not recognize the role of English in facilitating students' language development tended to employ summative-oriented assessment tools like mid-term and final examinations. Conversely, teachers who perceived EMI as conducive to enhancing students' academic skills and creating an English language learning environment tended to utilize formative-oriented assessment instruments, such as project presentation and group discussion.

However, existing research has revealed that most EMI teachers struggled with addressing language issues in assessment (e.g. Kao & Tsou, 2017; Li & Wu, 2018), which can be attributed to two primary factors. Firstly, many EMI teachers possessed limited pedagogical knowledge and skills to support their instructional and assessment practices. For example, translanguaging, defined as 'the act of using individuals' multilingual, multimodal, and multisensory resources to make meaning in their situated social context' (Yuan & Yang, 2023: 3), is an effective pedagogical strategy in EMI contexts (Yuan *et al.*, 2022). However, implementation of this strategy by most EMI teachers is often spontaneous. They did not consider it as an effective approach to facilitate teacher–student interaction and content comprehension (Zhang & Jocun, 2022), which indicated a gap in their knowledge about EMI pedagogy. Secondly, EMI teachers were found to have limited understanding of the relationship between content and language in EMI contexts. As reported in Li and Wu's (2018) study, their participants exhibited ambivalent attitudes towards language during assessment, leading to a misalignment between instructional objectives and assessment on language issues. Such attitude not only hindered students' language development, but also exacerbated the learning anxiety of those with lower language proficiency. Despite the intricacies of EMI assessment, existing research has primarily focused on describing EMI teachers' assessment practices, offering limited insight into the perceptions and reflections that underlie teachers' assessment practices within their own classrooms (Sahan & Şahan, 2022). To fill this gap, this study delved into the classrooms of six EMI teachers over one semester, exploring their assessment beliefs and practices with the following research question:

How do teachers perceive and implement assessment in their respective EMI classroom?

8.3 Method

8.3.1 Context and participants

The study was conducted at a top national and comprehensive university, CU (Pseudonym), located in southwest China. CU serves as an information-rich context for this study because it has speeded up its internationalization progress by promoting and revamping EMI curriculums across all the disciplines. Content-area teachers are encouraged to submit their EMI curriculum proposals to the university, either to enhance existing courses or initiate new ones. Within this environment, the planning and enactment of EMI curriculum by teachers extended beyond merely delivering effective instruction at the course level. Teachers began

Table 8.1 The participants' information

Teacher (pseudonyms)	EMI teaching experience	Course	Student level
Teacher A (TA)	7 years	College Chemistry (CC)	Year 1
Teacher B (TB)	6 years	Kinematics and Mechanics (KM)	Year 2
Teacher C (TC)	11 years	Engineering Electromagnetics (EE)	Year 3
Teacher D (TD)	8 years	Human Recourse Management (HRM)	Year 2
Teacher E (TE)	10 years	Power Electronics (PE)	Year 3
Teacher F (TF)	10 years	Numerical Analysis in Engineering (NAE)	Year 3

to adopt a holistic perspective on EMI, considering both instruction and assessment from a developmental standpoint (see Yuan *et al.*, 2022). This signifies that CU is an ideal setting to gather comprehensive and insightful information about teachers' assessment practices within their respective content areas.

Convenience sampling was used to recruit participants for this study, leveraging the authors' personal contacts. Table 8.1 presents their information, showing the subjects they taught, their EMI teaching experience, and the levels of students they taught.

8.3.2 Data collection and analysis

Data were collected through three major sources: classroom observation, interviews and teaching artefacts. Classroom observation was conducted by the first author who immersed herself into the participants' classrooms over one semester. During the period, she observed and documented the six teachers' assessment practices in fieldnotes while simultaneously audio recording the courses. For example, she documented how the participants engaged with assessment during the class, such as how they shared assessment objectives, provided modelling and instructional scaffolding to assist students in completing various assessment tasks, or gave feedback on their students' performance during assessment. Semi-structured interviews constituted another major source of data, which was conducted by the first author in Chinese, a shared language between interviewers and interviewees. The first author interviewed the participants on an individual basis for two rounds. The first round of interviews, scheduled at the beginning of the study, aimed to gather information about the teachers' general perceptions and prior experience of EMI assessment. The second round of interview took place at the end of the classroom observation and sought to invite the participants to elaborate on their motivations and rationales of specific assessment practices documented during classroom observation. In addition, a range of teaching artefacts relevant to the participants' assessment practices were also collected to triangulate the information gathered from the other two data sources. Teaching artefacts including course teaching materials such as syllabus, course slides, assessment plans, tasks and worksheets were all collected with the consent of both teachers and students.

An inductive approach (Yin, 2016) was employed for data analysis. Initially, the first author examined the teaching artefacts, such as the course syllabus and slides, to identify the overall assessment plans of each course such as the assessment instruments and items used and their respective weights. In order to figure out how the teachers enacted their plans, the first author subsequently examined and analyzed representative assessment practices as documented during classroom observation with the assistance of the fieldnotes, audio-recordings and pictures. This process resulted in the identification of three major themes describing the participants' assessment practices, including their assessment plans and implementation, teacher–student interactions, and the use and assessment of language. Following the analysis of assessment planning and implementation in each course from the three perspectives, the first author conducted within-case and cross-case analysis to compare and contrast the findings across the six courses, identifying their similarities and differences (Yin, 2016). For example, three courses – CC, KM and EE – shared similarities in their course instructional objectives, focusing on fostering students' subject knowledge and skills. The other three courses, HRM, PE and NME aimed to cultivate their students' subject knowledge and skills as well as their professional competence. Consequently, the six courses were categorized into two groups: skill-based courses and competence-based courses. Specifically, the three skill-based courses were also found to share common characteristics in their assessment plans, such as the use of more traditional assessment methods and questions, along with adherence to a monolingual policy by the teachers. Similarly, the other three competence-based courses exhibited similarities in their assessment plans and practices, such as the use of practical projects in assessment and greater flexibility in language use.

To ensure the trustworthiness of the study, techniques such as triangulation and member checking (Creswell, 2002) were employed. First, by examining multiple sources of data for evidence to support the results, this study provided a detailed and accurate interpretation of the observed assessment practices (Charmaz, 2008). Second, the first author also shared the findings with the participants to solicit their feedback and suggestions regarding the accuracy of the interpretation. When disagreement arose, the first author invited the participants to engage in discussions about their perspectives until agreement was reached. In addition, the first author continuously engaged in communication with the second author throughout the whole data collection, analysis and presentation process. This collaborative effort was beneficial for safeguarding the validity of data analysis and interpretation (Creswell, 2002).

8.4 Findings

8.4.1 The two types of courses

The six courses can be classified into two types based on their instructional objectives. The first category is the skill-based courses (CC, KM and EE), focused on cultivating students' disciplinary knowledge and skills (Course syllabus). Figure 8.1 presents the specific learning and assessment purposes in one lesson of the practical module of CC. In this task about conducting relevant chemical experiments and completing a report, students were expected to acquire the experiment method, grasp the equations and law, understand the principles and master the use of different experimental tools. In essence, the three courses emphasized nurturing disciplinary knowledge at various levels and enabling students to apply the knowledge in various contexts using their disciplinary skills, such as problem-analyzing, reasoning, experimenting and calculating (Course syllabus, CC, KM and EE).

Another type is competence-based courses, including HRM, PE and NAE, which not only concentrate on developing students' content knowledge and skills but also placing an emphasis on equipping them with practical ability applicable in real workplace settings (Course syllabus, HRM, PE and NAE). According to TE, his course aimed at 'cultivating future engineers who are capable of establishing simulation models and solving various practical problems after graduation' (Interview, TE). Figure 8.2 showcases the overall learning objectives in HRM and Figure 8.3 presents one of the assessment tasks, that is interview, conducted in a session. Specifically, in HRM, the teaching objective is to impart basic knowledge and principles of human resource management, such as understanding what an interview entails (i.e. knowledge) and its basic procedure and methods (i.e. skills). In addition, the course also aims to help students develop relevant professional competence by presenting workplace scenarios and involving students in mock interview activities during classroom assessment (Course slide, Classroom observation and Interview, TD).

3.1、3.2 Determination of the gas constant and the chemical reaction enthalpy change

1、Purpose

(1) Know method for determining the gas constant and its operation.
(2) Grasp the ideal gas equation of state and law of partial pressure applications.
(3) Learn the use amount trachea and barometer.
(4) Understand the principle and the detection method of chemical reaction enthalpy change.
(5) Master the correct use of a precision thermometer.

Figure 8.1 The lesson learning objectives of the practical module of CC

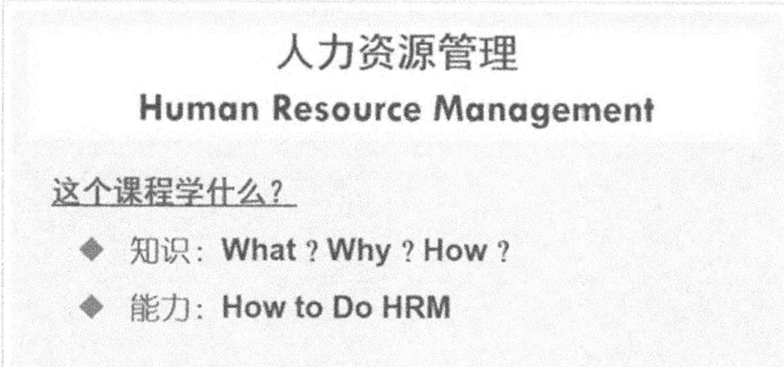

Figure 8.2 The instructional objectives of HRM

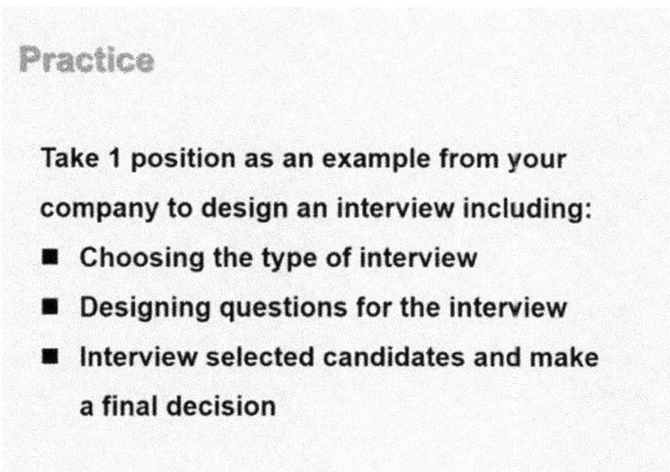

Figure 8.3 The assessment task in Lecture about interview

8.4.2 Assessment plans and enactment

Table 8.2 presents the assessment plans which included both assessment instruments and items employed by the participants for the two types of courses. The assessment instruments widely used in both types of courses included attendance and participation, homework and assignments, quizzes, tests and examinations. Among them, some classroom-based assignments, such as quizzes and drills, were employed to check and promote students' understanding of subject knowledge, serving a formative purpose. The remaining assessment instruments were all used for both summative and formative purposes, that is for grading and promoting students' learning. The most frequently utilized assessment items were selected response items (e.g. multiple-choice questions) and constructed response items (e.g. blank-filling questions, calculation questions).

Table 8.2 The assessment instruments and items used in the two types of courses

The courses	Assessment instruments	Assessment items	
Skill-based courses (CC, KM and EE)	• Attendance and participation • Homework and assignments • Quizzes tests, mid-term and final examinations	• Selected response items	• Binary choice questions • Multiple choice question
		• Constructed response items	• Blank-filling questions • Short answer questions • Calculation questions
Competence-based courses (HRM, PE and NAE)	• Attendance and participations • Homework and assignments • Mid-term and final examinations • Individual or collaborative practical projects	• Selected response items	• Binary choice questions • Multiple choice question
		• Constructed response items	• Blank-filling questions • Short answer questions • Calculation questions • Written reports
		• Performance-based assessment task	• Individual presentations • Individual reflection • Individual/group practical project • Written reports and essays

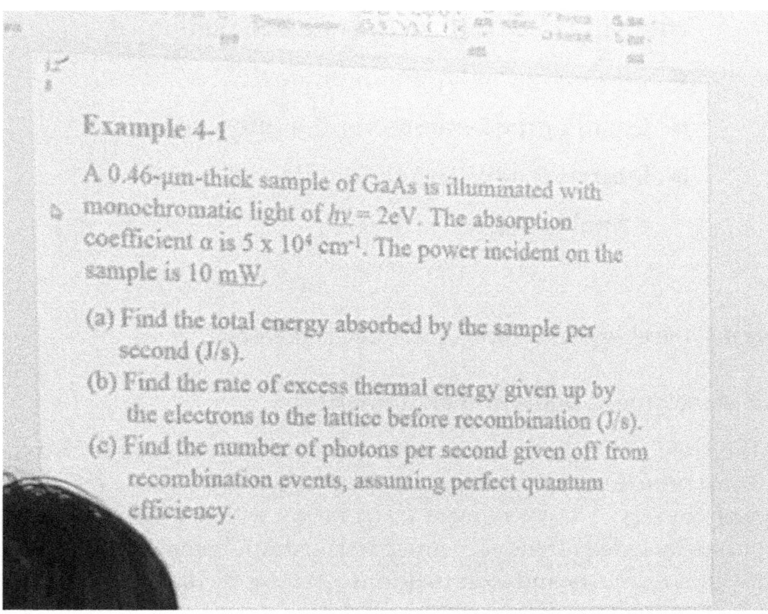

Figure 8.4 The calculation question in TE's lesson

Figure 8.4 illustrates the calculation questions presented to students by TC during his lesson. The calculation questions, comprising three sub-questions, aimed to gauge how well the students had comprehended and applied key concepts pertaining to the working principles of light in the

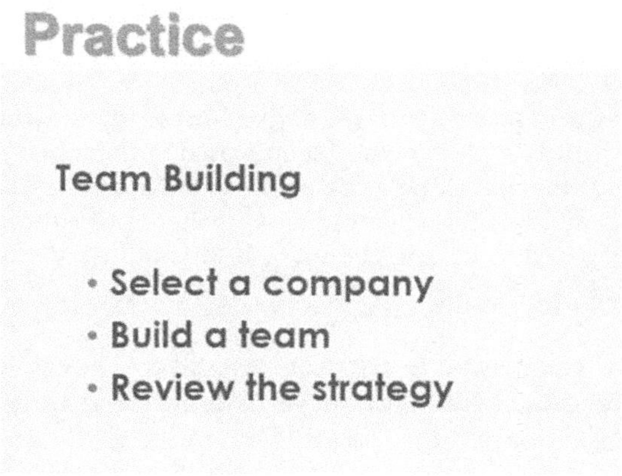

Figure 8.5 The performance-based assessment task in HR

electromagnetic field. As TC shared, to address these questions, students had to engage in problem analysis and reasoning for each question as well as developing a global understanding to approach the problems from an integrated perspective (Interview, TC).

In the competence-based courses, teachers' use of assessment instruments exhibited both similarities and differences compared to those in the skill-based courses. Similarly, the three participants in the competence-based courses utilized identical assessment instruments and items, aiming to enhance students' knowledge and skills acquisition. According to TD, examinations and tests were deemed essential in her course because 'without examination, the subject knowledge on the theoretical level might be overlooked by the students' (Interview, TD). However, given the emphasis on practical competence for future workplace in the three courses, the teachers also designed and implemented performance-based assessment tasks, such as individual or collaborative practical projects, to foster students' professional capabilities (Interview, TD, TE and TF). Figure 8.5 illustrates how TD simulated real-life work situations in her assessment tasks. She required students to select a company of interest and form groups representing a team in the company's HR department, tasked with reviewing and analyzing the corporate strategy.

Upon further inquiry regarding the rationales of their assessment design, all teachers concurred that their plans were principally influenced by the course learning objectives (Interviews). Specifically, when being asked why he did not incorporate performance-based assessment tasks, practical projects, into his assessment plan, TB explained:

> There's no need for projects in my course since the primary learning objectives focus on developing students' subject knowledge and skills. Hence various types of calculation questions, examinations, assignments, drills are sufficient. (Interview, TB)

TE, a teacher from one of the competence-based courses, also elaborated on his design of performance-based assessment tasks:

> These assessment tasks mirror the daily routines the students will encounter in their future work. The problems posed in these tasks are similar to those I faced when working as an engineer before. They are all practical issues. Students' successful completion of these tasks indicates that they are well-prepared to commence work in this industry after graduation. (Interview, TE)

To conclude, the assessment instruments and tasks teachers used were primarily determined by the course instructional objectives. If the goals revolved around subject knowledge and skills at a theoretical level, assessment instruments such as examinations, assignments and drills were effective. However, if the course teaching goals included a practical focus, teachers had to design assessment tasks with authenticity (Yuan, 2023) to provide students' opportunities to demonstrate their understanding and competence (Musial *et al.*, 2009; Popham, 2014).

8.4.3 Teacher–student interactions during assessment

With different learning and assessment objectives, teacher–student interactions in the two types of courses also varied. In the three skill-based courses, the participants predominantly guided teacher–student interactions in assessment. To initiate assessment tasks, they often utilized tools like PowerPoint, handouts or the blackboard to present questions. TA, for example, favored presenting questions on PowerPoint slides and reading them aloud in English (Classroom observation, TA). By doing this, TA attempted to 'enhance students' comprehension' and 'fostering an English learning environment' (Interview, TA). In contrast, TB and TC frequently visualized questions through translanguaging (Yuan & Yang, 2023), such as drawing diagrams together with verbal explanations in Chinese to facilitate students' comprehension of questions.

Following the clarification of questions, the three teachers allowed students time to respond, during which they monitored and observed students' progress. The nature of their monitoring varied, mainly depending on the difficulty level of the assessment tasks (Interview, TA, TB and TC). For simpler tasks like binary choice or multiple-choice questions, they observed the entire class in front of the classroom. Once most students stopped their calculations and put their pens and pencils on the table which indicated task completion, the teachers invited students' collective answer sharing and then provided feedback on their commonly made mistakes (Classroom observation, TA, TB and TC). In cases of more complex tasks, the teachers roamed the classrooms, observing students' real-time performance and providing individualized instructional scaffolding when needed. TB further elaborated why he did so during assessment:

> My student found the course content challenging. Thus, I offered them ample practices while moving around the classroom to monitor their actual learning conditions. When I noticed students struggling with certain questions, I often provided hints and clues tailored to their specific difficulties. (TB, Interview)

In the competence-based courses, the teacher–student interactions paralleled those in the skill-based courses in some respects but still exhibited distinct differences. In both course types, the teachers recognized the importance of clearly informing students about the task requirements, offering instructional scaffolding and modelling, and monitoring students' progress. However, differences emerged in the roles students played in assessment and in the strategies teachers employed for feedback. Notably, the students in the competence-based courses were afforded more opportunities to express their opinions and publicly demonstrate their work, leading to more immediate teacher feedback and enhanced teacher–student communications during assessment (Classroom observation, TD, TE and TF). When asked about why they deliberately initiated more student-sharing opportunities and teacher–student interactions, TF explained:

> If teachers want to ensure that students have truly mastered practical skills, the most effective and convenient way is to have students demonstrate what they've acquired in public... Through such demonstration, teachers can correct mistakes promptly and use face-to-face communication to help them improve, thereby gradually developing their abilities. (Interview, TF)

The approaches to providing feedback on students' assessment performance also varied among the participants. Given the constraint of class time, TE and TF often worked jointly with their students to complete the formative assessment tasks incrementally. For example, TE preferred to utilize Tencent meetings, a versatile video conferencing platform, where teachers could interact with their students in real time, to demonstrate how to construct or debug a simulation model. Throughout the process, he provided step-by-step scaffolding and regularly inquired about students' understanding. As shown in Figure 8.6, TE was working together with his students to draw the circuit diagram via this platform (Classroom observation, TE). By contrast, TD encouraged students to publicly present their group work, during which she positioned herself centrally in the classroom to interact with presenters and offered specific, constructive feedback to help them refine their work (Classroom observation, TD).

Although the students in the competence-based courses had ample opportunities for public expression, teacher feedback remained predominant (Classroom observation, TD, TE and TF). The teachers in the

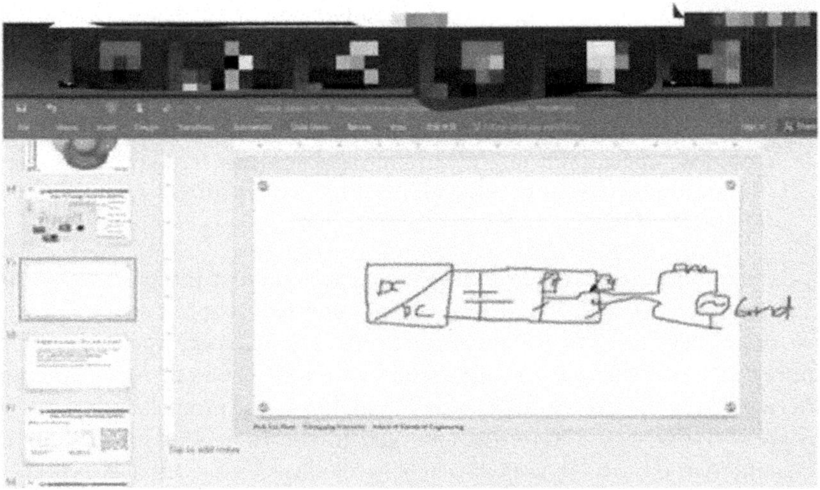

Figure 8.6 TE's demonstration of how to complete a task via Tencent meetings

competence-based courses also explained their action. For example, as TD shared:

> You know, there is no standard answer in most of my assessment tasks. It means that collective feedback is not effective in most cases because each student might have their own answer to the same question. In other words, I have to observe their performance, figure out their problems, tell them their own issues and guide them to rectify them. Only by doing this the learning objectives could be achieved. (Interview, TD)

8.4.4 The use and assessment of language

Language was identified as a critical factor that EMI teachers needed to consider in their assessment practices (Kao & Tsou, 2016). In this study, the interplay of language and assessment was reported from two perspectives: the usage and assessment of language. In the three skill-based courses, English was considered the only language for both summative and formative assessment (Classroom observation, TA, TB and TC). TA and TC even attempted to create an English language learning environment by adhering to a monolingual policy (Interview, TA and TC). Nonetheless, they rarely compelled students to use English in formative assessment, allowing them to switch to their L1, Chinese, for verbal responses and group discussions in various formative assessment tasks (Classroom observation, TA, TB and TC). The three teachers shared similar opinions towards such a decision, saying that their students' English language proficiency was not sufficient to articulate the problem-solving process explicitly. As TA stated:

> My students are freshmen with initial language proficiency challenges. In addition, the abundance of terminology in my course exacerbates these challenges, making it difficult for them to fully express themselves. (Interview, TA)

Mid-term project

Numerical Analysis

For spring 2022

You are required to select one of the two problems and complete the following three tasks:

1. Design a solver based on given requirements and write a brief report to introduce your solver and the process you design and refine it
2. Give a representation of 5 minutes to introduce your solver (with a PPT and a Word document for your detail procedure)

Problem I: Design a solver of numerical quadrature and a solver of numerical derivative.

Requirements: (1) your solver can obtain a numerical integral and derivative of a function in an interval or some discrete points. (2) your solver is fast and accurate (user can select tolerance of error). (3) your solver provides several methods for the problems. (4) you need illustrate why your solver works well, including speed and accuracy. (5) you must give many examples to show your solver's advantages.

Problem II: Design a solver of numerical ODEs.

Requirements: (1) your solver can solve ODE and ODEs, including initial-value and boundary-value problem. (2) your solver can solve include several methods, such as Euler's method, modified Euler's method, RK methods. (3) your solver can select step size or error tolerance for user's requirement. (4) you need illustrate why your solver works well, including speed and accuracy. (5) you must give many examples to show your solver's advantages.

Figure 8.7 The mid-term project in NAE

In contrast, in the competence-based courses, teachers adopted a more flexible approach to language use in assessment. While TE and TF mandated the use of English in summative assessment, TD afforded students more freedom in selecting which language to use, given the complexity of language within the subjects and her students' English language proficiency:

> In social sciences, the demands for students' language proficiency are often higher because the questions are more open-ended and rely more on students' expression. Considering my students are only sophomores, being overly strict with language use could result in their

> reluctance to participate, hindering the achievement of my teaching objectives. This is why I adopt a more flexible language policy. (Interview, TD)

To balance the relationship between content and language and ensure English remained a significant component in EMI assessment, TD introduced a compensatory strategy, awarding an additional five points for solely using English in assessment as a bonus policy (Interview, TD).

Although language development was not an explicit goal in the course learning and assessment objectives, the teachers in both types of courses still endeavored to evaluate and enhance students' language proficiency. Specifically, they intended to promote students' language development while aiding comprehension of course content along with subject learning simultaneously (Interview, TE and TF). The focus of language evaluation diverged between the two course types. In the skill-based courses, the evaluation primarily targeted students' memorization and understanding of specific concepts and terminology in quizzes or examinations (Classroom observation and Interview, TA and TC). For example, TA tested his students in remembering both the English and Chinese names of given chemical symbols in the first quiz (The first quiz, TA). TC asked his students to write down the terminology and its translation based on given definitions in different quizzes (Interview, TC). In the competence-based courses, assessment on language emphasized semantic and pragmatic aspects of language use. An illustrative case is the mid-term project in NAE (see Figure 8.7 for the task requirements and description), which included two sub-tasks involving students' academic speaking and writing skills. This project required students to draft English academic essays to articulate their products and then deliver a 5-minute English presentation introducing the assessment products (Classroom observation and Mid-term project, NAE). TF explicitly informed his students that their English language ability and academic literacy would be evaluated based on the given criteria such as language accuracy, writing styles, report format and presentation fluency.

8.5 Discussion and Implications

This study delved into six EMI teachers' classrooms and explored how they engaged with assessment in their respective courses under the influence of their pedagogical beliefs and other contextual factors. It illuminated the varying approaches to assessment across different course types and highlighted the significance of constructive alignment in EMI assessment (Biggs, 1996; Chan & Lee, 2020). Specifically, the differentiation between the skill-based and the competence-based courses, and their respective assessment approaches and language strategies, provided a rich context for understanding the multifaceted nature of EMI assessment and its unique features different from assessment in non-EMI contexts in higher education. First, the principle of constructive alignment (Biggs, 1996) was exemplified in how each course type aligned its assessment practices with its instructional goals. Similar to the constructive alignment in non-EMI contexts (Chan & Lee, 2020; Lawrence, 2018), the assessment practices of this study not only referred to the specific assessment tasks, instruments and items teachers used, but also included how teachers negotiated meaning and provide feedback during assessment. Specifically, the skill-based courses focused on the transmission of disciplinary knowledge and skills, employing summative-oriented assessment instruments and items like quizzes, tests and examinations. These methods were apt for evaluating students' understanding and retention of knowledge and their ability to apply knowledge in structured settings (Musial *et al.*, 2009; Popham, 2014; Winterson *et al.*, 2022). In contrast, the competence-based courses aimed to equip students with professional competencies. Accordingly, their assessment strategies extended beyond summative-oriented assessment instruments to include performance-based tasks like practical projects and authentic tasks. These tasks were more reflective of real-world scenarios and designed to assess not only students' subject knowledge and skills but also their ability to apply these skills in practical situations (Chan & Lee, 2020; Lawrence, 2018; Musial *et al.*, 2009).

The results also reflected the crucial role of language in EMI assessment, which is also a unique feature in EMI assessment (Sahan & Sahan, 2022). In the skill-based courses, English is predominantly used throughout the overall assessment process, underpinning a monolingual policy aimed at reinforcing students' acquisition of subject-specific English terminology and concepts in an English environment. This approach is consistent with the courses' focus on disciplinary knowledge and skills, where mastery of specific terminology is often a key to understanding core concepts. In the competence-based courses, however, the approach to language in assessment is more flexible, based on teachers' perception that performance-based assessment tasks often required more complex English language knowledge and skills as well as students' higher English language proficiency levels. This flexibility in language use did not diminish the importance of English but rather acknowledged its role as one among different tools (e.g. educational technology) in facilitating understanding and communication in professional contexts (Kao & Tsou, 2017; Li & Wu, 2018). Such an approach aligned with the courses' practical orientation, where effective communication and the ability to articulate ideas coherently are as important as technical knowledge and skills (Chan & Lee, 2021). The distinct assessment orientations and approaches to language in the two types of courses together provided a nuanced and in-depth interpretation of the rationale behind EMI teachers' assessment practices. As reported in Kao and Tsou's (2017) study, EMI teachers' perceptions and attitudes towards language influenced their assessment orientation, such as choosing between summative and formative assessments. The study further found that while teachers' perceptions of language did affect how they handled language in assessment (Mancho-Bares & Aguilar-Perez, 2020), they also actively considered other factors such as the course objectives and students' language levels to make a systematic evaluation that informed their assessment plans (Chan & Lee, 2020). Although some participants demonstrated certain language awareness in their assessment practices, the rubric provided by TE revealed a common issue among EMI teachers, that is a lack of understanding of effective integration of content and language in assessment, as the evaluation criteria presented overly focused on language aspects while overlooking the role of content (e.g. Kao & Tsou, 2017).

The study offers practical implications for EMI teachers in customizing assessment approaches and strategies in their courses. First, the two types of courses identified in this study essentially represent different instructional objectives. This differentiation aids teachers in formulating and implementing aligned and effective assessment plans. For example, in courses with a professional focus, EMI teachers should utilize performance-based assessment tasks that provide ample opportunities for students to demonstrate their learning outcomes throughout the instructional process, thereby promoting their learning and development. In addition, regarding the role of language in EMI contexts, it is crucial for teachers to thoughtfully address language issues in their assessment. This involves their contemplation about whether language should be treated as an instruction objective in their course, as this decision will subsequently influence how to align assessment tasks with teaching goals. If language development is a teaching goal, integrating the language component into assessment tasks becomes essential. Drawing from the findings, teachers can tailor assessment to students' language proficiency levels and focus on different language issues at various learning stages throughout the assessment process. For instance, for lower-grade students who are new to EMI, teachers might start by assessing their grasp of terminology and some basic language skills, such as listening and reading comprehension. As students progress to higher grades and their foundational language skills solidify, teachers can design complex assessment tasks, such as practical projects, presentation, essays, to promote students' academic English language ability, as well as enhance their English writing and speaking skills. This study also offers insights into how EMI teachers can engage in professional development in the realm of assessment. The findings show that in assessment, instructional objectives and activities, together with students' English language abilities, are important influencing factors. This further inspires EMI teachers, particularly those who were perceived to be lacking in sufficient pedagogical knowledge and skills, to cultivate their assessment capability from a holistic and integrated perspective. This encompasses developing skills in designing instructional activities, facilitating effective teacher–student interaction and giving meaningful feedback simultaneously. Only by doing so, can EMI teachers truly improve their capabilities in assessment.

8.6 Conclusion

This study provides empirical evidence concerning EMI teachers' assessment practices in the context of Chinese higher education. However, it is not without limitations. First, the majority of the participants in this study were from STEM disciplines, with only one from the social sciences. This imbalance was attributed to CU's strengths at STEM disciplines, where more EMI programs have been developed. Future research should aim to recruit participants from diverse academic backgrounds, including social sciences and liberal arts, to comprehensively explore varying characteristics of EMI assessment. Second, most of the participants in this study were experienced EMI teachers, each with over six years of teaching experience. It is recommended that future research endeavors extend their focus to examine the assessment practices of novice EMI teachers in higher education.

References

Biggs, J. (1996) Enhancing teaching through constructive alignment. *Higher Education* 32 (3), 347–364. https://doi.org/10.1007/BF00138871

Boon, J. and van der Klink, M. (2002) Competencies: The triumph of a fuzzy concept. *Academy of Human Resource Development Annual Conference*, February-March, Honolulu, HA.

Cao, H. and Yuan, R. (2020) Promoting English as a Medium of Instruction in university teaching: An action research experience. *Journal of Education for Teaching* 46 (2), 240–243. https://doi.org/10.1080/02607476.2020.1724657

Chan, C.K.Y. and Lee, K.K.W. (2021) Constructive alignment between holistic competency development and assessment in Hong Kong engineering education. *Journal of Engineering Education* 110 (2), 437–457. https://doi.org/10.1002/jee.20392

Charmaz, K. (2008) Constructionism and the grounded theory method. In J.F. Gubrium and J. Holstein (eds) *Handbook of Constructionist Research* (pp. 397–412). Guilford Press.

Creswell, J.W. (2002) *Educational Research: Planning, and Evaluating Quantitative Research.* Pearson Education.

Dafouz, E. and Camacho-Miñano, M.M. (2016) Exploring the impact of English-medium instruction on university student academic achievement: The case of accounting. *English for Specific Purposes* 44, 57–67. https://doi.org/10 1016/j.esp.2016.06.001

Dang, T.K.A., Bonar, G. and Yao, J. (2023) Professional learning for educators teaching in English-medium-instruction in higher education: A systematic review. *Teaching in Higher Education* 28 (4), 840–858. https://doi.org/10.1080/13562517.2020.1863350

De Costa, P., Green-Eneix, C. and Li, W. (2022) Problematizing EMI language policy in a transnational world: China's entry into the global higher education market. *English Today* 38 (2), 80–87. https://doi.org/10.1017/S026607842000005X

Doiz, A. and Lasagabaster, D. (2020) Dealing with language issues in English-medium instruction at university: A comprehensive approach. *International Journal of Bilingual Education and Bilingualism* 23 (3), 257–262. https://doi.org/10.1080/13670050.2020.1727409

Kao, Y.T. and Tsou, W. (2017) EMI Course assessment: A survey study of the issues. In W. Tsou and S.M. Kao (eds) *English as a Medium of Instruction in Higher Education. English Language Education* (pp. 183–205). Springer. https://doi.org/10.1007/978-981-10-4645-2_11

Lawrence, J.E. (2018) Designing a unit assessment using constructive alignment. *International Journal of Teacher Education and Professional Development* 2 (1), 30–51. https://doi.org/10.4018/ijtepd.2019010103

Li, N. and Wu, J. (2018) Exploring assessment for learning practices in the EMI classroom in the context of Taiwanese higher education. *Language Education and Assessment* 1 (1), 28–44. https://doi.org/10.29140/lea.v1n1.46

Macaro, E., Curle, S., Pun, J., *et al.* (2018) A systematic review of English medium instruction in higher education. *Language Teaching* 51 (1), 36–76.

Mancho-Barés, G. and Aguilar-Pérez, M. (2020) EMI lecturers' practices in correcting English: Resources for language teaching? *Journal of Immersion and Content-Based Language Education* 8 (2), 257–284. https://doi.org/10.1075/jicb.19011.man

McManus, S. (2008) Attributes of effective formative assessments. In the Council of Chief State School (ed.) Formative Assessment for Teachers and Students, State Collaboration on Assessment and Student Standards of the Council of Chief State School Officers.

Musial, D., Niemine, G., Thomas., J., Stoneman, R. and Burke, K. (2009) *Foundations of Meaningful Educational Assessment*. McGraw-Hill.

Pereira, D., Flores, M.A. and Niklasson, L. (2016) Assessment revisited: A review of research in Assessment and Evaluation in Higher Education. *Assessment & Evaluation in Higher Education* 41 (7), 1008–1032. https://doi.org/10.1080/02602938.2015.1055233

Popham, W.J. (2014) *Classroom Assessment: What Teachers Need to Know* (7th edn). Pearson.

Pun, J.K. and Thomas, N. (2020) English medium instruction: Teachers' challenges and coping strategies. *ELT Journal* 74 (3), 247–257. https://doi.org/10.1093/elt/ccaa024

Richards, J.C. and Pun, J. (2023) A typology of English-medium instruction. *RELC Journal* 54 (1), 216–240. https://doi.org/10.1177/0033688220968584

Sahan, K. and Şahan, Ö. (2022) Content and language in EMI assessment practices: Challenges and beliefs at an engineering faculty in Turkey. In Y. Kirkgöz and A. Karakaş (eds) *English as the Medium of Instruction in Turkish Higher Education Policy, Practice and Progress* (pp. 155–174). Springer International Publishing. https://doi.org/10.1007/978-3-030-88597-7_8

Shepard, L.A. (2000) The role of assessment in a learning culture. *Educational Researcher* 29 (7), 4–14. https://doi.org/10.3102/0013189X029007004

Wang, K. and Yuan, R. (2023) Towards an understanding of EMI teacher expertise in higher education: An intrinsic case study. *Journal of English for Academic Purposes* 101288. https://doi.org/10.1016/j.jeap.2023.101288

Winterton, J., Delamare-Le Deist, F. and Stringfellow, E. (2006) *Typology of Knowledge, Skills and Competences: Clarification of the Concept and Prototype*. Office for Official Publications of the European Communities.

Yin, R. (2016) *Qualitative Research: From Start to Finish*. The Guilford Press.

Yuan, R. (2023) Maximizing the potential of reflective practice in pre-service language teacher education: The issue of authenticity. *RELC Journal*. https://doi.org/00336882231157460.

Yuan, R. and Yang, M. (2023) Towards an understanding of translanguaging in EMI teacher education classrooms. *Language Teaching Research* 27 (4), 884–906. https://doi.org/10.1177/1362168820964123

Yuan, R., Li, M., Peng, J. and Qiu, X. (2022) English-medium instruction (EMI) teachers as 'curriculum makers' in Chinese higher education: A textual analysis. *Journal of Multilingual and Multicultural Development.* https://doi.org/10.1080/01434632.2022.2061268

Yuan, R., Liu, S. and Wang, Z. (2023) Humanising teacher education through translanguaging: Experiences from an online English-medium instruction (EMI) course. *International Journal of Multilingualism.* https://doi.org/10.1080/14790718.2023.2268120

Zhang, Y. and Jocuns, A. (2022) From natural translanguaging to planned translanguaging: Developing classroom translanguaging as pedagogy in a private university in China. *Irab World English Journal (AWEJ)* 13 (1), 313–329. https://doi.org/10.2139/ssrn.4085868

9 Established Conceptual Frameworks for Exploring English-as-a-Medium-of-Instruction and Classroom Assessment in Taiwan: New Perspectives for Reflecting on Assessment Practices

Barry Lee Reynolds and Melissa H. Yu

9.1 Introduction

This chapter discusses the established conceptual frameworks of classroom assessment in English-as-a-medium-of-instruction (EMI) contexts. Based on the discussion, this chapter aims to provide further questions and suggestions for EMI practitioners to reflect and practice in classrooms. To do so, this chapter begins with outlining the English language education and its use in Taiwanese contexts. Within such a context, the pros and cons of the established conceptual frameworks for exploring EMI classroom assessment will be analyzed to derive implications for EMI researchers and practitioners, when analyzing classroom assessments of their own. The next section summarizes, selects and synthesizes the points made by the questions, suggestions and implications emerging from the discussion in the first two sections, to highlight fundamental and practical issues for EMI practitioners to reflect on, and generate assessment ideas of their own. The conclusion suggests a new pedagogical and research direction toward triangulating EMI-relevant perspectives, such as English as an international language (EIL), bilingual education, sociolinguistics and assessment, to obtain a local–international integrated knowledge of teaching, learning, research and assessment for practice.

9.1.1 English language learning and use in Taiwan

Taiwanese students rarely have opportunities to use English outside the classroom because Taiwan is not an English-speaking context. For instance, there are only a few written English signs in Taiwan, such as 'Northbound' or 'Southbound' platforms at railway stations, or the English–Chinese bilingual names of schools and public sector institutions. English announcements are also sometimes made in shopping malls and public transport services. Other than these examples of limited visual or audio exposure to English, most Taiwanese do not listen to or speak English to communicate, study or work in their daily lives. Therefore, learning English relies heavily on English language education. However, as McKay and Brown (2016) observed, within the six-year compulsory English language education period in several countries, only a few students acquire high levels of English proficiency. The same holds true to the result of English language education in Taiwan.

For decades, English was the first and only foreign language introduced as a subject in compulsory education in Taiwan. To internationalize higher education, English language requirements were imposed at various levels, such as for course entry, school admission and university graduation. This means that students need to present the results of English language proficiency tests, proving that they have acquired certain levels of English language proficiency to become eligible for academic courses/programs. The washback effects of these language tests have encouraged examination-oriented teaching and learning. However, although the often-cited goal for Asian students learning English is to become fluent speakers (Brown & Muller, 2014), examination-oriented English language education has made it challenging for students to study English for the other purposes.

Despite the limitations of English language education, it has become the fundamental provider of learning resources for students to learn and practice English. Nevertheless, producing competent English users remains a challenge if English language education continues to be examination oriented. Additionally, as students rarely use English outside the classroom, it is reasonable to assume that learning and using English practically mostly occur inside classrooms, including using it as a medium for teaching, communicating and learning.

9.1.2 Evolving roles of English in Taiwanese educational settings

The global status of English is an impetus for educational reforms in non-English-speaking countries. One such example is the creation of a quasi-English-speaking environment in Taiwan. To this end, since the 2000s, the Ministry of Education (MOE) has introduced several language plans and programs to enhance the English language proficiency of students at all levels. These include Challenge 2008, the National Development Plan and the Aim for Top University Project (MOE, 2008), highlighting the English language's function as a medium of communication in (non)educational settings. Following this, universities were encouraged to establish 'a foreign student affairs section that assists foreign students with visa applications and extensions, as well as dealing with most matters relating to daily life' (MOE, 2008: 32) that operates in English or Chinese, depending on which language is chosen for communication. In 2021, the MOE launched the 'Program on Bilingual Education for Students in College' to continue establishing English–Chinese bilingual environments, which aimed at an 'overall enhancement of teachers' ability to teach in English,' 'students' ability to learn in English' and 'training bilingual professionals in specialized areas' (MOE, 2022: 77).

To create an English–Chinese bilingual environment, universities offer training courses to students and staff that enhance their English skills. For instance, universities provide students with the following courses: English for Specific Academic Purposes (Chou, 2018), English for General Academic Purposes (Chou, 2018) and first-year students' English. Extracurricular English language courses are also available to students or staff (MOE, 2022; Reynolds & Yu, 2018, 2021a, 2021b, 2022), focusing on communication or academic English proficiency development. All English language classes are provided in parallel with courses taught in English, to establish English-using contexts. Another example is the leading role in internationalizing higher education is played by EMI courses, in which the MOE encourages lecturers to conduct classes in English to attract international students, enhance Taiwanese universities' world competitiveness and benefit home students who plan for further study in Taiwan or abroad or to speak fluent English in the workplace (MOE, 2022).

As indicated, at universities in Taiwan, the role of English has shifted from simply a language subject to a medium for international communication, to being a gatekeeper for EMI course entry and, further, to a medium of instruction for teachers and a medium of education for students to study academic subjects. Thus, English has multiple functions and pragmatic dimensions, further highlighting the coexistent relationship between several roles and functions of English within a context (Chen & Kraklow, 2015). English as a medium for teaching, learning and assessment in EMI settings is one such example.

9.2 Literature Review

This literature review discusses how researchers have defined EMI to frame studies on classroom practice and assessment, with a focus on the limitations of the cited definitions and their impact on research. It also considers how researchers have related EMI to conceptual frameworks in other fields, such as EIL and authenticity, thereby expanding the scope of research. Finally, suggestions proposed by previous studies on classroom assessment in EMI or other contexts are reevaluated, aiming to highlight the compatibility of these suggestions with practical issues concerning teaching and assessment practices.

9.2.1 The established and emergent conceptual lens of EMI classroom practice

Researchers in Taiwan have defined EMI as conceptually framing studies of language use for teaching, learning and assessment (see Table 9.1). Most studies claimed that they defined EMI practices by referring to definitions of EMI given by Western researchers, such as Dearden (2014) and Macaro *et al.* (2018) (e.g. Chou, 2018; Li & Wu, 2018, 2021), to explore classroom assessment. In addition to direct citations of Western scholars' definitions (e.g. Chou, 2018), one approach to practice was that the studies touched on EMI by briefly stating that (1) EMI stood for English as the medium of instruction (e.g. Kao & Tsou, 2017) and (2) EMI was used as an alternative to other terminological counterparts, such as 'English-taught courses' (e.g. Chen, 2019: 987). These exemplified definitions by scholars appear to be consistent with those of EMI practices by the MOE, which focus on English language use.

Another approach to the practice was to reinterpret the definitions provided to various degrees. For instance, Li and Wu (2018: 2) claimed that they drew on Macaro *et al.*'s (2018) definition of EMI to frame their study of EMI classroom assessments. Nevertheless, Li and Wu (2018: 2)

Table 9.1 Examples of how the existing definitions of EMI were referred to or reinterpreted in studies on classroom assessment in Taiwan

Definitions of EMI	Studies
Direct quotation: 'The use of the English language to teach academic subjects in countries or jurisdictions where the first language (L1) of the majority of the population is not English' (Dearden, 2014: 4).	Chou (2018: 611)
Original definition of EMI: 'The use of the English language to teach academic subjects (other than English itself) in countries or jurisdictions where the first language of the majority of the population is not English' (Macaro *et al.*, 2018: 37). Reinterpretation: 'Despite variation in terminology and its form of application, EMI generally refers to the practice of using English as a vehicular language to transmit academic knowledge' (Li & Wu, 2018: 2).	Li and Wu (2018: 2).
Original definition of EMI: (see Dearden, 2014: 4; Macaro *et al.*, 2018: 37 above) Reinterpretation: 'The use of English to teach academic subjects in a setting where English is a second or a foreign language' (Li & Wu, 2021: 124).	Li and Wu (2021: 124)

reinterpreted the definition, stating, 'EMI generally refers to the practice of using English as a vehicular language to transmit academic knowledge', implying the naturalness of English as a tool for knowledge transmission. In this instance, Li and Wu (2018) did not specify the context in which the EMI practice occurred, who was involved, or the other relevant local variables. Three years later, Li and Wu (2021) pointed out the wide contexts in which EMI assessment may occur (see Table 9.1). The evolving notion of EMI in Li and Wu's studies on assessments from 2018 and 2021 echoed Macaro's (2018: 19) comment on the definitions of EMI: they were 'deliberately open to challenge'. Thus, the approach to EMI practice appears to be as open as possible, thereby yielding space for capturing the changeable nature of local EMI practices.

Observing the varying nature of EMI practices, Dimova and Kling (2022) analyzed the existing EMI conceptual framework by categorizing EMI contexts into three sociolinguistic categories: (a) non-English-medium universities in non-English-dominant settings; (b) Anglophone university branch campuses in non-English-dominant contexts; and (c) universities in English-dominant settings. These international categories of EMI practices illustrate the adaptable nature of the contexts in which the EMI courses were implemented. This further raised our awareness of the need to avoid being confined by preconceived notions of EMI practice when understanding EMI classroom assessments in Taiwanese contexts. Such awareness, for instance, helps to consider local EMI practice beyond the established scope. The review of Chou's (2018) study on EMI assessments below is a case in point.

Chou (2018) commented that Dearden's (2014) definition of EMI practice is broad, making it convenient to apply this conceptual framework to explore EMI in many contexts. Although this convenience was beneficial for providing a quick overview of EMI practices, it hindered studies from delving into the details of the adaptation of local EMI practices. Within the broad definition of EMI (see Table 9.1), Chou's (2018) research exemplified how universities offered partial and full EMI courses. Partial EMI courses allowed code-switching when lecturing; however, the learning materials and assessments needed to be in entirely in English. Full EMI courses were conducted only in English. These two types of EMI courses represent how the cited conceptual lens only roughly corresponded to local EMI practices. Simultaneously, they reveal the local adaptations of EMI practices. As can be seen, even though some definitions of EMI are well recognized, they are not limitation free.

The discussion above indicates a call for the conceptual openness of the research and pedagogical scope, allowing for a quick overview of EMI practice. Nevertheless, this openness in turn posed an obstacle for researchers or practitioners in obtaining local knowledge about the development of EMI practices, which have both international and national variations. Thus, a question for EMI assessment practitioners and researchers to consider was how classroom assessment was implemented: entirely in English; entirely in Chinese; half in English and half in Chinese (i.e. bilingual); partly in English or through context-dependent use of English or other alternatives, and why.

Reviewing more literature to address the abovementioned question, we observed there were alternative directions in which Western-related concepts of EMI were introduced into EMI practice in local settings. For instance, Chou (2018) identified the local varieties of EMI courses. Dimova and Kling (2022) also grouped varieties of EMI practices. Both demonstrated flexible adaptation to suit local contexts, covering a spectrum of EMI varieties. Local adaptations, in turn, have demonstrated how predefined conceptual frameworks failed to account for the adaptable or emergent nature of EMI practices. Existing studies often emphasize EMI to internationalize local higher education (e.g. Li & Wu, 2021) rather than localizing EMI as a part of internationalizing local higher education. The canonical stance toward EMI practice raises concerns about local needs when conducting classroom assessments in Taiwanese EMI settings. In this regard, McKay and Brown (2016) framed questions for EMI practitioners to analyze local needs when adapting Western-based EMI concepts and devise local EMI assessments.

Discussing local needs in EMI provision, McKay and Brown (2016) proposed that needs assessment should be conducted to address local pedagogical concerns, such as:

(1) whether using English to teach and learn increases educational burden or value;
(2) whether using English alone or English along with other languages for instruction is adjustable according to the local educational and social conditions;
(3) whether students have sufficient English language proficiency to meet their learning needs in EMI classes; and
(4) how students whose English language proficiency has not reached the level to apply for EMI entry benefit from EMI practice.

Inspired by McKay and Brown's (2016) inquiries, we consider the following questions to analyze local needs in implementing classroom assessment in Taiwanese EMI settings:

(1) whether assessment in English encourages or discourages learning;
(2) whether using English to undertake classroom assessment is a choice or necessity, that is, assessment in English only or English along with other language(s);
(3) whether the focus of classroom assessment is on the content of professional subjects, language, or both; and
(4) whether classroom assessment aims to adjust teaching, enhance learning, monitor the learning process/progress, know the learning results, etc.

EMI researchers and practitioners have raised these questions to consider the purposes and needs of classroom assessments. Non-EMI researchers have related EMI practices to language teaching or learning concepts, because of the broadening of the research scope of their fields. For instance, Pinner (2016) linked the concept of authenticity to learning English as a global language and learning academic subjects in EMI contexts. According to Pinner (2016: 142), 'Authenticity, as it relates to EMI, is not so much just about the process of authenticating the language but also it is a question of making the entire subject authentic'.

Pinner (2016: 143) regarded English as 'a basic skill' to increase learning value because English has made using language 'as a tool to understand the content' of academic subjects real. This has, in turn, added authenticity to learning academic subjects and languages. The win–win situation demonstrated that learning English did not necessarily rely on learning English as a subject. Instead, when English became an acquired skill for students, the 'content' of teaching and learning academic subjects, that is, advanced language acquisition through real-world pragmatic exposure, took place. This made it reasonable to assume that authenticating learning languages and academic subjects occurred independently and interdependently in EMI classroom assessment. In this case, classroom assessments took place in a real-world bilingual learning environment, as the MOE (2022) proposed, although not in a simulated one. The implication for EMI practitioners is to see classroom assessment as an opportunity for students who are competent bilingual users of English to undertake assessment, focusing on what they really know about the subjects through English in the real-world bilingual learning environment.

Another example of broadening the research scope is taking a translanguaging perspective to explore EMI practices in Taiwan. These studies have focused on how teachers (Kao *et al.*, 2021) and students (Huang, 2021) perceive EMI provisions. In these studies, translanguaging refers to the process in which bilinguals or multilinguals use language repertoires, which are syntheses of resources of all types, to negotiate meaning. This way of reconceptualizing EMI practices in Taiwan aligns with the aim of MOE programs, to create a bilingual environment and enhance bilingual education at the tertiary level (see 9.2.1 Evolving roles of English in Taiwanese educational settings). Therefore, to understand EMI assessment within the created but real-world bilingual classrooms in Taiwan, the following questions are worth rethinking:

(1) Are students encouraged to use Chinese, English or both, to complete assessment tasks?
(2) If students choose to use Chinese and/or English to undertake classroom assessments, do their choice(s) influence their learning and the final assessment results?

(3) Is pedagogical adjustment necessary to address students' testing needs in language?
(4) Finally, if advanced language acquisition was seen as an integral part of learning from classroom assessment (e.g. Kao & Tsou, 2017; Li & Wu, 2021), the pedagogical concern is: What kind of assessment tasks should be introduced in EMI contexts to increase learning value for lecturers?

As indicated, some researchers tended to frame studies on EMI practices by relying on established definitions of EMI, thereby resulting in a call for the reinterpretation of given knowledge about EMI practices. Nevertheless, the other scholars drew on other language- or education-related concepts that may not be directly related, but are relevant to EMI classroom assessments, to form an additional conceptual lens for capturing the nuances of studies in this area. In either way, we suggest that local EMI practice, including assessment, should be examined from multiple and mixed, local and international perspectives.

The above discussion reflects the addition of local innovations of EMI classroom assessment to the established theoretical constructs of EMI. Since there is no all-purpose approach to EMI in various contexts, any approach or suggestion, such as the Western-based test framework to build EMI assessment template below, in the existing literature may require adaption or innovations. These emergent theoretical innovations serve as an additional set of concepts through which the practical dimensions of EMI classroom assessments are examined next.

9.2.2 Classroom assessment in various contexts and its implications

In English as a Foreign Language (EFL) and English as a Second Language contexts, the established literature has discussed standardized, large-scale testing more than classroom assessments (Cheng *et al.*, 2008). The same holds for studies on assessments in the Taiwanese EMI context (Li & Wu, 2018). Thus far, existing studies have discussed the impact of standardized English language proficiency test results on EMI practice, such as setting course entry (e.g. Chou, 2018), and less about how EMI teachers assess students' learning (e.g. Kao & Tsou, 2017) or students' performance in EMI classroom assessment and its impact on content learning of subjects.

Additionally, studies on students' English learning or assessment have usually been framed within the scope of standardized testing systems. Examples of this are Chou's (2018) study on students' spoken performance in EMI classrooms, by grouping participants based on their university first-year 'English placement test scores'. Against this backdrop, the first pedagogical concern was how students' English, based on large-scale testing, reflected their actual use of English in classroom assessments and learning academic subjects in EMI contexts. For instance, did those students who obtained high listening and speaking scores guarantee their success in studying academic subjects in English?

Regarding teaching, the existing studies considerably rely on Western-based (e.g. International English Language Testing System (IELTS), Test of English as a Foreign Language (TOEFL), large-scale testing frameworks, such as Common European Framework of Reference (CEFR), or the other English language proficiency results to develop and explore EMI teaching and assessment materials. For instance, researchers make suggestions by providing teachers with a ready-to-use template to design classroom assessment activities according to the CEFR (Kao & Tsou, 2017: 198). This example pointed to a lack of EMI teaching, learning and assessment repertoire, which was built based on and for the local EMI practice. EMI assessment template proposed by Kao and Tsou (2017) provides a good example of assessment repertoire built by local EMI practitioners despite the fact that the assessment template was established within the Western-based testing framework.

However, building an assessment template within the testing framework of CEFR (Kao & Tsou, 2017) is not limitation-free and some pints need to be furthered below. The first point to be considered was what CEFR meant to local EMI teachers, whose professionalism had nothing to do with language. If teachers who worked in non-language disciplines were unfamiliar with what CEFR stood for, then the concern was whether they had a good understanding of testing frameworks for English language proficiency to design and implement classroom assessment activities (e.g. Kao & Tsuo, 2017). The second point is that since the assessment activities are planned within a large-scale testing framework, adaptation for local EMI practice is inevitably necessary. In this case, the question is whether local EMI practitioners have sufficient professional knowledge and skills to adapt ready-to-use test activities, and if not, what professional training they need in order to effectively adapt the existing EMI assessment activities.

Instead of suggesting classroom assessment activities based on standardized testing systems, an alternative was to give EMI teachers examples of local EMI classroom assessments drawn from a range of disciplines, to reflect on, adapt and generate assessment ideas that fit their own contexts. For example, EMI teachers who worked with the same group of students can share their ideas, activities and reflection for testing students within or across the disciplines in the same university. This can also be applied to EMI teachers who worked in the same discipline at different universities. By doing so, the EMI assessment template and repertoire was established by local EMI teachers collaboratively, catering for the group and individual needs in planning and implementing assessments.

As mentioned, English plays different roles in classroom assessments in the EIL and EMI contexts. English is an academic subject that is taught, learned, tested and practiced in EIL-oriented classroom practice, whereas it serves as a medium for teaching, learning and testing academic subjects in EMI classrooms. In EIL contexts, McKay and Brown (2016: 80) stressed that 'classroom tests are typically used to assess what students know or can do in the language regarding what is being taught in a specific classroom or program'. Borrowing McKay and Brown's (2016) point regarding the primary purpose of classroom assessment, the suggestion was that classroom assessment in the EMI context could also be seen as a test approach, through which students present what they know or can do with the professional knowledge and skills acquired in a subject or program. In this situation, the focus of classroom assessment in the context of EMI is primarily on professional subjects. English knowledge and skills are not a major concern here, although they have additional educational value. English in EMI classroom assessments plays a pragmatic role in helping teachers and students implement and undertake assessment tasks.

Furthermore, as McKay and Brown (2016: 80) argued, 'classroom tests are relatively low-stakes and can be used at the beginning of a course for diagnostic assessment purposes, middle of a course for progress assessment purposes and end of a course for achievement assessment purposes'. This has implications for EMI practitioners in considering the purposes of classroom assessment, such as diagnosing assessment at the beginning of an EMI course, monitoring the learning process and progress in the middle of an EMI course, and composing achievement assessments at the end of an EMI course. These purpose-oriented classroom assessments inspire EMI practitioners to view classroom assessment as a low-stakes testing method that gives teachers opportunities to adjust their teaching and allow students to make mistakes and try again with less anxiety about their final grades. In turn, low-stakes tests remind EMI teachers of the importance of contextual reasons for (re)planning and (re)adjusting for future classroom assessments and other practices.

As Davison and Leung (2009: 401) observed, 'teachers are involved at all stages of the assessment cycle', including planning assessments, developing test activities and grading students' performances in EFL contexts. In addition, it is common for EFL teachers to use English to assess students because they are language teachers. However, as EFL teacher education rarely provides pre-service teachers with training for classroom assessments, they tend to count on their experience in tests to develop (classroom) assessments (Berger, 2012). This is also true for EMI teachers who require professional training in classroom assessments. Most EMI teachers do not have language teaching experience, let alone any experience in planning assessments in English (e.g. Li & Wu, 2018, 2021). Therefore, it is necessary to conduct an assessment to understand why and on what EMI teachers want to test their students. Teachers' reasons for conducting tests influence the frequency and timing of assessments, the methods they use and how they implement an assessment (Cheng & Fox,

2017). It is also important to understand what knowledge and training EMI teachers prioritize when fulfilling their professional needs.

In EFL contexts, students' primary role is as language learners inside the classroom, while aiming to become users of the language outside it. For example, based on a four-skill curriculum, students learned skills, practiced using them (Hinkel, 2006) and were tested. Additionally, students acquired a prescribed knowledge of English from their teachers and textbooks. This perspective of English language teaching, learning, use and assessment forms an essential component of EFL education (Seidlhofer, 2011). In contrast, EMI education reflects a less prescriptive understanding of English language use. The focus of EMI education is on English as a skill, to convey the extent to which students have acquired the knowledge and skills of professional subjects (e.g. Pinner, 2016). Students in the EMI context are primarily English users; they learn academic subjects by listening to lecturers and peers, verbally responding to lecture content and learning activities, reading learning and assessment materials and writing assessment tasks (Kao & Tsou, 2017). Students' roles as learner-users provide them with ample exposure to immersion-based classroom practices, thereby facilitating language acquisition. In simple terms, students are assessed as language learners in EFL classrooms, but as language users in EMI classrooms. The key point is to view EMI classroom assessments not only as a testing method but also as an opportunity for students to use English as a skill for listening, speaking, reading and writing as professionals in real-world EMI class settings.

While it was acceptable to assume that 'learners have achieved the language proficiency needed to learn about the subject', which was usually high in an EMI context (Pinner, 2016: 138), it did not necessarily mean that all students in the same EMI class or context had the same language repertoire for learning and assessment. It was also uncertain how relevant the implications and suggestions from existing studies on EMI practice were to classroom assessments in other EMI contexts. Therefore, it became pedagogically significant to understand what transpired during classroom assessment and the underlying theories that supported this practice.

9.3 Rethinking Pedagogical Inquiries and Implications

The first two sections provided a contextual and conceptual background for implementing classroom assessments in the Taiwanese EMI setting. This section establishes theoretical and practical foundations for posing new questions and makes suggestions that are directly relevant to classroom assessment and its context. These synthesized questions and implications aim to become part of the teaching repertoire for EMI practitioners, encouraging them to reflect on their teaching contexts. By doing so, EMI teachers can consider their teaching environment, students' English proficiency, assessment purposes and appropriate assessment activities.

9.3.1 Syntheses and reappraisal of inquiries into and implications for EMI classroom assessment

Based on the above, the selected key points below are highlighted either because they have not been adequately addressed or because they carry fundamental pedagogical value. Although these points are selective, they are intended to provide EMI practitioners and researchers with a foundation to consider the concepts underlying classroom assessment. Furthermore, the synthesized points and questions form a collection of classroom assessment ideas and principles for teacher training or scholarly discussions in the context of EMI practice. This collection is not meant for EMI teachers from various disciplines to apply directly to their classroom assessment. Instead, it is a tool for EMI practitioners to reflect on and brainstorm their ideas, which are directly relevant to the specific learning needs of their students, the assessment process and teaching objectives and purposes. The following synthesis is divided into three subsections, and presented as bullet points and questions: EMI contexts, EMI practitioners and assessing bilingual/multilingual students and learning.

9.3.1.1 EMI contexts

Most of the following points were made based on the varying nature of EMI practices. The following points have been covered because one objective of the MOE is to create a bilingual learning environment:

- Some universities offer different types of EMI courses (e.g. partial- and full-EMI courses) (Chou, 2018), others only provide students with one type of EMI course (English-only courses), but Chinese is used when necessary (e.g. Kao & Tsou, 2017).
- A few universities have several international students in EMI courses, while others have a few international students (Li & Wu, 2018), and some have only Taiwanese (Li & Wu, 2018) or native Chinese-speaking students in EMI courses. The number of international students remains low (Chou, 2018; MOE, 2022).
- Most universities have Taiwanese EMI course teachers, while few have Taiwanese and international teachers.
- The MOE (2022) aims to create a bilingual learning environment for higher education. However, the extent to which university learning environments have become bilingual is uncertain. It is also uncertain whether students have the 'bilingual academic literacy' to undertake classroom assessments (Li & Wu, 2021: 133–134).

Guiding Questions:

Reflecting on the background information about Taiwanese EMI, consider the following questions in relation to your teaching or research context:

- To what extent is each of these points relevant to your research and/or teaching context(s), and how?

- At your institute, is there any top-down language policy to 'advise' teachers to teach and assess students in English, and how? For example, do institutes suggest that teachers teach and assess students entirely in (American) English, or do you believe you can adhere to the traditional concept of EMI – the English-only principle when teaching – as some teachers do (e.g. Li & Wu, 2018)?
- In your institute, is there any alternative to the so-called traditional EMI courses, 'Chinese is not allowed (Chou, 2018: 611)'? Are all assessments conducted in English? Is it likely to have approximately 80%, 60% or 50% of the assessment content in English as an alternative, depending on teachers' observations of students' English?
- Is it possible to 'customize' EMI courses/assessments for different groups of students with varying English language proficiencies? For example, how do Taiwanese students whose English language proficiency test results are insufficient for EMI courses benefit from EMI teaching and assessment?

9.3.1.2 EMI practitioners

Owing to a lack of teaching workforce to provide EMI, those 'who have obtained their doctoral degree from English-speaking countries' were often assigned as EMI teachers based on the assumption that they were immersed in English-speaking contexts and had become competent users of English to teach EMI courses (Tsui, 2017: 165). Approximately a decade ago, the MOE sponsored several faculty development programs to produce competent EMI practitioners (Tsui, 2017). The following points were crucial to these development programs:

- Taiwanese or international teachers from (non-)English-speaking countries constitute the teaching workforce for EMI courses. Taiwanese EMI teachers made up the majority of studies on EMI classroom assessments (e.g. Li & Wu, 2018).
- It seems that few needs assessments were conducted to understand what professional support EMI teachers need to plan and implement classroom assessments.
- Local EMI teachers were often required to acquire adequate English language proficiency to be able to use English to teach and assess students (Li & Wu, 2021; Tsui, 2017). However, what EMI teachers' English proficiency means for classroom practice and students has never been the focus.
- Teachers should be familiar with the purposes and benefits of classroom assessment for teaching and learning in any teaching context. They should also acquire a fundamental knowledge of classroom assessment. As Dimova and Kling (2022: 139–140) note, the 'evidence shows that in authentic content assessment situations, content teachers make ad hoc decisions based on personal interpretation of

institutional and/or departmental language policies and assessment'.

Guiding Questions:

- To what extent do Taiwanese and international EMI teachers agree that their English is internationally intelligible to bilingual and multilingual students, for teaching purposes or classroom assessments?
- What professional training do EMI teachers require to help them effectively plan and implement classroom assessments?
- To what extent do teachers feel confident about using English to implement classroom assessments, such as paraphrasing, clarifying test questions and giving feedback, and how?
- If students are competent Chinese–English bilinguals, is it possible to plan and implement bilingual classroom assessments, such as bilingual written or oral assessment tasks, and do students choose to undertake assessments in the language in which they feel confident?
- What do teachers want to learn from assessing students in EMI classrooms, and why? To what extent do teachers agree that assessing students helps in teaching, learning or both and how?
- If EMI teachers view classroom assessments as low-stakes, what do they benefit from? Do assessments help teachers teach (see 9.2.2 Classroom assessment in various contexts and its implications) an EMI course, to diagnose teaching, monitor the progress of teaching/learning and examine students' learning achievements?

9.3.1.3 Assessing bilingual/multilingual students and learning

It is unlikely that students who attend EMI classes come from similar linguistic backgrounds. For example, an EMI class may comprise monolingual, bilingual or multilingual English speakers. It is not easy for EMI teachers to assess such mixed groups, which adds to their teaching workload. Thus, the following points and questions cater to classroom assessment in relation to learning:

- In EMI classrooms, students are typically English users, sometimes learners and/or both.
- In EMI classrooms, students listen, speak, read and write while undertaking classroom assessments. EMI practitioners should be aware of students' English language proficiency and the four skills required to learn professional subjects (Le & Tang, 2022) and use English as a professional skill.
- Language assessment has been identified as a way to facilitate language learning (e.g. Berger, 2012; Cheng & Fox, 2017).
- EMI classroom assessment has been approved for consolidating academic subject learning (e.g. Li & Wu, 2021).

- EMI classroom assessment provides students with opportunities to authenticate their learning of academic subjects and English simultaneously (Pinner, 2016).

Guiding Questions:

- Who makes up most of the EMI classroom, and what is their professional and linguistic background?
- Are students in EMI classrooms treated as learners or users of knowledge and skills about academic subjects in addition to English, and why? How does this relate to classroom assessment?
- Is learning English or an academic subject the major objective of EMI classroom assessment? What does assessment-based learning prioritize? In this case, what should EMI teachers do to make learning subject knowledge and skills a learning priority, learning language as an additional educational value, or both?
- If EMI teachers use presentations as a classroom assessment activity, to what extent do teachers agree that students should discuss academic subjects as professionals? Does this so-called authentic learning through assessments use the acquired professional knowledge of academic subjects for presentations and use English to discuss professional subjects?

9.4 Conclusion

The points and questions above aim to help EMI practitioners and researchers reflect on, and consider classroom assessment, from the perspective of learning context, national curriculum, EMI teachers' and students' need for EMI courses, and other variables specific to teaching/researching conditions. This chapter identifies that adaptation and variation in EMI practices are inevitable in Taiwanese contexts. The adaptations and variations discussed here make EMI a new teaching approach for local teachers, to use their acquired professional and language skills to deliver instruction, conduct assessments and make adjustments according to local variables. Moreover, EMI is a learning approach that encourages students to play dual user–learner roles in English, and to use their professional knowledge and language to engage in various academic and assessment tasks. In such EMI classrooms, teachers and students should no longer be passive education providers and receivers, respectively, but become autonomous educational participants and partners.

As discussed, although the concept of EMI is internationally established, restructuring EMI practices is inevitable when it is realized in several parts of the world, to address local teachers' and students' needs. Therefore, pedagogically, the transmission approach is not recommended because local EMI course tutors should not be only (1) consumers of

Western, institution-based knowledge about EMI practice; (2) teaching technicians to conform to a set of professional knowledge and transmit such a knowledge base to their students without any adaptation; and (3) proponents of the one-size-fits-all teaching method. Instead, EMI teachers should become familiar with a wide range of pedagogical methods and resources available, have the autonomy to teach beyond external constraints imposed and take a reflective approach to observe, reflect on and change teaching to respond to teaching/learning needs. Rejecting the former three and accepting the latter three roles, EMI practitioners should be able to independently seek pedagogical alternatives, (re)theorize their EMI practice to engage in context-sensitive practices and understand locally applicable ways to conduct EMI courses and assessments, which can be altered when necessary. This continual cycle of seeking pedagogical alternatives, (re)theorizing teaching and classroom assessment to produce context-sensitive practice and consistently reflecting on EMI practice and altering it for improvement, should be able to maximize the quality of EMI practice.

Living in the postmethod era, we acknowledge the multiple phases and diversity of local EMI classroom assessments, and thereby the difficulties in exemplifying all practical techniques to help EMI practitioners assess students. This chapter also rejects a unifying approach to EMI classroom assessment, because knowledge about EMI classroom assessment is always local, representing alternative forms of interpretation and realization of EMI assessment from one discipline to another. Hence, this chapter does not aim to provide EMI practitioners with prepackaged knowledge and ideas about assessing students in EMI classes. Instead, it poses several questions to challenge any normative assumptions about EMI classroom assessment. The questions further serve as a starting point from which EMI teachers can adapt existing classroom assessment ideas, or generate new assessment ideas that suit their teaching contexts.

In terms of research, we recommend that multiple ethnographic case studies, within a single institute or across institutes, be conducted and comprehensive techniques be applied to collect data about local classroom assessment in local EMI settings (i.e. multiple data sources). Such a suggestion is made based on a call for providing insiders' (local teachers/students') perspectives on their needs for teaching and learning in EMI settings. After all, EMI practitioners and students are the participants of EMI classroom assessments, not others. Finally, we recommend the necessity of problematizing the givens (i.e. the established knowledge about EMI classroom assessment) and questioning the terms/frames (i.e. the definitions of EMI) that researchers deal with. Thus, it will be beneficial for researchers to look into alternative research directions that best serve their interests.

Acknowledgement

The research reported in this article was supported by the Education Fund of the Macao SAR (HSS-UMAC-2021-02).

References

Berger, A. (2012) Creating language-assessment literacy: A model for teacher education. In J. Hüttner, B. Mehlmauer-Larcher, S. Reichl and B. Schiftner (eds) *Theory and Practice in EFL Teacher Education: Bridging the Gap* (pp. 57–82). Multilingual Matters.

Brown, P.S. and Muller, T. (2014) Introduction. In M. Theron, J. Adamson, P.S. Brown and S. Herder (eds) *Exploring EFL Fluency in Asia* (pp. 1–7). Palgrave MacMillan.

Chen, R.T.H. (2019) University lecturers' experiences of teaching in English in an international classroom. *Teaching in Higher Education* 24 (8), 987–999. https://doi.org/10.1080/13562517.2018.1527764

Chen, Y.-L. and Kraklow, D. (2015) Taiwanese college students' motivation and engagement for English learning in the context of internationalization at home: A comparison of students in EMI and non-EMI programs. *Journal of Studies in International Education* 19, 46–64. https://doi.org/10.1177/1028315314533607

Cheng, L.Y. and Fox, J. (2017) *Assessment in the Language Classroom: Teachers Supporting Student Learning*. Palgrave Macmillan.

Cheng, L., Rogers, W.T. and Wang, X. (2008) Assessment purposes and procedures in ESL/EFL classrooms. *Assessment & Evaluation in Higher Education* 33 (1), 9–32. https://doi.org/10.1080/02602930601122555

Chou, M.H. (2018) Speaking anxiety and strategy use for learning English as a foreign language in full and partial English-medium instruction contexts. *TESOL Quarterly* 52 (3), 611–633. https://doi.org/10.1002/tesq.455

Davison, C. and Leung, C. (2009) Current issues in English language teacher-based assessment. *TESOL Quarterly* 43 (3), 393–415. https://doi.org/10.1002/j.1545-7249.2009.tb00242.x

Dearden, J. (2014) *English as a Medium of Instruction: A Growing Global Phenomenon*. British Council. https://www.britishcouncil.org/education/ihe/knowledge-centre/english-language-higher-education/report-english-medium-instruction

Dimova, S. and Kling, J. (2022) Emerging assessment needs and solutions in EMI in higher education. *Journal of English-Medium Instruction* 1 (2), 137–152. https://doi.org/10.1075/jemi.00002.edi

Hinkel, E. (2006) Current perspectives on teaching the four skills. *TESOL Quarterly* 40, 109–131. https://doi.org/10.2307/40264513

Huang, Y.P. (2021) Translanguaging in EMI higher education in Taiwan: Learner perception an agency. In B. Will and T. Wenli (eds) *Translanguaging Practices in Asia: Theories, Frameworks and Implementation in Higher Education* (pp. 163–180). Springer.

Kao, S.M., Tsuo, W. and Chen, F. (2021) Translanguaging strategies for EMI instruction in Taiwanese higher education. In W. Tsou and W. Baker (eds) *Translanguaging Practices in Asia: Theories, Frameworks and Implementation in Higher Education* (pp. 81–100). Springer.

Kao, Y.T. and Tsou, W. (2017) EMI course assessment: A survey study of the issues. In W. Tsou and S.M. Kao (eds) *English as a Medium of Instruction in Higher Education: Implementations and Classroom Practices in Taiwan English Language Education* (Vol. 8, pp. 183–205). Springer. https://doi.org/10.1007/978-981-10-4645-2_11

Le, T. and Tang, C.W. (2022) Towards a comprehensive effectiveness scale for university students' perception of English medium instruction in Vietnam and Taiwan: An importance-performance analysis. *Journal of Multilingual and Multicultural Development* 1–18. https://doi.org/10.1080/01434632.2022.2117366

Li, N. and Wu, J. (2018) Exploring assessment for learning practices in the EMI classroom in the context of Taiwanese higher education. *Language Education & Assessment* 1 (1), 28–44. http://dx.doi.org/10.29140/lea.v1n1.46

Li, N. and Wu, J. (2021) Assessment practices in the EMI classroom in Chinese-speaking higher education contexts: Challenges and considerations. In L.I.-W. Su, H. Cheung and J.R.W. Wu (eds) *Rethinking EMI: Multidisciplinary Perspectives from Chinese Speaking Regions* (pp. 124–140). Routledge.

Macaro, E. (2018) *English Medium Instruction*. Oxford University Press.

Macaro, E., Curle, S., Pun, J., An, J. and Dearden, J. (2018) A systematic review of English medium instruction in higher education. *Language Teaching* 51, 36–76. https://doi.org/10.1017/S0261444817000350

McKay, S.L. and Brown, D.J. (2016) *Teaching and Assessing EIL in Local Contexts Around the World*. Routledge.

Ministry of Education (MOE) (2008) *2008 Education in Taiwan*. Ministry of Education. https://stats.moe.gov.tw/files/ebook/Education_in_Taiwan/2008-2009_Education_in_Taiwan.pdf

Ministry of Education (MOE) (2022) *2022 Education in Taiwan*. Ministry of Education. https://stats.moe.gov.tw/files/ebook/Education_in_Taiwan/2022-2023_Education_in_Taiwan.pdf

Reynolds, B.L. and Yu, M.H. (2018) Addressing the language needs of administrative staff in Taiwan's internationalised higher education: Call for an English as a lingua franca curriculum to increase communicative competence and willingness to communicate. *Language and Education* 32 (2), 147–166. https://doi.org/10.1080/09500782.2017.1405017

Reynolds, B.L. and Yu, M.H. (2021a) A language course to teach administrative staff English for communication in an international university. *Education as Change* 25, 1–29. https://doi.org/10.25159/1947-9417/8749

Reynolds, B.L. and Yu, M.H. (2021b) The hiring and management practices of a seven-year extracurricular program to enhance Asian undergraduates' English as an international language communication skills. *Asian Englishes* 25 (3), 391–406. https://doi.org/10.1080/13488678.2021.1961183

Reynolds, B.L. and Yu, M.H. (2022) Using English as an international language for fluency development in the internationalised Asian university context. *The Asia-Pacific Education Researcher* 31 (1), 11–21. https://doi.org/10.1007/s40299-020-00534-w

Pinner, R.S. (2016) *Reconceptualising Authenticity for English as a Global Language*. Multilingual Matters.

Seidlhofer, B. (2011) *Understanding English as a Lingua Franca*. Oxford University Press.

Tsui, C. (2017) EMI teacher development programs in Taiwan. In W. Tsou and S.M. Kao (eds) *English as a Medium of Instruction in Higher Education: Implementations and Classroom Practices in Taiwan* (Vol. 8, pp. 165–182). Springer.

10 An Exploratory Study to Examine the Role of Assessment Literacy in the EMI Classroom

Joyce Kling and Slobodanka Dimova

10.1 Introduction

In its early evolution, key voices in the integration of content and language in higher education (ICLHE) movement identified a need for focused attention to questions of language and/or content assessment and feedback in disciplinary content courses taught in a foreign language (e.g. English-medium instruction (EMI)) (van Leeuwen *et al.*, 2006). Unfortunately, nearly two decades later, research on reliable and valid approaches to assessment, both formative and summative, of students in EMI courses is scant. Current discussions focus on the need for testing of both language and content, and the challenges related to implementation of assessment practices in institutional practices (Hultgren *et al.*, 2022; Kao & Tsou, 2017; Molino *et al.*, 2022). Although there has been considerable emphasis on content teachers' needs related to language in EMI teaching practices (Dimova & Kling, 2022a), limited attention has been given to the role of language in their assessment practices, usually related to students' achievement of course goals, that may or may not involve integration of content and language. This has resulted in researchers struggling to determine the focus of assessment in EMI (language and/or content), as well as language choice, that is should translanguaging be allowed in assessment or is English only the necessary approach (Lasagabaster, 2022). Additionally, there has been an ongoing call for increased development of disciplinary content teachers' EMI assessment literacy (EMIAL), that is the ability and confidence to understand and effectively interpret, design and use information on student performance on classroom assignments and/or exams to improve teaching and learning, as well as general principles of assessment for learning in EMI educational contexts – contextual and policy literacies, language and content learning, formative assessment and awareness of students' learning needs (Inbar-Lourie, 2022). These calls include enhanced focus on English language proficiency development and feedback for students, as well as collaborative assessment practices between disciplinary content teachers and language teachers (Hultgren *et al.*, 2022).

The span of assessment practices in higher education across disciplines, not to mention academic cultures and contexts, run the gamut from summative to formative approaches, as a means for 'fostering, facilitating, and improving learning and instruction' (Inbar-Lourie, 2022: 210). Naturally, the addition of a language element in EMI context only adds to the mix. In the EMI classroom, students are tasked with grasping disciplinary content, with or without explicit emphasis on language development. Distinguishing between language-related difficulties and disciplinary knowledge challenges becomes particularly complex. Consequently, content instructors may struggle to accurately identify whether students' struggles stem from language proficiency or comprehension of the subject matter. This ambiguity makes it difficult for teachers to offer pertinent feedback during class and assess students' performance (Dimova & Kling, 2022b). Differences in educational cultures across different contexts add to the complexity of the assessment practices in EMI. Exam formats, exam performance expectations, presence or absence of continuous assessment, and grading systems vary greatly among universities as they are embedded within the local assessment traditions. International students may lack experience with some assessment types and procedures that are taken for granted in the local educational context. Students' inexperience with assessment procedures may affect their exam performance and consequently their grades.

To address these conceptual considerations, in this chapter we consider EMI content teachers' perceptions about balancing teaching and integrated assessment of language and disciplinary content, as well as their awareness of the role of educational culture in assessment practices and their confidence with assessing students in a multilingual, multicultural academic context. The study includes teachers' confidence with assessment as it is commonly associated with teacher assessment literacy (Harding & Kremmel, 2020). In the following, we present findings from an international study investigating business management content teachers' responses to questions related to their instruction and assessment practices in a global dual-degree graduate business program.

10.2 Literature Review

Given that the twofold desired educational goals for EMI of both language and content are conceptually supported (Malmström & Pecorari, 2021), we should expect that they are represented in teaching and learning practices, as well as in assessment. However, while EMI content teachers in Europe emphasize their disciplinary focus on instruction, they have maintained a consistent mantra denouncing their role in supporting students' language development (Aguilar Pérez, 2018; Airey, 2012; Block & Comas, 2019; Costa, 2013). For example, in interviews with EMI STEM (science, technology, engineering and mathematics) content teachers in Spain, Block and Comas (2019) found a steady distancing in self-positioning of academic professionals who identified primarily as disciplinary experts and not as language teachers. The rationale for this positioning mirrored Airey's (2012) findings in that the teachers declare competence as proficient English speakers and as disciplinary experts, but not as trained language instructors. Although the 'I don't teach language' (Airey, 2012) mantra continues, as noted above, there are those content teachers who embrace the role of language mentor and advocate for an English-only teaching strategy in the EMI classroom. With over a decade of experience teaching business administration in Spain, del Campo (2020) argues for modeling of language use in all interactions with students to support goals of multilingual, multicultural education. Students draw on this type of modeling to develop their language skills and disciplinary literacy through teachers' explicit guidance (Muir *et al.*, 2019).

The *not a language teacher* stance and suggested division of labor, i.e. disciplinary experts teaching content, leaving language support and instruction to the language experts, may stem directly from policies at the macro-, meso- or micro-levels. The implementation of English-taught courses, including full-degree EMI in higher education is guided by explicit and/or implicit policies of internationalization and globalization. Policy decisions in local EMI contexts are influenced by a range of factors, including stakeholders' perceptions, values and experiences (Molino *et al.*, 2022). At the departmental or classroom level, decisions and actions of stakeholders, such as students and teachers, shape EMI implementation in relation to classroom communication, teaching/learning and assessment. While macro-level drivers like international, national and regional factors have been extensively researched, meso-level policies often face execution challenges. Institutional strategies related to internationalization and EMI frequently go unheeded (Chopin, 2016) or lack specificity, resulting in varied interpretations of language selection and use at the classroom and assessment level. Therefore, at the classroom level, language choice beyond English only and translanguaging affordances in the EMI context have been documented (Molino *et al.*, 2022). Drawing on students' extended linguistic repertoires, i.e. all languages beyond English that students have in their repertoire, has been advocated as an approach to equalizing the playing field for assessment in EMI contexts (Carroll & Mazak, 2017). When it comes to assessment, this approach allows students with English language proficiency challenges to demonstrate content knowledge, though it may penalize those students who do not share a [second] common language with their examiner.

For example, Nissen (2018) investigated a bottom-up implementation of an institutional language policy by analyzing student language use in both classroom group activities and oral examinations at the University of Copenhagen. For EMI courses, the curriculum clearly states that the language of instruction and examination is English, despite a university-wide policy of parallel language use, i.e. the choice of language when two languages are considered equal within a particular domain or context. In her research, Nissen observed a loose interpretation at the interaction level. Using a linguistic ethnographic perspective, she found that students were allowed to strategically employ Danish (L1) and English (L2) in academic situations, including interactions with peers and teachers. Notably, during EMI oral examinations where English responses were expected, Nissen presented examples of code-switching to Danish by students with two different results. The examiner accepted the use of the shared L1 to facilitate the students' responses. However, whereas the first student's switch was accepted positively – with explanation in the L1 suggesting a nuanced understanding – the second student's switch led to a perception of lacking content knowledge and language proficiency. Both students, sharing the L1 with their examiner, chose to use Danish, reflecting a local decision to optimize communicative efficiency rather than strictly adhering to the imposed language policy. Nissen suggests that this pragmatic choice may risk exclusion and unfair practices in EMI courses, similar to the challenges faced by non-Danish speaking students in other studies.

An example of a top-down implementation of EMI incentivized by external socioeconomics is the tendency in some institutions to prioritize internationalization and rankings over student learning needs (Molino & Campagna, 2014). As institutions promote opportunities for desirable workforce competence development, criticism has been raised regarding specific and appropriate prerequisite language proficiency and academic disciplinary requirements for students, as well as directed learning outcomes (Molino *et al.*, 2022).

A number of researchers have questioned student achievement when learning in the L2 (see e.g. Dafouz *et al.*, 2014; Dafouz & Camacho-Miñano, 2016; De Vos *et al.*, 2020; Klaassen, 2001). To address whether studying through the medium of English (as an L2) affects academic performance, researchers have investigated the impact of English L2 instruction on content learning. Results from studies in the Netherlands suggest negative differences in quality between lectures and classroom interactions held in English versus Dutch (de Vos *et al.*, 2020). Similarly, in a recent large-scale empirical investigation of students participating in a comparable Swedish and EMI massive open online course (MOOC), Bälter *et al.* (2023) found that the EMI students answered significantly fewer test questions correctly and also dropped out of the course at a significantly higher rate compared to students in the Swedish-medium instruction course.

However, as early as 2001, Klaasen (2001) observed no adverse effects of EMI on Dutch and international students' academic performance when assessed in naturalistic environments. Given these findings, Klaasen suggested that factors other than language may play a role in student achievement. Similarly, several studies from Spain and Italy have explicitly investigated assessment types academic results. When comparing EMI and non-EMI students, empirical studies addressing student academic achievement across a range of disciplines have documented similar assessment outcomes, and even superior achievement (Costa & Mariotti, 2017; Dafouz *et al.*, 2014; Dafouz & Camacho-Miñano, 2016; Del Campo *et al.*, 2015; Hernandez-Nanclares & Jimenez-Munoz, 2017).

In Spain, Dafouz and Camacho-Miñano (2016) conducted a study on students of financial accounting, analyzing 383 first-year students' academic performance over four years, comparing language of instruction (L2 English or L1 Spanish) and types of assessment. They ensured equivalence in course content and assessment between L1 and L2 courses taught by the same teacher. Despite variations in assessment performance between EMI and non-EMI students, statistical tests did not reveal significant differences in final grades or distribution of marks by performance level between the two groups. Dafouz and Camacho-Miñano's (2016) research underscores significant inquiries in EMI content learning. They found that even students with limited English proficiency, particularly in fields like financial accounting, could pass exams with predominantly receptive linguistic demands. In their discussion, the authors emphasize the necessity for both EMI and non-EMI students to develop academic literacy in their discipline's language, suggesting that the absence of significant final grade differences between EMI and non-EMI students may stem from their familiarity with local educational practices and assessment criteria. In Italy, delving slightly deeper into disciplinary differences, Costa and Mariotti (2017) discovered variations in final exam scores between EMI and non-EMI students across subjects (general physiopathology, geometry, economics and international relations), suggesting that the nature of the subject may influence learning outcomes in EMI settings and warranting further investigation into the role of discipline beyond language proficiency.

In addition to findings on performance, researchers in Chinese-speaking contexts have also sought to investigate the approaches and methods of assessment in EMI (Kao & Tsou, 2017; Li & Wu, 2018). Results from these small-scale studies suggest that there is lack of consensus as to the role of English as a focus of assessment, the amount of support and feedback EMI teachers should provide when language difficulties affect student performance outcomes, and that the use of English for assessment does affect how assessment is implemented in these context (China and Taiwan) (Li & Wu, 2021).

Overall, as Macaro *et al.* (2018) point out in their systematic review of EMI research, evidence between content learning in students L1 and EMI (i.e. L2 learners) is inconclusive since the contexts and conditions varied greatly. However, what is apparent from the noted findings and discussions in the systematic review about content learning and assessment is a clear focus on student achievement and grades. Yet, with all the focus on student performance, there is limited discussion on how this achievement is actually assessed by EMI content teachers (Sahan & Şahan, 2022). This has led to a call for more focused investigation of EMI content teachers' assessment literacy (Dimova & Kling, 2022; Inbar-Lourie, 2022) and inclusion of explicit language learning outcomes in course goals (Li & Wu, 2021).

Thus, the tension between EMI teachers' stance as *content experts* and not *language experts* becomes exacerbated when student content achievement is in focus. Research has shown that EMI teachers do not distinguish between L1 and EMI assessment practices (in non-English-dominant contexts), but instead their practices conform strongly to the institutional norm for all subjects (Moore, 2017). Ignoring students' language proficiency as a factor in content assessment is problematic at best, and may be discriminatory at worst. Therefore, Inbar-Lourie (2022) advocates specifically for strengthening content teachers' EMI assessment literacies related to four relevant areas, namely 'contextual and policy literacies; the role of language in facilitating content learning; formative assessment for learning orientations; and awareness and understanding of students' linguistic and content needs' (2022: 218).

To move beyond comparative reporting of EMI vs. non-EMI student achievement we investigate teachers' perceptions of their own assessment practices in an international graduate degree program in international management. The context for this study offers a unique insight into EMI assessment across a broad range of educational contexts.

10.3 Context: EMI and the CEMS-MIM

The CEMS Master's in International Management (MIM) is a prestigious global alliance of 33 leading business schools across six continents and over 70 multinational companies. The CEMS-MIM offers a dual MSc degree focused on the development of academic and practical skills for a global business environment. Launched in 1988, the CEMS-MIM was built on multilingual, multicultural curricular goals. Students seeking to enhance their language proficiency in one or more European languages sought out this elite program to highlight their multilingual, multicultural portfolios.

When it was established, the CEMS-MIM was an early adopter of an immersion model (Swain & Lapkin, 2005) that supported the development of students' language proficiency for both academic and business purposes. Students were rigorously pre-tested in two foreign languages prior to admission to the dual degree program to determine status of proficiency for academic and business purposes, as well as to identify foreign language development needs. Students were required to enroll in advanced level business courses that were primarily taught in the national language of a partner university. Additionally, students' language proficiency development was supported through participation in educational curricular activities, internship work, as well as targeted (business) language for specific purposes courses. Finally, students were tested in their two foreign languages for proficiency in business communication prior to graduation (Kling, 2006).

At present, CEMS-MIM students still participate in internationally focused business courses and internships. Admission to the dual-degree continues to be rigorous. To be qualified to apply students must be concurrently enrolled in a graduate business studies program at one of the partner universities. Additionally, students must provide evidence of strong academic performance (i.e. grade point average) and complete personality tests and individual interviews with academic coordinators and corporate partners. In regard to foreign language proficiency, the English language proficiency requirements for admission (Language 1) is C1 on the Common European Framework of Reference (CEFR) scale (Council of Europe, 2020) (documented through commercial test results or the equivalent). Graduation requirements include documented competency in two additional languages in addition to English. Language 2 (any language) must be documented at B1, and Language 3 can be either a declared mother tongue or any language at the elementary level. Documentation of Languages 2 and 3 can take place at any point of the two-year degree program. The CEMS-MIM language requirement reflects the international and cross-cultural focus of the program (CEMS, 2024).

Though originally developed as a trilingual program, with content courses taught and assessed in a range of languages, the CEMS-MIM is now fully EMI. All courses in the CEMS-MIM are conducted in English at institutions around the world in English-dominant and non-English-dominant settings. CEMS-MIM universities do not promote explicit language instruction in the program. The shift to EMI in the global CEMS-MIM has been gradual and replaces what was previously a European focused mother-tongue-plus-two initiative (European Parliament, 2017). As the CEMS-MIM community grew and spread beyond Europe, EMI became a natural default option with English as the academic lingua franca. This shift to EMI eliminated explicit language for specific purpose post-program testing (e.g. English for specific purposes oral and written exams). Instead, focus has shifted to business communication training through workshops and student internship experience.

10.4 Methods

To improve our understanding of EMI teachers' perceptions of their own assessment practices in the EMI classroom, the current study was guided by the following research questions:

(1) What is the teachers' perceived interplay between language, content and academic expectations in teaching and assessment?
(2) How confident are teachers in assessing students in multilingual, multicultural EMI courses?

Given the specific international focus and multilingual, multicultural educational goals of the CEMS-MIM program, a survey questionnaire was sent to business management content teachers working in business schools around the world that offer the dual Master's degree program in International Management.

10.4.1 Instrument

Data were collected through an online survey questionnaire designed in Sunet Survey. The 20-item questionnaire was divided into five sections: (1) background information, (2) students, (3) teaching practices, (4) assessment practices and (5) English proficiency. Given that teachers' characteristics and teaching experience may influence their perspectives on EMI, the background information section included seven multiple-choice items eliciting data regarding their teaching experience in higher education, first language(s), academic position and type of courses that content teachers teach. To obtain sufficient contextual information about the CEMS-MIM programs, the survey also included a section related to students. This section consisted of five-point Likert-type questions that focused on teachers' perceptions of their students' English proficiency, prerequisite disciplinary knowledge and preparation to succeed in the local academic culture.

Based on previous research findings that teachers tend to view assessment as part of teaching (Black & Wiliam, 2018; Dimova & Kling, 2022), the survey included sections both on their perspectives on teaching and on assessment in their EMI classrooms. Using matrices with Likert-type items, the section on teaching practices elicited information regarding the teaching activities and languages used in different teaching situations. Similarly, the section dealing with teachers' assessment practices comprised multiple-choice items and matrices with Likert-type items to elicit data regarding types of assessment the teachers engage in and their confidence levels with administering and grading student work. Both sections included open-ended questions to obtain more detailed answers to some of the Likert-type items.

Finally, as EMI teachers' English proficiency tends to be associated with the selection of their teaching and assessment perceptions and practices in EMI (Li & Wu, 2021), the last section included a single item related to teachers' self-evaluation of their own English proficiency based on the levels of the CEFR scale (Council of Europe, 2020).

We performed a descriptive analysis of the survey data, i.e. we calculated raw distribution frequencies of respondent data.

10.4.2 Participants

The CEMS Global Office distributed the survey to the academic directors of the institutions that are members of the CEMS-MIM global alliance, who, then, forwarded the invitation for participation to the teachers in their programs. The EMI teachers who replied to the survey (n = 30) came from universities in North (n = 3) and South America (n = 9), Europe (n = 9), Asia (n = 4), Africa (n = 3) and Australia (n = 2), and had various language backgrounds (Portuguese = 9, English = 7; German = 5; Finnish = 2; and 1 from each Arabic, Russian, Spanish, French, Korean, Cantonese). Only one respondent reported being English-French bilingual. All participants who were second language (L2) speakers of English reported high proficiency levels (C2 on CEFR), while eight participants considered themselves first language (L1) speakers of English.

The respondents held different positions at their institutions, ranging from Assistant (n = 2), Associate (n = 9) and Full Professors (n = 13), senior lecturers (n = 2), as well as deans, study coordinators and academic directors (n = 4). Fifty-seven percent of the respondents were aged 51 or older, while 17% were aged 30–40 and 27% aged 41–50. Most respondents (69%) were experienced teachers who have taught in higher education and in English for over 16 years. The least experienced lecturers (19%) had at least three years of teaching in EMI in higher education.

10.5 Results

In order to understand teachers' perspectives on their own assessment practices, especially in relation to their awareness of the interplay between language, content and academic expectations, it was important to examine their perceptions of their students' disciplinary, linguistic and cultural preparedness for studying in an internationalized EMI program. Results suggest that all respondents had either a mix of domestic and international students (63%) or predominantly international students (37%) in their classes. Teachers believed that both their domestic and international students possess the necessary disciplinary, linguistic and cultural prerequisites to study in their courses, but domestic students seemed to have an advantage in all three areas. The difference between domestic and international students was most obvious in their preparedness to succeed in the academic culture, where 93% of the respondents strongly agreed (60%) or agreed (33%) that domestic students are prepared, while 23% strongly

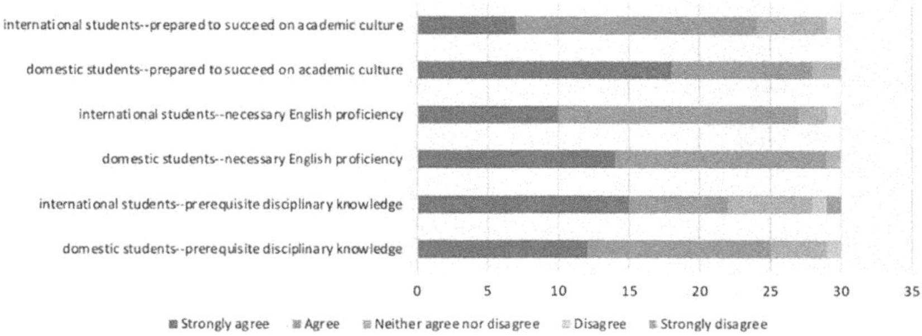

Figure 10.1 Domestic and international students' disciplinary, linguistic and cultural preparedness

agreed and 57% agreed that international students are prepared to succeed in the academic culture at their university. Although domestic students also have an advantage in relation to linguistic (strongly agree/agree = 96% vs. 90%) and disciplinary preparedness (strongly agree/agree = 83% vs. 73%), the differences are not as great as with their cultural preparedness (see Figure 10.1).

When looking at the reported intended learning objectives (ILO) for the disciplinary courses that the respondents taught, it is obvious that the primary focus is on development of disciplinary knowledge, for example: 'Recognize the role of national and regional institutional environments in the conduct of business. Recognize the significant influence of culture in the conduct of business and organizational life' (Respondent 4). Among the competences found among the reported learning goals and objectives were critical thinking and analytical skills, as well as problem-solving and leadership/management skills, for example: 'To demonstrate critical thinking and problem solving and analysis skills' (Respondent 30). While teachers mentioned communication skills, e.g. 'acquiring subject-related knowledge; acquiring analytical and critical thinking skills; enhancing communication skills' (Respondent 24), specific language development learning objectives were absent. Instead, the role of language and awareness and understanding of students' linguistic and content needs appears to lie implicitly in ILOs such as: participation in 'class discussions, written assignments, presentations, applied final project' (Respondent 19); and 'General competence in: Advanced research ability, problem solving and critical reflection; Planning and executing project work in an international team during the length of the semester; Communicating findings of the project in a clear and engaging manner' (Respondent 28). However, the teachers also note that ILOs for the degree courses may implicitly drive cross-cultural awareness and intercultural communicative competence assessment of the CEMS-MIM students. A word frequency analysis of the reported course ILOs finds that

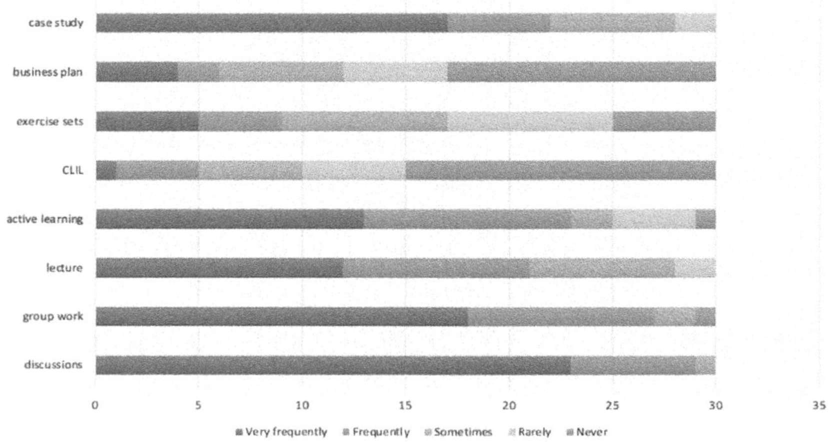

Figure 10.2 Teaching practices

terms such as *understand(ing) (n = 24), global (n = 18), and international (n = 12)* dominate.

Given the lack of linguistic focus in the intended learning outcomes as well as teachers' beliefs that their students' English language proficiency is sufficient to succeed in the course, many claimed that they never (50%) or rarely (17%) apply content and language integrated learning (CLIL) in their teaching, while 33% did use CLIL sometimes or frequently. As shown in Figure 10.2, the most widely used teaching activity in the classroom that respondents reported was discussions (very frequently = 77%; frequently = 20%), followed by group work (very frequently = 60%; frequently = 30%; sometimes = 7%) and case studies (very frequently = 57%; frequently = 17%; sometimes = 7%; sometimes = 20%). Although a large percentage of teachers use active learning activities (very frequently = 43%; frequently = 33%; sometimes = 7%), many of them also give lectures (very frequently = 40%; frequently = 30%; sometimes = 23%).

Owing to the international nature of the CEMS program, the purpose of which is to promote multilingual, multicultural education, it was important to ask about the use of English in relation to other languages in different academic situations, i.e. lecturing, group discussions, assessment and interaction with students. Based on teachers' responses (see Figure 10.3), English tends to dominate in all communicative situations in the academic setting. For instance, most teachers did not agree with the statement regarding allowing students to use languages other than English in exams (strongly disagree = 67%; disagree = 30%) or the statement about using a shared language to explain difficult concepts when teaching (strongly disagree = 57%; disagree = 37%). The only situation in which some teachers allow students to use languages other than English is in group discussions (strongly agree = 37%; agree = 20%). A small

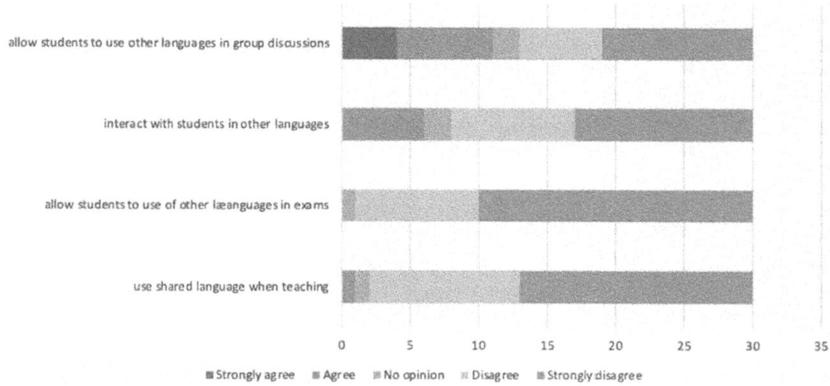

Figure 10.3 Use of other languages than English

percentage of the respondents use other languages when they interact with students during supervision or advising (strongly agree = 0%; agree = 20%).

The dominance of English seems also governed by the department/institutional language policy for teaching and assessment. Although most indicated the existence of a specific language policy for teaching at their institutions (70%), only 30% reported the existence of a specific policy for language use in assessment (30% reported no policy and 27% did not know). Most respondents reported that English is the default language for international courses, and that the teachers must use the language indicated in the syllabus for teaching and assessment. Some respondents indicated, though, that at their institutions, undergraduate courses tend to be taught in the local language and graduate courses in English.

Additionally, teachers acknowledged an awareness of programmatic and contextual policies specific to this degree program. In describing the ILOs of their courses, teachers noted how program policies served as drivers of content delivery and assessment. The learning objectives are reported to be designed and assessed in alignment with the nature of the CEMS-MIM program design, namely, an ethos of international understanding and critical analysis. For example, ILOs were described as: 'Following the particular CEMS learning outcomes of the course in question or business project' (Respondent 27); and 'the learning outcomes follow the ones for the CEMS program' (Respondent 28).

Formative assessment is used to provide feedback to students regarding their progression towards the ILOs. Therefore, the survey included questions about teachers' feedback practices. Most teachers reported giving written feedback (strongly agree = 47%; agree = 30%; sometimes = 16%). They engage in the other feedback types less frequently: group oral feedback (strongly agree = 17%; agree = 47%; sometimes = 7%), individual oral feedback (strongly agree = 20%; agree = 20%;

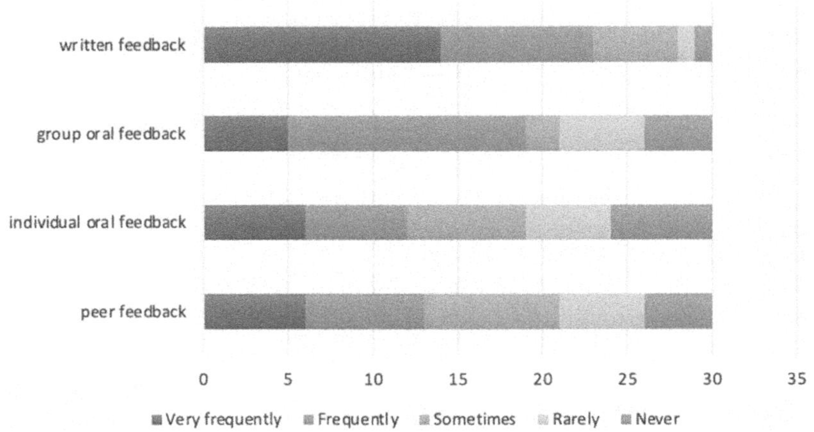

Figure 10.4 Reported feedback practices

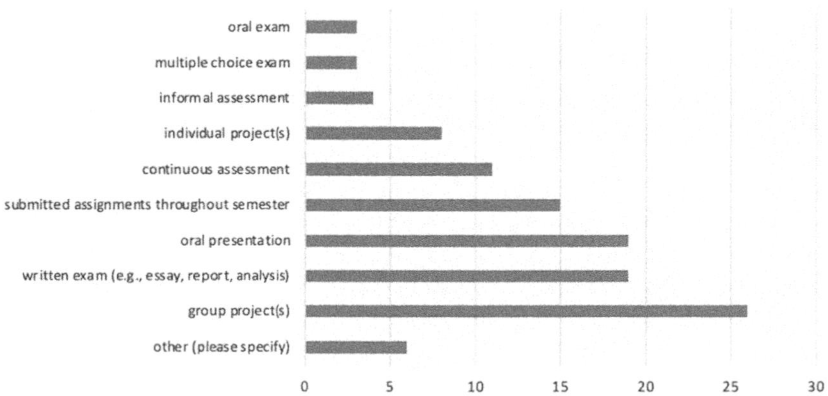

Figure 10.5 Reported assessment methods

sometimes = 23%; rarely = 17%; never = 20%) and peer feedback (strongly agree = 20%; agree = 23%; sometimes = 27%; rarely = 17%; never = 13%) (see Figure 10.4).

Regarding assessment, the lectures reported using mostly performance-based assessment methods based on group projects (87%), written exams (e.g. essay, reports, analyses) (63%) and oral presentations (63%), as well as projects submitted during the semester (50%) and continuous assessment (37%) (see Figure 10.5). Individual projects (27%), informal assessments (13%) and oral exams (10%) were used only by few of the respondents.

Previous research suggests that language proficiency can affect students' performance on exams and that an integrated content and language perspective in assessment poses challenges for teachers (Inbar-Lourie,

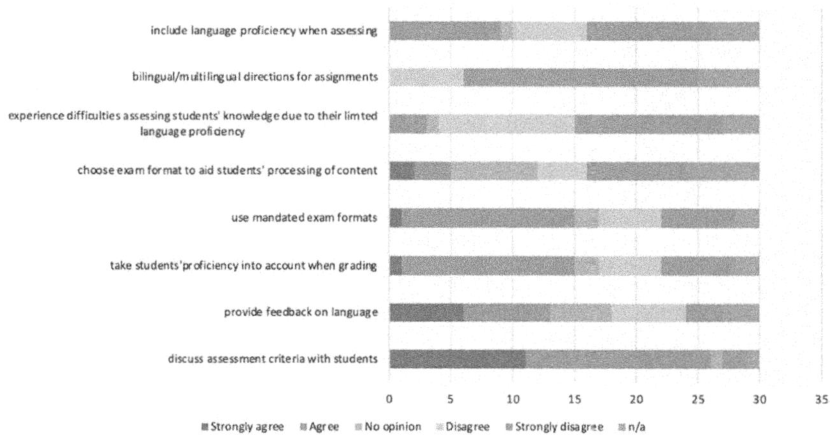

Figure 10.6 Reported assessment practices

2022). Therefore, the questions related to teachers' assessment practices and their confidence with assessment were related to the role of language and educational culture in assessment of content. As shown in Figure 10.6, most teachers did not report experiencing difficulties assessing content knowledge due to the students' limited English proficiency (strongly disagree = 40%; disagree = 37%), and they did not use bilingual/multilingual directions for assignments to ensure that students understand the assignment (strongly disagree = 63%; disagree = 20%). However, some teachers did report that they provided feedback on language (strongly agree = 20%; agree = 23%), took students' proficiency into account when grading (strongly agree = 3%; agree = 47%) and included language proficiency as part of their assessment (strongly agree = 0%; agree = 30%). Regardless of whether teachers considered language proficiency during their assessment, the majority respondents claimed that they presented and/or discussed their assessment criteria with their students (strongly agree = 37%; agree = 50%). Only a few teachers reported choosing an exam format to aid students' process content in a foreign language (strongly agree = 7%; agree = 10%), while many of them used the exam formats mandated by their departments/programs (strongly agree = 3%; agree = 47%).

As can be seen from Figure 10.7, most teachers felt confident with different aspects of assessment, including designing assessment materials (mean = 4.7), assessing students' content knowledge (mean = 4.5), designing assessment criteria (mean = 4.6), giving grades (mean = 4.5), providing feedback (mean = 4.7) and explaining test results to students (mean = 4.6). Teachers felt less confident identifying students' English proficiency issues (mean = 3.9), or cultural aspects of exams (mean = 3.9) that may affect their exam performance. Teachers felt the least confident with using AI for grading (mean = 1.8) or assessment design (mean = 2.9).

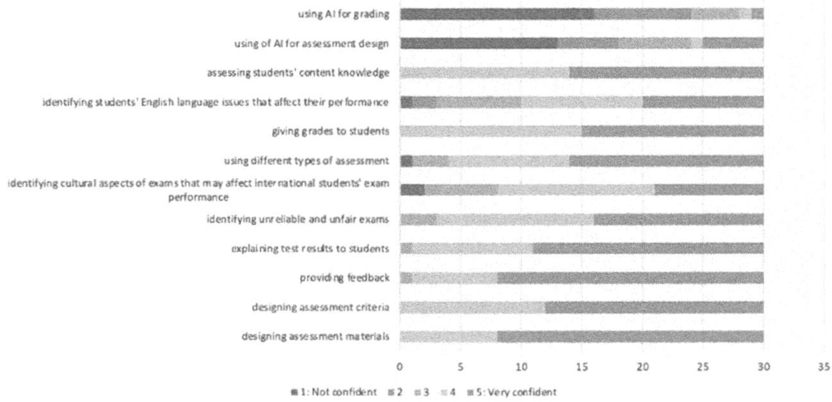

Figure 10.7 Teachers' confidence with assessment practices

10.6 Discussion

In this section, we discuss our survey results vis-a-vis our two research questions. More specifically, we discuss the teachers' approaches to balancing teaching and assessment of language, culture and disciplinary content, as well as their confidence with assessing students in a multilingual, multicultural academic context.

10.6.1 Balance between teaching and assessment of language, culture and disciplinary content

Results support previous research findings that EMI teachers tend to focus on the disciplinary content rather than language development (Kao & Tsou, 2017) despite the fact that many EMI programs promote students' development of English proficiency alongside content learning (Mancho-Barés & Aguilar-Pérez, 2020). In addition to content knowledge development, intended learning goals also include competences in critical thinking and problem solving, as well as analytical and reflective skills. Language is not mentioned explicitly although communication, often in intercultural context, tends to be included as one of the goals. In that sense, language becomes an implicit, rather than explicit, learning and assessment goal (Gronchi, 2023).

Teachers tend to be quite satisfied with students' language skills, be they domestic or international. Perhaps that represents one of the reasons why they do not focus explicitly on integration of content and language in their classes. However, despite the lack of focus on language in teaching, teachers report that they consider language proficiency and the role of language in assessing content and providing feedback to students. However, they find it difficult to identify how language influences students' ability to show their disciplinary content knowledge in assessment situations.

Given explicit and implicit language policies in their institutions, which seem to tend to be monolingual (e.g. if the syllabus states English as a medium of instruction, the exam must also be in English; or, undergraduate courses are in the local languages and graduate are in English), teachers report complying with the policies and sticking to English in both teaching and assessment. Teachers rarely report using more than one language (e.g. English and a shared language) in formal teaching and assessment situations, while other languages may come into play in individual encounters with students or student group work. These findings support previous studies that show that teachers use only English for assessment purposes (Li & Wu, 2017, 2018). However, this contradicts findings that suggest that teachers apply accommodation strategies during exams (Nissen, 2018).

Regardless that the teachers acknowledge students' educational cultural backgrounds and disciplinary preparedness as potential challenges for students, they may draw their perceptions from the idea that the CEMS-MIM is considered an elite degree program. As noted above, admission is selective. Thus, the CEMS-MIM population is deemed academically experienced and culturally savvy. Although the teachers in both English-dominant and non-English-dominant partner institutions may dismiss culture and linguistic as challenges, when asked explicitly about specific groups, they indicate that international students may have issues dealing with transitioning into educational contexts (Molino *et al.*, 2022). Though they are aware of these challenges, no compensation or assistance is described in the assessment of disciplinary content.

10.6.2 Teachers' confidence with assessing students in multilingual, multicultural EMI courses

The teachers who responded to the survey for this study self-describe as experienced educators who have taught a wide range of international business studies in English for several years. This experience feeds into a perceived sense of confidence in educational choices, in terms of both instruction and assessment. Based on reported self-perceptions, the teachers in this program align with the four EMI assessment literacy (EMIAL) competences suggested by Inbar-Lourie's (2022), namely contextual and policy literacies, language and content learning, formative assessment and awareness of students' learning needs.

To begin with, the data shows that those teaching in the CEMS-MIM are aware of the specific context in which they teach, including both programmatic and institutional policies for teaching EMI, and more specifically the international management courses. However, though there are suggestions in their responses to aspects related to language, these are couched in focused development of students' higher order thinking skills, critical analysis and communication.

When it comes to awareness of the role of language in facilitating content learning, the data from the survey align with much of the previous research. These teachers do not describe activities that support language learning. English dominates all communication and instruction, and the teachers reject the use of any language other than English for assessment or instruction. Thus, though the CEMS-MIM is built on a foundation of multilingualism and multiculturalism, the language of the instruction is English-only. Instructional language support is not suggested, nor is the role of language beyond implied expectations in summative assessment practices (e.g. final reports, group projects, written assignments).

Interestingly, teachers also felt confident with inclusion of formative assessment for learning orientations, the third EMIAL competence (see Figure 10.5). The ILO that emphasizes communication and negotiation goals is assessed through student-centered assessment in the form of group projects and oral presentations, both of which require development of communicative competences. Continuous assessment through assignments throughout the semester and group projects allows for formative feedback and scaffolding of content.

Finally, in their responses, the teachers claim to be aware of their students' content and linguistics needs, the last EMIAL competence. However, unlike previous findings that report on the challenges faced by EMI students in international contexts (Molino *et al.*, 2022), this cohort of respondents overwhelmingly reports confidence that both the domestic and local students are able to manage in their educational culture (see Figure 10.1). This may stem from the international, multilingual design of the CEMS-MIM. Unlike much of the research that reports on teaching and assessment of L1 linguistically homogeneous students (see e.g. DeVos *et al.*, 2020; Li & Wu, 2017, 2018; Mancho-Barés & Aguilar-Pérez, 2020; Moore, 2017), the teachers in this study report that their students are a mix of domestic and international students, or predominantly international students. Also, the international nature of this study that includes teacher responses from English-dominant and non-English-dominant contexts offers a new perspective on perceptions of student needs.

Therefore, these data from the CEMS-MIM teachers point to strong reported EMIAL for traditional classroom teaching in a well-established international program. However, one aspect of assessment that is not captured through Inbar-Lourie's model (2022) is related to teachers' confidence applying the latest technological advances such as AI to assist their assessment practices. Findings suggest that the teachers in this study do report uncertainties and lack of confidence implementing artificial intelligence (AI) for grading or for designing assessment tools (see Figure 10.7). Overall, these are the areas of least confidence. Thus far, technology and the use of AI has not been discussed in relation to EMIAL. However, advances in technology are inevitable components of education, particularly in an international program such as the CEMS-MIM. Global changes (e.g. related to health, climate change, sustainability, etc.) require reconsideration of approaches to assessment, particularly in EMI. The results from this study consequently highlight the need for inclusion of AI and digital literacy competences within assessment literacy models.

10.7 Conclusion

Previous findings suggest that EMI teachers lack confidence in teaching and assessment of students in the context, which has raised questions related to the quality of EMI education (Molino *et al.*, 2022). Data from this study challenge the previous findings in that the teachers' reported assessment literacy appears to be strong. It could be hypothesized that this result is due to the fact that those who responded to the survey were experienced educators with years of EMI teaching. Additionally, the data was collected from a well-established degree program founded by principles of international education and multilingualism.

The main implication from the results, given the experience of the respondents, is that with time, EMI lectures gain confidence in their teaching and assessment practices. Previous research has noted concerns and lack of confidence of less experienced teachers in these areas (Airey, 2011). However, the results of this study also imply that if teachers' confidence is reliant on experience, new practices are challenging. In this study, for example, we can see that EMI teachers report lack of confidence in relation to using AI in their assessment practices, most likely due to a lack of familiarity or training.

It is important to note that the purpose of this study was to investigate EMI teachers' perceptions of and confidence with assessment practices in EMI from one specific degree program. To examine the relationship between EMI teachers' reported assessment literacy and their actual assessment practices, observational data are required.

References

Aguilar Pérez, M. (2018) Integrating intercultural competence in ESP and EMI: From theory to practice. *ESP Today* 6 (1), 25–43.

Airey, J. (2011) Talking about teaching in English: Swedish university lecturers? Experiences of changing teaching language. *Ibérica: Revista de La Asociación Europea de Lenguas Para Fines Específicos (AELFE)* 22, 35–54.

Airey, J. (2012) "I don't teach language." The linguistic attitudes of physics lecturers in Sweden. *AILA Review* 25 (25), 64–79.

Bälter, O., Kann, V., Mutimukwe, C. and Malmström, H. (2023) English-medium instruction and impact on academic performance: A randomized control study. *Applied Linguistics Review* 15 (6), 2373–2396.

Black, P. and Wiliam, D. (2018) Classroom assessment and pedagogy. *Assessment in Education: Principles, Policy & Practice* 25 (6), 551–575. https://doi.org/10.1080/0969594X.2018.1441807

Block, D. and Comas, B.M. (2019) English-medium instruction in higher education and the ELT gaze: STEM lecturers' self-positioning as NOT English language teachers. *International Journal of Bilingual Education and Bilingualism* 1–17. https://doi.org/10.1080/13670050.2019.1689917

Carroll, K.S. and Mazak, C.M. (2017) Language policy in Puerto Rico's higher education: Opening the door for translanguaging practices. *Anthropology & Education Quarterly* 48 (1), 4–22.

CEMS (2024) Language Requirements: Possess three languages upon graduation. Retrieved from https://cems.org/cems-mim/programme-description/language-requirements.

Chopin, K.R. (2016) More Danish, More English: Language Policy, Language Use, and Medium of Instruction at a Danish University [Faculty of Humanities, University of Copenhagen]. https://curis.ku.dk/portal/files/170476653/Ph.d._afhandling_2016_Chopin.pdf

Costa, F. (2013) Dealing with the language aspect? Personally, no. Content lecturers' views of teaching through English in a ICLHE context. In S.V.B. Breidbach (ed.) *Content and Language Integrated Learning in Europe* (pp. 117–127). Peter Lang.

Costa, F. and Mariotti, C. (2017) Students' profiles and their reception of English-medium instruction in Italian universities. In J. Valcke, A.C. Murphy and F. Costa (eds) *L'Analisi Linguistica e Letteraria, Supplement 2. Critical Issues in English Medium Instruction at University* (pp. 361–371). Università Cattolica del Sacro Coure.

Council of Europe (2020) Common European Framework of Reference for languages: Learning, teaching, assessment — Companion volume. Council of Europe Publishing. https://rm.coe.int/common-european-framework-of-reference-for-languages-learning-teaching/16809ea0d4

Dafouz, E., Camacho, M. and Urquia, E. (2014) 'Surely they can't do as well': A comparison of business students' academic performance in English-medium and Spanish-as-first-language-medium programmes. *Language and Education* 28 (3), 223–236.

Dafouz, E. and Camacho-Miñano, M.M. (2016) Exploring the impact of English-medium instruction on university student academic achievement: The case of accounting. *English for Specific Purposes* 44, 57–67.

De Vos, J.F., Schriefers, H. and Lemhöfer, K. (2020) Does study language (Dutch versus English) influence study success of Dutch and German students in the Netherlands? *Dutch Journal of Applied Linguistics* 9 (1–2), 60–78.

del Campo, C. (2020) English medium instruction through the lens of a content teacher: Challenges, adjustments, and opportunities. In S. Dimova and J. Kling (eds) *Integrating Content and Language in Multilingual Universities* (pp. 167–177). Springer. https://doi.org/10.1007/978-3-030-46947-4_10

Del Campo, C., Cancer, A., Pascual-Ezama, D. and Urquía-Grande, E. (2015) EMI vs. Non-EMI: Preliminary analysis of the academic output within the INTE-R-LICA Project. *Procedia-Social and Behavioral Sciences* 212, 74–79.

Dimova, S. and Kling, J. (2022a) Emerging assessment needs and solutions in EMI in higher education. *Journal of English-Medium Instruction* 1 (2), 137–152.

Dimova, S. and Kling, J. (2022b) Lærerkognition i sprogevaluering [Teacher cognition about language assessment]. *Sprogforum. Tidsskrift for Sprog-Og Kulturpædagogik* 28 (75), 53–61

European Parliament (2017) Language policy. https://www.europarl.europa.eu/RegData/etudes/fiches_techniques/2013/051306/04A_FT(2013)051306_EN.pdf

Gronchi, M. (2023) Language assessment in EMI: Unravelling the implicit-explicit dichotomy. *Educational Linguistics*. https://doi.org/10.1515/eduling-2023-0011

Kremmel, B. and Harding, L. (2020) Towards a comprehensive, empirical model of language assessment literacy across stakeholder groups: Developing the language assessment literacy survey. *Language Assessment Quarterly* 17 (1), 100–120.

Hernandez-Nanclares, N. and Jimenez-Munoz, A. (2017) English as a medium of instruction: Evidence for language and content targets in bilingual education in economics. *International Journal of Bilingual Education and Bilingualism* 20 (7), 883–896.
Hultgren, A.K., Owen, N., Shrestha, P., Kuteeva, M. and Mežek, Š. (2022) Assessment and English as a medium of instruction: Challenges and opportunities. *Journal of English-Medium Instruction* 1 (1), 105–123.
Inbar-Lourie, O. (2022) EMI programs and formative assessment: Implications for the assessment literacy of content lecturers. *Journal of English-Medium Instruction* 1 (2), 204–231.
Kao, Y.-T. and Tsou, W. (2017) EMI course assessment: A survey study of the issues. In W. Tsou and S.M. Kao (eds) *English as a Medium of Instruction in Higher Education* (pp. 183–205). Springer.
Klaassen, R. (2001) The international university curriculum: Challenges in English-medium engineering education [PhD thesis, Technische Universiteit Delft]. http://repository.tudelft.nl/view/ir/uuid%3Adea78484-b8c2-40d0-9677-6a508878e3d9/
Kling, J. (2006) Evaluating foreign language skills for communication in management: Application of CEF criteria. In C. van Leeuwen, R. Wilkinson and V. Zegars (eds) *Bridging the Assessment Gap in English-Medium Higher Education* (pp. 161–178). AKS-Verlag.
Lasagabaster, D. (2022) *English-Medium Instruction in Higher Education*. Cambridge University Press.
Li, N. and Wu, J. (2018) Exploring assessment for learning practices in the EMI classroom in the context of Taiwanese higher education. *Language Education & Assessment* 1 (1), 28–44.
Li, N. and Wu, J.R. (2021) Assessment practices in the EMI classroom in Chinese-speaking higher education contexts: Challenges and considerations. In L.I.-W. Su, H. Cheung and J.R.W. Wu (eds) *Rethinking EMI: Multidisciplinary Perspectives from Chinese-Speaking Regions* (pp. 124–140). Routledge.
Macaro, E., Curle, S., Pun, J., An, J. and Dearden, J. (2018) A systematic review of English medium instruction in higher education. *Language Teaching* 51 (1), 36–76.
Malmström, H. and Pecorari, D. (2021) Disciplinary literacies as a nexus for content and language teacher practice. In D. Lasagabaster and A. Doiz (eds) *Language Use in English Medium Instruction at University* (pp. 213–221). Routledge.
Mancho-Barés, G. and Aguilar-Pérez, M. (2020) EMI lecturers' practices in correcting English: Resources for language teaching? *Journal of Immersion and Content-Based Language Education* 8 (2), 257–284.
Molino, A., Dimova, S., Kling, J. and Larsen, S. (2022) *The Evolution of EMI Research in European Higher Education*. Routledge.
Moore, S.H. (2017) A case study of assessment in English medium instruction in Cambodia. In B. Fenton-Smith, P. Humphreys and I. Walkinshaw (eds) *English Medium Instruction in Higher Education in Asia-Pacific: From Policy to Pedagogy* (pp. 173–191). Springer.
Muir, C., Dörnyei, Z. and Adolphs, S. (2019) Role models in language learning: Results of a large-scale international survey. *Applied Linguistics* 42 (1), 1–23. https://doi.org/10.1093/applin/amz056
Nissen, C.F.R. (2018) Language policy in reality–A study of language use in two English-taught courses at University of Copenhagen. In M. Siiner, F.M. Hult and T. Kupish (eds) *Language Policy and Language Acquisition Planning* (pp. 187–199). Springer.
Sahan, K. and Şahan, Ö. (2022) Content and language in EMI assessment practices: Challenges and beliefs at an Engineering Faculty in Turkey. In A. Karakaş and Y. Kirkgöz (eds) *English as the Medium of Instruction in Turkish Higher Education: Policy, Practice and Progress* (pp. 155–174). Springer.
van Leeuwen, C., Wilkinson, R. and Zegers, V. (eds) (2006) *Bridging the Assessment Gap in English-Medium Higher Education*. AKS-Verlag.

11 Perceptions of English Medium Instruction in Brazil: How do Students and Instructors of Varying English Proficiency Levels Experience EMI?

Ron Martinez and Larissa Giordani Schmitt

11.1 Introduction

English medium instruction (EMI) involves delivering university courses through the English language in countries where it is not the primary institutional language. One important prerequisite to offering classes in English is, of course, the availability and interest of those who would teach and learn through that language, which presupposes a certain degree of linguistic proficiency. In some countries, such as the Netherlands (Klaassen & Bos, 2010) and Belgium (Guimarães & Kremer, 2020), there is evidence that it is not uncommon to find faculty and students at the higher levels (i.e. C1–C2) on the Common European Framework of Reference (CEFR). Indeed, some authors have supported this higher proficiency band as a requisite minimum for teaching a class through English (Margić & Vodopija-Krstanović, 2018). If so, some countries are failing to meet that putative standard. For example, close to half of Spanish universities allow instructors to teach with levels of B2 or less (Halbach & Lazaro, 2015).

In short, there seems to be little consensus around a recommended level to teach through English. In a review of EMI research worldwide, Macaro *et al.* (2018: 54) conclude that 'there is no (higher education) research ... that matches some kind of language proficiency test with actual practice in order to determine a minimum level to teach (in EMI contexts)'. In a survey of EMI policy in European universities, O'Dowd (2018: 9) remarks that the 'lack of consensus among universities regarding the minimum level of English a teacher should have' to teach in EMI settings is 'remarkable' and 'disconcerting', and points to a need for research that could delineate proficiency guidelines.

Likewise, there may not be a singular solution for students that fits all EMI contexts. Dimova (2020) explored the usefulness of standardized English test scores (e.g. TOEFL, IELTS) for admission to EMI graduate programs at the University of Copenhagen (UCPH), a non-Anglophone university in Denmark. Surveys and interviews with UCPH instructors found they believe English proficiency is important for EMI programs but see tests as a formality. Overall, the study concluded standardized test scores provide a limited solution. Aizawa *et al.* (2020: 855) arrive at a similar conclusion. In their survey of language skills of Japanese students in EMI programs and the challenges they face, the authors observe that 'there appears to be no discernible threshold at which students have "enough" proficiency' and 'it is difficult to establish whether a clear "threshold" of proficiency exists for EMI'. They add that the test scores do not reveal the complex nature of what students feel about studying through English which, according to the authors, is better evinced through qualitative data.

Therefore, further research is needed to elucidate whether certain proficiency thresholds may be prohibitively low for positive EMI experiences, or if indeed factors like pedagogy, content knowledge and time may mitigate ability gaps. The current study helps address this need through an in-depth qualitative exploration of perceptions of EMI instruction among students and instructors at varying levels of English proficiency. Brazil provided a fitting setting as a country that has recently increased its efforts to internationalize through English (Finardi & Archanjo, 2018), is a relative newcomer to EMI growth in higher education (Martínez, 2016) and is still developing relevant language policy (Martinez & Palma, 2022).

Our study was guided by the following broad research question:

How do students and faculty of varying English proficiency levels experience EMI?

11.2 Methodology

11.2.1 Research design and methods

This research adopted an exploratory, multiple case study design in which 'a number of cases are studied jointly in order to investigate a phenomenon or general condition' (Dörnyei, 2007: 152). Data collection focused on eliciting detailed perspectives from multiple sources to provide a contextualized understanding of each bounded case. The inclusion of three cases allowed for cross-case comparison during analysis to identify convergences and differences in EMI implementations across varying institutional settings. The multiple case study structure also helped provide the contextualization necessary to illuminate local particularities of EMI experiences in Brazil. Altogether, this pragmatic approach acknowledges that integrating different forms of data provides a more comprehensive understanding of complex research problems than relying solely on one method (Yin, 2017).

11.2.2 Participants

Convenience and snowball sampling methods were used to recruit participants at several Brazilian institutions where the researchers had existing contacts. Inclusion criteria for instructors stipulated:

- EMI course lasting at least 8 weeks;
- minimum 5 enrolled students;
- in-person delivery;
- sole course instructor.

Participants ultimately included[1] 3 university instructors and 11 graduate students that would start their EMI courses at three different Brazilian public universities. Sampling aimed to include both students and faculty across a range of English proficiency levels. Instructors averaged 15 years of university teaching but no prior EMI experience. Graduate students were distributed as shown in Table 11.1. All were native Portuguese speakers undertaking EMI for the first time.

Information on the EMI classes delivered is in Table 11.2.

Henceforth, the participating instructor at UnB will be identified as 'Instructor 1', the UFPR instructor will be identified as 'Instructor 2' and the instructor at Unioeste will be named 'Instructor 3'.

Table 11.1 Summary of participant demographics

Type	N	Gender	Age	Location in Brazil
Instructors	3	2 female, 1 male	31–46	South, Midwest
Students	11	7 female, 4 male	23–35	South, Midwest

Table 11.2 Overview of EMI classes included in the study

Instructor	Discipline	Course name	Duration (hrs)	University
1	Statistics	Complex sampling	30	Universidade de Brasilia (UnB)
2	Genetics	Epigenetics	60	Universidade Federal do Parana (UFPR)
3	Agronomy	Supply chains in Brazil	30	Unioeste

Instructor 1 and Instructor 2 both had periods of study in other countries in which at least part of their programs was delivered in English (Instructor 1, USA; Instructor 2, Germany). However, only Instructor 2 had already delivered a class through English once, and therefore the offering represented in this study was her second time delivering a class in the same subject, but not the specific version taught for the present study. None of the faculty had ever had specific instruction on how to teach in EMI contexts.

In terms of English proficiency level, this was initially self-reported (see *Questionnaires* under Materials), and this self-report was later able to be checked against the TOEFL score (see Results). Instructor 1 and Instructor 3, after using the CEFR grid (the version in Portuguese, available through the Council of Europe), declared their proficiency to be at B1. Instructor 2 reported her CEFR level to be C1.

An overview of the number of students that were initially enrolled in the three participating classes is presented in Table 11.3. Note that although all participants took the first questionnaire, only the data of those who were interviewed are included in this report. All students were postgraduate (doctoral level).

It is also worth noting that attendance declined over time in all three courses. (The ethics review purview of present study did not include a protocol for interviewing students not enrolled in the course, so the reasons for course abandonment are unknown.)

11.2.3 Materials

11.2.3.1 TOEFL iBT

Participants' English proficiency was assessed using the TOEFL iBT, a standardized test of academic language skills covering reading, listening, speaking and writing. TOEFL scores range from 0 to 120, and ETS reports alignment with CEFR benchmarks (which may facilitate comparison with findings from other EMI research). The TOEFL iBT provided an objective measure of participants' English proficiency. Faculty took the test once prior to teaching their EMI course. Students took the TOEFL twice – once at the start of their EMI course and again after concluding. TOEFL scores were used to categorize participants' proficiency levels according to the CEFR.

Table 11.3 Number of participating students per class and completed instruments

Students	Class: Statistics (Instructor 1)	Class: Genetics (Instructor 2)	Class: Agronomy (Instructor 3)	Total
Initially enrolled	7	12	7	26

11.2.3.2 Questionnaires

Before and after courses, students and faculty completed online questionnaires, rating perceptions of English abilities, teaching skills, EMI expectations and experiences. Initial questionnaires gathered information on demographics, prior English learning experiences, self-perceived proficiency and confidence levels, and expectations for the EMI course. End-of-course questionnaires asked student participants to retrospectively rate dimensions like the instructor's teaching and English proficiency, their own learning engagement and comprehension, and compare their experience to initial expectations. Questionnaires utilized 5-point Likert scale ratings and open-ended responses.

11.2.3.3 Interviews

Instructors′ responses to questionnaires were used to help conduct semi-structured interviews via Zoom before and after their course, and with three to four students per class after conclusion.[2] Pre-course instructor interviews[3] focused on motivations for teaching EMI and anticipated challenges. Questions elicited perspectives on EMI experiences, factors impacting teaching and learning, challenges encountered and pedagogical strategies. Participants completed post-course interviews reflecting on their EMI experience, teaching or learning outcomes, shifts in confidence and factors impacting engagement. Interviews lasted 40–60 minutes and were recorded and transcribed.

11.2.4 Procedure

After enrollment in the study, participants first completed the initial questionnaire and TOEFL test. Instructors had entry interviews prior to starting their courses and at the conclusion. Shortly after beginning their courses, students took the first questionnaire. Finally, all participants finished the end-point questionnaire and TOEFL re-test. Instructors had exit interviews, and 3–4 students per class were interviewed based on perceived weaker/stronger English abilities as judged by their instructors.

TOEFL scores were analyzed for central tendency and variation across proficiency levels. Questionnaire results were analyzed for descriptive statistics.

The 17 total interview transcripts (3 instructor pre-course, 3 instructor post-course, 11 student post-course) were thematically coded by the researchers following established guidelines for rigorous qualitative research (Nowell *et al.*, 2017). Transcripts were first read thoroughly to gain immersion and take open-ended notes on impressions. These notes were then collated into a shared document. Next, we collaboratively generated initial codes using an inductive approach, staying close to participants' own language (instructors were interviewed in English; students in Portuguese). Using *Google Jamboard*, codes were organized into categories based on connections to the research question.[4] We discussed discrepancies in interpretive coding until reaching consensus.

11.3 Results

To answer the research question, it was first important to establish participants' level of proficiency in English. TOEFL iBT, scores of all participants (as well as self-estimated proficiency) are therefore reported in Table 11.4. As can be seen, most student participants were assessed at B1 or lower, and only one of the instructors reached C1. In addition, students took the TOEFL at the beginning and after the conclusion of their courses, and those scores, divided by skill, are shown in Table 11.5.

In-depth thematic analysis of the 17 interview transcripts revealed three prevalent themes related to how students and faculty experienced

Table 11.4 Participant TOEFL scores (Time 1*) and self-reported CEFR levels

Participant	Overall score	CEFR	Self-reported
Instructor 1	86	B2	B1
Instructor 2	111	C1	C1
Instructor 3	68	B1	B1
Student 1A	23	<B1	A2
Student 1B	97	C1	B2
Student 1C	79	B2	B2
Student 2A	105	C1	B2
Student 2B	67	B1	B1
Student 2C	78	B2	B1
Student 2D	76	B2	B1
Student 3A	34	<B1	B1
Student 3B	31	<B1	A2
Student 3C	4	<B1	A1
Student 3D	36	<B1	A2

*Only student participants who were interviewed have been included in Table 11.4.

Table 11.5 Summary of TOEFL scores by skill (only students retested)

Participant	Reading (0–30)	Listening (0–30)	Writing (0–30)	Speaking (0–30)	Total (0–120)	CEFR level
Instructor 1	26	18	22	20	86	B2
Instructor 2	29	29	29	24	111	C1
Instructor 3	19	21	14	14	68	B1
Students T1	M = 12.57 SD = 9.07	M = 12.78 SD = 9.51	M = 15.92 SD = 7.57	M = 11.04 SD = 4.06	M = 52.42 SD = 29.45	M = B1
Students T2	M = 15.40 SD = 7.76	M = 17.30 SD = 9.49	M = 13.90 SD = 7.89	M = 11.60 SD = 6.26	M = 58.20 SD = 29.19	M = B1

EMI across a spectrum of proficiency levels ranging from A1 to C1 on the CEFR scale:

(1) *Language challenges eased through acclimation over time*
(2) *Interactive strategies supported comprehension*
(3) *Positive motivations and perceptions of EMI*

These themes will be elaborated on below, exemplified through the students' and instructors' voiced perspectives. Note that the CEFR levels reported in this section reflect participants' actual TOEFL iBT scores, not their self-reported proficiency estimates.

11.3.1 Theme 1: Language challenges eased through acclimation over time

This theme was expressed by 12 of the 14 participants, including all three instructors and most students.

11.3.1.1 Theme 1 instructor findings

All three instructors expressed in interviews how continual EMI practice and experience facilitated language development and increased their confidence over time. As Instructor 2 (CEFR C1) explained: 'In the beginning I felt a little nervous, I think. But the more you use a language, I think, you're doing better and better ... After a few weeks I could perceive it was easier, you know, no problems'. This point of perceived improvement through continual usage of the language was echoed by Instructor 1 (CEFR B2): 'The more you speak, the more your English is going to be better, right? So, it's good, natural. [...] I start to speak slowly, try to remember the words, and after, at the end I can speak like that.'

Instructor 3 (CEFR B1) remarked that around 40 days into her course, she became conscious of her own improvement: '('T)he last five classes, I felt that I was more comfortable. I could speak with them without reading the slides [...] And it's, I felt free to talk with them'.

These impressions, as voiced by all three instructors, align with questionnaire data showing all instructors, regardless of proficiency (self-reported and TOEFL) initially felt their English was sufficient for EMI teaching. By the course conclusion, all instructors again reported in questionnaires that their English was sufficient, but had also improved (according to their own perceptions) over time through EMI practice.

11.3.1.2 Theme 1 student findings

This theme also emerged in 9 of 11 student interviews, as they described classroom immersion expanding their language skills. As Student 3C (CEFR <B1) shared: 'Yeah, and it's' funny. I don't know if

maybe my ear got used to it, right, I can't say, but I thought that, wow, the last classes were really much more understandable for me'.

On the productive skills side of proficiency, students also reported also noticing growth in speaking fluency: 'I realized that not only in the course, but also in conversations, in movies and series, in music, understanding improved a lot too...I think that my biggest problem is speaking, so, like, I thought that with the course my confidence in speaking improved' (Student 2B, CEFR B2).

The instructor with the lowest rating of interactivity on the student questionnaire had one student that had a lower TOEFL score (CEFR <B1), and that student remarked how inhibited they felt to speak. Nonetheless, even that student noticed a greater willingness to participate as the course went on: 'You know, like, much more towards the end of the course, from the middle to the end of the course, like that. I can't tell you if the difficulty, if this inhibition is because of the English language, for me it was, for others I don't know' (Student 1A, CEFR <B1). That student also seemed to attribute a lack of participation on her part to not being able to follow well initially, but appeared to blame her own lower level of proficiency: 'And I can't tell you if his pronunciation was..., because my English is terrible. So I can't judge whether his pronunciation is good or not'.

Interestingly, the reported level of confidence in English actually went down for some students in their final questionnaires relative to their first. This was the case for three of the student participants, who reported noticing a 'gap' (e.g. Schmidt, 1990) between their proficiency as originally perceived by them, and where they realized they had some linguistic ground to make up.

Students often mentioned that their comprehension of discipline-specific vocabulary improved noticeably as a function of time and contact with the EMI classes, as exemplified by Student 1A (CEFR <B1): '('T) hroughout the course it became comfortable because those words were no longer strange. So they started to be better assimilated, right? So, from that point of view, yes, but I believe that's why, because of the contact, because you're always using the same vocabulary...'

Thus, though students frequently spoke of initial difficulties with unfamiliar vocabulary, accents, spontaneous speaking and listening comprehension, these reported difficulties were regularly qualified with some note of (self-reported) improvement. This improvement among students was also noticed by instructors: '('S)ome students in the beginning didn't understand what I said, but at the middle, pretty nice, they understood everything, the questions...' (Instructor 1).

These impressions are further corroborated by the student questionnaire responses, which revealed student confidence in comprehension grew over time (initial M = 3.1 out of 5; final M = 4.0), with most students (9/11) agreeing in questionnaires that their understanding of the instructor's English had improved over time.

11.4.1 Theme 2: Interactive strategies supported comprehension

All 14 interviewed participants emphasized the key role of interactive, student-centered teaching techniques in boosting engagement and learning.

11.4.1.1 Theme 2 instructor findings

All three instructors emphasized interactive, student-centered pedagogy in interviews as beneficial for EMI engagement and comprehension. As Instructor 1 described: 'I explained, then I stopped, "Did you understand? If you don't understand I'll come back" ... I asked them what they think, engaged them in discussion'.

Engaging students was a facet of teaching that seemed prominent in the minds of all three instructors, and the very experience of EMI seemed to foster among the instructors a desire to break from their usual approach to teaching. Instructor 2, for example, mentioned how she wanted to promote ludic learning, and tried using the app *Kahoot* (an online interactive and collaborative teaching resource) in her classes: 'So, I try to explain something in a funny way, and I'm' also using some tools for the class like *Kahoot* ...' In essence, such engagement was a way to monitor comprehension, since responses by students (e.g. in the form of collective laughter or smiles, or by way of online responses) were indicative of following the class.

Another strategy that instructors deployed was checking understanding using Portuguese (e.g. eliciting the translation of an English term), or even by involving students when lexical gaps occurred in their own teaching. Instructor 3 also consciously employed such a strategy:

> Instructor 3: If I can't remember the word, first, I tried to explain in English, but if I was not successful I translate to Portuguese.
>
> (*Interviewer: Oh okay. Did the students ever help you?*)
>
> Instructor 3: I had, but I asked them to look for the term in *Google Translator.*

Indeed, all three instructors reported that occasional use of or reference to Portuguese occurred.

11.4.1.2 Theme 2 student findings

This theme unanimously emerged from student interviews as they appreciated instructors' use of strategies like continual comprehension checks, visual aids and collaborative learning. As Student 2D (CEFR B2) explained: 'She would ask questions or, sometimes, like, she also asked so that when someone wants to make a comment, a question, they could interrupt her at any time and leave it very free, like, for whoever needed it'.

Student 3A (CEFR <B1) also commented: '('The class) dynamics, taking an article in English and having people read it, identifying phrases

that we know and then finding out if the introduction is correct, if there is a clear objective in this article'.

This kind of scaffolding was broadly employed by all three professors, and was noticed by the students. Student 1C (CEFR B2), for example, remarked how she appreciated the teacher-led lecturing, which itself was well organized, was followed by hands-on student-centered exercises.

Student 3B (CEFR <B1) also talked about how having hands-on tasks helped, and also breaking down larger chunks of content in English into smaller ones with specific foci (e.g. 'What is the author's main objective?').

Confirming what was mentioned by Instructor 2 in the context of ludic learning (in 'Instructor results' above), students pointed to whole-class interaction as important to following the class and overall engagement: '('I)n my perception I think that there was part of the class that was able to follow well, especially those who were in all classes. This was more noticeable to me when we had games where there was interaction, so it was possible that they were able to follow the games' (Student 2B, CEFR B1).

On the student questionnaire, there was an item that was intended to elicit impressions of teacher-centeredness, with students asked to offer estimated percentages of how much they (the instructors) spoke vis-à-vis student talking time. Instructor 2 reported the lowest percentage of her own talking time (70–79%), while both Instructor 1 and 3 stated that their lecturing occupied '90–90%' of the class. In reading the student interviews, there was evidence of how this difference between Instructor 2 and the others may have impacted student impressions. This was especially true in one of Instructor 1's students, who said 'I'm going to say something I missed here (in his class): it was interaction, even with those who knew English' (Student 1A, CEFR <B1). The student reported that it sometimes seemed that her classmates – two of whom in particular that had higher TOEFL scores than her – seemed to be the only ones following the instructor's class. It is also worth noting that Instructor 1 believed that engaging students through talking would be motivating. (A related note on Instructor 1 and his student's attitudes toward his speaking style will be explored in the next theme presented.)

Interactivity was often helped by making use of Portuguese. Students, like their instructors, also occasionally drew on their L1s, which also helped their comprehension. Notably, in all cases, it was the instructors that set the tone in that regard by explicitly discussing the role of Portuguese in their classes.

11.5.1 Theme 3: Positive motivations and perceptions of EMI

This theme also emerged in different ways across all interviews.

11.5.1.1 Theme 3 instructor findings

In all cases, instructors spoke about offering the course again sometime because of the positive experience: 'That's why I said I'm satisfied with my English. Probably next year, I have some time, I need some time, one week to take fluency again, but this is my first time teaching in English. So, I'm pretty confident to speak. Sometimes I have some mistakes, and you know, but I think I can conduct the class, in this case' (Instructor 1). Instructor 2 shared a similar sentiment: 'So, this makes everything so interesting, I loved it, yeah. It was really a nice experience and I hope to go on, you know, doing these classes'.

For all three instructors, their teaching in EMI was also a boost in self-efficacy, and validation that they can deliver effective classes through English. Instructor 3, who had the lowest TOEFL score among faculty participants (CEFR B1), also reported that she had a positive experience, but qualified that statement: 'I think that I have more positive experience than my, my students. I felt that not the majority of them, but some students suffered a lot with the classes in English. Maybe half of them didn't understand many things that I, I explained to them'.

Motivation also emerged as a theme involving instructors trying to motivate their students. Instructor 1, for example reported how he tried to challenge students to use English more, apparently with some success:

> I had another student, a girl, very shy. I knew that English was good but she's just speaking in Portuguese. Sometime, I said: no, you can't help me, because here we are all learning. I'm practicing only my speak. I would like to, to train my listen (in English), so if you do not speak English to me I cannot train my listen. So, he tried to speak to me in English at the end she spoke to me only in English. So, it was nice. (Instructor 1)

As will be reported in the student findings below, there were students that appeared to appreciate such challenging.

All instructors also responded in the affirmative in the questionnaires when asked if they planned to offer the course again, which seems to support the instructors' motivation to continue in EMI.

11.5.1.2 Theme 3 student findings

This theme also emerged strongly in student interviews and questionnaires (9 of 11). Students expressed varied motivations for enrolling in EMI courses, including career goals, instructor reputation, novelty and practical application of English, as exemplified by Student 3D (CEFR <B1): 'I realized that this subject... aroused a desire, not only in me, but in all the students in the room, you can tell, to want to learn more about the language, to want... less for you to achieve, within your area, a better performance, not only within the graduate program, but in the job market or when visiting a university or receiving students'.

Many students found that the content was 'better' in English because the literature in the discipline is predominantly in that language: 'I think it's even better, I found it even better in English because the reference is all in English, which we already follow' (Student 1B, CEFR C1).

Similarly, students also often spoke favorably about the maintenance of academic rigor and consistency in subject matter expertise, despite the language transition. As Student 3D (CEFR <3D) explained: 'She maintained, like, a very good level (of the course content), because some words, like, that she didn't know how to speak, one or two here and there, but it was very little, did not affect my understanding (of the subject)'. Student 2B's (CEFR B1) impressions are representative of other students who were 'pleasantly surprised' by their ability to follow along despite maintenance of discipline-related challenge: 'I was very impressed with the range of topics it addressed within the course, it went far beyond what I expected, not that I had low expectations, but it surprised me very positively. I was also surprised by the technical depth she gave to the themes'.

Thus, students who expressed that the EMI course was 'challenging' also conveyed that the challenge was also motivating. However, the inverse also was apparent. If a student perceived a lower degree of rigor, that seemed to have a negative effect on motivation. This was the case of Student 1A (CEFR <B1), for example. 'My expectation regarding the course ... in fact, I thought it was a kind of undergraduate-level course. I expected it to be more applied statistics, in the sense of forms of research that use statistics and the way we choose'. This caused her to disengage in the class, according to the student.

Beyond disciplinary content, there is no question that English language per se was often a main motivator for students. As a student whose English proficiency was already relatively high commented:

> Me, I was more willing because I think it's an extra challenge, I think it's a testing moment, like English training, we don't have the opportunity to speak English, practically nowhere. And then, you had the opportunity there, during class, to talk in English, to have an immersion there, in English. (Student 1B, CEFR C1)

Student 1B therefore appreciated his instructor's style, which involved much extemporaneous speech, including telling anecdotes and jokes. Note again, however, that Student 1B also had the highest TOEFL score among students in his class; this positive impression cannot be said to be totally generalizable to Student 1B's entire class. (The possible implications of this will be revisited in the Discussion.)

Nevertheless, EMI as a motivator due to the opportunity to practice the skill of speaking in English, in particular, was widely cited by students. This seemed to be the case even when the instructors directly challenged their students linguistically, drawing attention to areas in which they could improve their English: 'She corrected our presentations, our pronunciation, she stopped a lot to tell us that, like, in the middle of class.

Table 11.6 Summary of questionnaire findings

Time 1 Questionnaire*	Time 2 Questionnaire
• Instructors received high average ratings for teaching (4.5/5) and English proficiency (4.6/5) • Most students (n = 9) reported understanding instructors completely or with little effort • Only 2 reported occasional difficulty due to pronunciation (self-reported CEFR all B1 or <B1) • 1 felt grade could suffer due to instructor's English • Most felt instructors were interactive and used extensive English • Main English areas needing improvement (self-reported) were vocabulary, speaking, listening • Confidence levels ranged from 1 to 5 (mean 3.7)	• Instructors again received high marks for teaching (4.7/5) and English proficiency (4.9/5) • Most (9) agreed their understanding of instructor's English improved • 11 agreed instructor's English improved during course • Only 1 reported occasional difficulty with pronunciation (all TOEFL-measured B1 or lower) • None felt grade impacted by English • Key perceived improvements (self-reported) were in vocabulary, speaking, listening • Confidence levels increased slightly (mean 4.0)

*Only participants that completed all phases of the research, including interview, are included here.

We were saying something, she corrected that pronunciation and told us to pay close attention to the grammar, how we were pronouncing it' (Student 3D, CEFR <B1).

Questionnaire data revealed no students felt EMI impacted grades negatively (Table 11.6), and were satisfied that their and their instructors' English were ultimately sufficient to follow the classes – which in general students reported enjoying. This triangulation helps validate the overall positive perceptions expressed in interviews, which appears generalizable to a diverse range of proficiency levels in English.

11.6 Discussion

Our analysis that encompassed data from TOEFL scores, questionnaires and interviews uncovered key themes around teaching practices, student engagement and content needs that influence EMI experiences across a spectrum of proficiency levels ranging from CEFR A1 to C1. In terms of how instructors and students experienced EMI, the wide variance in proficiency did not preclude them from reporting positive EMI outcomes. As presented in Theme 1 (*Language challenges eased through acclimation over time*), initial impressions evolved with time and classroom experience.

As Table 11.5 reveals, TOEFL did not detect any quantifiable change in their proficiency, but what often appeared to grow over the many class meetings was their self-efficacy (e.g. Mercer, 2008). As argued in Chang *et al.* (2017), even though actual proficiency may not increase, students may perceive that their ability to successfully tackle certain academic tasks (e.g. participate in class discussion, understand their professors and assigned readings) may have positive impacts. The present study corroborates this notion. In Thompson *et al.* (2022), the authors found that lower proficiency negatively impacted self-efficacy, but in that cross-sectional study there was no repeated measure protocol to examine change in self-efficacy over time.

Thus, the findings presented in Theme 1 can be said to add to our understanding of how (self)perceptions may change over time, and can also be usefully compared to Zhang and Pladevall-Ballester's recent (2022) EMI research in China. In that study, the authors also administered questionnaires at the beginning and end of an EMI course (but unlike the present study, did not deploy an interview protocol or proficiency measurements). Zhang and Pladevall-Ballester (2022: 211) also found that attitudes of their participants changed over time, but for the worse. One aspect in that study the authors say can explain that trend is the lack of opportunity for student involvement, stating that the classroom observations they conducted 'showed that the three classes were all teacher-centered, and students had only limited opportunities to practice English'.

In such a light, the findings that emerged in Theme 2 (*Interactive strategies supported comprehension*) make sense. The interview and questionnaire data show that the faculty participants regularly received positive comments for incorporating activities that helped students feel involved. Notably, Instructor 1 was the faculty participant with the highest degree of student attrition. As seen in the Results section, when interviewed, Instructor 1's students seemed sometimes to tell a conflicting story: some loved his classes, mentioning that he did not use PowerPoint slides hardly at all, but did use humor and told interesting stories; yet one student (CEFR <B1)in particular was disappointed, noting that she noticed that Instructor 1 talked a lot, often telling stories, but she 'missed interaction.' In other words, Instructor 1's teacher-centered style, relying heavily on his own ability to engage through stories and humor, could work as long as students were able to comprehend well.

Interviews revealed that instructors' interactive teaching, use of multimedia and vocabulary support facilitated student comprehension and lowered anxiety (Morell, 2018). Allowing flexible use of Portuguese in class also helped, enabling conceptual understanding of vocabulary in particular. As has been reported elsewhere in the context of so-called *language-related episodes* in EMI classes (e.g. Martinez *et al.*, 2021), instructors sometimes deploy a kind of preemptive focus on form in their classes, in particular when they want to draw attention to a particularly important concept or term, and/or when they anticipate possible confusion or misunderstanding. Our data here support such findings, and back recent calls to further explore the incorporation of translanguaging practices in EMI (Yuan *et al.*, 2023). Time and again, students reported appreciating it when instructors held open and frank conversations about their role, encouraging the use of English, but permitting the use of Portuguese. It would seem that at least an open and frank discussion about L1 use in EMI would also be helpful in EMI faculty development.

At the same time, it was also clear that it was the English language element of EMI was often most important to participants, and a recurring element in Theme 3 (*Positive motivations and perceptions of EMI*). Instructors sometimes assumed roles of not only teachers of the discipline, but also English language. This is perhaps unusual, as there it has been reported elsewhere that EMI instructors do not typically see themselves in the role of integrating content *and* language (e.g. Lasagabaster & Doiz, 2021), but what is most relevant is the classroom climate that apparently was developed by the instructor. Many students spoke of feeling motivated when feeling challenged.

That challenge was evinced in the way they and their instructors approached both content and language, and even how they integrated the two. There has been growing interest in content and language-integrated learning (CLIL) in higher education (e.g. Valcke & Wilkinson, 2017), and the results reported in Theme 3 seem to point to potential in exploring this kind of direction in EMI. Students in our study often reported feeling a sense of accomplishment, even excitement, upon noticing they could use their English successfully. However, students also noted that they perceived 'gaps' in their current proficiency that they were not aware of at the beginning of the course. Rather than discourage them (these same students also reported a decline in confidence in their English), such awareness was seen as an opportunity to improve, having been shown where there can develop and perhaps would not have known about if not for the EMI opportunity.

At the same time, this positive perception seemed to be sensitive to the degree of challenge perceived by the students in terms of the course content itself. Students that reported that the 'level' was high, also seemed especially excited to report that their English was sufficient to successfully follow along and participate in the course. As a reminder, all participants in the present study were enrolled in EMI classes they chose to take (i.e. electives). Students often expressed intrinsic motivation around the content itself and appreciated activities building academic literacy like analyzing research articles in their discipline. This passion for the subject matter sustained engagement in EMI despite linguistic obstacles, and may have positively affected strategic behavior on the part of the students. This is consistent with research (Li *et al.*, 2022; MacIntyre, 2019) that has shown the power of motivation as an important variable in compensating for and overcoming proficiency weaknesses (real or perceived).

For that reason, the notion of challenge – in both English language and disciplinary content – seems to have played such an important role in Theme 3. One of Instructor 1's students (who described the level of the class as 'undergraduate'), and who noticed lighter demands compared to previous courses with the same instructor (or what they had heard about the instructor), also reported feeling disengaged and unmotivated to participate. Though not definitive evidence, the findings are similar to Yeh's (2014) insights into EMI in Taiwan, and these observations provide impetus for future research on possible 'sheltered' teaching in EMI, which could shortchange student learning (Echevarria & Short, 2010).

Specifically with respect to challenges experienced by students at different levels of proficiency, our study is consistent with Aizawa *et al.* (2020) in that all participants reported challenges irrespective of level of language ability. One interesting result that emerged, particularly in Theme 1 in the present study, was related to attributions, i.e. student participants at the lower CEFR levels tended to attribute comprehension difficulties to their own deficiencies, which corroborates findings in other EMI contexts (e.g. Yeh, 2014). As reported in the Results (in Theme 1), student 3C (CEFR <B1) initially found it challenging to follow the class but improved over time, adding that her early lack of comprehension was 'not because of her', but because of her lack of experience with English. Similarly, student 1C could not tell if her instructor's English was good or not because, according to her, her proficiency 'is terrible'.

Overall, it can be said that challenge was actually discussed often, by both instructors and students, in a positive and even motivating light. Most participants ultimately felt that EMI had been worth the time spent and would like to try another EMI class in the future. This reported impression is consistent with Thompson *et al.* (2022), whose participants, like those in the present study, possessed mostly lower levels of proficiency, and yet felt EMI was 'worth the extra effort' for them.

In terms of pedagogical implications of the findings presented here, this study reinforces the importance of teacher development for EMI. Martinez and Fernandes (2020) describe an EMI faculty development course in which they emphasize the importance of encouraging interaction with students, and de-emphasize focusing on putative language deficiencies on the part of instructors. Similarly, in a recent review of faculty development in EMI, Deroey (2023) shows that the encouragement of such methods in EMI instructor-training courses is not uncommon, and the findings presented in this report can be seen as further validation of the usefulness of that approach. (Though Deroey also cautions that local cultures need to be respected in which teacher-student interactivity is not the custom.) Trained EMI instructors may employ strategies like comprehension checks, paraphrasing, pacing modifications, visual aids and vocabulary adjustment to aid student understanding, especially early on (Costa & Coleman, 2013; Dafouz, 2018; Lasagabaster, 2018). As Rose (2021: 161) advises, 'EMI teachers should employ more student-centered approaches in their classes, moving away from lecture-style delivery' since 'students generally learn more through discussion and discovery'. Student interviews and questionnaire data in this study suggest that such approaches can lower the risks that students may feel left out and disappointed. Preparation can enhance teaching self-efficacy to deploy linguistic and didactic supports, including the use of L1 and even direct correction, shown to be of perceived value in the comments made by student participants.

However, this exploratory multi-case study also has several limitations. The small sample of participants from just three Brazilian universities constrains generalizability of findings. Additional research should include more participants across diverse institutional types and regions in Brazil to determine if similar themes emerge. Our analysis drew heavily on self-reported data from interviews and questionnaires. Incorporating direct classroom observations and content analysis of course materials in future research could provide more objective insights into actual teaching practices and academic rigor in EMI. It should also be noted that the only participants interviewed or who completed questionnaires were those who did not drop out of their respective courses. Put another way, while we have some degree of insight about why the student participants that stayed on decided to do so, we were unable to reach students that had dropped out of their courses (and therefore, the study) to ascertain their reasons for leaving. It is thus entirely possible that the sample collected for our data represents a bias toward positivity, since it is plausible that the students that left the courses did not feel as positively about their EMI experience. Future research should endeavor to incorporate a contingency protocol for such students, who could then volunteer their reasons for leaving if they so concede.

It is nevertheless hoped that the Brazilian cases presented and explored here spur similar investigations across expanding EMI landscapes worldwide, especially in still under-studied regions like Latin America and Africa. Further scholarship in Brazil should continue to explore comparisons of EMI experiences and outcomes between students at varying initial proficiency levels. This study also points to a need for more research on how Brazilian instructors adjust pedagogical practices within EMI, and the potential impacts on content level and rigor Additional studies could investigate the long-term trajectories of students in Brazil exposed to EMI using longitudinal data on outcomes like publications, careers and graduate research pursuits, building on initial connections suggested in the student questionnaire and interview data between EMI and student aspirations. As suggested by Martinez *et al.* (2019), it would also be informative to analyze EMI and non-EMI courses taught by the same instructors using classroom observations to systematically compare instructional quality. Such studies can guide context-specific EMI development to fulfill the oft-repeated promise (e.g. by university administrators) of greater access and inclusion through English, rather than replicating inequities.

This exploratory research shows that locally attuned policies and teaching practices may matter more than language proficiency thresholds in enabling quality EMI implementation in diverse global settings.

Notes

(1) Although there were more instructors and their respective students that agreed to participate, the 14 participants included here are those that completed all research phases including the interview.
(2) One class, Statistics, was left with just three students at the end of the course. The other two classes had four students from which to sample.
(3) Students were not interviewed before their courses because of logistics (for example, enrolment remained open until the first day of classes, and students did not enroll early enough).
(4) *Google Jamboard* uses virtual sticky notes that can be moved around and reorganized. The 'sticky note' approach to thematic analysis has been long described elsewhere, however, using real adhesive paper (e.g. Braun & Clarke, 2006), and in fact has been shown to possess properties that favor more scaffolded academic rigor (Maher *et al.*, 2018).

An acknowledgment is required: This research was funded by ETS under a TOEFL Committee of Examiners research grant. ETS does not discount or endorse the methodology, results, implications or opinions presented by the researchers.

References

Aizawa, I., Rose, H., Thompson, G. and Yanagisawa, S. (2020) Developing academic literacy through English-medium instruction: Learning experiences of Japanese undergraduates. *TESOL Quarterly* 54 (3), 657–680.
Braun, V. and Clarke, V. (2006) Using thematic analysis in psychology. *Qualitative Research in Psychology* 3 (2), 77–101.
Chang, J.-Y., Kim, W. and Lee, H. (2017) A language support program for English medium instruction courses: Its development and evaluation in an EFL setting. *International Journal of Bilingual Education and Bilingualism* 20 (5), 510–528.
Costa, F. and Coleman, J.A. (2013) A survey of English-medium instruction in Italian higher education. *International Journal of Bilingual Education and Bilingualism* 16 (1), 3–19.
Dafouz, E. (2018) English-medium instruction and teacher education programmes in higher education: Ideological forces and imagined identities at work. *International Journal of Bilingual Education and Bilingualism* 21 (5), 540–552.
Dafouz, E. and Smit, U. (2016) Towards a dynamic conceptual framework for English-medium education in multilingual university settings. *Applied Linguistics* 37 (3), 397–415.
Deroey, K.L. (2023) English medium instruction lecturer training programmes: Content, delivery, ways forward. *Journal of English for Academic Purposes* 62, 101223.
Dimova, S. (2020) English language requirements for enrolment in EMI programs in higher education: A European case. *Journal of English for Academic Purposes* 47, 100896.
Dörnyei, Z. (2007) *Research Methods in Applied Linguistics: Quantitative, Qualitative and Mixed Methodologies.* Oxford University Press.
Echevarria, J. and Short, D. (2010) Programs and practices for effective sheltered content instruction. *Improving Education for English Learners: Research-Based Approaches*, 250–321. California Department of Education.

Finardi, K. and Archanjo, R. (2018) Washback effects of the science without borders, English without borders and language without borders programs in Brazilian language policies and rights. *Language Policy and Language Acquisition Planning* 173–185.

Guimarães, F.F. and Kremer, M.M. (2020) Adopting English as a medium of instruction (EMI) in Brazil and Flanders (Belgium): A comparative study. *Ilha do Desterro* 73, 217–246.

Halbach A. and Lázaro A. (2015) *La acreditación del nivel de lengua inglesa en las universidades españolas: Actualización 2015* [The accreditation of the level of English language in Spanish universities: Update 2015]. *The British Council.* Available at: https://www.researchgate.net/publication/268502491_La_acreditacion_del_nivel_de_lengua_inglesa_en_las_universidades_espanolas.

Klaassen R.G., Bos M. (2010) English language screening for scientific staff at Delft University of Technology. *Hermes-Journal of Language and Communication Studies* 45, 61–75.

Lasagabaster, D. (2018) Fostering team teaching: Mapping out a research agenda for English-medium instruction at university level. *Language Teaching* 51 (3), 400–416.

Lasagabaster, D and Doiz, A. (eds) (2021) *Language Use in English-Medium Instruction at University: International Perspectives on Teacher Practice.* Routledge.

Li, J., King, R.B. and Wang, C. (2022) Profiles of motivation and engagement in foreign language learning: Associations with emotional factors, academic achievement, and demographic features. *System* 108, 102820.

Macaro, E., Curle, S., Pun, J., An, J. and Dearden, J. (2018) A systematic review of English medium instruction in higher education. *Language Teaching* 51 (1), 36–76.

MacIntyre, P.D., Ross, J. and Clément, R. (2019) Emotions are motivating. In M. Lamb, K. Csizér, A. Henry and S. Ryan (eds) *The Palgrave Handbook of Motivation for Language Learning* (pp. 183–202). Palgrave.

Maher, C., Hadfield, M., Hutchings, M. and De Eyto, A. (2018) Ensuring rigor in qualitative data analysis: A design research approach to coding combining NVivo with traditional material methods. *International Journal of Qualitative Methods* 17 (1), 23–34,

Margić, B.D. and Vodopija-Krstanović, I. (2018) Language development for English-medium instruction: Teachers' perceptions, reflections and learning. *Journal of English for Academic Purposes* 35, 31–41.

Martínez, R. (2016) English as a Medium of Instruction (EMI) in Brazilian higher education: challenges and opportunities. In K. Finardi (ed.) *English in Brazil: Views, Policies and Programs* (pp. 191–228). Eduel.

Martinez, R., Machado, P. and Palma, C. (2021) An exploratory analysis of language related episodes (LREs) in a Brazilian EMI context: Lecturers' and students' perspectives. In D. Lasagabaster and A. Doiz (eds) *Language Use in English-Medium Instruction at University* (pp. 11–33). Routledge.

Martinez, R. and Palma, A.C. (2022) Brazil trying English-Medium Instruction on for size: Emerging trends and policy. In J. McKinley and N. Galloway (eds) *English-Medium Instruction Practices in Higher Education: International Perspectives* (pp. 14–25). Bloomsbury.

Martinez, R. and Fernandes, K. (2020) Development of a teacher training course for English medium instruction for higher education professors in Brazil. In M. Sanchez-Perez (ed.) *Teacher Training for English-Medium Instruction in Higher Education* (pp. 125–152). IGI Global.

Martinez, R., Fogaça, F. and de Figueiredo, E.H.D. (2019) An instrument for English Medium Instruction (EMI) classroom observation in higher education. *Caderno de Letras* 35, 221–234.

Mercer, S. (2008) Learner self-beliefs. *ELT Journal* 62 (2), 182–183.

Morell, T. (2018) Multimodal competence and effective interactive lecturing. *System* 77, 70–79.

Nowell, L.S., Norris, J.M., White, D.E. and Moules, N.J. (2017) Thematic analysis: Striving to meet the trustworthiness criteria. *International Journal of Qualitative Methods* 16 (1), 1–13.

O'Dowd, R. (2018) The training and accreditation of teachers for English medium instruction: An overview of practice in European universities. *International Journal of Bilingual Education and Bilingualism* 21 (5), 553–563.

Rose, H. (2021) Students' language-related challenges of studying through English: What EMI teachers can do. In D. Lasagabaster and A. Doiz (eds) *Language Use in English-Medium Instruction at University: International Perspectives on Teacher Practice* (pp. 145–166). Routledge.

Schmidt, R.W. (1990) The role of consciousness in second language learning. *Applied Linguistics* 11 (2), 129–158.

Thompson, G., Aizawa, I., Curle, S. and Rose, H. (2022) Exploring the role of self-efficacy beliefs and learner success in English medium instruction. *International Journal of Bilingual Education and Bilingualism* 25 (1), 196–20.

Thompson, G., Curle, S. and Aizawa, I. (2022) It's worth the extra effort: Behind student perceptions of success in the study of content via English medium instruction in Japan. In J. McKinley and N. Galloway (eds) *English-Medium Instruction Practices in Higher Education: International Perspectives* (pp. 213–224). Bloomsbury.

Valcke, J. and Wilkinson, R. (2017) *Integrating Content and Language in Higher Education: Perspectives on Professional Practice*. Peter Lang.

Yeh, C.C. (2014) Taiwanese students' experiences and attitudes towards English-medium courses in tertiary education. *RELC Journal* 45 (3), 305–319.

Yin, R.K. (2017) *Case Study Research: Design and Methods* (6th edn). Sage.

Yuan, R., Liu, S. and Wang, Z. (2023) Humanising teacher education through translanguaging: Experiences from an online English-medium instruction (EMI) course. *International Journal of Multilingualism* 1–23.

Zhang, M. and Pladevall-Ballester, E. (2022) Students' attitudes and perceptions towards three EMI courses in mainland China. *Language, Culture and Curriculum* 35 (2), 200–216.

12 Assessing Students' Discipline-Specific Comprehension Ability in a Secondary English Medium Instruction Economics Classroom: The Role of Teacher–Researcher Collaboration

Wenyun Jia and Qiuyi Zhu

12.1 Introduction

In recent years, the global expansion of English-medium instruction (EMI) has been observed at the secondary level, especially in the Asian context (Gilanyi *et al.*, 2023). In mainland China (hereafter China), over 330,000 students have enrolled in EMI secondary-level courses by 2021 (Guojixuexiao, 2022). The institutions that offer these courses are also known as non-traditional international high schools (Poole, 2020). In these classrooms, English and Putonghua are used in content subject teaching and learning, to foster both subject knowledge and English language skills development. The dual curriculum model is popular in these EMI programmes (Center for China & Globalization, 2018). Some subjects are taught in Chinese following the national curriculum, while others (e.g. economics) are instructed in English or bilingually, aligning with an Anglophone curriculum such as the IGCSE (International General Certificate of Secondary Education) and A-level (Advanced level). Many high school students choose EMI, due to their aspirations to pursue overseas studies to gain global capital and to bypass the intense competition of the Chinese university entrance exam (Lu *et al.*, 2023). For example, some are concerned that their lower scores in middle school will restrict their eligibility to attend a higher-tier traditional high school, making it harder to secure admission to a reputable university in China.

In these EMI contexts, the curriculum and assessment requirements create a significant demand for students to read English-written textbooks and other materials to acquire knowledge and thrive in school life (Xiong *et al.*, 2023). For these EMI newcomers who possess basic English language abilities, it is critical to develop their ability to comprehend disciplinary-specific texts in English so that they can understand subject matter and participate in authentic English-mediated learning situations and disciplinary community practices (Airey, 2023; Shanahan & Shanahan, 2008).

Supporting EMI high school students' L2 (second language, which is English in this study) disciplinary reading ability poses the question of how well these students can comprehend L2 disciplinary texts. This leads to learning-oriented assessments that highlight the process of seeking and interpreting results to decide where students are now and how to scaffold next (Schellekens *et al.*, 2021). EMI scholars have also emphasised that assessment should inform decisions on learning rather than just admission (Aizawa *et al.*, 2020; Hultgren *et al.*, 2022). In this sense, assessment plays a vital role in diagnosing students' L2 disciplinary reading strengths and weaknesses, enabling teachers to identify what they need to work on.

However, EMI content teachers may find it difficult to implement effective L2 content reading assessments given the intricate relationship between language and content (Lo, 2021). These challenges are particularly pronounced for EMI high school content teachers in China due to the lack of systematic curriculum planning, the underdeveloped localised assessment resources and the challenges associated with content-language collaboration (Lu *et al.*, 2023; Poole *et al.*, 2022).

Implementing assessment and alleviating teacher challenges may benefit from teacher–researcher collaboration (TRC), because teachers' expertise, perspectives and knowledge of their classroom contexts may complement researchers' ideas and resources and thereby lead to significant pedagogical change. In particular, the potential of TRC to support the enhancement of EMI teaching and learning is increasingly discussed (e.g. Macaro *et al.*, 2016).

However, very few EMI studies have investigated fine-grain assessment that specifies language and content constructs in disciplinary-specific tasks (e.g. reading), nor has discussed how to implement and interpret the assessment results in learning-oriented and teacher–researcher collaborative ways (Li & Wu, 2018). More generally, much is unknown about the pedagogical concerns in EMI secondary contexts, specifically with regard to optimising academic environments for students with inadequate English abilities (Gilanyi *et al.*, 2023).

To address these gaps, this study aimed to understand how teachers and researchers collaborate to assess L2 disciplinary-specific comprehension ability in an EMI high school economics course in China. We examined the process of collaboration between two researchers and two EMI economics teachers in four collaboration phases (Fine, 2021; McKenney & Reeves, 2018) and the symmetrical and complementary roles played by the researchers and teachers throughout this collaborative process (Reimer & Bruce, 1994). The four collaboration phases are as follows:

(1) Co-exploration of problems: The team collaboratively identified key challenges related to assessing and reading in EMI classrooms.
(2) Co-design of assessments: The team collaboratively designed assessment instruments to evaluate EMI students' English reading ability in the context of economics learning.
(3) Co-evaluation of outcomes: The team collaboratively analysed the assessment results after the tests were administered.
(4) Co-reflection on instruction: The team collaboratively revisited the initial assessment and teaching challenges, discussing lessons learned from the assessment process and results to inform and improve future instruction.

12.2 Literature Review

12.2.1 Assessing EMI students

Assessment deeply influences teaching and learning. A high-quality assessment not only informs students about what is important but also direct teaching toward worthy and meaningful goals that benefit learning conditions of students (Lambert & Lines, 2013). Assessment has received growing interests in EMI contexts. Scholars have found that, English proficiency threshold is essential but not sufficient to predict success in EMI (e.g. Aizawa *et al.*, 2023). This emphasises the need for assessments that meticulously evaluate specific aspects of English proficiency in content learning and prioritise students' continuous learning process (Lambert & Lines, 2013).

This learning-oriented assessment, or assessment for/as learning (Schellekens *et al.*, 2021), refers to 'the process of seeking and interpreting evidence for use by students and their teachers to decide where the students are in their learning, where they need to go and how best to get there' (Assessment Reform Group, 2002: 1). It echoes the call for more studies to investigate how assessment can enhance learning and teaching in EMI classrooms (Hultgren *et al.*, 2022). For instance, Kao and Tsou (2017) promoted 'assessment as learning' in EMI by understanding the source of students' learning difficulties.

However, one challenge of implementing this learning-oriented assessment in EMI is how to assess and interpret results because it is difficult to discern the mastery of content knowledge and the mastery of L2 when the content knowledge is often tested in L2 (Lo, 2021). This informs the interrelated nature of language and content in EMI assessments to identify students' learning confusion and drive instruction multidimensionally (Hultgren *et al.*, 2022). Another challenge relates to EMI content teachers' awareness and perceived competence. Studies have found that many EMI teachers undervalued the importance of English proficiency in specific language skills for student success and faced difficulties in evaluating language components in their courses (Kao & Tsou, 2017; Li & Wu, 2018).

Knowledge from content-language integrated learning (CLIL) has responded to these challenges, suggesting that assessments should be fine-tuned with integrated language and content elements in each disciplinary-specific task (Xavier, 2020). This involves determining what to test (e.g. comprehension skills) and how to assess students (e.g. student interviews) while considering language competence in terms of subject-specific literacy (Xavier, 2020). These assessment approaches can be informative for EMI, as language proficiency is an integral yet often overlooked aspect of academic content learning. However, there is a lack of research examining the assessment of high school EMI students' comprehension in specific content domains.

12.2.2 Assessing L2 reading from a disciplinary literacy perspective

To EMI students, comprehending content in a foreign language is one of the major challenges with unheeded care. Scholars have found that many EMI students were struggling and passive readers (Soruç *et al.*, 2021). Specific to EMI high school students in China, learning content through their L2 was the major obstacle to their lack of adequate English ability (Poole *et al.*, 2022); and the comprehension challenges were found relating to technical vocabulary, normalisation and dense information in sentences (Lu *et al.*, 2023). Unfortunately, these problems have not been effectively addressed in the classroom (Pun & Thomas, 2020). Considering the role of learning-oriented assessment mentioned above, assessing disciplinary-specific L2 reading can be a valuable approach to improving EMI teaching.

From the disciplinary literacy perspective, reading competence can be understood as one literacy ability to 'engage in social, semiotic, and cognitive practices consistent with those of content experts' (Fang, 2012: 19). Therefore, the reading skills that are assessed should align with the skills required for disciplinary learning in order to ensure content validity (Behrman, 2000). When designing the test and interpreting the results, one needs to consider the current reading instruction in subject classes, the characteristics of disciplinary-specific text (e.g. genres and specialised language) and habit of mind associated with the discipline (e.g. reasoned thinking) (Fang & Pace, 2013; Massey, 2015; Uccelli *et al.*, 2015). Take economics reading, for example; one should be capable of explaining, discussing and applying economic issues based on their reading (Yuan, 2019).

Furthermore, disciplinary-specific L2 reading assessment requires an authentic and in-depth understanding of the comprehension process (Watkins & Lindahl, 2010). Therefore, a qualitative investigation of the reading process, such as the stimulated recall method, can provide valuable information on readers' sense-making, as verbalisation of their thoughts can provide an introspective view of their cognitive processes during reading (Gass & Mackey, 2016). For instance, Arkın and Osam (2015), using the stimulated recall method, revealed that EMI students were at risk of limited comprehension and misunderstanding of disciplinary content.

Collectively, these understandings support the teachers and researchers in designing and using assessments that go beyond mere memorisation of isolated facts and emphasise inquiry and thinking processes with suitable language required to analyse disciplinary-specific texts.

12.2.3 Teacher–researcher collaboration in assessment

EMI scholars have highlighted the vital role of collaboration in identifying students' linguistic needs and motivating teachers to perceive themselves as capable of integrating content and language (Liu *et al.*, 2020; Lo, 2014; Macaro *et al.*, 2016; Maxwell-Reid & Lau, 2024; Nguyen *et al.*, 2023). Although these studies did not focus on assessment issues, some relevant episodes can shed light on how TRC could be more effective during assessment. For instance, Macaro *et al.* (2016) reported that EMI teachers gained a better understanding of addressing lexical issues and the interplay between language and content through collaboration. English teachers also became more aware of the language used in specific subjects. Maxwell-Reid and Lau (2014) described a collaboration between a linguist and a science teacher, where the science teacher contributed content knowledge and evaluated students' difficulties related to curriculum objectives, while the linguist explained those difficulties in terms of language resources needed. Regarding collaboration in reading assessment, But (2020) reported a disciplinary-specific reading assessment under the collaboration between content area faculty and literacy specialists. They coordinated to select texts (e.g. considering content relevance, readability level, text features), create and revise questions, and design scoring.

These studies imply two key points: firstly, the dual significance of content and language in EMI assessment necessitated collaboration between literacy and subject area experts; the second is about the complementary and symmetrical dynamics between linguistic and content specialists. Symmetry refers to the equal responsibilities throughout the entire processes (Andrée *et al.*, 2020). Despite some criticism, this notion is valuable in seeking common goals and making processes explicit to each party during collaboration (Herrenkohl *et al.*, 2010). Complementarity stresses the complementary strengths of each party (e.g. researchers' theoretical understanding can be practicalised with teachers' knowledge of students and curriculum) (McKenney & Reeves, 2018). Therefore, collaborative assessment design should involve joint and iterative negotiation, shared authority, open discussion of conflicts and mutual utilisation and appreciation of each other's knowledge and expertise (Olin *et al.*, 2023; Reimer & Bruce, 1994; Säfström *et al.*, 2021).

Still, little TRC research can be found targeting assessment in the EMI context, except for Li and Wu (2018), who provided materials for EMI teachers to evaluate their students' understanding of content and English receptive skills. The potential that TRC may offer for assessment in EMI classrooms underscores the need for more research to understand how TRC can be effectively conducted.

12.3 Methodology

12.3.1 Research context

The setting of this study was an EMI programme at a high school in a Tier 3 city in China. At this school, IGCSE economics courses were taught in a combination of English and Chinese by two Chinese economics content teachers who possessed basic skills in delivering lessons in English. The student participants were pursuing IGCSE and IELTS qualifications (at least 5.5) for future college entrance. All of them had begun learning economics in an EMI context in the 10th grade.

12.3.2 Teacher–researcher collaboration

The key endeavour of this collaboration was the joint design and interpretation of an English reading assessment, specifically the L2 reading ability of 10th- and 11th-grade students studying economics in EMI classrooms.

The study involved four collaborators: two teachers and two researchers. The teacher collaborators from the targeted school, Lin and Xing, had each taught 10th- and 11th-grade economics for over two years, respectively. At the time of the study, Qiuyi, a former high school EMI economics teacher in China, was a student researcher in EMI education; and Wenyun, a doctoral researcher, specialised in applied linguistics and EMI education.

The collaboration team worked together for three months, from October 2023 to January 2024, applying the collaboration protocol adapted from the educational design study (McKenney & Reeves, 2018) and the co-designing assessment framework (Fine, 2021). The four collaboration phases and their purposes are shown in Table 12.1.

Table 12.1 Four teacher–researcher collaboration phases and purposes

Collaboration phase	Purpose Teacher–researcher work together to:
Co-exploration of problems	Explore the assessment challenges to be addressed.
Co-design of assessments	Design economics reading assessments with a learning-oriented end goal.
Co-evaluation of outcomes	Evaluate the reading assessment results from a comprehension test and stimulated recall.
Co-reflection on instruction	Reflect on the initial identified classroom challenge and lessons learned.

12.3.3 Data collection

To address the research question of how teachers and researchers collaboratively assess students' reading ability, the researchers collected data during each of four above-specified phases of collaboration. The data collected to depict TRC activities included approximately 400 minutes of audio recordings capturing teacher–researcher and researcher–researcher communication (e.g. conversations during each of four phrases); two collaboration documents (i.e. one for test design, one for results evaluation and reflection) with notes from both sides.

12.3.4 Data analysis

The first author engaged in qualitative data analysis, guided by Miles *et al.* (2014) at the end of each phase of the TRC. First, the researcher familiarised herself with the verbatim transcriptions of audio recorded meetings with the teachers and with the organised collaboration documents (Yin, 2010).

The aim of the first cycle of coding was to generate codes to separate the data into chunks based on the TRC framework. Structural coding was adopted because it is suitable for gaining an overview of specific segments framed by the research purpose (Saldaña, 2016). Four structural codes were identified based on the TRC framework: problem exploration, solution design, outcome evaluation and reflection. The subcoding method was then used to tag codes under these four structural codes (Saldaña, 2016). The subcodes were derived from the literature on the two types of relationships involved in TRC: symmetrical and complementary. 'Symmetrical' describes the development of a shared aim of activities or the understanding of each other's practices. 'Complementary' describes one party's contribution of perspectives, knowledge and experience that complement those of another party. For instance, the subcode 'problem exploration–complementary–teacher' referred to an episode in which one

TRC phases	Symmetrical	Complementary	
		T helps R by...	R helps T by...
Co-exploration of problems	• Forming a shared understanding of research objectives and research context. • R helps T understand research aim and process. • T helps R understand the education context.	• Sharing challenges related to reading, context issues, their perceptions of the importance of reading, and their current teaching and assessing challenges.	• Providing discussion topics and prompts. • Proposing several key education problems for further discussion.
Co-design of assessments	• Forming a shared goal of developing reliable assessments. • R familiarise T with assessment design approaches. • Reaching agreement of the two assessment methods to be used (one reading test and one stimulated recall).	• Defining constructs in content domain. • Evaluating constructs in language domain relating to their knowledge of key language features in economic learning. • Suggesting texts based on students' current knowledge. • Revising and evaluating items. • Devising questions for stimulated recall. • Matching items under each construct for content validity.	• Defining constructs in language domain. • Providing resources for Ts in text selection. • Providing text complexity analysis for T's reference. • Designing test items based on language assessment principles. • Designing stimulated recall.
Co-evaluation of outcomes	• Ensuring the transparent test analysis process. • R shares and explains quantitative and qualitative analysis results to T.	• Reviewing and refining the qualitative coding. • Interpreting results based on their understanding of students.	• Analyzing quantitative reading assessment results. • Selecting six students for stimulated recall. • Analyzing qualitative data.
Co-reflection on instruction	• Possessing a shared aim of using the result to inform teaching practices. • R understands T's constraints when reflecting on their previous teaching methods.	• Reflecting on how the results develop their understanding of students, which areas they overlooked. • Planning what they will do in the future based on test results and contextual considerations.	• Facilitating discussion and T's reflections through prompting questions and discussion themes. • Proposing some instructional methods when T lacks relevant information.

Note: T stands for "teachers." R stands for "researchers."

Figure 12.1 Major processes in four teacher–researcher collaborative phases

teacher used her practical knowledge to complement the researchers' understanding of the reading assessment context.

Next, inductive codes, which emerged from the study data, were generated and collated with the subcodes. The researcher paid attention to observable actions and specific activities during TRC, such as 'sharing current assessments' and 'asking the researchers questions'. The second author conducted member-checking until the consensus reached (Cronbach's alpha reliability (a) = 0.956).

During the second cycle of coding, two patterns were identified across the individual codes (Saldaña, 2016): teachers helping researchers and researchers helping teachers. For instance, when co-designing the assessments, the teachers assisted the researchers in evaluating the relationship between the assessment constructs with their knowledge of key language features in economics learning, while the researchers aided the teachers by providing resources for text selection. A comprehensive overview of the codes can be found in Figure 12.1.

12.3.5 Reading assessment instruments

This study focuses on reporting the processes involved in TRC rather than the assessment results. For clarity, however, we now briefly introduce the instruments used to assess the students' L2 economics reading ability. The instruments used consisted of one multiple-choice test and one stimulated recall interview. The development of the test and interview and the evaluation of their results were a joint effort by the teachers and researchers and are presented in more detail in the Findings section.

12.3.5.1 Multiple-choice test

A total of 31 students (15 from 10th grade; 16 from 11th grade) were assessed with a reading comprehension test, which was an assessment collaboratively developed by the teachers and researchers to measure the students' English reading ability in economics. The text (525 words in English) used in the test was entitled 'Seasonal flavours bring in millions of dollars in sales every year'. This text was chosen for the following reasons.

(1) The chosen text discussed scarcity and customer behaviour, which are the topics covered in the grade 10–11 IGCSE curriculum.
(2) The passage consisted of economic discourse patterns, such as economics-related arguments and explanations. Although it was not a typical journal article, it served as an illustration of how concepts from economics can be applied in real-life situations. It offered the students the chance to apply their economics knowledge in new contexts for the purpose of evaluating their English reading skills alongside their understanding of economics.
(3) The researchers quantitatively analysed the difficulty of the text to strike an appropriate balance between the text's content and the students' reading skills (Fisher *et al.*, 2012). The Coleman–Liau readability index, which was used to assess readability (index = 8), indicated that this text was suited to English language learners with a low to moderate level of English proficiency, which were the target group of this study.

The multiple-choice items were designed to include content and language domains, with 10 items in each domain. The language domain tested three levels of ability: lexical level, sentence level and discourse level. These three levels were chosen based on a review of the literature on key factors influencing L2 readers' comprehension in specific discipline areas. Language features of school disciplinary texts, such as technical vocabulary, normalisation and intricate grammar, have been found to significantly hinder L2 students' comprehension (Schleppegrell, 2004; Snow & Uccelli, 2009), including EMI students (Uchihara & Harada, 2018). Discourse-level language skills, such as text organisation and tracking themes, have also been posited to influence scientific thinking, including in economics (Yuan, 2020); and to be associated with L2 students' reading development in school-relevant literacy practices (Uccelli *et al.*, 2015).

The content domain included three levels based on the students' knowledge of economics discourse patterns (Yuan, 2019) and economic literacy (Walstad *et al.*, 2013). Specifically, the knowledge level pertained to the students' ability to understand the economics facts or definitions and to describe them in a form close to the way they were presented. The comprehension level pertained to the students' understanding of the economics discourse patterns, including their ability to explain, reason about, compare and summarise the content. The application level pertained to the students' ability to apply the information from the text to new situations and real-life circumstances.

12.3.5.2 Stimulated recall

A qualitative approach was then used to assess the students' reading comprehension to reach a deeper understanding of their cognitive processes when reading this text and to avoid biased interpretations of the test results. In each grade level, we randomly chose three students who had obtained high, middle and low scores in the multiple-choice test, for a total of six participants (two for each test score level).

The first artefact prompt was each participant's own reading test paper, on which they had marked their choices and taken notes. The second artefact prompt comprised verbatim transcriptions of the students' audio-recorded retelling of the text in Chinese. Prompt questions were designed to elicit the students' descriptions and interpretations of their reading and test-taking process (Gass & Mackey, 2016). These included questions on how they had selected their answers (e.g. 'What support you on this answer selection?), whether they could recall the content knowledge based on the text information (e.g. 'Is the idea of scarcity in this text similar to what you have learned from the textbook') and whether they could explain real-life economics events drawing on the text.

12.4 Findings

To illustrate the process of TRC-based assessment, this section describes the work in which the teachers and researchers engaged in each of the four phases. In particular, the symmetrical and complementary relationships between the teachers and researchers and the ways in which they helped each other are highlighted.

12.4.1 Phase 1: Co-exploration of problems

Phase 1 aimed to gain a holistic understanding of the challenges involved in assessing and reading in EMI classrooms. From a symmetry perspective, the researchers and teachers formed a shared understanding, with the teachers helping the researchers understand the observed EMI programme and current assessments and the researchers clarifying the research aims and plans with the teachers. From a complementary standpoint, the researchers facilitated the discussion by organising one meeting where all team members discussed current teaching and assessment issues devising discussion topics, asking guiding questions and sharing relevant literature. The teachers shared their on-the-ground understanding and experience.

The researchers first shared existing findings on the L2 disciplinary reading issues EMI teachers and students had encountered, asking the teachers if they resonated with these studies. The teachers stressed the importance of reading in learning economics:

> *Because the majority of them want to study economics in university, reading the [economics] textbook will prepare them for a smoother university experience and familiarise them with foreign materials and learning environments. (Lin)*

The researchers expressed agreement with the teachers' perceptions of the importance of reading. The researchers then asked about how these perceptions had been put into practice, teachers both admitted to lacking relevant pedagogical knowledge and methods beyond translation and vocabulary instruction.

The challenges the students faced raised by both teachers were students lacked English abilities and awareness of the importance of English economics reading. The researcher further prompted the teachers to analyse the reasons for this, which were related to the current exams:

> *The exam (English mediated) mainly consists of multiple-choice and short-answer questions, which are usually not very long. So, students only need to master the key words to read the questions. (Xing)*

The researcher then asked the teachers to explain how they assessed their students' reading ability in economics. According to the teachers, they used self-designed tests that included some translation items, asking students to translate key economics concepts from English into Chinese or vice versa. The researchers further prompted the teachers to elaborate on why they primarily focused on translation in their assessments:

> *I want to provide them with more opportunities to be exposed to key vocabularies. Because their English abilities are poor, they need to memorise these keywords first. (Lin)*

Researchers shared concerns about this approach. For instance, one of the researchers mentioned that while Lin recognised the role of language and literacy ability in content learning, the language assessment component seemed to be an addition rather than an integrated aspect. Another researcher stated that directly equating discrete vocabulary knowledge to reading ability would be biased, as this would overlook other important comprehension skills in economics learning, such as the ability to recall economics concepts and models to explain economics issues raised in texts. The teachers argued that despite many other important competencies, the students' English proficiency was too limited to allow them to develop these more challenging skills. Nevertheless, the teachers admitted that they were not well aware of their students' specific English reading proficiencies needed for economics learning.

In summary, the meeting revealed that the teachers were confused about how to facilitate their students' economics reading ability and that they lacked information about the students' reading ability based on current assessments. It is noteworthy that the two teachers' issues and thoughts were nearly identical, which may be attributable to their sharing the same school context and their students' similar levels of English language proficiency between the two grades.

12.4.2 Phase 2: Co-design of assessments

Phase 2 aimed to design assessments of the students' English reading ability for economics learning. The symmetrical roles of the teachers and researchers were evident in their shared commitment to a learning-oriented assessment principle. This approach emphasised that assessment results should guide and enhance instructional practices, rather than merely provide a static, numerical snapshot of student abilities. To achieve this, the team recognised that despite designing a single reading test comprising multiple-choice questions, stimulated recall interviews was essential to gain deeper insights into individual students' thought processes during the reading test and to understand the comprehension challenges they faced, which could not be captured through multiple-choice questions alone.

When developing key constructs (i.e. language and content domains) for the assessment, in which researchers took the lead with teachers' suggestions and feedback. The researchers explained to the teachers how the language and content domains (mentioned in the Methodology section) were constructed according to the relevant literature. The teachers provided insights into how to adapt this knowledge to this school context, because they were familiar with the UK-based economics examinations that these students would take and the skills their students would need in developing content knowledge. For instance, Lin argued for the applicability of a three-level economics literacy schema (Walstad *et al.*, 2013):

> *This could reflect the skills our students need to understand the basic economic concepts and effectively prepare them for future economic activities.*

The teachers also offered insights into the selection of the text, based on their knowledge of what the students had learned, the prior knowledge they should have, the typical genres they frequently encountered in economics studies and how this co-designed assessment could fit into the school curriculum. For instance, the teachers noted several key text topics (e.g. scarcity; demand and supply) that their students had learnt. This helped the researchers to control the variable of background knowledge in the interpretation of reading scores. Furthermore, the teachers preferred microeconomics texts and economics reports over textbooks or academic journals because 'recent exams incorporate more current economics topics' (Xing) and 'journal articles might pose a challenge for students at their current level of understanding'(Ling).

In designing the reading test items and stimulated recall prompt questions (see details in the Methodology section), the researchers initially drafted the items based on predetermined constructs. The prompt questions specifically targeted students' higher-order thinking abilities to gain a deeper understanding of their potential comprehension challenges in content reading. For instance, many of these questions focused on 'why' and 'how' aspects (e.g. How did you locate the answer for this question? Why do you choose this item?). Then, the teachers helped the researchers by suggesting the order of items, improving test validity and refining prompting questions. For instance, Lin evaluated the test to ascertain its relevance to the students' coursework and whether its level of difficulty was appropriate. Xing suggested some prompts used in the stimulated recall to investigate how certain expressions (e.g. 'in other words') impacted the students' understanding.

12.4.3 Phase 3: Co-evaluation of outcomes

In Phase 3, the teachers and researchers collaboratively analysed the assessment results. The extent of symmetry (seeking common goals and making processes explicit to each party) between the teachers and researchers was characterised by a transparent test result analysis process, in which the researchers helped the teachers to understand the test scoring and stimulated recall analysis processes. From a complementary standpoint, which stresses the distinct contributions stemming from various areas of expertise, the researchers took the lead in analysing the students' test scores and stimulated recall responses.

The researchers shared the results with the teachers and the teachers' roles in reviewing these researcher-generated results were crucial and contributed to the accuracy of the results. For instance, one student said in the stimulated recall interview, 'because this paragraph mentioned consumers many times, I think this section is something about this economic agent'. The researchers interpreted this as the student's formulating semantic predictions with separating known words. Xing further added to this interpretation: 'They simply overlook unfamiliar words, reading in a fragmented manner and making unreasonable guesses'.

As this study focuses on exploring TRC processes, we do not elaborate on the test analysis; however, some details are provided here for clarity. In general, the reading test showed that the accuracy rate was significant low in the sentence and discourse levels of the language domain. The performance in the content domain was lower than that in the language domain. The prominent issues observed in the stimulated recall, across the low, middle and high achievers, comprising the following.

(A) Language domain:
   (1) Confusing words with others that sound or look alike (e.g. customers and company).
   (2) Trying to make sense based on separate words.
   (3) Inability to unpack dense information presented with complex syntactic grammatical features.
   (4) Lack of awareness regarding logical flow between sentences and paragraph-level relationships.
   (5) Failing to identify reading confusion.
(B) Content domain:
   (1) Failing to identify and understand key economic knowledge.
   (2) Bing constrained by textbook definitions, preventing application to specific scenarios in readings.
   (3) Lack of critical analysis (e.g. unidimensional analysis of economic behaviours).
   (4) Heavy reliance on personal experience rather than rigorous reasoning when inferring economics behaviours and impacts.

12.4.4 Phase 4: Co-reflection on instruction

In Phase 4, the teachers and researchers discussed how the assessment results served as a meaningful source in identifying what the teachers needed to work on and how this TRC affected the teachers' views on instruction and assessment. Symmetry was exemplified through the shared objective of using this assessment to shape future instructional practices.

Regarding their complementary roles, the researchers facilitated the discussion by asking the teachers the following questions: Which results surprise you? How do the results alter or confirm your perspective on the students? In what areas would you like to make changes to your teaching? The researchers also specifically inquired as to whether the teachers would allocate more attention to language-related issues in future economics classroom instruction.

As to the teachers' contributions, their reflections deepened their own and the researchers' understanding of these EMI students, which led to informed instructional change. The teachers collectively acknowledged this TRC experience as providing thoughtful and effective input, filling the gap created by previously unavailable resources for testing their students' language proficiency in EMI learning and bolstering their attention to facilitating their students' specific linguistic competence.

Accordingly, the teachers revisited their prior teaching approaches. The first notable change was their re-evaluation of self-perceived accountability in language teaching:

> *I used to prioritise content before seeing these results. But now I think it's important to highlight things [language] that are easy to overlook. (Lin)*

They highlighted the students' ability at the previously overlooked lexical level, particularly regarding issues of word confusion, especially among the low and middle achievers.

> *This assessment told me that many students confused high-frequency simple words and lacked grammatical knowledge. Perhaps, I just based on high achievers and assumed everyone knew these words. (Lin)*

They particularly mentioned the useful information obtained from the discourse domain results, including the language used to unpack dense information, track themes, connect ideas logically and organise analytic texts:

> *Understanding the logical relationships between paragraphs is important. I didn't pay much attention to this before because the textbooks typically provide clear subtitles that indicate paragraph functions, such as definition, pros and cons. (Xing)*

Based on the stimulated recall results, which revealed that the low and mid-achievers lacked the metacognitive ability to identify confusion:

> *I will ask these students to think aloud and inquire about where they did not understand. (Lin)*

The researchers also prompted teachers to consider how to achieve the balance between content and language learning. The teachers realised that bolstering the students' academic English repertoires and awareness could act as a vehicle to enhance their economics knowledge learning and reasoning.

The researchers and teachers then discussed how to translate these reflections into practice. While challenges existed (e.g. the constraints of limited classroom time), the teachers mentioned that the results made the need to engage the students in interactive sense-making processes more evident:

> *Previous lessons were all about me translating English sentences. The students didn't get a chance to participate in the process of comprehending or to think about how they should understand it. I will group them to discuss their comprehension in future classes. (Xing)*

They also emphasised the need to use multiple resources to expand the students' genre awareness and ability to apply economics knowledge:

> *I will expose them to economics articles beyond textbooks, like case studies. (Lin)*

12.5 Discussion

Situated in the context of an EMI secondary economics course in China, this study sought to understand TRC in designing and interpreting reading assessments of students' L2 economics comprehension ability. This four-phase TRC-based assessment featured a shared commitment between the researchers and teachers to using assessment to drive instruction through a rich, detailed understanding of the students' weaknesses in L2 economics reading (Reimer & Bruce, 2006; Schellekens *et al.*, 2021). The findings highlighted the processes of transforming and leveraging content and language expertise, as well as teaching and research experience (Säfström *et al.*, 2021).

Figure 12.1 displays the major processes in each collaborative stage. The symmetry principle guiding this TRC laid the foundation for smooth interaction and reciprocal exchange (Andrée *et al.*, 2020). At each stage, the team emphasised the learning-oriented goals of this assessment, focusing on what the students lacked and how instruction should proceed. Attention was paid to both parties' needs and conditions. In contrast to the approach taken in Li and Wu's (2018) study, where researchers provided assessment resources to EMI teachers, this study's collaboration emphasised teachers' voices and ideas throughout the entail process of assessment design and interpretation (e.g. their specific reading assessment needs and current assessment challenges). This shared focus and understanding served as a motivating force for collaboration, because this goal was meaningful to both sides by addressing teaching practice issues while also contributing to the research domain (Herrenkohl *et al.*, 2010).

Regarding their complementary roles, the researchers took the lead in initiating and planning a collaboration-based assessment study, analysing assessment results and organising discussions of outcome evaluation and reflection, drawing on their expertise in systemic functional linguistics, EMI education and language assessment. The content teachers proved to be indispensable, given their content knowledge and teaching experience, in enabling a deeper understanding of the assessment context and the examinee. This enhanced the design of appropriate reading assessments and assisted with outcome evaluation. The teachers' work experience in the underexplored EMI secondary context and experience of teaching young EMI students addressed gaps in the researchers' knowledge, mitigated the risk of context irrelevance and made the assessment process authentic and meaningful. Specifically, the teachers brought insights into how these students were assessed through IGCSE for overseas study, as well as foreign curriculum requirements, the students' prior English and content learning experience and their daily learning habits. Similar findings regarding the complementary roles of the researchers and teachers who coordinated with and helped each other with their respective areas of expertise were also identified in studies by But (2020) and Maxwell-Reid and Lau (2024), as mentioned in the literature review.

Nonetheless, tension emerged during the collaboration – a finding also reported in other collaboration studies (Olin *et al.*, 2023; Säfström *et al.*, 2021), in which they suggest recognising the complexity inherent in real teaching practices and emphasise the need for ongoing dialogue between both parties to develop teachers' readiness for a changed practice. In this study, when students' academic shortcomings were disclosed by the assessment, the teachers initially emphasised the students' limitations, such as their laziness. After the researchers further developed the conversation with sympathy, the teachers started discussing how to customise instruction based on the students' current English proficiency levels and individual differences. The complexity and challenges inherent in this case of TRC may imply that a broader discourse on effective collaboration is needed in future EMI research (McKinley, 2019).

Perhaps a more interesting finding lies in the reflective lessons learned from the assessment results, which can inform teaching and research alike. In terms of research, studies have discussed the reading difficulties that EMI students face, as mentioned in the literature review (Lu *et al.*, 2023; Soruç *et al.*, 2021). By using a contextualised and fine-tuned assessment to measure students' reading ability from a disciplinary literacy perspective and with attention to language–content relationships, this study develops our understanding of what such students currently lack for their successful EMI learning. This knowledge can inform teachers in developing their students' L2 disciplinary reading ability to enhance their skills in solving content problems and cultivating a discipline-specific way of understanding and thinking (Airey, 2023; Shanahan & Shanahan, 2008).

Notably, we revealed a substantial reading ability gap among these students, partly attributable to the absence of an entrance threshold for EMI classes. It was also concerning that most of the students confused non-technical vocabulary frequently used in economics learning (e.g. experts and exports), struggled to unpack dense information and lacked awareness of and language ability to identify logical relationships. They also had troubles in economic reasoning and faced challenges in relating knowledge gained from the text to school knowledge. These issues may have been related to the fact that these EMI newcomers were expected to study content knowledge in a foreign language, and their language ability and literacy skills had not been calibrated for this purpose in their previous schooling. Moreover, as found in similar EMI high school programmes in China (Lu *et al.*, 2023; Poole *et al.*, 2022), the participating content teachers had been left to develop their own methods in dealing with the challenges brought about by this situation.

In terms of teaching, reflecting on teaching approaches in response to assessment results holds promise for addressing the aforementioned issues. As in other collaborative research mentioned in literature review, where teachers were found to transform their previous perceptions (Liu *et al.*, 2020; Macaro *et al.*, 2016), the teachers from this study also re-examined their responsibilities as content teachers. They realised that their previous approaches to language scaffolding, such as excessive teacher-fed translation with insufficient teacher–student interaction, were not conducive to facilitating their students' reading ability. This indicates that TRC-based assessment may address the commonly observed teacher-centred and non-supportive dynamics in EMI classrooms.

The teachers in this study also experienced a notable shift in their language awareness, especially regarding language functions within and across disciplines. For instance, they said that they would vocalise to their students about how cohesive language functions in economics texts and how reading involves piecing ideas into a logical course of action (Yuan, 2019). This indicates that although they had recognised the importance of English, the assessment design process and results clarified their uncertainty about whether teaching language in content classrooms truly works, which inspired them to find ways to incorporate content and language learning. It could be argued that the TRC-based assessment process empowered the content teachers to legitimise themselves as EMI teachers who can explicitly incorporate language instruction into content classrooms with less uncertainty.

However, the teachers also expressed concern about the challenge of continuing to learn about students' reading, writing and other language skills on their own. This illustrates the importance of long-term TRC, especially in these emerging secondary EMI classrooms, where content teachers are not trained as language or EMI teachers and systematic political and professional development is still lacking.

12.6 Conclusion

In this article, we have investigated the process of TRC in designing and interpreting L2 economics assessments in a EMI secondary-level context. By reflecting on teachers' and researchers' roles from symmetry and complementarity perspectives and the lessons learned from the assessments, this study demonstrates the potential advantage of TRC-based learning-oriented assessment in improving content teachers' perception of the language–content relationship, their understanding of students' language abilities for content learning and their instructional approaches.

We also acknowledge the limitations of our work. Firstly, the present co-designed reading assessment did not consider students' proficiency in interpreting visual representations in economics. Moreover, English teachers' and students' perspectives on the assessment processes and results can provide more valuable information on how to support L2 disciplinary literacy abilities. For a more informative evaluation, tracking the results of the TRC on the actual changes in teachers' daily instruction and assessment would be valuable.

References

Airey, J. (2023) Disciplinary literacy and English-medium instruction. In *Language Issues in English-Medium Instruction 22nd–23rd April 2023 Keynote speaker.* National Science and Technology Council.

Aizawa, I., Rose, H., Thompson, G. and Curle, S. (2020) Beyond the threshold: Exploring English language proficiency, linguistic challenges, and academic language skills of Japanese students in an English medium instruction programme. *Language Teaching Research* 27 (4), 837–861. https://doi.org/10.1177/1362168820965510

Andrée, M., Danckwardt-Lilliestrӧm, K. and Wiblom, J. (2020) Ethical challenges of symmetry in participatory science education research–Proposing a heuristic for ethical reflection. In K. Otrel-Cass, M. Ándrée and M. Ryu (eds) *Examining Ethics in Contemporary Science Education Research: Being Responsive and Responsible* (pp. 123–141). Springer International Publishing.

Arkın, E. and Osam, N. (2015) English-medium higher education. A case study in a Turkish university context. In S. Dimova, A.K. Hultgren and C. Jensen (eds) *English-Medium Instruction in European Higher Education* (pp. 177–200). De Gruyter Mouton.

Assessment Reform Group (2002) *Assessment for Learning: 10 Principles.* Available at http://www.assessment-reform-group.org/CIE3.PDF

Behrman, E.H. (2000) Developmental placement decisions: Content-specific reading assessment. *Journal of Developmental Education* 23 (3), 12.

But, J.C. (2020) Assessment: A tool for improving disciplinary literacy. In J. But (ed.) *Teaching College-Level Disciplinary Literacy.* Palgrave Macmillan.

Center for China and Globalization (2018) *China International School Blue Book 2018.* Center for China and Globalization.

Fang, Z. (2012) Language correlates of disciplinary literacy. *Topics in Language Disorders* 32 (1), 19–34.

Fang, Z. and Pace, B.G. (2013) Teaching with challenging texts in the disciplines: Text complexity and close reading. *Journal of Adolescent & Adult Literacy* 57 (2), 104–108.

Fine, C.G. B.M. (2021) Co-designing for translanguaging in middle school science formative assessment. PhD thesis, University of Colorado at Boulder.

Fisher, D., Frey, N. and Lapp, D. (2012) *Text Complexity: Raising Rigor in Reading.* International Reading Association.

Gass, S.M. and Mackey, A. (2016) *Stimulated Recall Methodology in Applied Linguistics and L2 Research.* Routledge.

Gilanyi, L., Gao, X.A. and Wang, S. (2023) EMI and CLIL in Asian schools: A scoping review of empirical research between 2015 and 2022. *Heliyon.*

Guojixuexiao (2022) *2022 China Internationalized School Admission Guide Blue Book.* Available at http://www.guojixuexiao.org/ieiczx/ieic14688.html

Herrenkohl, L.R., Kawasaki, K. and Dewater, L.S. (2010) Inside and outside: Teacher-researcher collaboration. *The New Educator* 6 (1), 74–92.

Hultgren, A.K., Owen, N., Shrestha, P., Kuteeva, M. and Mežek, Š. (2022) Assessment and English as a medium of instruction: Challenges and opportunities. *Journal of English-Medium Instruction* 1 (1), 105–123.

Kao, Y.T. and Tsou, W. (2017) EMI course assessment: A survey study of the issues. In W.L. Tsou and S.M. Kao (eds) *English as a Medium of Instruction in Higher Education: Implementations and Classroom Practices in Taiwan* (pp. 183–205). Springer.

Lambert, D. and Lines, D. (2013) *Understanding Assessment: Purposes, Perceptions, Practice*. Routledge.

Li, N. and Wu, J. (2018) Exploring assessment for learning practices in the EMI classroom in the context of Taiwanese higher education. *Language Education & Assessment* 1 (1), 28–44.

Lo, Y.Y. (2014) Collaboration between L2 and content subject teachers in CBI: Contrasting beliefs and attitudes. *RELC Journal* 45, 181–196.

Lo, Y.Y. (2021) Researching assessment in EMI. In J.K.H. Pun and S.M. Curle (eds) *Research Methods in English Medium Instruction*. Routledge.

Lu, C., So, W.W. M., Lee, Y.C. and Yeung, Y.Y. (2023) Exploring the problems of learning science in the English medium: A study on high school students' perceptions and attitudes in China. *Asia Pacific Journal of Education* 43 (4), 1224–1239.

Macaro, E., Akincioglu, M. and Dearden, J. (2016) English-medium instruction in universities: A collaborative experiment in Turkey. *Studies in English Language Teaching* 4 (1), 51.

Massey, D.D. (2015) Reading history: Moving from memorizing facts to critical thinking. In K.L. Santi and D.K. Reed (eds) *Improving Reading Comprehension of Middle and High School Students* (Vol. 10). Springer International.

Maxwell-Reid, C. and Lau, K.C. (2024) Investigating student difficulties in English-medium secondary classes: A functional linguist and a science educator in collaboration. *Journal of English for Academic Purposes* 67, 101315.

McKenney, S. and Reeves, T.C. (2018) *Conducting Educational Design Research*. Routledge.

McKinley, J. (2019) Evolving the TESOL teaching-research nexus. *TESOL Quarterly* 53 (3), 875–884. https://doi.org/10.1002/tesq.509

Miles, M.B., Huberman, M.A. and Saldaña, J. (2014) *Qualitative Data Analysis. A Methods Sourcebook* (3rd edn). SAGE Publications.

Nguyen, M.H., Turner, M. and Premier, J. (2023) The distributed knowledge base: Preservice language teachers' positioning in language–content teacher collaboration. *System* 114, 103022.

Olin, A., Almqvist, J. and Hamza, K. (2023) To recognize oneself and others in teacher-researcher collaboration. *Educational Action Research* 31 (2), 248–264.

Poole, A. (2020) Decoupling Chinese internationalised schools from normative constructions of the international school. *Compare: A Journal of Comparative and International Education* 50 (3), 447–454.

Poole, A., Liujinya, Y. and Yue, S. (2022) 'We're away from everything': Understanding the struggles faced by internationalized schools in non-urban contexts in China. *Sage Open* 12 (1), 21582440221081026.

Pun, J.K. and Thomas, N. (2020) English medium instruction: Teachers' challenges and coping strategies. *ELT Journal* 74 (3), 247–257.

Reimer, K.M. and Bruce, B. (1994) Building teacher-researcher collaboration: Dilemmas and strategies. *Educational Action Research* 2 (2), 211–221.

Säfström, A.I., Palmberg, B., Granberg, C., Sidenvall, J. and Lithner, J. (2021) Initiating teacher-researcher collaboration to support students' mathematical problem-solving. *Mathematics Education* 26 (3–4), 131–151.

Saldaña, J. (2016) *The Coding Manual for Qualitative Researchers* (2nd edn). SAGE.

Schellekens, L.H., Bok, H.G., de Jong, L.H., van der Schaaf, M.F., Kremer, W.D. and van der Vleuten, C.P. (2021) A scoping review on the notions of Assessment as Learning

(AaL), Assessment for Learning (AfL), and Assessment of Learning (AoL). *Studies in Educational Evaluation* 71, 101094.

Schleppegrell, M.J. (2004) *The Language of Schooling: A Functional Linguistics Perspective*. Routledge.

Shanahan, T. and Shanahan, C. (2008) Teaching disciplinary literacy to adolescents: Rethinking content-area literacy. *Harvard Educational Review* 78 (1), 40–59.

Snow, C.E. and Uccelli, P. (2009) The challenge of academic language. In D.R. Olson and N. Torrance (eds) *The Cambridge Handbook of Literacy*. Cambridge University Press.

Soruç, A., Altay, M., Curle, S. and Yuksel, D. (2021) Students' academic language-related challenges in English medium instruction: The role of English proficiency and language gain. *System* 103, 102651.

Uccelli, P., Galloway, E.P., Barr, C.D., Meneses, A. and Dobbs, C.L. (2015) Beyond vocabulary: Exploring cross-disciplinary academic-language proficiency and its association with reading comprehension. *Reading Research Quarterly* 50 (3), 337–356.

Uchihara, T. and Harada, T. (2018) Roles of vocabulary knowledge for success in English-medium instruction: Self-perceptions and academic outcomes of Japanese undergraduates. *TESOL Quarterly* 52 (3), 564–587.

Walstad, W.B., Rebeck, K. and Butters, R.B. (2013) The test of economic literacy: Development and results. *The Journal of Economic Education* 44 (3), 298–309.

Watkins, N.M. and Lindahl, K.M. (2010) Targeting content area literacy instruction to meet the needs of adolescent English language learners. *Middle School Journal* 41 (3), 23–32.

Xavier, A. (2020) Assessment for learning in bilingual education/CLIL: A learning-oriented approach to assessing English language skills and curriculum content in Portuguese primary schools. In M. deBoer and D. Leontjev (eds) *Assessment and Learning in CLIL Classrooms: Approaches and Conceptualisations*. Springer.

Xiong, T., Song, Z., Zhou, A. and Huang, X. (2023) EMI teachers' agency in the context of international education in China: Language choice, identity construction, and cultural negotiation. *International Journal of Bilingual Education and Bilingualism* 27 (4),472–486.

Yin, R.K. (2010) *Qualitative Research from Start to Finish*. The Guilford Press.

Yuan, C. (2019) Teaching disciplinary literacy in high school Economics classrooms: A dual-case study. PhD thesis, North Carolina State University.

13 Assessment in English-Medium Instruction in Higher Education: Current Research and Future Considerations

Slobodanka Dimova

13.1 Introduction

Much of the research in the area of English-medium instruction (EMI) in higher education has focused on identifying stakeholders' (e.g. students, lecturers, management) attitudes towards the implementation of EMI programs and their perspectives on the effectiveness of teaching and learning disciplinary content in a second/foreign language (L2), analyses of EMI learning outcomes and pedagogies, as well as the effectiveness of various EMI teacher training endeavors (Molino *et al.*, 2022). *Assessment* tends to be a recurring theme in a number of these studies, but it rarely is the main, or the sole, focus of investigation. In the literature, *assessment* tends to appear in passing when the focus is on teaching practices in EMI (Dafouz *et al.*, 2016). However, a number of emerging assessment needs in EMI university contexts require closer attention both in EMI research and practice; thus, the purpose of this chapter is to take stock of the current status of research in EMI assessment, identify research gaps and offer future directions for research.

Given that some of the emerging assessment needs in EMI include design and use of assessment for admission to EMI programs and design and administrations of classroom assessment (Dimova & Kling, 2022), this chapter provides an overview of findings in these areas and identifies thematic and methodological gaps. The chapter ends with a discussion on the importance of identifying and describing new disciplinary and communicative constructs that emerge from the non-English-dominant EMI contexts as well as the need to strengthen stakeholders' (students, teachers, administration) EMI assessment literacy (EMIAL, Inbar-Lourie, 2022).

13.2 Language Assessment for University Entry

Many institutions have established policies that require evidence of English proficiency for admission to EMI courses and programs at non-English-dominant universities, i.e. universities that have traditionally offered instruction in languages other than English. Although there are exceptions, most university policies require that prospective students have at least a B2 level on the Common European Framework of Reference (CEFR) (Council of Europe, 2020) which has been established as the minimum proficiency to learn disciplinary material in an L2.

However, how the language requirements are implemented varies among institutions, and in many cases, it differs between domestic and international students. For instance, in some institutions, all applicants must submit evidence of their proficiency level based on one of the international standardized English tests that were originally designed for university entry in the United Kingdom (UK), Canada, the United States (US), Australia and New Zealand. Such tests include International English Learning Testing System (IELTS), Test of English as a Foreign Language (TOEFL), the Cambridge exams and, more recently, the Duolingo English Test (DET), which gained popularity due to the possibility for a distant administration during the COVID-19 restrictions (Breeze & Miller, 2011; Isaacs *et al.*, 2023; Saarinen & Nikula, 2013). In some Asian institutions, Test of English for International Communication (TOEIC) has also been used for admission purposes even though the test was originally designed to measure the everyday English skills of those working in an international environment (Duong & Chua, 2016; Rose & McKinley, 2018). An alternative to this requirement is evidence that the student has completed previous education in EMI programs in an English-dominant higher education institution. Some Asian universities (e.g. Japan, Vietnam) require TOEFL, IELTS or TOEIC scores also for domestic students (Duong & Chua, 2016; Rose & McKinley, 2018).

In many university contexts (especially in Europe), however, domestic students are not required to take an international standardized test in English. Instead, they can provide evidence of English proficiency by showing that they completed English courses, took a school-leaving exam in English in upper secondary education (e.g. matura exam), or a university entrance exam (Dimova, 2020). Although in many European countries the curriculum for English in upper secondary education is aligned with the B2 level on the CEFR, school-leaving exams and grades fail to fully differentiate between students who have reached a B2 proficiency level and those who have not (Harsch & Hartig, 2022). This mismatch between expected and actual English proficiency of students could potentially lead to educational challenges, both for lectures and students (Harsch & Hartig, 2022).

Previous research has focused on the predictive validity of international standardized tests (e.g. TOEFL, IELTS) for university entry in English-dominant contexts (Bridgeman *et al.*, 2016; Cho & Bridgeman, 2012; O'Loughlin, 2011) as well as test score use and interpretation (Ginther & Elder, 2014; Rea-Dickins *et al.*, 2007; Wait & Gressel, 2009). Results have not been consistent in that some suggest none to weak or moderate association between test scores and students graduate point average (GPA), while others suggest negative associations. More meaningful patterns regarding associations between test scores and academic success have been found through analyses of student subgroups (e.g. based on score profiles, degree level, nationality, subject area) (Bridgeman *et al.*, 2016; Ginther & Yan, 2018; Harsch *et al.*, 2017). In addition, research has examined various stakeholders' (students, lecturers, administration) perceptions of the usefulness of test scores (IELTS, TOEFL) to predict students' readiness to study in English (e.g. Breeze & Miller, 2011; Coleman *et al.*, 2003; Schoepp, 2018).

The COVID-19 pandemic has changed the established university admissions practices due to the need for automated, distantly administered tests. This has led to the rise of the DET for university entrance purposes. DET departs from the traditional testing methods, given its fully automated, easily accessible format (LaFlair *et al.*, 2022). With the increased use of DET for university entry in English-dominant contexts, studies that focused on its validity for the admissions purpose have increased in the recent years (Isbell & Kremmel, 2020; Isbell *et al.*, 2023; Wagner, 2020; Wagner & Kunnan, 2015).

Two main issues arise from the current assessment practices associated with student admission to EMI programs in non-English-dominant higher education: lack of validation of existing tests for uses in EMI programs in non-English-dominant university contexts and the need for local post-entry assessment in order to identify students who may need additional language support for academic success.

Compared with the scope of validation research in English-dominant contexts regarding international standardized English tests for university entry, research in non-English-dominant contexts remains quite limited (Dimova, 2020). Only a handful of studies deal with the predictive validity or the suitability of existing international standardized tests of English in the emerging EMI contexts. Some research suggests significant association between TOEFL internet-based tests (iBT) or IELTS scores and students' GPAs (see, e.g. O'Dwyer *et al.*, 2018 regarding Turkey; Schoepp, 2018 about the United Arab Emirates), and findings from a Spanish and a Japanese university contexts suggest that higher scores on international English tests (IELTS and TOEIC, respectively) can be associated with students' ability to cope with EMI lectures. However, in both cases, test scores could not predict student success in EMI courses (Aizava *et al.*, 2020; Breeze & Miller, 2011; Rose *et al.*, 2020).

EMI scholars have criticized the adequacy of existing international English tests that have been designed to reflect the communicative realities in English-dominant universities, arguing that instead of embracing English as a lingua franca in academia, the tests promote native-speaker norms (Galloway *et al.*, 2020; Saarinen & Nikula, 2013). This criticism is supported by research based on description of communicative practices in EMI classrooms, which suggests that lecturers and students increasingly engage in multilingual and translingual practices (Haberland & Mortensen, 2012; Kuteeva, 2023; Smit, 2018). For example, in terms of productive skills (speaking and writing) in a Danish university context, Dimova (2020) found that lecturers reported to purposely involve students' L1 in different communicative situations because it allowed them to process difficult disciplinary materials. Moreover, lecturers did not only use students' L1 (and other languages) for scaffolding purposes but also to ensure that students develop disciplinary literacy in both languages. Based on micro- and macro-analyses of filed-note observations and video recordings at a Lebanese university, Iliovits *et al.* (2022) also found communicative patterns characterized by translingual and ELF features that are not represented in the underlying construct of TOEFL iBT.

Regarding receptive skills (reading and listening), comparing data from three EMI university contexts (in Austria, Egypt and Lithuania), Holzknecht *et al.* (2022) found great contextual variation in terms of text complexity and students' reading proficiency, although the common text difficulty factors were related to students' topical knowledge, text length, as well as text structure and organization in addition to word frequency and sentence length. Therefore, they recommend assessments that consider reading ability separately, include tasks that integrate reading with productive skills, and ensure variation in text length and text complexity level. In addition, Fung and Chung (2023) investigated the language demands of EMI assessment in Hong Kong by drawing upon the test forms of the Hong Kong Diploma of Secondary Education Examination (HKDSE). They found that the tests vary across disciplines in relation to the vocabulary levels that the tests demand, which may require explicit focus on students' disciplinary, academic and general vocabulary in instruction. Owen *et al.*'s study (2021), on the other hand, examined the relevance of the TOEFL iBT reading section for EMI programs in two distinct contexts, Nepal and Sweden. They found that despite the representation of the core reading construct in the TOEFL iBT reading tasks, academic reading in these contexts (especially in Nepal) involved a great deal of translating both individually and with peers.

To overcome these issues, some universities have developed local English assessments for university admissions to EMI programs. Examples of such assessments are the Interuniversity Test of Academic English (ITACE) for Students developed by IUTC (the Interuniversity Testing Consortium) in Flanders (Ghent University, KU Leuven, University of

Antwerp and Vrije University Brussels) (Inter University Testing Consortium, 2022), Proficiency in Academic English (PAE) Examination at Bilkent University in Turkey (Kantarcıoğlu *et al.*, 2010) and the American University Beirut English Entrance Examination (AUB-EN) (Pill, 2016a, 2016b). However, despite the attempt of local tests to allow for a greater representation of the local *target language use domain*, they tend to remain quite conservative in the representation of the contextual communicative characteristics of EMI (see, e.g. Iliovits *et al.*, 2022).

In some cases, implementing an admissions test for EMI programs may seem inappropriate as it may exacerbate practices of exclusion in higher education spurred by implementation of a foreign language as a medium of instruction (Dimova, 2020). There is disagreement in the literature regarding what could provide more relevant language proficiency evidence. Research does suggest that grades from exams at the end of upper secondary education may also lack relevance because they assess general, rather than academic English skills (Hellekjær, 2009; Wilkinson & Zegers, 2006). Therefore, scholarly discussions have included the possibility for implementation of post-entry assessments the main purpose of which would be identification of students who need linguistic support to succeed in their EMI courses or study programs (Dimova & Kling, 2022; Kurtán, 2006; Lockwood, 2013). For example, Harsch and Hartig (2022) discuss the development of an online post-entry diagnostic test to support newly enrolled students' academic English through (semi-) automatized diagnosis and automated feedback and feedforward. In order to strengthen the formative aspect of the local assessment, the test could be accompanied by self-learning modules and materials. However, the field lacks an accurate picture of how widespread such diagnostic tests are because studies on EMI diagnostic test development and validation are rare.

Given that English language proficiency is considered a prerequisite for students' success in EMI courses and programs, assessments used for university admissions and diagnostic purposes tend to have a broader scope, i.e. assessment of applicants/students across a variety of academic disciplines, and to focus primarily on general or academic language skills. Classroom-based assessment in EMI courses poses an additional challenge for lecturers because it tends to include different levels of content and language integration (Moore, 2017; Zhao & Dixon, 2017).

13.3 Classroom Assessment in EMI

Engagement in classroom-based assessment is central in university lecturers' teaching practice because it allows lecturers to track their students' progress and assess their achievement. When it comes to classroom assessment in EMI, the literature has identified several issues that need further consideration: assessment of disciplinary literacy, understanding of the construct of integrated language and content, and implementing task design with scaffolding features.

Traditionally, the two main types of assessment lecturers engage with in the classroom are formative and summative assessment; formative refers to ongoing assessment that supports students' learning, while summative refers to end-of-course assessment, usually associated with grade assignment (William, 2011). Another tripartite categorization has also been used in the literature: assessment *of* learning, assessment *as* learning and assessment *for* learning. The intention behind this categorization is to emphasize the assessment purpose and provide a more precise description of the different classroom assessment practices (Harlen, 2009). Assessment *of* learning tends to be used interchangeably with summative assessment because its focus is on collecting evidence of student learning through formal assessment methods (e.g. exams, tests) in order to make judgements regarding students' achievement against intended learning goals of the course and, more broadly, educational standards (Black & William, 2018; Carless, 2005).

Assessment *for* learning and assessment *as* learning, on the other hand, tend to be used synonymously with formative assessment because they emphasize the integration of teaching and learning, in that their purpose is enhancement of the learning process (Black & William, 2018). More specifically, in assessment *for* learning practices, lecturers apply different assessment methods that allow students to demonstrate their learning. This allows teachers to identify students' strengths and weaknesses and adjust their teaching approaches to address students' needs. Moreover, lecturers can use this assessment approach to provide useful feedback that can serve as the basis for students' continuous improvement. Assessment *as* learning also tends to be viewed as formative assessment although here the purpose of this assessment is to assist students to set goals and engage in metacognitive processes (e.g. self-reflection, understanding of the learning process, awareness of own development). Self- and peer-assessment can be considered assessment *as* learning because they help students to use the assessment process as an opportunity for students to become aware of their own learning stages (Earl & Katz, 2006; Jones, 2010).

Research suggests that higher education institutions across the globe subscribe to summative assessment, given the focus on large-scale data as evidence for program evaluation and accreditation (Hultgren *et al.*, 2022). The preponderance of test-oriented assessment practices is reflected in classroom assessment where lecturers focus on assessment for grading purposes rather than as an integrative part of teaching (Inbar-Lourie, 2022). This common trend in assessment in higher education does not escape non-English-dominant EMI contexts. For example, Kao and Tsou (2017) found that the vast majority of the lecturers they surveyed employed summative assessments, such as term projects and exams, with the purpose to compare students' achievements against certain educational standards. Li and Wu (2021) call for a more learner-oriented assessment in EMI claiming that it helps teachers monitor students' progress continuously in order to help them develop disciplinary literacy, as well as content learning and language proficiency.

13.4 Disciplinary Literacy

Literature abounds with findings that content teachers reject the idea of teaching (and assessing) language because their professional identity is associated with their disciplinary expertise (Airey, 2012; Doiz *et al.*, 2013). However, findings also suggest that lecturers engage in activities that help students develop disciplinary literacy (Breeze & Dafouz, 2017; Sánchez-Pérez, 2021). They guide students' disciplinary acculturation through expansion of their disciplinary terminology and genres, both from a receptive and productive perspective. It is not unusual that content lecturers hold journal reading meetings and seminars in order to help students understand the moves of the research genres in the field (Kling *et al.*, 2017) or to provide specific guidelines about the format and the structure of various texts the students produce during classes (Mancho-Barés *et al.*, 2022). Focus on development of disciplinary literacy is crucial because an indirect approach to students' development of their literacy skills is insufficient, especially when they are supposed to engage in independent writing processes, such as their Master's theses (Chell *et al.*, 2021).

Despite the increased focus on genre approach to understanding students' disciplinary literacy development, not much research focuses on lecturers' assessment practices regarding both formative and summative classroom assessment. An example of such research is a study in the Catalan context that draws on genre analysis in order to understand the effectiveness of formative assessment intended to help students' development of disciplinary literacy (Mancho-Barés *et al.*, 2022). They found that despite the lecturer's intention to help students develop competence in writing laboratory reports, her task instructions and feedback focused primarily on content and format rather than the characteristics of the report genre. In addition, they found discrepancies between the instructions, the assessment rubric and the feedback given, which could lead to students' confusion. These discrepancies emerged from the unclear relationship between content knowledge and language.

13.5 Integrating Content and Language in Rubrics

Although some lecturers try to strike a balance between content and language, they find themselves focusing mostly on content even though they acknowledge the fact that language is central to teaching content (Moore, 2017). In their study on the assessment practices in a Taiwanese university context, Kao and Tsou (2017) found that EMI lecturers' assessment instruments could be broadly divided into three types, none of which explicitly includes language: (1) examination focusing only on content knowledge; (2) evaluation that includes students' class participation and content-based examination; and (3) multiple assessment instruments that also include both students' participation and content-based examination. The EMI lecturers who participated in the study were aware of the importance of language proficiency in students' learning, as well as the importance of improving students' English proficiency through assessments.

One of the reasons why lecturers avoid the inclusion of language in their assessment tasks and criteria is that they find it difficult to disentangle language and content when assessing (Kao & Tsou, 2017). More specifically, they cannot identify to what degree language skills contribute to students' ability to demonstrate their content knowledge (Otto & Estrada Chichón, 2021). Therefore, lecturers' inclusion of language in the assessment criteria varies. In some cases, lecturers stated that they focused on content when they assessed their students, and some of them stated that language was also included in their assessment (Aguilar & Rodriguez, 2012; Li & Wu, 2018). Some lecturers assessed language intuitively, while others tried to design rubrics that included language as a grading criterion. Lecturers reiterate, though, that their focus is on content because they are not trained to assess language and because they take into consideration the fact that students are L2 users of English (Otto & Estrada Chichón, 2021).

Given this tension between content and language in EMI lecturer assessment practices, some studies focused on the level of explicitness of language proficiency in learning objectives, assessment criteria and actual assessment practices. In a study that analyzed learning objectives and assessment rubrics in an EMI setting in Italy, Gronchi (2023) found that although language-related objectives remained implicit in both course descriptions and assessment, they were explicitly used in the assessment rubrics. Gronchi attributed these findings to the tension between language policy constructs, academic literacies and internationalization. Similarly, in a Spanish EMI university context, Rodriguez Melchor and Walsh (2022) found that although lecturers declared that their assessment focused only on content, data also revealed an implicit linguistic bias in their assessment. Students who produced texts with better organization and clarity in English had an increased ability to display their content knowledge. This lack of explicitness leads to a misalignment that occurs between lecturers instructional and assessment goals, which in turn may lead to confusion among students and affect their ability to rely on assessment for learning purposes (Li & Wu, 2018).

From the students' perspective, English skills play a different role across various university contexts. Results from a study conducted in a Turkish EMI context suggest that students believed that high English proficiency represented an advantage for academic success even though their lecturers may not use rubrics that include language proficiency among the assessment criteria (Sahan & Şahan, 2022). In some cases, students believed that they could capitalize on their English proficiency to pass their exams even if they did not put in much effort in exam preparation. Students' strategy to show their high proficiency in English included using long and complex sentences and indirect answers. The implications of these findings are that the lack of explicit focus on English proficiency in teaching and assessment may lead to unfair assessment, and that the exam validity could be questioned if language proficiency overshadows students' disciplinary knowledge.

Despite students' perceptions about the important role of English proficiency in academic success, lecturers claimed that knowledge of disciplinary terminology in English may be sufficient for students to show their knowledge even if students struggle expressing themselves in English. Similar results were found in a comparative study that explored EMI settings in Austria, Thailand and the UK (Baker & Hüttner, 2017). While lecturers claimed that linguistic mistakes in students' exam performance did not influence grades, students felt that their English was assessed anyway.

Students from a Vietnamese context, on the other hand, believed that the role of English proficiency was not as prominent in their assessments as long as they could demonstrate their content knowledge (Truong *et al.*, 2020). Compared to their experiences with EMI programs in France, the UK and Australia, where language plays a role in longer written assignments, lecturers in Vietnamese EMI programs allowed short, bullet-point answers instead of full sentences.

The tension between content and language could also be seen in assessment task design and administration, especially in the role of English.

13.6 Task Design and Scaffolding

When it comes to task design and expected student performance, approaches to assessment task and rubric design tend to vary. For instance, while in some contexts (e.g. Finland, Spain, the UK), lecturers tend to use identical assessment tasks and criteria in both EMI and non-EMI contexts, in others (e.g. Austria), lecturers tend to be more flexible in assessment design to accommodate students (Dafouz *et al.*, 2016). One reason why some lecturers do not adjust their assessment practices to accommodate EMI students, even if they are aware of their students' challenges, is because they use assessment methods that they are familiar with rather than assessment methods that serve a particular purpose in the EMI course (Li & Wu, 2018).

The role of English in the design of assessment tasks and rubrics also varies across university settings. In some EMI contexts, lecturers tend to report using an English-only approach to task design and assessment, despite lecturers' awareness of potential struggles due to students' proficiency levels (Li & Wu, 2018; Sahan & Şahan, 2022), and in others, a more fluid approach to language use is incorporated (Dafouz *et al.*, 2016). These practices may be governed by institutional and departmental policies that require a certain percentage of courses and/or exams to be administered in English (Dafouz *et al.*, 2016; Li & Wu, 2018).

In terms of accommodation strategies both in terms of task design and assessment administration, studies from Spanish and Taiwanese university contexts found that teachers are cognizant of students' challenges and therefore establish accommodation strategies that help scaffold the tasks for students (Dafouz *et al.*, 2016; Li & Wu, 2018; Otto & Estrada Chicón, 2021). For instance, research suggests that lecturers provide glossaries with English terminology, translation of texts and additional aids that can help students optimize their performance on the assessment (Otto & Estrada Chicón, 2021; Sahan & Şahan, 2022). Kao and Tsou (2017) also found that lecturers allowed code-switching and peer collaboration to support students' exam completion.

In Denmark, research has documented instances of allowing students to select the language for their written assignments (Dimova, 2020), and instances of translanguaging during formal exams in order to support students' ability to display their knowledge (Nissen, 2019). Whether or not lecturers allow translanguaging during examinations can vary among contexts, but also among lecturers based on their educational ideologies. Sahan and Şahan (2022), for example, found that each lecturer they interviewed had a different perspective on whether and to what degree using students' L1 during exams is acceptable in a Turkish university context. One of the teachers expected that students used only English and therefore he marked down students' exams if they used their L1 even if the answers were correct. Another teacher established a firm English-only requirement and graded students' language, including grammar. A third lecturer from the same institution allowed students to use their L1 if it helped them show their disciplinary knowledge.

Li and Wu (2021) argue that regardless of the assessment task type, the medium of instruction plays a role in students' performance, and, therefore, lecturers should take it into consideration when designing assessments in EMI classrooms. Given students' challenges with learning through English, assessment should support their learning experiences rather than represent a source of struggle and frustration. Focus on scaffolding and accommodation in assessment task design could alleviate some of learners' challenges.

13.7 English-Medium Instruction Assessment Literacy (EMIAL)

Some of the assessment challenges EMI lecturers experience stem from the limited training they receive in terms of assessment overall, but even less in terms of language assessment practices (Inbar-Lourie, 2022). In recent years, language assessment literacy (LAL) has received increasing attention with the intention to define the construct and its components (Fulcher, 2021; Inbar-Lourie, 2008; Kremmel & Harding, 2020; Taylor, 2013). The conceptualizations of LAL have shifted from bare focus on stakeholders' knowledge of the fundamentals of measurement, practical assessment development skills and assessment consequences (Davies, 2008), to increased focus on social and experiential factors within a particular educational context (Levi & Inbar-Lourie, 2020; Yan & Fan, 2021).

Based on findings related to the pedagogical and assessment characteristics of the EMI contexts, Inbar-Lourie (2022) has identified an emerging construct of EMIAL that comprises four partially overlapping domains to be taken into consideration: (1) understanding of context and policy; (2) the relationship between language proficiency and content learning as part of pedagogical and assessment practices; (3) assessment for learning; and (4) awareness and understanding of EMI students' linguistic and content needs. She argues that lecturers need to be cognizant of the characteristics of the local EMI context, including the makeup of the student population (e.g. background of their domestic and international students), as well as explicit or implicit language and educational policies that govern educational practices at the local institution. Although language tends to be subsumed in the assessment of disciplinary content, lecturers need to develop awareness of the role of language in content learning, as well as in students' ability to display their content knowledge they have acquired. Building an ability to identify and address students' linguistic issues can enhance lecturers' endeavors to develop both students' content knowledge and disciplinary literacy. Although scholars have taken a constructivist perspective on assessment and emphasized the need for EMI lecturers to develop their competence on implementing assessment-for-learning practices (Hultgren *et al.*, 2022; Inbar-Lourie; 2022), many still need to consider how their assessment of learning should be adjusted to accommodate the unique EMI context in which they are administered.

13.8 Conclusion

This chapter is intended to provide an overview of existing research related to assessment in non-English-dominant university contexts and reveal issues that need further attention in order to achieve theoretical and practical advancement in this area. More specifically, these issues are related to both methodology and focus of research.

Current research is based on a limited variation of research methods and on small-scale studies that remain descriptive in nature. Most research studies draw on survey data and focus group or individual interviews. This means that findings rely on lecturers' and students' reports that show their perceptions rather than their actual assessment practices. Although understanding different stakeholders' perspectives represents valuable data, especially when it comes to understanding underlying assessment ideologies, analysis of actual assessment methods and practices would help gauge the validity of assessment methods, the use and misuse of assessment results, and the influence of assessment practices on teaching and learning. While some emerging research on construct validity of existing assessment methods for non-English-dominant EMI contexts (Iliovits *et al.*, 2022; Schoepp, 2020) is available in the literature, research on the consequences of assessment on teaching and learning, as well as its impact on individual, societal and educational level is lacking.

While some research has examined EMI lecturers' and students' perceptions of assessment practices, the field falls short of a solid empirical foundation that will help theorize various constructs that underlie assessment in EMI. Although multilingual and translingual communicative practices have been identified in EMI communicative settings (Kuteeva, 2023), there is an absence of theoretical models of multilingual competence that can be used to inform the design of assessment tasks and rubrics. Moreover, despite the essence of both content and language especially in classroom assessment, discussions still refer to content-based (i.e. cognitive) and linguistic skills as separate or, perhaps, complementary abilities rather than an integrated skill construct (see, e.g. Lo & Lin, 2014). The field could benefit from research on integrated assessment in elementary and secondary education, both in CLIL and immersion contexts (see, e.g. Grapin & Llosa, 2020; Lee *et al.*, 2019; Lo, 2021).

Finally, this edited volume represents an important step forward towards the actualization of research on assessment in EMI university contexts, which hopefully will inspire scholars to contribute to the development of this underrepresented area. Understanding the purposes and the characteristics of local language testing and assessments and assessments embedded in various educational contexts will allow us to identify common patterns identified across higher education institutions and idiosyncratic characteristics of individual institutions influenced by local contextual, educational and social factors (Dimova *et al.*, 2020, 2022).

References

Aguilar, M. and Rodriguez, R. (2012) Lecturer and student perceptions on CLIL at a Spanish university. *International Journal of Bilingual Education and Bilingualism* 15 (2), 183–197.

Airey, J. (2012) I don't teach language. The linguistic attitudes of physics lecturers in Sweden. *AILA Review* (25), 64–79.

Aizawa, I. and McKinley, J. (2020) EMI challenges in Japan's internationalization of higher education. In H. Bowles and A.C. Murphy (eds) *English-Medium Instruction and The Internationalization of Universities* (pp. 27–48). Springer.

Baker, W. and Hüttner, J. (2017) English and more: A multisite study of roles and conceptualisations of language in English medium multilingual universities from Europe to Asia. *Journal of Multilingual and Multicultural Development* 38 (6), 50516. https://doi.org/10.1080/01434632.2016.1207183.

Black, P. and Wiliam, D. (2018) Classroom assessment and pedagogy. *Assessment in Education: Principles, Policy & Practice* 25 (6), 551–575.

Breeze, R. and Dafouz, E. (2017) Constructing complex cognitive discourse functions in higher education: An exploratory study of exam answers in Spanish- and English-medium instruction settings. *System* 70, 81–91. https://doi.org/10.1016/j.system.2017.09.024

Breeze, R. and Miller, P. (2011) Predictive validity of the IELTS Listening Test as an indicator of student coping ability in Spain. In *IELTS Research Reports Volume 12, 2011* (pp. 1–34). IELTS Australia and British Council.

Bridgeman, B., Cho, Y. and DiPietro, S. (2016) Predicting grades from an English language assessment: The importance of peeling the onion. *Language Testing* 33 (3), 307–318.

Carless, D. (2005) Prospects for the implementation of assessment for learning. *Assessment in Education: Principles, Policy & Practice* 12 (1), 39–54.

Chell, G., Mikkilä-Erdmann, M., Iiskala, T. and Dillon, A. (2021) A comparative study of academic literacy in English medium instruction programs in UAE and Finland. *Issues in Educational Research* 31 (1), 56–75. http://www.iier.org.au/iier31/2021conts.html

Cho, Y. and Bridgeman, B. (2012) Relationship of TOEFL iBT® scores to academic performance: Some evidence from American universities. *Language Testing* 29 (3), 421–442.

Coleman, D., Starfield, S. and Hagan, A. (2003) The attitudes of IELTS stakeholders: Student and staff perceptions of IELTS in Australian, UK and Chinese tertiary institutions. In *International English Language Testing System (IELTS) Research Reports 2003: Volume 5* (pp. 160–235). IELTS Australia.

Council of Europe (2020) *Common European Framework of Reference for Languages: Learning, Teaching, Assessment. Companion Volume.* Council of Europe.

Dafouz, E., Hüttner, J. and Smit, U. (2016) University teachers' beliefs of language and content integration in English-medium education in multilingual university settings. In T. Nikula, E. Dafouz, P. Moore and U. Smit (eds) *Conceptualising Integration in CLIL and Multilingual Education* (pp. 123–143). Multilingual Matters.

Davies, A. (2008) Textbook trends in teaching language testing. *Language Testing* 25 (3), 327–347. https://doi.org/10.1177/0265532208090156

Dimova, S. (2020) English language requirements for enrolment in EMI programs in higher education: A European case. *Journal of English for Academic Purposes* 47, 100896.

Dimova, S. and Kling, J. (2022) Emerging assessment needs and solutions in EMI in higher education. *Journal of English-Medium Instruction* 1 (2), 137–152.

Dimova, S., Yan, X. and Ginther, A. (2022) Local tests, local contexts. *Language Testing* 39 (3), 341–354.

Dimova, S., Yan, X. and Ginther, A. (2020) *Local Language Testing: Design, Implementation, and Development.* Routledge.

Doiz, A., Lasagabaster, D. and Sierra, J. (2013) Globalisation, internationalisation, multilingualism and linguistic strains in higher education. *Studies in Higher Education* 38 (9), 1407–1421.

Duong, V.A. and Chua, C.S. (2016) English as a symbol of internationalization in higher education: A case study of Vietnam. *Higher Education Research & Development* 35 (4), 669–683.

Earl, L.M. and Katz, S. (eds) (2006) *Leading Schools in a Data-Rich World: Harnessing Data for School Improvement.* Corwin Press.

Fulcher, G. (2021) Language assessment literacy in a learning-oriented assessment framework. In A. Gebril (ed.) *Learning-Oriented Language Assessment* (pp. 34–48). Routledge. https://doi. org/10.4324/9781003014102

Fung, D. and Chung, E. (2023) Defining language goals in EMI: Vocabulary demand in a high-stakes assessment in Hong Kong. *Language and Education*, 1–15.

Galloway, N., Numajiri, T. and Rees, N. (2020) The 'internationalisation', or 'Englishisation', of higher education in East Asia. *Higher Education* 80 (3) 395–414.

Ginther, A. and Elder, C. (2014) A comparative investigation into understandings and uses of the TOEFL iBT® Test, the International English Language Testing Service (Academic) test, and the Pearson Test of English for graduate admissions in the United States and Australia: A case study of two university contexts. *ETS Research Report Series* 2014 (2), 1–39.

Ginther, A. and Yan, X. (2018) Interpreting the relationships between TOEFL iBT scores and GPA: Language proficiency, policy, and profiles. *Language Testing* 35 (2), 271–295.

Grapin, S.E. and Llosa, L. (2020) Toward an integrative framework for understanding multimodal L2 writing in the content areas. *Journal of Second Language Writing* 47, 100711.

Gronchi, M. (2023) Language assessment in EMI: Unravelling the implicit-explicit dichotomy. *Educational Linguistics* (0).

Haberland, H. and Mortensen, J. (2012) Language variety, language hierarchy and language choice in the international university. *International Journal of the Sociology of Language* 2012 (216), 1–6.

Harlen, W. (2009) Improving assessment of learning and for learning. *Education 3–13* 37 (3), 247–257.

Harsch, C. and Hartig, J. (2022) Linguistic preparedness in EMI contexts. 'Language assessment in EMI: Linking assessment to learning in new domains' Symposium at LTRC conference (online).

Harsch, C., Ushioda, E. and Ladroue, C. (2017) *Investigating the Predictive Validity of TOEFL iBT® Scores and Their Use in Informing Policy in a UK University Setting* (TOEFL iBT Research Report No. 30, ETS Research Report No. RR-17–41). ETS. https://files.eric.ed.gov/fulltext/EJ1168729.pdf

Hellekjear, G.O. (2009) Academic English reading proficiency at the university level: A Norwegian case study. *Reading in a Foreign Language* 21 (2), 198–222

Holzknecht, F., Guggenbichler, E., Zehentner, M., Yoder, M., Konrad, E. and Kremmel, B. (2022) Comparing EMI university reading materials with students' reading proficiency: Implications for admission testing. *Journal of English-Medium Instruction* 1 (2), 180–203.

Hultgren, A.K., Owen, N., Shrestha, P., Kuteeva, M. and Mežek, Š. (2022) Assessment and English as a medium of instruction: Challenges and opportunities. *Journal of English-Medium Instruction* 1 (1), 105–123.

Iliovits, M., Harding, L. and Pill, J. (2022) Language use in an English-medium instruction university in Lebanon: Implications for the validity of international and local English tests for admissions. *Journal of English-Medium Instruction* 1 (2), 153–179. https://doi.org/10.1075/jemi.21009.ili

Inbar-Lourie, O. (2022) EMI programs and formative assessment: Implications for the assessment literacy of content lecturers. *Journal of English-Medium Instruction* 1 (2), 204–231.

Inbar-Lourie, O. (2008) Constructing a language assessment knowledge base: A focus on language assessment courses. *Language Testing* 25 (3), 385–402. https://doi.org/10.1177/0265532208090158

InterUniversity Testing Consortium (2022) *ITACE for Students*. Retrieved from https://www.itace.be/students/

Isaacs, T., Hu, R., Trenkic, D. and Varga, J. (2023) Examining the predictive validity of the Duolingo English Test: Evidence from a major UK university. *Language Testing*, 02655322231158550.

Isbell D.R. and Kremmel B. (2020) Test review: Current options in at-home language proficiency tests for making high-stakes decisions. *Language Testing* 37 (4), 600–619. https://doi.org/10.1177/0265532220943483

Isbell, D.R., Kremmel, B. and Kim, J. (2023) Remote proctoring in language testing: Implications for fairness and justice. *Language Assessment Quarterly* 20 (4–5), 469–487.

Jones, J. (2010) The role of Assessment for Learning in the management of primary to secondary transition: Implications for language teachers. *Language Learning Journal* 38 (2), 175–191.

Kantarcıoğlu, E., Thomas, C., O'Dwyer, J. and O'Sullivan, B. (2010) The COPE linking project: A case study. In W. Martyniuk (ed.) *Relating Language Examinations to the Common European Framework of Reference for Languages: Case Studies and Reflections on the Use of the Council of Europe's Draft Manual* (pp. 102–116). Cambridge University Press.

Kao, Y.T. and Tsou, W. (2017) EMI course assessment: A survey study of the issues. In W. Tsou and S.M. Kao (eds) *English as a Medium of Instruction in Higher Education: Implementations and Classroom Practices in Taiwan* (pp. 183–205). Springer.

Kling, J., Larsen, S. and Thomsen, S.F. (2017) The need for focused literacy training in the medical school curriculum: A cross-sectional study of undergraduate students. *Education Research International* 2017, 1–6.

Kremmel, B. and Harding, L. (2020) Towards a comprehensive, empirical model of language assessment literacy across stakeholder groups: Developing the language assessment literacy survey. *Language Assessment Quarterly* 17 (1), 100–120. https://doi.org/10.1080/15434303 .2019.1674855

Kurtán, Z. (2006) On assessing students' entry competences for English medium higher education programmes in Hungary. In R. Wilkinson and V. Zegers (eds) *Bridging the Assessment Gap in English-Medium Higher Education* (pp. 77–91). AKS-Verlag.

Kuteeva, M. (2023) *Tension-Filled English at the Multilingual University: A Bakhtinian Perspective*. Multilingual Matters.

LaFlair, G.T., Langenfeld, T., Baig, B., Horie, A.K., Attali, Y. and von Davier, A.A. (2022) Digital-first assessments: A security framework. *Journal of Computer Assisted Learning* 38 (4), 1077–1086.

Lee, O., Llosa, L., Grapin, S., Haas, A. and Goggins, M. (2019) Science and language integration with English learners: A conceptual framework guiding instructional materials development. *Science Education* 103 (2), 317–337.

Levi, T. and Inbar-Lourie, O. (2020) Assessment literacy or language assessment literacy: Learning from the teachers. *Language Assessment Quarterly* 17 (2), 168–182. https://doi.org/10.1080 /15434303.2019.1692347

Li, N. and Wu, J.R. (2021) Assessment practices in the EMI classroom in Chinese-speaking higher education contexts: Challenges and considerations. In L.I. Su, H. Cheung and J.R.W. Wu (eds) *Rethinking EMI: Multidisciplinary Perspectives from Chinese-Speaking Regions* (pp. 124–140). Springer.

Li, N. and Wu, J. (2018) Exploring assessment for learning practices in the EMI classroom in the context of Taiwanese higher education. *Language Education & Assessment* 1 (1), 28–44.

Lo, Y.Y. (2021) Researching assessment in EMI. In J.K.H. Pun and S.M. Curle (eds) *Research Methods in English Medium Instruction* (pp. 61–74). Routledge.

Lo, Y.Y. and Lin, A.M.Y. (2014) Designing assessment tasks with language awareness: Balancing cognitive and linguistic demands. *Assessment and Learning* 3 (3), 97–119.

Lockwood, J. (2013) The Diagnostic English Language Tracking Assessment (DELTA) writing project: A case for post-entry assessment policies and practices in Hong Kong universities. *Papers in Language Testing and Assessment* 2 (1), 30–49.

Grapin, S.E. and Llosa, L. (2020) Toward an integrative framework for understanding multimodal L2 writing in the content areas. *Journal of Second Language Writing* 47, 100711.

Mancho-Barés, G. and Aguilar-Pérez, M. (2020) EMI lecturers' practices in correcting English: Resources for language teaching? *Journal of Immersion and Content-Based Language Education* 8 (2), 257–284.

Molino, A., Dimova, S., Kling, J. and Larsen, S. (2022) *The Evolution of EMI Research in European Higher Education*. Routledge.

Moore, S.H. (2017) A case study of assessment in English medium instruction in Cambodia. In B. Fenton-Smith, P. Humphreys and I. Walkinshaw (eds) *English Medium Instruction in Higher Education in Asia-Pacific: From Policy to Pedagogy* (pp. 173–191). Springer.

Nissen, C.F.R. (2019) Blind spots of internationalization of higher education. Unpublished doctoral thesis, Department of Nordic Studies and Linguistics, University of Copenhagen. https://static-curis.ku.dk/portal/files/222323139/Ph.d._afhandling_2019_Nissen.pdf.

O'Dwyer, J., Kantarcıoğlu, E. and Thomas, C. (2018) An investigation of the predictive validity of the TOEFL iBT® test at an english-medium university in Turkey. *ETS Research Report Series* 2018 (1), 1–13.

O'Loughlin, K. (2011) The interpretation and use of proficiency test scores in university selection: How valid and ethical are they? *Language Assessment Quarterly* 8 (2), 146–160.

Otto, A. and Estrada Chichón, J.L. (2021) Analysing EMI Assessment in Higher Education. *Revista Tempos e Espaços em Educação* 14 (33), e15475. http://dx.doi.org/10.20952/revtee.v14i33.15475

Owen, N., Shrestha, P.N. and Hultgren, A.K. (2021) Researching academic reading in two contrasting English as a medium of instruction contexts at a university level. *ETS Research Report Series* 2021 (1), 1–28.

Pill, J. (2016a) *American University of Beirut English Entrance Examination (AUB-EN): New Test Specifications*. American University of Beirut.

Pill, J. (2016b) Maintaining the connection between test and context: A language test for university admission. *Papers in Language Testing and Assessment* 5 (1), 66–89. https://arts.unimelb.edu.au/__data/assets/pdf_file/0006/2190642/4_Pill.pdf

Rea-Dickins, P., Kiely, R. and Yu, G. (2007) Student identity, learning and progression: The affective and academic impact of IELTS on 'successful' candidates. In *International English Language Testing System (IELTS) Research Reports 2007: Volume 7* (pp. 1–78). IELTS Australia and British Council.

Rodriguez Melchor, M.D. and Walsh, A.S. (2022) I'm really not assessing the language. *Ibérica* 44, 345–368. https://doi.org/10.17398/2340–2784.44.345

Rose, H. and McKinley, J. (2018) Japan's English-medium instruction initiatives and the globalization of higher education. *Higher Education* 75, 111–129.

Rose, H., Curle, S., Aizawa, I. and Thompson, G. (2020) What drives success in English medium taught courses? The interplay between language proficiency, academic skills, and motivation. *Studies in Higher Education* 45 (11), 2149–2161.

Saarinen, T. and Nikula, T. (2013) Implicit policy, invisible language: Policies and practices of international degree programmes in Finnish higher education. In A. Doiz, D. Lasagabaster and J.M. Sierra (eds) *English-Medium Instruction at Universities: Global Challenges* (pp. 131–150). Multilingual Matters.

Sánchez-Pérez, M. (2021) Predicting content proficiency through disciplinary-literacy variables in English-medium writing. *System* 97, 1–12. https://doi.org/10.1016/j.system.2021.102463

Sahan, K. and Şahan, Ö. (2022) Content and language in EMI assessment practices: Challenges and beliefs at an Engineering Faculty in Turkey. In Y. Kirkgöz and A. Karakaş (eds) *English as the Medium of Instruction in Turkish Higher Education: Policy, Practice and Progress* (pp. 155–174). Springer.

Schoepp, K. (2018) Predictive validity of the IELTS in an English as a medium of instruction environment. *Higher Education Quarterly* 72 (4), 271–285.

Smit, U. (2018) Classroom discourse in EMI: On the dynamics of multilingual practices. In K. Murata (ed.) *English-Medium Instruction from an English as a Lingua Franca Perspective* (pp. 99–122). Routledge.

Taylor, L. (2013) Communicating the theory, practice and principles of language testing to test stakeholders: Some reflections. *Language Testing* 30 (3), 403–412. https://doi.org/10.1177/0265532213480338

Truong, L.T.T., Ngo, P.L.H. and Nguyen, M.X.N.C. (2020) Assessment practices in local and international EMI programmes: Perspectives of Vietnamese students. In P. Le Ha and D. Ba Ngoc (eds) *Higher Education in Market-Oriented Socialist Vietnam*. Palgrave Macmillan. https://doi.org/10.1007/978-3-030-46912-2_16

Wagner, E. (2020) Duolingo English test, revised version July 2019. *Language Assessment Quarterly* 17 (3), 300–315.

Wagner, E. and Kunnan, A.J. (2015) The Duolingo English test. *Language Assessment Quarterly* 12 (3), 320–331.

Wait, I.W. and Gressel, J.W. (2009) Relationship between TOEFL score and academic success for international engineering students. *Journal of Engineering Education* 98 (4), 389–398.

Wilkinson, R. and Zegers, V. (2006) Assessing incipient linguistic competences: An institutional perspective. In R. Wilkinson and V. Zegers (eds) *Bridging the Assessment Gap in English-Medium Higher Education* (pp. 61–76). AKS-Verlag.

Yan, X. and Fan, J. (2021) 'Am I qualified to be a language tester?': Understanding the development of language assessment literacy across three stakeholder groups. *Language Testing* 38 (2), 219–246. https://doi.org/10.1177/0265532220929924

Zhao, J. and Dixon, L.Q. (eds) (2017) *English-Medium Instruction in Chinese Universities: Perspectives, Discourse and Evaluation*. Routledge.

Index

Page numbers in italic type refer to tables and figures.

For Product Safety Concerns and Information please contact our EU Authorised Representative:

Easy Access System Europe

Mustamäe tee 50

10621 Tallinn

Estonia

gpsr.requests@easproject.com

www.ingramcontent.com/pod-product-compliance
Ingram Content Group UK Ltd.
Pitfield, Milton Keynes, MK11 3LW, UK
UKHW021828100926
8556IPUK00003B/221

* 9 7 8 1 8 0 0 4 1 9 1 7 9 *